The Biblical Seminar
70

THE MATERIAL CULTURE OF THE BIBLE

THE MATERIAL CULTURE OF THE BIBLE

An Introduction

Ferdinand E. Deist
Edited with a Preface by Robert P. Carroll

Sheffield Academic Press

BS
670
.D45
2000

For Henriette

Copyright © 2000 Sheffield Academic Press (*A Continuum imprint*)
Reprinted 2002

Published by Sheffield Academic Press Ltd
The Tower Building, 11 York Road, London SE1 7NX
370 Lexington Avenue, New York, NY 10017-6550

www.continuumbooks.com

All rights reserved. No part of this publication may be reproduced or transmitted in any form or by any means, electronic or mechanical, including photocopying, recording or any information storage or retrieval system, without permission in writing from the publishers.

British Library Cataloguing-in-Publication Data
A catalogue record for this book is available from the British Library

Typeset by Sheffield Academic Press
Printed on acid-free paper in Great Britain by Bookcraft Ltd, Midsomer Norton, Bath

ISBN 1-84127-098-9

CONTENTS

Foreword	9
Abbreviations	17
Introduction	19

Chapter 1
CULTURE AND INTERPRETATION 23
   1. Formulating Hypotheses on the Authors' Intention,
      or Identifying Relevant Intertexts 24
   2. The Necessity of Cultural Information for Synchronic
      Interpretation 33
   3. The Validation of Interpretation and Cultural Information   39
   4. Looking for Discriminatory Indicators in Interpretation   47
   5. Self-Awareness and Cultural Information 48
   6. 'Biblical' Culture 50

Chapter 2
WHAT DO WE MEAN BY 'CULTURE'? 78
   1. Renewed Interest in Culture 79
   2. Anthropological Approaches to the Study of Culture 82
   3. Choosing a Model for the Study of Biblical Literature . . . 94
   4. Pitfalls in the Study of Culture 96

Chapter 3
CULTURE, LANGUAGE AND MEANING 102
   1. Cultural Domains, Function and Meaning 102
   2. Language and Meaning 105
   3. Custom and Meaning 116

Chapter 4
ENVIRONMENT AND MEANING 118
   1. Heavenly Bodies 119

2. Natural Forces and Climate   121
3. Water Sources   124
4. Fauna   128
5. Flora   137

Chapter 5
ECONOMY AND MEANING   143
1. Property   143
2. Labour   146
3. Distribution   165
4. Consumption   182
5. Conclusion   188

Chapter 6
TECHNOLOGY AND MEANING   189
1. Agricultural Technology   189
2. The Technology of Subsistence   193
3. Architectural Technology   195
4. Mining Technology   209
5. Manufacturing Technology   211
6. The Technology of War   220
7. The Technology of Measurement   223
8. The Technology of Writing   226
9. Conclusion   232

Chapter 7
SOCIAL ORGANIZATION AND MEANING   233
1. Collective Goals   233
2. Mechanisms for Achieving Goals   235
3. Organizational Units and Strategies   244
4. Status Groups, Social Roles and Symbols 260

Chapter 8
POLITICAL ORGANIZATION AND MEANING   276
1. Tribal Authorities   277
2. Chiefdoms   278
3. States   281

Chapter 9
SOCIAL CONTROL AND MEANING   291

Concluding Editorial Remarks   299
Bibliography   300
Index of References   322
Index of Subjects   339
Index of Hebrew Terms   341
Index of Authors   346

FOREWORD

Ferdinand Etienne Deist died suddenly of a heart attack on 12 July 1997, while on study leave in Heidelberg, leaving the incompleted manuscript of this book at the time of his death. Appropriately enough I had spent that day at Joseph Henry Magill's funeral—the father of my good friend and colleague Father Tom Magill—a good old-fashioned Catholic Scoto-Irish day-long series of celebrations of the departed's life after the proper religious ceremonies (Mass followed by graveside prayers and a decade of the Rosary) had been observed during the first half of the day. Yet I was not really prepared for the shock of hearing the very next day about Ferdinand's sudden death just short of his 53rd birthday. He was far too young to die and far too important a scholar for South African Biblical Studies to go so soon—and besides, he had so much to live for, including a loving wife and children, and he was a man of great intelligence, ability and integrity. But the angel of death spares nobody, nor does she operate according to a rational list of humane values. Ferdinand is gone now and the preparation of his unfinished manuscript for publication has fallen to me, for reasons outwith my knowledge. While I do not know why this should have been the case, I do embrace the opportunity to bring my friend's final manuscript to published fruition. For Ferdinand and I were friends and I consider it an honour, as well as an act of *pietas* and friendship, to take up the task on behalf of my dead friend and also for Henriette his widow, and to give to the world as complete a volume as I can manage in circumstances which are less than ideal.

He and Henriette had visited us in Glasgow only some three months before his untimely death, when we had discussed plans for another visit to South Africa the following year in order to give some lectures there. That visit was never made—will now never be made—so in its place I offer the editing of this book as my final act for Ferdinand, both to his memory and as a gesture of the strength of our friendship and the depth of my high regard for him as scholar, intellectual, friend and, above all else, a very fine man. He will be missed by very many of us in the years to come. Fortunately a Festschrift had been written for him when he moved from UNISA to Stellenbosch at the end of 1991 (Wessels and Scheffler 1992) and since his death a Memorial Volume of the *Journal of Northwest Semitic Languages* has also been produced for him (Cook, Kruger and Cornelius 1998), so he is not without witnesses in the after life (*Nachleben*) of his influence (see esp. le Roux in Wessels and Scheffler 1992).

The substance of Ferdinand's book may accurately be described as an attempt to provide a thoroughgoing cultural materialist account of the world reflected in the Hebrew Bible and from such an account to allow readers to be able to construct their own formation and understanding of biblical culture. His premature death prevented him from completing the book, so now readers will have to extrapolate from what he has written to what he might have written on the cultural production of biblical religion. This book then should be thought of as being an 'interactive' book: that is, readers are invited to complete its argumentation for themselves in the unwritten final chapter by writing that chapter for themselves. My part in this book production, apart from all the usual editing activities of grammatical, spelling and stylistic changes—for Ferdinand was primarily an Afrikaans and German speaker, with English only as a third language—has been to provide the nine-tenths of the book completed by Ferdinand with the information that will enable readers to complete it themselves. I have added very little of substance to the argument of the book, but I have enhanced and updated the Bibliography, which also was incomplete at Ferdinand's death. While I was a great admirer of Ferdinand's academic and intellectual work and was heavily influenced by his writings on Ideological Criticism (*Ideologiekritik*: cf. Carroll 1998), our approaches to and thinking about the Hebrew Bible were so very different that I could not in all good conscience interpolate or traduce his book with my rewritings of it. The book as it stands is very much all Ferdinand's work, with my editorial fiddlings only evident around the edges and as a framework for the book.

There is a brief 'Introduction' to the book by Ferdinand himself (see pp. 19-22), so my Foreword is only intended to put the whole book in context and to spell out what I think are the main implications for Biblical Studies of what Ferdinand has written. So what appears in this Foreword should be read as one reader's reading of another writer's work and as a guide for readers wishing to have some instruction about 'what follows' from a work such as this. Ferdinand was a brilliant intellectual and an excellent scholar, so readers will find running through his book a number of insightful and significant forays into current issues in contemporary Biblical Studies. There are in this book some fine takes on such important topics as biblical hermeneutics (how should one read and interpret the Bible?), the role of history in biblical historiography, the contribution cultural origins makes to the generation of meaning and the currently much debated matter of whether the Hebrew Bible was produced in the Persian period or in later eras. Ferdinand was one of the most well-informed scholars it has been my pleasure and privilege to have known personally and he always had such pertinent observations to make on all such matters. He was always his own man—the highest compliment I can pay a fellow scholar—so read and thought for himself, and this, his final book, provides ample evidence of his own thoroughgoing knowledge and independence of judgment.

The first chapter of the book, on 'Culture and Interpretation', raises the issue of the indispensability of culture for meaning. In effect, this means that readers of the Bible need to know the kinds of culture from whence the writers of documents that later came to be incorporated into the collection of writings we know as 'The Bible' (or The Books) wrote and also the cultural assumptions and presuppositions built into these biblical writings. At the same time, theories of discourse and understanding are important for the interpretation of the Bible. Deist favours 'relevance theory' in relation to positing rational communicators communicating to rational interpreters where anticipation of shared meaning is fundamental to successful communication. Relevance theory involves 'the cognitive worlds of the speaker and hearer', worlds that are culturally and locally constituted. Hence, according to this theoretical approach

> the degree of validity of a particular interpretation may, among other things, be measured against certain indicators, such as the degree of which the principles of recency, frequency, effective encyclopaedic memory, hierarchy of communicated knowledge, and the closeness of cognitive resemblance can be shown to apply (p. 48).

In this, perhaps the densest and most interesting part of the book, Deist offers a percipient and profound introduction to hermeneutics in relation to reading the Bible and gives evidence of what has been lost to scholarship with his demise.

It would, on the other hand, be unwise of me to offer readers just an uncritical representation of the main points made by Deist in his book. In the area of biblical hermeneutics—both in terms of understanding what the writers of the Bible may have meant by what they wrote and of understanding such writings in the light of our own contemporary hermeneutic holdings—it is always a wise procedure to allow the horizons of the text and our own horizons to be brought together whatever the tensions there may be between the two. In giving an account of what the ancient writers appear to have believed was the case according to their writings, modern readers are not bound to replicate such beliefs within their own belief system. It is also very necessary to provide a critical account and analysis of such beliefs (cf. Bauman 1978: 62-68). It does therefore seem to me that 'relevance theory' in application to the biblical writings may itself become problematical if it is used simply to underwrite whatever is imagined to have been the writers' points of view. I will not pursue this critical approach to reading Deist on cultural materialist approaches to reading the Bible, but I would like to remind readers of the necessity of taking seriously the need for critical reading of the Bible.

One of the most interesting features of Deist's first chapter is his engagement with the current debate about the sociopolitical period of the production of the text of the Bible. In recent years the European Seminar in Historical Methodology has focused on this issue in a very big way (see Grabbe 1997, 1998). Opposing the so-called 'Persian fiction theory' (cf. Davies 1992) Deist offers a number of reasons for dissenting from Davies's point of view and also distances himself from Joel Weinberg's *Bürger-Tempel-Gemeinde* ('civic-temple-community') thesis (Weinberg 1992). Here Deist is able to make use of his own deep knowledge of Afrikaner life to provide an analogy for the discussion. With a series of counter-indications he offers a very interesting and critical take on the discussion, favouring a more conservative and more mainstream approach to the debate. So, as this debate proceeds through the early years of the next century (and millennium), Deist's voice may be added to it in favour of the position that claims that 'even though the present text had been compiled and tuned to address post-exilic situations, its authors had access to quite substantial Judaean oral and written sources that had originated between the eighth and sixth centuries BCE' (p. 77). Had he lived his would have been a dominant voice in that discussion, a voice against which others would have been able to strengthen their positions with the construction of better arguments.

In his second chapter Deist concentrates on culture, defining it in anthropological, structuralist and ethnohistorical terms. But what model should be chosen for the study of biblical literature? Because interpretation is an act of communication and has to do with understanding the cognitive worlds of the original speakers and hearers, perhaps the best anthropological approach to biblical interpretation would be a focus on the cognitive side of culture. So Deist favours using an evolutionary model that could account for cultural development *and* also explain cultural change. Stressing the importance of empiricism, Deist also recognizes that the opportunity for extended first-hand exposure to biblical culture is not possible for biblical scholars. There will always be huge gaps in our knowledge of the biblical past and its culture (there are times when this editor wonders whether biblical scholarship as practised by the 'compact majority' of scholars is not in reality the practice of the invention of material to fill those huge gaps!) even though Deist is confident that there is such a vast amount of cultural information available from the Hebrew Bible that we may generate a coherent explanation of elements of Israelite culture using anthropological theories at our disposal. However, the existence of subcultures within any culture may entail the impossibility of speaking usefully of 'Israelite culture', as if there only was one such unified culture. At the same time it must be recognized that we 'invent' the culture we are studying—but not as an invention of free fantasy. Our inventing of culture consists of a complex reciprocal relationship between constructing the imagined past culture and constructing ourselves. Deist wisely concludes his second chapter on a note of the necessity for recognizing the problematic nature of culture construction and the need for being aware of what we are doing. Such recognition and awareness will not guarantee that we will get our constructions of past culture right, but they are a substantial improvement on not being aware or not even caring about such lack of awareness.

Throughout his book Deist provides a wide range of diagrams and figures, grids and references, bibliographical discussions and biblical textual analyses. Hence his book is at one level an invaluable *vade mecum* of all the complexities of anthropology, culture and hermeneutics relating to the Bible and to a wide selection of biblical texts. In a brief chapter on 'culture, language and meaning' Deist offers some wise counsel about the cultural community that produced the Bible in the first place. Such cultural production takes place in specific languages—the biblical languages (Aramaic, Hebrew)—but the long history of the Bible's transmission has severed the Bible from its original languages and replaced it *by means of translation* as an object in languages and cultures other than its own. The necessity for knowing the customs and value system of a culture is an absolute for any intelligent attempt at interpreting and understanding that culture. Ignorance of such custom and value can lead to extra processing efforts whereby modern interpreters add to the text or give it an allegorical interpretation or seek to harmonize its contradictory reports. With such brief remarks Deist alludes to a vast industry and history of biblical exegesis that has been such a negative stain on rational cultural understanding of the ancient biblical text.

In the chapter on 'environment and meaning' Deist discusses ecological anthropology and, in particular, considers such phenomena as the heavenly bodies, natural forces and climate, water sources, fauna and flora as represented by the biblical text. Such sweeps of the material culture embedded in the Bible are indicative of the rich imagery available to the biblical writers and with which they produced such a densely and richly layered collection of writings. The very lengthy chapter on 'economy and meaning' provides readers with a comprehensive introduction to the socioeconomic world of biblical writers. Matters having to do with property and labour, especially in relation to a farming economy, provide some insight into the basic economic systems operative behind (or in) the biblical text. From all these data Deist constructs an account of a mixed economy, that is, one of reciprocity and redistribution. These two systems are not easily translated into one another, so there may be found throughout biblical writings a confusing shift between each system. Such economic systems also provide concepts and metaphors used in the religious language of the Bible. Thus the god of the Bible—whose personal name is very frequently used and represented as the tetragrammaton Yahweh (out of respect for Jewish readers of the Bible I shall not attempt to profane the name by pronouncing it)—is represented as owning heavenly stores, making grants of land to his people, a redistributor of booty and, being the people's king, makes a levy of ten per cent to be brought to his storehouse to sustain the temple service there. Such specific economic contexts of production, distribution and consumption in the Bible demonstrate how deeply embedded in economics is the culture reflected in the Bible and especially in the construction of cultural meaning.

The chapter on 'technology and meaning' looks at the technology of agriculture, of subsistence, architecture, mining, manufacturing (smelting, pottery, fabric), war, metrology and the technology of writing. Deist argues that without a sound knowledge of the technological environment of the Bible comprehending the book will become very difficult and its interpretation well-nigh impossible. From much of this technological culture comes language for representing the deity in the text. A further lengthy chapter on 'social and political organization' offers a considerable vocabulary for developing cultural descriptions of the Bible and also provides more technical language for the representation of the deity. Religion is here intimately bound up with the cultural structures of biblical society, and the language of the world of the biblical writers provides the resources for constructing numerous pictures (images) of the god Yahweh.

The final chapters on 'social political organization and meaning', and 'social control and meaning' unfortunately are only available in the sketchiest of forms. There are sufficient clues in what is available for readers to have some firm ideas about where Deist is driving with his analysis here. But it is deeply unfortunate that just as he approached the climax of the work the angel of death should have intervened and removed him from our midst. I cannot make good that loss. I would indeed prefer to leave the work as unfinished so that readers can internalize Deist's arguments over the long run of the book and then work out for themselves what the biblical world view(s) might look like given the huge amount of data and analysis already provided by the author. In my own judgment I feel that the final chapter would need to have taken into account the kinds of religious world views represented by the great imperial systems of Egypt, Assyria, Babylon and Persia with which the writers of the biblical texts came into contact and which greatly shaped their representations of the deity. Because, of course, there were many cultural influences on the biblical writers that fed into their construction of culture and value as we find them in the Bible and a considerable amount of such influence helped to shape their representations of Yahweh, the god of Israel. Deist gives us a huge amount of cultural data, with considerable analysis of such data, but in the final analysis it is for readers to bring the book to conclusion and fruition by extrapolating from his analysed data to imagined conclusions of his work.

I have devoted a considerable amount of time to editing Ferdinand Deist's final book and it is my firm judgment that in due course its publication will provide scholars and readers with a fine opportunity for building on his work and producing a much more comprehensive account of the material culture of the Bible. Out of the data and analyses provided by Deist will come, I hope, more realistic accounts of how meaning was constructed and produced by the biblical writers and as a consequence of such improved models of understanding readers of the Bible will have a better sense of the cultural elements which helped to forge the biblical images of the deity Yahweh and the religious cosmos over which this god reigned and within which the people of the Bible were expected to worship and to serve. It would be a magnificent jump forward for biblical scholarship if readers of the Bible were helped to abandon the dogmatic structures of later religious systems which for so long have been imposed on the Bible as alien meaning systems and enabled to go back to the Bible in order to construct meaning from its own material cultural content. To this end this book has been edited and I look forward to the years to come when 'Deist on Material Culture of the Bible' will be looked back on as setting a benchmark for the discipline.

Robert P. Carroll
Glasgow
November 1999

During the final stages of editing this book, and by a most dreadful coincidence, Robert Carroll died, suddenly and unexpectedly, on 12 May 2000. The remaining tasks of editing, chiefly in Chapter 7, were completed by me. This volume is thus doubly marked by tragedy and the marks of both losses are evident in the editing as well as the authoring. Despite the death of Robert Carroll, it was decided to proceed with the original publication deadline, marking the third anniversary of Deist's death. I would like to thank all those at Sheffield Academic Press who undertook, in these circumstances, to produce this book to its schedule.

Philip R. Davies
Sheffield
May 2000

ABBREVIATIONS

BARev	*Biblical Archaeology Review*
BASOR	*Bulletin of the American Schools of Oriental Research*
BibInt	*Biblical Interpretation: A Journal of Contemporary Approaches*
BZ	*Biblische Zeitschrift*
FRLANT	Forschungen zur Religion und Literatur des Alten und Neuen Testaments
GCT	Gender, Culture, Theory
HR	*History of Religions*
IDB	George Arthur Buttrick (ed.), *The Interpreter's Dictionary of the Bible* (4 vols.; Nashville: Abingdon Press, 1962)
IEJ	*Israel Exploration Journal*
JANES	*Journal of Ancient Near Eastern Studies*
JBL	*Journal of Biblical Literature*
JNES	*Journal of Near Eastern Studies*
JNSL	*Journal of Northwest Semitic Languages*
JSOTSup	*Journal for the Study of the Old Testament*, Supplement Series
OBO	Orbis biblicus et orientalis
OTE	Old Testament Essays
PEQ	*Palestine Exploration Quarterly*
ResQ	*Restoration Quarterly*
RSV	Revised Standard Version
SBL	Society of Biblical Literature
SJOT	*Scandinavian Journal of the Old Testament*
VT	*Vetus Testamentum*
ZAW	*Zeitschrift für die alttestamentliche Wissenschaft*
ZDPV	*Zeitschrift des deutschen Palästina-Vereins*

INTRODUCTION

Biblical interpretation has since the 1960s been inundated with new exegetical methods, some as rivals to traditional methods, others as 'complementary' to or refinements of them. Most of these methods set out a sequence of steps to be taken in exegeting a text. It is, however, at the least debatable whether exegesis, like baking a cake, is or can be done by following certain methodical 'steps'. If exegesis has to do with understanding, and has, consequently, something in common with the way human beings come to understand each other's talk, one would perhaps be better off in taking one's cue on interpretation from conversations at coffee tables than from neat 'steps' prescribed by some academic soliloquy.

What happens at a coffee table? Surely, one thing that does not happen there is that everybody is consciously analysing the flow of a speaker's speech (or the linear sequence of letters in the newspaper on the table) by carrying out a logically or chronologically ordered sequence of operations. Interpretation occurs spontaneously, automatically, and instantaneously. There is no way of preventing the understanding of intelligible talk. Also not of 'freezing' or putting the process in slow motion to enable one carefully to observe and describe it in sequence. There is also no way of preventing ordinary people reading the Bible from forming an understanding of what they read. Like professional exegetes, they spontaneously, automatically and instantaneously, and without having read a single book on exegetical method, understand what they read.

Exegetical 'methods' rather serve two quite different and, *nota bene*, academic purposes. On the one hand, they avail professionals with an argumentative framework with reference to which they may *post factum* demonstrate to their critics that everything the branch of their guild accepts at the time as criteria for *correct, valid, responsible, answerable* interpretation (call it what you like) has in fact been taken into consideration. Any argument in favour or against a particular interpretation is measured against such criteria. Thus, logically and chronologically ordered exegetical 'procedures' are, at least for professionals, an output system rather than an input system. And in any critical assessment of results one can hardly do without such an agreed frame of reference, especially not with deconstruction in the air. For this reason, books on exegetical method, rather than explaining *how* understanding 'really' takes place, have to do with (very important) *meta*-exegetical issues and with drawing frames around a text in order to prevent it, for the purpose of the discussion, from deferring *ad infinitum*. Ordinary readers do the same, but they make use of frames of a different kind, such as experience, their denomination's dogma, the consensus of their Bible study group, etc. Professionals usually find such frames inadequate, draw up their own and call them 'exegetical methods'. Academics in medicine, engineering, psychology, and all the rest, also find popular frames of mind inadequate and put *their* frames around the slices from reality that form their fields of expertise.

On the other hand, books on 'exegetical methods' aim at introducing novices to the guild of professionals to the rules of the game. These books say to them, 'If you want to be taken seriously in these circles, here are the requirements. To be acceptable an interpretation should meet them. So, make sure you pay attention to all these things and to measure your interpretation of a text against them before publishing it or presenting it as a paper at a congress.' And there is nothing wrong with that. This is what mathematicians, physicists, sociologists, psychologists, linguists, and all other guilds do. For scholarship to draw any conclusions and conduct any meaningful debate there *should* be agreed rules and accepted criteria.

This is, however, not really a book on 'method' in biblical interpretation, although it does have somewhat of a forked tongue. On the one hand, it is a book on *how* understanding takes place, and is therefore about a kind of consciousness or awareness, specifically a cultural awareness, on the part of the exegete that may enable her or him to intuitively, spontaneously, automatically and instantaneously understand the sequence of letters she or he reads in the Bible in the same way as one understands texts in one's own language. In this sense the book has more to do with hermeneutics than with method. However, it will, on the other hand, also argue that this cultural awareness may be extrapolated and 'formalized' as an important element in the process of arguing one's case and validating an interpretation of a particular biblical text. In this sense it has in fact something to say on method.

The title of the book does not purport to suggest that the social dimension of the biblical text has as yet not received the attention of biblical scholars. On the contrary. Apart from the fact that not only 'culture' but specifically anthropological conceptions of culture had already in the nineteenth century formed part of (at least German) Hebrew Bible scholarship, the present scene of Hebrew Bible studies is buzzing with cultural and anthropological talk of all sorts. The aim of this book is therefore to join critically in the buzz with a view to establishing at least some kind of a framework within which the ongoing discussion on especially biblical *interpretation* may be interpreted and evaluated.

Although it may be putting the cart before the horse, a provisional agreement of some sort has to be struck on the meaning of the concept 'culture'. Quite generally speaking one may distinguish between material, habitual and mental culture. The first concerns the things people do: for example, feed and shelter themselves, procreate, dress, mourn, rejoice, work their land, fight, etc. The second has to do with how they do things or get them done: for instance, through distributing labour and responsibilities, marrying, trading, making war, solving disputes, and so on. The third is about their reasons for doing these things in the way they do: for example, why they prefer a particular kind of social or economic organization, bring sacrifices, marry the way they do, organize inheritance in a particular manner, and so forth. The reasons for some actions may be fairly obvious (e.g. to satisfy basic human needs), or be deeply embedded in their own philosophies on the construction of the universe. Risking a dangerous term, on which some constraints will be put later, culture is what defines, in the eyes of an outsider, a particular group of people as a recognizable 'identity'.

The argument of the book is that, when people speak, they are not merely uttering sounds with structure and meaning. They *intend* something, and that intention is entrenched in their whole material, habitual and mental world. Language is *part* of culture. People socialized in the culture of a speaker need not be reminded of this. Under ideal circumstances they understand her or his speech spontaneously, automatically and instantaneously. For outsiders to understand that same speech, they have to acquire as much as they can of the intimate knowledge *presupposed* by the speaker. What is presupposed is of course linguistic proficiency, but also, and importantly, knowledge of the relevant culture of which the language forms an integral part.

Chapter 1

CULTURE AND INTERPRETATION

This chapter discusses, first, the advantages for biblical interpretation of a critical awareness of the cultures of which the biblical languages formed a part. Secondly, attention is paid to the definition of the term '*biblical* culture' and the consequences of such a definition for biblical interpretation. (The definition of 'culture' in the context of the present-day 'cultural studies' debate, sometimes also referred to as the debate on 'multi-culturalism' or 'culture criticism', will be dealt with in Chapter 2.)

A critical awareness of the cultures of biblical times may play an important role in biblical interpretation. First, acquaintance with these cultures has a heuristic function in that it enhances the readers' intuitive ability to formulate relevant hypotheses about the speakers' intentions *also*, and even if, the exegete chooses a synchronic or immanent approach. Secondly, cultural knowledge has a validatory function in that it avails the exegete of a range of arguments that may assist in arguing about a particular interpretation. Thirdly, cultural knowledge has a hermeneutical function in creating an opportunity for a reader to discover the features of the world she thinks she inhabits,[1] thereby preventing her from substituting her own cultural (religious, political and social) orientation for that of the biblical text.

While the third advantage of a cultural awareness mentioned above may partly slip through as fairly postmodern, the first and second seem to be fundamentally modernist—if not positivist. They may therefore

---

1. To avoid the boring he/she style, I shall speak of speakers and writers as 'he' and of hearers and readers as 'she'. Depending on one's approach to textual interpretation (author/text/reader) 'he' may be considered more important than 'she', or vice versa. In the end, I trust, though, that the approaches subscribed to by the readership of this book will balance out their relative importance so that neither male or female readers need to take offence.

seem a little awkward, perhaps even backward, in the light of postmodernist thinking. Although 'postmodernism' should not be employed as a kind of shibboleth for academic acceptability (which would, of course, amount to sound modernism), such a view of these criteria will be shown not to be the case.

1. *Formulating Hypotheses on the Authors' Intention, or Identifying Relevant Intertexts*

The first advantage of a sound knowledge of the cultural world of the biblical text is that it may assist the reader to formulate germane hypotheses on the intentions of the authors responsible for these texts. It may sound surprising in this day and age still to speak of 'author's intention' in the context of literary interpretation. After all, already in 1968 Wimsatt (1968: 221-24) said,

> The design or intention of the author is neither available nor desirable as a standard for judging the success of a work of literary art... [T]he closest one could ever get to the artist's intending or meaning, outside of his work, would still be short of his effective intention or operative mind as it appears in the work itself and can be read from the work.

And Jacques Derrida (1996: 84) would hardly be wrong when he says,

> To produce this signifying structure [i.e. to interpret] obviously cannot consist of reproducing, by the effaced and respectful doubling of commentary, the conscious, voluntary, intentional relationship that the writer institutes in his exchanges with the history to which he belongs thanks to the element of language.

Much depends, however, on whether one takes one's cue from philosophical soliloquies on meaning or from ordinary conversations conducted at coffee tables.[2] The ordinary hearer or reader *is* and remains

---

2. This is said in full knowledge of the dangers of an appeal to 'common knowledge'. The appeal here is a very pragmatic one and should *not* be viewed in the light of, for instance, common sense philosophy. Common-sense philosophy aims at precluding doubt and producing certitude, which, as will become clear, is not at all the aim of the present argument. I fully agree with Routledge (1995: 43) that a major problem with an appeal to 'common knowledge' is that, 'should the experience/knowledge of the reader not coincide with that of the writer, there is no means provided to convince the reader through demonstration'. Not to walk into this trap, I shall introduce relevance theory as 'demonstration'. The point here merely is that academic pronouncements on the indeterminacy of language some-

interested in the intention of the person addressing her at the coffee table. Otherwise she would never have interrupted his speech with 'What do you mean?', 'Do I understand you correctly?' or 'Are you mad?' The first question implies that she is not clear about the speaker's real intention, or that she cannot believe that he intended what she understood him to say. The second question politely requests the speaker to confirm her interpretation of his intention. The third question asserts her certainty that she understood the speaker's intention and that she sharply disagrees with it. Equally, a speaker may object to a wrong construction of his intention by saying 'You got me wrong' or 'But that is not what I said' or 'You are reading into my words what is not there'.

Everybody would naturally agree that the 'intention' of an author and the 'effect' of his speech may differ widely. That is why in defamation lawsuits a court of law takes the effect of a newspaper report more seriously than the author's intention. But 'effect' cannot without any further ado be equated with 'meaning'. On the one hand, a particular effect may be based on an interpretation that can be shown to be at fault. On the other hand, the fact that an utterance may be ambiguous (what the speaker intended and what the hearer took it to mean) does not rule out or erase the author's intended meaning as a *legitimate* meaning of the utterance. Of course, only a die-hard positivist of the dinosaur type would still believe that a hearer can really get into the head of a speaker to retrace his thoughts. However, if one *could* look into the speaker's mind, one would be inclined to say that his intention (i.e. the meaning he thought he was verbalizing) is the meaning of the utterance. This is at least the case in ordinary conversation. If a speaker corrects a misunderstanding of his intention, the hearer normally accepts his explanation and that her interpretation was at fault. The problem is of course that the Hebrew Bible, as Freedman (1978: 87) reminds us with reference to the past in general, 'cannot talk back; it is exotic and dumb'. Which leaves us only with its *readers* to work with.

In view of the fact that 'authorial intention' is alive, operative *and* functional in ordinary conversation, and seeing that one may avoid the 'intentional fallacy' by involving the *perspective of a reader* in the argument (as will be shown below), one would perhaps be well advised not to dump the term.

times tend to ignore the fact that these statements are *intended* to communicate some thing very *specific* about language.

'Intention phobia' is one of the by-products of the heavy emphasis, especially of some forms of 'immanent' exegetical methods, put on the purely linguistic and formal side of texts. There has been a trend in the last 30 or 40 years of literary criticism which manifests itself in an emphasis on the structure of a literary work as a *autonomous entity*. This trend, present in 'immanent', 'structural' or 'close reading' approaches, depends among other things, on the code model of communication, with its narrow focus on linguistic matters.

According to the code model of communication, a speaker, employing the linguistic code (phonology, syntax, semantics, literary forms, etc.) of a particular language and using a particular medium (e.g. oral or written prose or poetry), encodes his message and sends it through a channel. At the other end of the channel the receiver employs the particular language's linguistic decoding rules to retrieve the coded message. In this view, communication consists of the *linguistic* encoding and decoding of meaning. What is recovered in the process of decoding is the *semantic representation* of an utterance. This process may be graphically represented as follows.

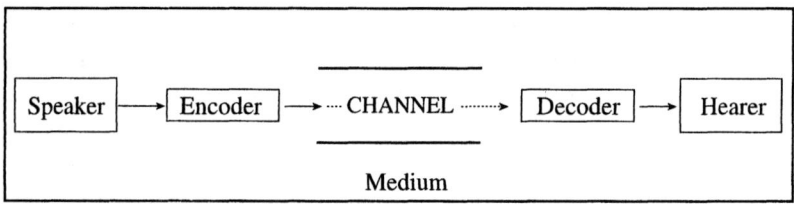

It is precisely the purely linguistic basis of the model that makes its explanation of successful communication problematic. Given the overlap among the semantic components of terms and linguistic structures, and the consequent associative play of meaning these overlaps allow, it becomes extremely problematic to 'pinpoint' the meaning of an utterance.

Jakobson (1960) may be right that, in ordinary speech, a person selects one member of a (paradigmatic) class of terms and combines it (syntagmatically) with terms selected from other paradigms to form a sentence. This procedure may, with Posner (1971: 236-37), be graphically represented as follows:

1. Culture and Interpretation

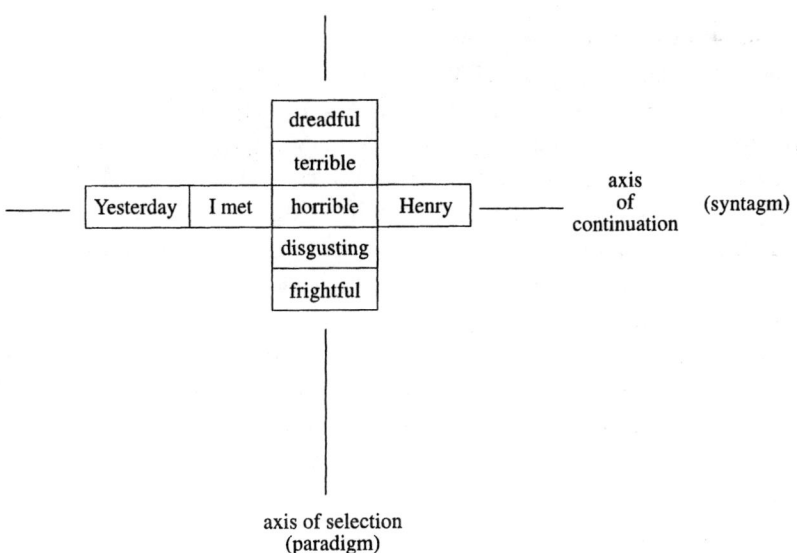

The problem is, however, that the meaning of one selected term from a class in a way implies or 'activates' the meanings of other members of the paradigm. It is in this context that deconstructionists speak of meaning with reference to 'deferring', 'effacing' or 'replacement'. Risking oversimplification, one may illustrate the point by trying to locate the meaning of 'infer'.

Looking up this word in a thesaurus reveals a series of terms in its immediate surroundings (Jakobson's 'paradigm'), such as 'deduce, conclude, induce, reason, presume, conjecture'. On looking up these terms, one is confronted with yet another series of terms, for example, a 'conjecture' occurs with terms like 'speculate, imagine, guess, surmise, *conclude*, venture, hypothesise'. One can continue along this line virtually *ad infinitum* without ever getting at the 'meaning' of 'infer', because 'infer' is merely replaced by other terms, which are in their turn replaced by yet other terms. This is, despite Ayer's belief in the existence of true synonyms (Ayer 1974: 80), true of all linguistic meaning. Linguistic context puts but a weak restriction on the possible associations a reader might make in reading a text containing the term 'infer'. Had linguistic structure and semantics been all that we had to work with in communication there would, for this reason, hardly be any communication going on at all. That is why the 'meaning' of a text, if approached purely linguistically, may be construed in a variety of directions, and why the logical positivists finally had to revert to symbolic logic to achieve explicitness.

However, in real communication people not only follow the rules of language but also certain pragmatic principles. This means recognizing presuppositions and implications behind the actual words used... Understanding a text means comprehending more than the logical structure and the purely designative or defining meanings of the lexical and grammatical structures. A listener or reader is usually engaged in a several operations almost simultaneously: (1) the literal, propositional content, (2) the relevance and impact of that content, (3) the aesthetic character of the rhetorical structures, (4) the motivations and background of the writer or speaker, (5) the intertextuality of the discourse, and (6) the frame of reference which provides coherence within the text and with the real or imagined world.

Given these shortcomings, it would be wise to look for an alternative model of communication that can better explain why successful communication takes place *in spite* of the indeterminacy of linguistic expression.

Without claiming universal validity for the model, it would seem that, compared to the code model, relevance theory, formulated by Sperber and Wilson in the mid 1980s, not only better explains the success and failure of human communication but also aptly illustrates the wisdom of viewing *author's intention* and *cultural information* as constituents of human communication, and therefore of interpretation. What follows is but the skeleton of a complex and elaborate theory.

The role assigned in relevance theory to the recovery of the semantic representation of utterances marks one of its major deviations from the code model. The semantic representation recovered by the hearer through the linguistic decoding system merely forms the *starting point* for the process of utterance interpretation. It is an input system rather than a central processing system. Communication is achieved not by coding and decoding messages, but by constructing a hypothesis about the communicator's intentions. Relevance theory has it that, in listening to speakers, hearers continuously *formulate and validate hypotheses regarding the rational intentions of speakers*.

Two kinds of communicative stimuli 'invite' attention from hearers. The first kind is stimuli with 'innate' relevance. That is, stimuli to which people react spontaneously, such as any noise that signals a life-threatening situation. The second kind is ostensive stimuli, that is,

1. Culture and Interpretation

stimuli that *intentionally* direct a hearer's attention. Relevance theory deals specifically with the way in which hearers 'recover' the meaning of ostensive stimuli.

In the process of human communication, speakers tacitly guarantee the optimal relevance of ostensive stimuli and hearers assume them to be optimally relevant. It is precisely the assumption that an ostensive stimulus optimally 'points to' something relevant that invites hearers to process the information imparted by it. However, in any particular context of communication a hearer expects more than just 'optimal' or 'general' relevance from an ostensive stimulus. She expects *adequate* relevance.

'Relevance', the key concept in this theory of communication, rests on two pillars. First, the relevance of an utterance's meaning depends on the adequacy of its effect on a hearer's *cognitive world*, that is, the cognitive 'picture' of the world in terms of which she interprets and speaks about reality. An effect may be achieved by effectively affirming, challenging or broadening the content and structure of the hearer's cognitive world. Where this does indeed happen, communication is said to have had *adequate* contextual effect.

A hearer's cognitive world exhibits a *particular* content and structure. Consequently, the criteria for deciding whether a particular communication has adequate contextual effect vary from (social) situation to situation, and, perhaps of greater consequence for the present discussion, from culture to culture.

Second, 'relevance' involves the amount of effort a hearer has to devote to process the information imparted by an utterance. For example, the less processing effort is required the greater the chances are that the intended effect will be achieved. But also, if a particular utterance requires more processing effort to have a contextual effect, such extra effort should be 'rewarded' with *greater* contextual effect, or meaning. In this connection one may speak of *justifiable* processing effort.

In the process of listening to a speaker the hearer constantly formulates hypotheses regarding the speaker's intention. And she accepts as the speaker's intention that interpretation that achieves a *maximal contextual effect* in exchange for *a minimum amount of processing effort*. In short, she takes as the correct interpretation of an utterance that interpretation that is consistent with the principle of relevance.

The discussion thus far may be summarized as follows:

Speaker ←	→ Hearer
By speaking, tacitly guarantees relevance	Assumes relevance of ostensive stimulus and formulates hypotheses on the intended meaning on the basis of: • the contextual effect the communication has on her • cognitive world, and selects that interpretation that • requires the least processing effort, or • rewards extra processing effort with extra relevance

This does not mean that every ostensive stimulus is necessarily intended to have contextual effect, or that every hearer will in every case infer meaning from an ostensive stimulus. An utterance might, for example, be intentionally misleading, or a hearer may fail to infer the meaning of a particular utterance. But in such cases the principle of relevance does not apply. In the case of misleading statements the speaker does not fulfil the expectation of optimal relevance, and in the case of a hearer failing to infer contextually relevant information from an utterance no communication takes place. *Meaning* can only be intended and recovered if, and only if, the principle of relevance applies. However, wherever this principle does apply, an utterance has, from the perspective of the hearer, *at the most one (intended) meaning*.

From the presentation of the theory above it might seem as if relevance theory puts its foot right into the trap of the intentional fallacy. This is, however, not the case. It is not even suggested that a hearer can 'read' a speaker's mind. What a hearer does while listening to a speaker, is to

(a) *assume* the ostensive stimulus to be intended to have optimal contextual effect,
(b) constantly formulate, test, and evaluate *hypotheses* on the meaning of an utterance with reference to the principle of relevance, and
(c) accept as the best hypothesis on the intended meaning *that* hypothesis that requires the least processing effort *and* yields adequate contextual effect.

There is thus no guarantee *other than the principle of relevance* that the hypothesis accepted by the hearer as the correct interpretation of the utterance is in fact the intended meaning. As soon as a hearer is satisfied that her interpretation is consistent with the principle of relevance, she accepts *that meaning to be the intended meaning*. Not even Wimsatt (1968) could have trouble with this view of authorial intention, since he talked about the author's intention 'as it appears in the work itself *and can be read from the work*'. Relevance theory also speaks about author's intention in terms of *hearers/readers*. But, contrary to Wimsatt, it encourages us to accept that, because meaning is more than mere semantics, *language* and *linguistic structures* are not all that readers have to judge authorial intention by.

In deciding which hypothesis represents the 'most readily accessible interpretation', the reader's culturally constituted *cognitive world* is deeply involved. Moreover, the principles she applies in taking a decision on a speaker's intended meaning are, according to relevance theory, for the most part not of a linguistic, but rather of a contextual and cultural nature. These criteria include the following:

(a) The more processed information links up with recently processed information the more easily accessible new information will be (the principle of recency). In the case of biblical interpretation this principle would involve the immediate context of a sentence, paragraph or text, events immediately preceding an utterance, also employed in forms of 'immanent' exegesis.

(b) The more stereotyped the processed information is the more accessible it will be (the principle of frequency). In the case of biblical literature this principle would involve tradition, values and customs relevant to the original situation of speaker and hearer, stereotyped literary forms (or a play on them), etc.

(c) The more extensive the hearer's encyclopaedic memory the less effort is required to process new information and the better the chances are that communication will have a contextual effect. In biblical literature this principle would involve the question of who is speaking to whom and what the structure of their respective cognitive worlds could have been.

(d) The higher the ranking of communicated knowledge is in the hearer's conceptual hierarchy, the better the chances are that less processing effort will be required and that related information will have a contextual effect. In the case of biblical literature this principle would involve the status of the hearer, her interests, needs, convictions, fears, beliefs, etc.

(e) The closer the resemblance between the speaker's assumptions about the cognitive world of the hearer and her real cognitive world, the less processing effort is required and the more apparent the contextual effect of the communication will be. In biblical literature this principle would once again involve questions like who is speaking to whom? what is the relevant status of the hearer in relation to the speaker? etc.

The more of these principles that apply to a particular interpretation the more the reader becomes convinced that *that* interpretation *is* the intended meaning.

Without claiming messianic status for relevance theory, it may be said to be more adequate than the traditional code model of communication in explaining *success and failure* in human communication. Applied to biblical interpretation, successful interpretation implies the availability to the interpreter of information regarding, for instance, the cognitive worlds of the speakers and hearers in biblical times.[3]

Chapter 3 will argue that the (re)construction of those cognitive worlds involves knowledge of the *whole cultural system* of the time, for example; customs, institutions, social relations, political system, control systems, social values and religious convictions.

One could present a similar argument from a quite different angle. It was argued earlier that linguistic meaning has the habit of deferring meaning. To afford understanding a linguistic community must have ways of 'framing' conversations so as to curb the constant process of replacement. Put differently, the hearer must be able to select those intertexts for the speaker's text that would make successful communication possible. For example, the way speakers formulate their intentions and the linguistic registers they choose depend very much on the social situation in which communication takes place. One situation, for example, during rituals, may imply a high frequency of metaphors, which can only be interpreted if the hearer has sufficient knowledge of the speaker's culture. Another situation, such as praising a king, might call for the use of hyperbole. Equally, to be able to follow an argument, the reader has to be acquainted with the criteria for classification and

---

3. Henceforth I shall, for the sake of brevity and convenience, merely speak of the different cultures relevant to Syro-Palestine of biblical times as if they constituted one culture, and therefore of the culture of biblical times. Section 6 of this chapter will deal more pertinently with the problem of 'biblical culture'.

1. *Culture and Interpretation*

the logic applicable in the particular culture. Not being able to select the suitable intertext(s) for the interpretation of a text will lead to misunderstanding or incomprehension. Successful communication therefore implies the ability on the side of the hearer/reader to select suitable intertext(s) that will sufficiently 'frame' a text for the purpose of sensible interpretation in a particular situation.

Also, from the perspective of sociology of knowledge, acquaintance with the culture of which a text is part is indispensable for understanding it. Although arguing from a rather old-fashioned definition of 'authorial intention', Mannheim attacked the doctrine of semantic autonomy. For him 'semantic autonomy' *surrendered the ideal of successful communication*, because in this view every interpretation that can be shown to be consistent with the norms of the relevant language has an equal claim to authenticity. Commenting on the implications of Mannheim's theory of knowledge for hermeneutics, Simonds (1975: 83) writes,

> To secure full understanding of the meaning of a cultural product we must recognize that it is presented not only immediately, in the determinate physical, structural, temporal, etc. properties of the product as 'something in itself', but also immediately: that is, the product also stands for and points to meanings which transcend whatever is given directly. For this reason, adequate interpretation of an object of this kind requires us constantly to look beyond the work in two different directions: first, to the specific intentional act by which meaning was conferred upon the work by its author, and second, to the larger (but still historically specific) context of intersubjective meanings which that intentional act reflected and also presupposed.

Viewed from this perspective successful communication also *implies* the cultural complex of which a text and its language formed a part.

2. *The Necessity of Cultural Information for Synchronic Interpretation*

Even those who choose to adopt a synchronic, immanent or close reading approach to interpretation cannot do without cultural knowledge, not merely because immanent interpretation is unavoidably involved in a process of communication, but also because synchronic interpretation—in so far as this term is not a misnomer—by definition *implies* the cultural context of texts.

Since the 1960s there has been a heated debate among biblical scholars on whether diachronic textual analysis has anything to contribute to answer the question, 'What does *this text* mean?' Much of what has been said in favour of synchronic analysis and about reading the Bible 'as literature' is, without a doubt, valuable and helpful, perhaps even true. The main problem, however, is that the overt or covert suggestion in many of these studies seems to be that, apart from outlawing diachronic strategies of interpretation, a mere appeal to 'synchronic' analysis, or a mere dropping of the name of Ferdinand de Saussure, justified the exclusion of cultural and historical arguments in the process of interpretation. But a reference to either synchronic analysis in general, or to de Saussure in particular, does not justify either of the two suppositions.

Since any method is constituted by a coherent ideological context integrating particular methodical procedures (Maren-Grisebach 1970: 5), it is necessary to construct the ideological context of de Saussure's notion of 'synchrony' (Deist 1995).[4]

Having been trained by neo-grammarians acquainted with natural evolutionist linguistics as well as with Gilliéron's linguistic geography, and having had a lively interest in the Slavic linguistic schools as well as in Durkheim's views on sociology, de Saussure nevertheless chose not to explain linguistic data with reference to non-linguistic phenomena, such as nation, geography and history. He rather chose to apply his mind to what he called 'pure linguistics' (de Saussure 1983 [1922]: par. 143).

His famous analogy of a chess game to explain what synchronic linguistics was about is sometimes misinterpreted by biblical scholars.

---

4. At the time a major methodological shift was taking place in various disciplines, for example, in philosophy, psychology, historiography and literary interpretation. Leo Pohlmann (1971: 105) aptly calls this shift 'die Wende nach innen' and typifies it as follows (my translation), 'Something similar to what was happening in psychology and philosophy had to take place [in literary studies]. Nietzsche, Freud, Bergson and Husserl turned the perspective around to constitute the world afresh from the perspective of...intentionality.' Leo Spitzer (quoted by Hough 1969: 13) said it a nutshell, '[As students] we were never allowed to contemplate a phenomenon in its pure being, to look into its face: we always looked at its neighbours or at its predecessors.' De Saussure (1983 [1922]: 34, my emphasis) expressed the same idea, saying that 'nothing is more appropriate than the study of language to bring out the nature of the semiological problem. But to formulate the problem suitably, it would be necessary to study what language is *in itself...whereas hitherto a language has usually been considered as a function of something else*, from other points of view.'

The analogy is used in order to to make a few points. First of all, just as the material and the form of the chessmen are 'arbitrary' in relation to their ascribed function in the system of the game, so the meaning of a linguistic sign is arbitrary in relation to its history or form. This observation is not meant as a generalization, though. The 'arbitrariness' of sound-form-meaning combinations in language draws on *comparativist* linguistics. The combinations making up the vocabulary and grammar of a particular language are arbitrary *only* when they are compared with the combinations in another language. The combinations in a particular language are *obligatory* and prescribed by the particular linguistic *community*. In this regard de Saussure (1983 [1922]: par. 104) said that 'from the point of view of the linguistic community the signal is imposed rather than freely chosen... The community, as much as the individual, is bound to its language.' There is thus no way in which a *particular* 'chess game' (e.g. Israelite literature) can be understood (and described) without reference to these obligatory rules, dictated by that *particular linguistic community*.

The second point of the analogy is that, just as a particular move in a chess game *changes* the scene on the board, so every linguistic change (following the rules for linguistic change) somehow affects the complete linguistic system. Such a change may be very marginal or it may reshape the whole system. But, and this is where de Saussure deviated from the comparativists, each new situation on the chessboard can be observed and described without reference to the positions of the chessmen prior to the move that brought about that particular arrangement. What he was interested in were the *relations* between the chessmen on the board. However, this observation did not imply or mean that evolutionary explanations of linguistic phenomena were wrong. Levinson (1994: 39, 57) rightly observes,

> Both synchrony and diachrony...are interpretative constructs... [I]t is simply unjustified to claim that an immanent approach to biblical and cuneiform law mandates synchronic analysis. Such a claim overlooks the extent to which synchronic analysis is itself an interpretative construction that strives to explain the evidence.

But there is another important aspect of the synchronic approach that should not be overlooked. Following Hermann Paul, de Saussure distinguished between observing the concrete speech of different individuals (*parole*) and an average abstract type of the language they speak (*langue*). *Langue*, as the institutionalized repository of a speech community, dictates the rules of the language at any given stage, while *parole* consists of particular speech actions. In order to eliminate the changing influence and unstable nature of *la parole* on the rules of *la langue*, de Saussure focused, and this is important, on *la langue* at a *specific point in time*. He explains,

> In the synchronic study of Old French, the linguist uses facts and principles which have nothing in common with those which would be revealed by the history of the same language from the thirteenth to the twentieth century, but are comparable to those which would emerge from the description of a *modern* Bantu language, or Attic Greek *in 400 BC*, or French at the *present day* (de Saussure 1983 [1922]: par. 139, my emphasis).

As Wells (1966: 9-11) pointed out, synchronic linguistics was methodologically opposed to at least two other (equally legitimate) approaches to linguistics: on the one hand, to dialect geography, which need not concern us here; and, on the other hand, to diachronic linguistics. In this connection Wells (1966: 9, my emphasis) remarks

> On the one hand, synchronic linguistics abstracts from time and change *not by treating facts of different times as though they were simultaneous*—doing this has been a common mistake, sometimes deliberate; but by considering a langue during a *span of time too short to show any appreciable change*.

What biblical scholars often do in the name of 'synchronic' interpretation, is precisely to treat facts of different times as though they were simultaneous. This cannot be done with an appeal to de Saussure.

For de Saussure, at least, synchrony meant that *langue* is studied with reference to a particular point in time. To choose a synchronic approach and to then ignore the 'chronic' dimension (i.e. reference to time), as so often happens in synchronic biblical studies, is to misuse the method. *Syn*chrony is not the same as *a*chrony. A really synchronic approach to the 'final text' of the Hebrew Bible (which has become so popular over the last decades) should, for example, treat the text as a product of the eleventh century CE and as reflecting the linguistic rules of *that* time. However much one may differ from Labuschagne's conclusions regarding the numerical patterns in the Pentateuch (Labuschagne 1982, 1984), these patterns, as far as they do in fact exist, are most probably cabbalistic inventions of mediaeval Massoretes, who produced that text (see, however, Rand 1991–92). They are, so to speak, the fingerprints of the time in which the 'final text' had been 'published'. Any interpreter purporting to read these texts 'asynchronically' but at the same time treating them as 'Israelite' literature of a pre-Christian date commits a methodological mistake or employs a crypto-diachronic approach.

There is no way in which an appeal to a synchronic approach can become an excuse for not *dating* a text in question or ignoring its social setting. Synchrony, in its strict as well as its more generic sense, demands a statement on the date of the 'textual state' under investigation. But to date a text is to speak about it in relation to other texts of the particular community, that is, to imply diachronic and social information.

Ironically, if the time and society from which a text originated are ignored, as often happens in synchronic interpretations, a social (and mental) framework foreign to the text itself is substituted as interpretative context. This is not only a problem in present-day 'synchronic' studies, though. The same problem also often manifests itself in historical critical studies. In deciding whether a particular phrase or section in a text does or does not 'fit the context' or constitutes a contradiction, one has to be acutely aware of the criteria of *logic* employed. It is, for example, more than merely debatable whether the logic of text construction *at the time and in the culture in which biblical texts originated* was compatible with post-enlightenment linear logic, on which historical critical decisions depend. Historical critics have seldom looked into this problem and have often substituted their own logic for that of ancient authors, who seemed to have been quite capable of living with what we would look upon as blatant logical contradictions. Not every logical contradiction or textual unevenness has to point to redactional activity. But it would, for the same reason, be equally wrong to defend the 'integrity' of a text by *rationalizing* and *harmonizing* contradictions in order to warrant a 'synchronic' approach.

Still within the orbit of synchrony, but viewed from another angle, it might even become problematic to employ de Saussure's method in an act of *interpretation*. Apart from the fact that his synchronic approach was not at all interested in *meaning* or the interpretation of texts,[5] two more serious, objections may be raised against 'synchronic' *interpretation*.

---

5. For him 'linguistics' formed *part* of the study of semiology, which deals with the role of signs as part of social life (de Saussure 1983 [1922]: par. 33).

First, synchronic linguistics is by definition not interested in specific instances of *parole*. On the contrary, it focuses exclusively on *langue*. Any literary text is, however, an instance of *parole*, because it is the product of the individual use of *langue*. It is in this context of some interest to note that de Saussure's pupil Bally, in discussing stylistics, heavily emphasized *parole*. Hough (1969: 25-26) summarizes Bally's views as follows, 'At the base of Bally's thought is the idea of language in the service of life, language as a function of life, soaked in human affections, mingled with human strivings, existing only to fulfil the purposes of life itself'. De Saussure himself (1983 [1922]: par. 31) said of *parole* that it was (my emphasis)

> an *individual act of the will and the intelligence*, in which we must distinguish: (1) the combination through which the speaker uses the code provided by the language (*langue*) in order to express his own thought, and (2) the psycho-physical mechanism which enables him to externalise these combinations.

Apart from the element of individual 'phonation', texts are also realizations of individual choice, which lie outside the scope of synchronic analysis.

Secondly, for the very reason that *parole* is 'in the service of life', and is a 'function of life, soaked in human affections' and 'mingled with human strivings', interpreting an instance of *parole* necessarily involves language-external factors deriving from the complexities of life itself. Literary interpretation is not interested in language for the sake of language itself, but, in the words of de Saussure (1983 [1922]: par. 34), in language as a 'function of something else', for instance, as the carrier of religious and social ideas. Interpretation *has* to take into account language external factors. But any approach to language that involves language-external factors disqualifies it as an instance of 'synchronic' analysis in de Saussure's sense of the term.

What has been said thus far, does not in any way invalidate literary interpretations of biblical texts that are called 'synchronic' (but should rather have been referred to as 'phenomenological'). Even a literary interpretation that completely ignores the social setting of a text is at least a partial interpretation that may be of great value. The point rather is that a quick reference to de Saussure or 'synchronic analysis' as an excuse for ignoring the historical and cultural dimensions of a biblical text will not do. Moreover, de Saussure's use of the term 'synchronic' *demands* that texts should be viewed as instances of *parole*, which, as an instance of the use of *langue*, forms an integral part of a complete local social system. Even if an interpreter chooses to follow the road of synchronic analysis, texts therefore *ought* to be interpreted with reference to their extra-linguistic environment.

3. *The Validation of Interpretation and Cultural Information*

Impressed by the achievements of the natural sciences, humanist scholars have for a considerable time cherished the ideals of objectivity in observation, theory construction and verification. In this tradition 'facts' are spoken of as tangible things and 'theories' as buildings. A fact should, for instance, be 'hard' in order to function as a 'building block' in the 'construction' of theories. To avoid the label 'shaky' or 'falling apart' a theory should have a sound 'foundation' and be 'buttressed' with 'solid' arguments. Depending on the degree of objectivity that may be achieved in a particular field of enquiry the ensuing science may be 'hard' or 'soft'. Such are the metaphors modernist Western science had traditionally been living by, and to an extent is still living by. This sentiment is, for instance, shared by Wolfgang Richter (1989: 12, my translation, incorporating also n. 13), 'It is...clear that [the Hebrew Bible] may and should be studied through the application of the same [natural scientific] empirical-rational methods as all other literatures.' It is, however, precisely the sentiment challenged by postmodernism.

Postmodernism has many faces. Some even doubt whether it does in fact constitute a new movement or merely represents a revival of old-fashioned romanticism. One may, however, safely say that, compared to earlier ideals of knowledge, the second half of the twentieth century, more particularly the last three decades, has seen a major shift in opinion. The ideal of objectively verified knowledge has in many minds made way for a much more modest (if any) claim to certainty. Consider, for instance, the following remark by Paul Feyerabend (1996: 195-96):

> To those who look at the rich material provided by history, and who are not intent on impoverishing it in order to please their lower instincts, their craving for intellectual security in the form of clarity, precision, 'objectivity', 'truth', it will become clear that there is only one principle that can be defended under *all* circumstances and in *all* stages of human development. It is the principle: *anything goes*.

This change of mind is not a mere fantasy of a small number of cranky, subversive, leftist academics. The academic debate rather reflects a global *cultural* tendency parented by two forces, the one political and the other economic. On the one hand, the notion of the political state as a tightly knit homogeneous national unit (symbolizing converging interests and certainties) has, at least since the demise of colonialism, been crumbling under the pressure of the assertiveness of (cultural, sexual and religious) diversity *within* the state, and is merely mirrored in the ongoing debate on multiculturalism. As previously voiceless minorities intensify their struggle to be *who they are and to see things their own way*, it became increasingly difficult to align 'the public' behind any single 'national interest' or 'truth'. The former unified national state is steadily changing into an aggregation of identities and views.

The second force, more powerful than the national state, namely economic globalization, is pressing for more than just 'national unity'. It presses for the local accommodation of foreign—even alien—mores, views of the world and truths from far away places. As the effacing effect of this drive for universality and similarity increases and, as a consequence, threatens smaller identities (even national states) with absorption into a faceless regional or global humanity, these smaller identities defend themselves by intensifying their insistence on locality, contingency and individuality. Therefore, although there is on the economic front a drive towards universalization, the cultural reaction is away from universalization towards emphasizing local identity, values and truths.

Under these circumstances there is little sense or salvation in pretending that nothing has changed in the world and that it can be (epistemological) business as usual. Neither is there an easy way 'around' these issues. Diversity of viewpoints is the name of the game. If one wishes to speak about *knowledge*, one has to reckon and deal with the 'erosive' power of perspectivism.

The scholarly community—also in the field of biblical exegesis—has over the past few decades sought to stem the erosive effect of perspectivism by making the formerly hard borders of its disciplines more fluffy so as to enable it to embrace an inter- and multidisciplinary approach. Even though this approach has often been adopted with the view to ensuring greater objectivity in uncovering the 'real' state of affairs, it often transpired that different disciplinary perspectives, each with its own set of criteria and values, yield results that are not easily collapsible into one sound and universal 'truth'. Rather than unveiling the truth this approach often demonstrated the *complexity* of 'reality' and the difficulty of telling and verifying statements on 'how things really are'. Oversimplifying, one may visually represent the preceding discussion as follows:

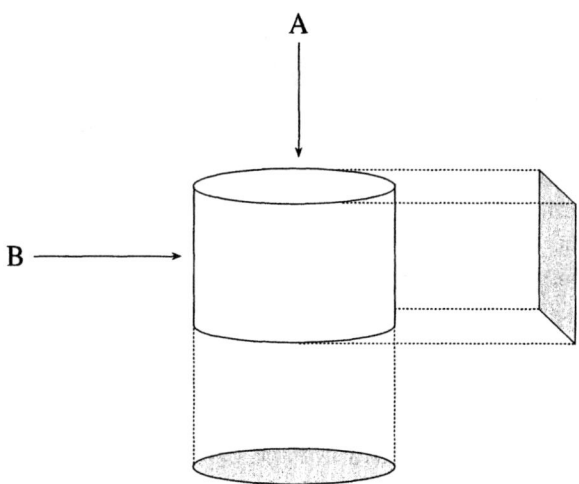

Projected from two perspectives (A and B), a three-dimensional object casts different shadows on a two-dimensional surface. Should observer A or B view his or her observational position as the only true one, he or she may take that particular projection to represent 'reality' and proceed to 'verify' his or her conclusion regarding the shape of the object by observing, measuring, and describing the shadow. Should A and B decide to apply a multidisciplinary approach, they may end up with two mutually exclusive conclusions. With the 'real' world out of sight the two observers seem to be 'doomed' to perspectivism.

But is this necessarily the case? Even Jacques Derrida, who is sometimes (mistakenly) construed as a representative of the 'anything goes' mood, acknowledges the necessity of curbing the productive power of interpretation, lest 'critical production would risk developing in any direction at all and authorize itself to say almost anything' (Derrida 1996: 85). And Feyerabend, whose 'anything goes' phrase was quoted earlier on, does not wish to make a matter-of-fact statement. The point he wishes to make is that no theory can lead to certitude because 'all methodologies, even the most obvious ones, have their limits' and 'how easy it is to lead people by the nose in a rational way' (1996: 199). Perspectivism does not by itself imply radical relativism in knowledge construction.

Kant had argued that we do not have access to reality itself. We work with *medially observed* and *perceived* reality. Had we—in godlike fashion—known the true dimensions of the *projected* (perceived) object in the sketch above we would have known that both perceptions of it were wrong, *and yet not altogether wrong*. We would also have known that it would have been better to accept both perceptions, even though they would, from the point of view of the observers, seem to be mutually exclusive. If both parties would accept the *relativity* of their observational perspectives, an opportunity could have been created for them to *argue* about the better observational position, to formulate *hypotheses* on the shape of the perceived object, or to accept their views to be complementary. It is therefore possible wholeheartedly to endorse the relativity of observation *without* giving up the search for validity. Once one has accepted the relativity of one's own perspective as well as the (equal) right of other observers to have genuine perceptions that may differ, the playing fields are levelled for a constructive debate.

Such a debate probably will not and cannot lead to the discovery or formulation of a 'universal truth', but it may, at the very least, allow for a *better argued option*, since in confrontation with alternative views different observers will, if they are honestly in search of truth, at least be forced to scrutinize their respective observational positions and strategies. But this is not all that can be won. It also becomes possible from this position to discriminate between better and worse interpretations.

In this context the term 'validity' becomes important. Any dictionary will tell that *validity* has to do with plausibility, effectiveness, genuineness, and the like, and that its opposites have to do with deceitfulness, delusiveness, beguiling, and so on. 'Plausibility' refers to the evidence presented in favour of a view held, and together with 'effectiveness' points to the *convincing* power of the presentation of a case, while 'genuineness' indicates the more ethical side of the presentation involving good old honesty (as compared to deceitfulness).

The convincingness or otherwise of a presentation depends on its plausibility and its effectiveness. While effectiveness has to do with the important issue of the rhetoric and aesthetics of the presented argument, plausibility involves the degree to which the presentation succeeds in explaining observations with reference to the relevant cognitive struc-

1. *Culture and Interpretation*

tures of the observers, that is, their way of seeing the world, or in effectively changing that view to make room for accepting the explanation as plausible. For example, the *observation* of similarities and differences among various living organisms may be *explained* with reference to at least two cognitive structures, namely with reference to biological evolution or creationism. The evolutionary explanation of the observations will only be plausible for people sharing a more or less naturalistic world view, while the creationist explanation will only make sense for people sharing a (literalist) biblicistic world view. That is why debates between biological evolutionists and creationists are usually fairly futile. Since some explanations may be *more* plausible than others, the plausibility of an explanation involves more than a mere shared frame of reference. It also involves an agreed set of criteria with reference to which degrees of plausibility may be measured. Such criteria sometimes, if not mostly, are context specific, contingent, transient and perhaps even ideological. But that does not disqualify them as criteria (see, in this context, Shmueli 1970).

One may graphically represent the preceding argument as follows:

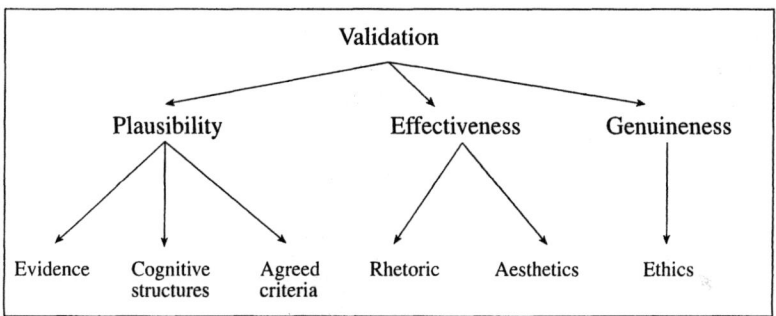

Paul Moser (1986) and Willern Verloren van Themaat (1989) would strongly object to the idea of 'justification by consensus' implied here and promoted by philosophers of science like Stephen Toulmin, Thomas Kuhn and Harold Brown. For Moser (1986: 158), consensus as a basis for the validation of propositions, if it could be shown to exist anywhere, would deprive one of any ground for holding views that are at variance with the consensus view, for, 'If one has no good reason to believe that such a consensus supports one's beliefs, then one will have no good reasons for one's beliefs.' This argument is problematic. On the one hand, *consensus* is not a substitute word for 'universality of acclaim'. On the other hand, the argument confuses 'certitude' and 'conviction'.

Richard Rorty (1996: 96-97) mentions a series of 'final' words typical of the vocabulary of justification. Some of them, such as 'good', 'right' and 'beautiful' are flexible and ubiquitous. Others, such as 'professional standards', 'progressive' and 'rigorous' are more rigid and parochial. He explains, 'These words are "final" in the sense that if doubt is cast on the worth of these words, their user has no noncircular argumentative recourse.' He might have included 'universal' under the set of parochial terms, for scholars for whom 'justification' or 'verification' is all-important (because these processes are believed to secure certitude of knowledge) greatly value *universally* acceptable epistemological criteria. However, as Sandra Harding (1994) and Hans-Martin Sass (1980) convincingly argue, the epistemological standard of 'rationality' that is supposed to ensure certitude of knowledge may not be as universal, and their products not as beneficial, as many of these scholars seem to take for granted. Bernstein (1983: 74-75) would say that, even though it is possible to reconstruct the rational basis on which choices between theories have been made over the centuries, there is no 'algorithm of truth' available. For this reason, an appeal to universal 'rationality' is perhaps no less shaky than an appeal to local 'consensus'.

This kind of argument is not very effective, though. What is more important is that Moser seems to caricature the strategy of justification by consensus. He asks,

> [W]hat constitutes a *consensus* of the scientific community? Must there be a unanimous decision in favour of the acceptability of a theory? Or is a simple majority decision sufficient? Further, what if the scientific community has a split decision on the acceptability of a particular theory? Should we then say that both the theory and its denial are rationally acceptable? In any case, there is rarely, if ever, complete agreement among the members of a scientific community, and even if there were such agreement, it would be very difficult to verify (1986: 158).

As Moser admits, there are 'schools of thought' in all fields of knowledge, some holding views contradicting or complementing views held by other schools. Consider, for example, the contradictory statements made by various schools of medicine on what causes cancer, heart attacks and whatnot. Since *all* of them appeal to rationality, that appeal does not assist us very much in finding 'the rational truth' of the kind

Moser is after. We are left with *variety of plausible opinions.*

The appeal to scholarly consensus does not and cannot imply universal assent, as Moser would prefer. Scholars preferring immanent textual interpretation may, for example, be said to have reached consensus on many issues regarding textual analysis. For that reason exegetes in that school of thought do not invent the wheel every time they set out to interpret a text. Through references and footnotes they appeal to *locally* achieved *consensus.* The locus here refers to an academic approach (to exegesis). It may, however, also be constituted by a particular paradigm in the Kuhnian sense of the word, a theory, or even consensus reached at some academic institution. Consider, for example, terms like the 'Amsterdam school' or the 'Göttingen school', the existence of which cannot be explained as instances of irrationality or poor rationality. Consensus cannot be universal and cannot claim 'majority opinion'. Neither can it ever 'verify' anything, as Moser wants it to do. The 'local' nature of consensus precludes any claim to certitude. Routledge (1995: 48) says in this regard, 'In such a context the contention between knowledge claims is not an unfortunate by-product of human imperfection, but rather a central act in the shaping of knowledge.' Consensus cannot therefore lead to certitude. What it can do however, is invite the mustering of support for a particular *conviction.*

A conviction is something one is persuaded of. Even though the support of a consensus opinion may strengthen one's conviction, the lack of consensus does not, as Moser holds, by definition invalidate the conviction. The practice of everyday life may once again show the way here, since people daily take important decisions without being certain that they are absolutely right. They take decisions because they are *convinced* that A is a better option than B.

There are at least two ways in which a person may 'justify' a conviction that is at variance with a consensus opinion. The first way is in some way related to 'verification', although less 'scientific'. People tend to work with what Tadeusz Buksinski (1985) calls 'indicators' and judge them according to 'qualitative probabalism'. Whenever a desired insight cannot be obtained through direct observation of 'facts' (e.g. the meaning of a written text or a historical event) people revert to 'indicators', that is, observable things that 'indicate' the presence of something invisible. Such indicators are of the type 'If A, B, C, then X or V'. Experience tells what, under particular circumstances, the probability would be of A, B and C producing X or producing Y. Because the probability of A, B, C producing X or Y cannot, because of a lack or information, be calculated statistically, it is expressed in qualitative terms, such as, 'If A, B, C, then [always/often/sometimes/seldom] X'). Without having obtained certitude through verification a person may still validate their conviction with reference to the occurrence of a number of observed indicators and the probability of their positive or negative relatedness in the situation. In similar vein Routledge (1995) presents an excellent example of how archaeologists (should) argue their way towards consensus on the interpretation of, for instance, excavated architectural structures.

The second basis for holding a conviction is supplied by what has earlier been referred to as the 'ethical side' of validation. Convictions are often based on lived *values* rather than on epistemologically safeguarded universal principles. One such value is honesty. Honesty, for example, requires that one gets informed as best one can and does not shut one's eyes to contradictory observations, variant opinions or alternative instruments for weighing opinions, and obliges one to change one's mind should another view seem more plausible under the circumstances. Another such value is openness. Especially in the academic field, frankness about the criteria one employed in arriving at a decision is important. It is therefore unfortunate that Glock (1985: 470) had to establish that, in many academic debates, explicit statements of presuppositions are 'as rare as fish in the Dead Sea'. Frankness affords not only the consensus community, but also one's opponents, of a line of support or attack, so that the reasons one supplies for holding a conviction may be scrutinized. Such openness distinguishes a conviction from an ideology in the negative sense of the word. It is in this connection that Long (1997: 83) observes, 'Speaking about [implied suppositions] in all their particularity ought to be a more routine part of our critical discourse than it is...'

Even if one has secured the backing of a traditional consensus group *and* succeeded in persuading a hundred former opponents of the validity of one's conviction, one would only have succeeded in making a local truth out of a personal conviction. And why would one want more than that? Certitude, so it would seem, can only be relatively achieved in areas where trivial laws apply to fairly simple systems. As soon as a system really becomes complex (like in subatomic particles, the cosmos at large, or even in human culture and literary texts) facts have to give way to indicators, and certitudes to convictions.

1. *Culture and Interpretation*

Perhaps Richard Rorty's description of the make-up of an 'ironist' (as compared to a 'metaphysician') best sums up the difference between 'conviction' and 'certitude'. An 'ironist', he says (Rorty 1996: 97),

> is someone who fulfils three conditions: (1) She has radical and continuing doubts about the final vocabulary she currently uses, because she has been impressed by other vocabularies, vocabularies taken as final by people or books she has encountered; (2) she realizes that argument phrased in her present vocabulary can neither underwrite nor dissolve these doubts; (3) insofar as she philosophizes about her situation, she does not think that her vocabulary is closer to reality than others, that it is in touch with a power not herself.

This book also does not lay any claim to certitude. It rather seeks to supply reasons for holding the conviction that cultural information is indispensable for textual interpretation. Further, that cultural information may supply the exegete with good arguments for being convinced that interpretation A is better than interpretation B. Finally, that the *way* in which cultural arguments are constructed has a bearing upon the validity of that part of the argument.

An argument that seeks consensus on what would distinguish better interpretations of biblical texts from poorer implies at least a dialogue. For this reason a monologue such as this book cannot even hope to 'formulate' a set of indicators. But it could join in the debate.

While the remainder of this chapter deals with arguments for the inclusion of cultural indicators in the validation of biblical interpretation, and in creating a self-awareness in interpreters of their perspectivist observational position, the next four chapters will deal with the construction and presentation of cultural arguments in interpretation.

4. *Looking for Discriminatory Indicators in Interpretation*

There is a fairly common acceptance among biblical scholars that a knowledge of the language and linguistic structure of biblical texts is a must for plausible interpretation. While agreeing that linguistic competence truly is an important indicator of the validity in interpretation (and would have prevented some of the implausible interpretations by 'the Bible as literature' scholars without linguistic training), I would submit that knowledge of the anthropology of the biblical world provides *at least* equally important indicators. Just as interpretations based on cultural knowledge may be invalidated on the basis of the linguistic structure of a text, interpretations based on Hebrew, Aramaic and Greek may be shown to be implausible from the perspective of culture.

According to relevance theory a reader interprets an act of communication by formulating hypotheses on its intended meaning and accepts as the intended meaning that interpretation that satisfies the principle of relevance. 'Relevance' minimally involves the *cognitive worlds* of the speaker and hearer. And those cognitive worlds, as will be argued in the next two chapters, are by definition culturally and locally constituted. A modern reader of biblical texts, even if she has a proficiency in Hebrew or Greek, will, if she is not *also* versed in the cognitive world of the intended (or implied) reader, as a matter of course substitute her own cognitive world for that of the intended or implied hearer. The result of such a substitution may, in many instances, result in accepting an interpretation as the 'most readily accessible meaning' that the original hearer could not have deemed relevant (in the technical sense of the word). This is most obvious in so-called dogmatic interpretation, such as to take רוח in Gen. 1.2 as referring to 'the Holy Spirit' in the sense of the second person in the Trinity, or to read Genesis 1 in the way creationists do, as a scientific treatise on the history of creation.

From this observation flow two further observations. First, if an interpreter is knowledgeable in the field of the anthropology of the biblical world, she is in a better position to formulate and weigh hypotheses on the intended meaning than a person without such knowledge. Secondly, if it can be shown that an interpretation, however sound its semantic analysis may be, could not have adequately effected the cognitive world of the original reader, such an interpretation could be said to be implausible, or invalid.

In terms of relevance theory, the degree of validity of a particular interpretation may, among other things, be measured against certain indicators, such as the degree to which the principles of recency, frequency, effective encyclopaedic memory, hierarchy of communicated knowledge, and the closeness of cognitive resemblance can be shown to apply.

5. *Self-Awareness and Cultural Information*

Apart from the heuristic function of cultural information in the interpretation of texts and its validatory role in the evaluation of exegetical arguments, confrontation with the cultural facet of a text may serve another, more hermeneutical, goal.

1. *Culture and Interpretation*

Critiquing the epistemological stance in relation to secured knowledge, Feyerabend (1996: 198) argues that it is impossible to examine something we are using all the time (e.g. a particular methodology) and to discover the kind of world we presuppose in doing so. One of the major obstacles in literary and theological interpretation is precisely that a present-day reader's 'taste' for literature, her traditional theological constructions, in short, her cultural heritage, cannot be 'bracketed' while she is interpreting—that is the fallacy of objectivism. Yet, without knowledge of 'who she is' and what kind of cognitive world she inhabits, and, for that reason, presupposes, communication cannot take place and exegesis becomes a soliloquy.

Feyerabend suggests that one cannot discover oneself through introspection.

> We need an *external* standard of criticism, we need an alternative set of assumptions or, as these assumptions will be quite general, constituting, as it were, an entire alternative world, *we need a dream-world in order to discover the features of the real world we think we inhabit*... The first step in our criticism of familiar concepts and procedures, the first step in our criticism of 'facts', must therefore be an attempt to break the circle.

He then goes on to show how this alternative world may supply us with 'counterinductive' arguments that may enable us to become aware of the world we live in and the kind of criteria that world forces on us.

In biblical literature, the interpreter, very much like an anthropologist doing fieldwork, is confronted with such an alternative, 'external' world. In this regard Roy Wagner (1996: 52-53) writes,

> In experiencing a new culture, the fieldworker comes to realize new potentialities and possibilities for the living of life, and may undergo a personality change himself. The subject becomes 'visible,' and then 'believable' to him, he apprehends it first as a distinct entity, a way of doing things, and then secondly as a way in which he could be doing things. Thus he comprehends for the first time, through the intimacy of his own mistakes and triumphs, what anthropologists speak of when they speak of 'culture'. Before this he had no culture, as we might say, since the culture in which he grows up is never really 'visible'—it is taken for granted, and its assumptions are felt to be self-evident.

Taking the cultural dimension of biblical texts seriously and endeavouring to get to know that culture as best one can may provide one with that external standard of criticism. The foreign culture of the biblical world has the ability to produce the kind of counterinductive arguments

Feyerabend speaks about that are necessary to break the circle of the self-evident notions and ways of looking at the world inherent in one's own invisible culture.

As will be argued further on, this confrontation with 'the other' never is an 'objective' encounter. In the words of Wagner (1996: 52-53), we do in a sense 'invent' the culture we are studying. Yet our description of it does not become a free fantasy. Of crucial importance in a confrontation with a foreign culture is the *relation*ship developed between the own and the foreign in the process of observing and learning. It is this relationship that has the potential of making one's own culture 'visible' and opens up a way for critiquing its complacency and self-evidencies.

Although made in a somewhat different context, two remarks by Robert Carroll (1991: 124, 147) may neatly sum up this section.

> It must be said that *reading is a dangerous thing*. It can harm your physical health. It certainly can change your life. Of course, whether it does or not depends on your situation and *how* you read. The thing written need not be profound but because it is always *other* than oneself its alterity can penetrate consciousness and radically alter how one thinks, behave or lives.
>
> If you can tolerate contradiction and contrariety and can handle hyperbolic drive and chaotic manipulation of metaphor, then the Bible will burn your mind.

6. 'Biblical' Culture

In considering the role of cultural information in exegesis, we have up to this point been talking about 'biblical culture' as if the referent of this term was self-evident. But it is not. In speaking about 'biblical culture' one has, on the one hand, to distinguish with Davies (1994: 23) between the society *in* the biblical text and the society *of* the text. That is, one has to distinguish between the cultural world *pictured* in the narratives, prophecies, poems and proverbs collected in the biblical text and the cultural surroundings in which these texts were *produced*. Dever (1997: 292) remarks in this regard, 'Literature is not life, but rather the product of the intellectual and literary imagination of a creative few'. And Long (1997: 89) would say that one has to read the text not *against* but *in* its environment, that is, as a product and/or function of it. Important as Margaret Davies's distinction between the world *in* the text and the world *of* the text is for discerning the cultural *function* of a text in its world of origin (or later reception), it neglects a very important aspect of the cultural world of the biblical text, namely the cultural worlds discussed in or presupposed by these texts—which is what this book actually is about. One therefore has to distinguish between the cultural world *pictured, discussed* and *affected* by a text. One can only begin to speak of or evaluate the (rhetorical/ideological) function of a text in a particular cultural environment once one has established the relationship between the cultural world *pictured* in the text and the real world *discussed* in the text. It is in this regard that Davies (1995: 228) remarks, 'The texts create a world and we do not know how far they reflect reality.'

The distinctions drawn above may be graphically represented as follows:

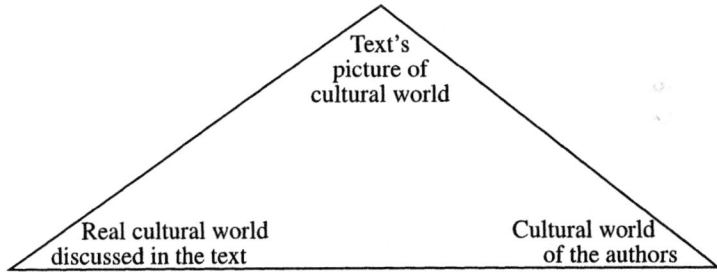

The Cultural World(s) Pictured and Discussed by the Biblical Text
In view of the processes involved in literary representation, it would be a methodological mistake simply to equate the cultural world pictured *in* a text with the cultural reality it discusses—a mistake that has often been made by scholars using the biblical text as a source of knowledge for the culture of 'ancient Israel'. The *literary* world in biblical texts may, but need not be a 'picture' of the real world. A few examples may illustrate the point.

Psalm 48.1-7 paints a picture of the city of Jerusalem as a city 'beautiful in elevation' and 'the joy of all the earth', at whose sight kings are astounded, panic, and take flight. This picture does not at all match the geography or physical features of the real, tiny, walled settlement of a few hundred square metres. However, the reference in the psalm to Mount Zion as situated 'in the far north' betrays the perspective of the poet. By employing the traditional Canaanite idea of Mount Zaphon (the northern mountain) as the *divine* abode he pictures Mount Zion not as a mere physical place but as God's *residence*.

Consider also the picture Isa. 51.9-10 draws of the exodus from Egypt:

> Awake, awake, put on strength, O arm of the LORD; awake, as in days of old, the generations of long ago. Was it not you that had cut *Rahab in pieces, that had pierced the dragon*? Was it not you that had *dried up the sea, the waters of the great deep*; that had made the depths of the sea a passage for the redeemed?

By juxtaposing the killing of the sea monster Rahab (a motif from creation narratives) with the drying up of the sea at the time of the exodus, the poet *reinterprets* a story of divine liberation as an act of divine *creation*. Something similar happens in Psalm 105. Lee (1990) presents the following graphical comparison between Psalm 105 and Genesis 1:

Day	Genesis 1	Psalm 105
1 + 4 Heaven	Light + luminaries (Sun, Moon, Stars)	Darkness (v. 28a) It became dark (v. 28b)
2 + 5 Waters	Water separated + Life populates water	Waters turned into blood (v. 29a) Fish in water died (v. 29b)
3 + 6 Earth	(a) Dry land made + Living creatures according to their kinds (b) Vegetation multiplies + Man was created	(a) Land swarmed with frogs, flies and gnats (vv. 30-31) (b) Vegetation destroyed (vv. 32-35) + Egyptian firstborn died (v. 36)

The poet of Psalm 105 obviously pictured the Egyptian plagues as creation-in-reverse. Here we have a *literary* picture of the plagues that differs from the tradition recorded in the book of Exodus (several plagues are not even mentioned) with a view to reinterpreting the tradition.

At some stage scribes supplied the psalms of superscripts, indicating the 'historical circumstances' in which these poems had supposedly been written (e.g. Ps. 3 in the time 'when David fled before Absalom'). This 'dating' procedure had not resulted from critical historical research but involved a study of the purely *linguistic* similarities between the psalms and narrative portions of the Hebrew Bible, as Childs (1971–72) and Slomovic (1979) have shown. Carasik (1994) argues that the superscript in Proverbs 25, ascribing a certain collection of proverbs to

1. *Culture and Interpretation*

'the men of Hezekiah' equally resulted from linking expressions occurring in Proverbs 25 and 2 Kings 18–19.

Some of these 'literary' representations are not altogether 'innocent'. Laato (1995: 210-13) points out a few devices Assyrian scribes employed in the 'historical records' of Sennacherib to hush up a military defeat or setback of the king. They sometimes simply omitted facts from their reports. At other times they combined a report on a victory with that of a defeat in such a manner that the defeat becomes part of the victory. Sometimes they boasted of major victories but failed to indicate what the actual political gain was—like they normally did when a real victory had in fact been won. Finally, if a foreign army dealt the Assyrian army a severe blow, they pictured the victorious king through insults, like when Sennacherib's scribes called the victorious Humban-ninema 'a rash fellow who had neither insight nor counsel'.

If poets and narrators had the licence to 'distort' reality in order to make their hearers and readers view it from a different angle (e.g. Jerusalem as *more* than just another city, or the exodus as a *creative* rather than a liberative act), to assign fictitious dates to poems or even to mislead their readers with regard to the 'actual state of affairs', the cultural set-up presented in a text could equally be a distortion of real cultural reality. This is why Margaret Davies (1995: 228) says, 'The texts create a world and we do not know how far they reflect reality.'

Micah's presentation of the upper-class society of his time, for example, does not present us with an 'objective' picture of their cultural values, but with his *polemical* picture of it:

> those who devise wickedness and work evil upon their beds! When the morning dawns, they perform it, because it is in the power of their hand. They covet fields, and seize them; and houses, and take them away; they oppress a man and his house, a man and his inheritance (Mic. 2.1-2).

To take this picture as a *description* of Micah's society would be to misunderstand the rhetorical function of hyperbole in polemical language. Exactly the *difference* between the literary and the real cultural worlds of a text often provides a powerful generator of meaning as well as important clues regarding the text's social or ideological function. To involve in the process of interpretation the difference between the cultural situation pictured and discussed in a text requires placing the text with reference to time and space (e.g. in eighth-century Ephraimite economy)—a problem to which we shall return below.

The observation that texts sometimes (or even often) distort the discussed cultural circumstances in their representation of that cultural situation should not, however, lead to the generalization that every textual world of necessity differs from or distorts the discussed cultural world. Because of the polemical stance of prophetic literature one may, for example, expect this *kind* of literature to paint an ironically twisted picture of Israelite or Judaean society. One may also expect a praise song (exalting the king or a capital city) largely to exaggerate the real situation. But this possibility cannot be turned into a rule, as if all texts *should* be approached with suspicion.

The principle of relevance applies here. A hearer's first hypothesis on the meaning of a text always is its *most readily accessible* (literal) meaning. If *that* meaning belies the hearer's encyclopaedic knowledge of the cultural situation (e.g. in cases of intentional irony), that non-fit makes her reject the literal hypothesis as the utterance's intended meaning. She then puts in more processing effort by, for example, interpreting the utterance as *irony*. If this extra effort is rewarded with an adequate contextual effect, the hypothesis of 'ironic meaning' is validated and accepted as the intended meaning. Often, however, an adequate contextual effect is produced by the hypothesis that a story (literally) reflects or closely resembles the real cultural world. Such may be the case in a romantic or picaresque story. The story of Jacob's wheeling and dealing, for example, probably presupposes, and therefore reflects, ordinary family life and clan custom. In such cases the cultural world in the text may thus closely resemble the real (discussed) cultural world (see Halpern 1997: 339).

To avoid possible misunderstanding at this point, one should perhaps rephrase and say the cultural world pictured in one text may be more *realistic* than in another text. Realism should not, however, be confused with 'historicity'. Even if the story of Jacob could be shown to reflect, say, Iron Age family custom up to 90 per cent, it might still be 100 per cent fictitious and a highly ideologically involved narrative at that. To decide whether a (realistic) story is also *historically* reliable requires the application of a totally different set of criteria, while the question of a story's social *function* requires yet another set of criteria. These decisions have to be based on three different procedures. Consider, for example, the procedures followed by Smelik (1992) and Laato (1995) for establishing historical reality from literary sources. However, 'historical reality' is not what interests us in this study.

Since modern readers of the Bible do not possess the ready encyclopaedic memory intuitively to decide whether the social world pictured in a text is realistic or not, and since the Hebrew Bible nowhere presents them with a comprehensive and coherent description of the social realities its literature discusses, their safest criterion for assessing the degree of realism of biblical representations is archaeological evidence. But since the archaeological evidence is also partial and, above all, dumb they have to resort to anthropological theory and comparative studies to obtain some form of a coherent and meaningful picture of 'Israelite' society.

The Cultural World(s) of the Biblical Text
If we have, on the one hand, to discern the degree of realism of the cultural reality pictured in a text compared to the discussed cultural world, and, on the other hand, need to know the cultural world *intended* or *effected* by a text in order to establish its function in society, it becomes important to know at what stage of Israel's history a particular text originated.

A hundred years of historical (critical) research culminated round about the middle of the twentieth century in a fairly general scholarly consensus that at least the narrative texts of the Hebrew Bible related events that, in so far as they were historical, had occurred long before they were actually narrated. Even if one believed that Moses wrote the whole Pentateuch, one has to concede that, for example, the patriarchal narratives could only have been committed to writing centuries after the time about which they purport to tell. This circumstance sometimes confronts exegetes with difficult decisions. First, are these texts fictions, merely presupposing the culture of the time of their creation, or do they perhaps rest on and rework older traditions or written sources? If they do indeed depend on older traditions or texts, does the *present* text, in those instances where older portions have been incorporated, presuppose or discuss the cultural situation of the time of their incorporation (e.g. 450 BCE), the time when these sources had been committed to writing (e.g. 750 BCE), the time of their original, say oral, creation (e.g. 850), or do they perhaps conserve some memory of the culture about which they tell (e.g. 1000 BCE)? If one accepts that older sources had in fact been incorporated in the present text and that these sources (at least) discuss the cultural situation of at least their time or *written* origin, the cultural interpretation of the biblical text may in theory become quite complicated in some instances.

Traditional historical-critical consensus has it that the Hebrew Bible not only originated over a long period (e.g. between the eighth and the second centuries BCE), but also that individual narratives or poems might have had a complicated history. A narrative might, for example, have been based on different sources that had originated at *various stages* of Israelite cultural history. In the flood narrative in Genesis, for example, one might have to reckon with J and P sections that might have originated as far apart as the eighth and the sixth centuries BCE, as well as with later editorial sections and phrases joining the various sources into one narrative. The implication of all this is that a particular text may discuss *various* cultural situations, as illustrated by the following diagram:

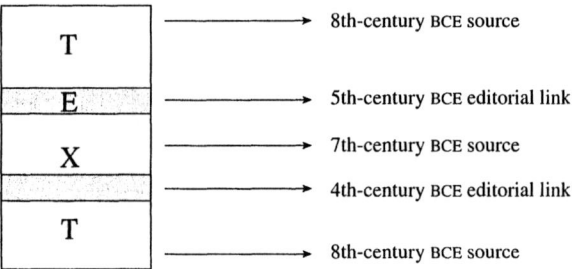

Sources dating from the eighth century BCE may, in this view, theoretically presuppose a socio-economic, political and religious system differing from that of texts or editorial sections that originated during the seventh century BCE, and even more from texts that were written during the Hellenistic period. On the whole, however, the question whether a source has to be dated in, for example, the ninth- or seventh-century Judah would not trouble the *cultural interpretation* of such a text too much. Even though one has to be very wary of the functionalist anthropological trap of conceiving of any culture as an unchanging, static world (Grimshaw and Hart 1996: 25) the available evidence seems to indicate that a substantial *cultural* break with Iron Age II Israel and Judah only occurred towards the beginning of the sixth century BCE (Kempinski 1966) or perhaps even as late as the later Persian period (Dar 1986; Carter 1994). If this is so, a substantial difference in the *discussed* cultural worlds of Hebrew Bible texts will probably only be noticeable in texts produced either outside of Judah (e.g. among the Babylonian exiles) or towards the *late* Persian period, and, of course, even more so in texts of a Hellenistic-Roman origin.

1. Culture and Interpretation

The traditional historical-critical consensus on the redactional history of the Hebrew Bible (see, e.g., Weippert 1985b) has, however, over the past three decades been challenged from four sides. The first two challenges came from within the ranks of historical criticism itself. On the one hand scholars started dating the hypothetical sources substantially later than had been the consensus opinion for quite some time. The Yahwist source had, for example, for quite some time been accepted to have originated in the tenth or eighth century BCE. Presently, many scholars date the bulk of this 'source' in exilic times (e.g. Levin 1993). More than this, a continuous 'refinement' of the supposed redactional process has proliferated the number of hypothetical 'sources', editorial additions and glosses to such an extent that it is no longer possible to speak of a consensus of any sort within historical-critical ranks. The result of this proliferation has (at least outside Germany) been a widespread scepticism of the plausibility of literary and redaction criticism as a basis for constructing the history of the formation of the Hebrew Bible. (Interestingly enough many scholars outside Germany still consciously or subconsciously, openly or clandestinely, presuppose in their work the older broad historical critical picture of the Hebrew Bible's historical evolution.) On the other hand, some scholars (e.g. Rendtorff, Childs), while to a greater or lesser extent still presupposing a fairly long history of textual formation for the Hebrew Bible and sometimes involving this history in the process of interpretation, came to focus more and more on the (exilic/post-exilic) final redactional organization or 'canonical shape' of the Hebrew Bible.

From outside the circle of historical criticism the consensus has, secondly, been challenged from two sides (see Gottwald 1985: 22-29). The first challenge came from a group of scholars (e.g. Weiss, Alter, Sternberg) emphasizing a phenomenological rather than a historical approach to Hebrew Bible texts. For them the evolutionary history and cultural embeddedness of a text had little if any relevance for its interpretation. In this view the Hebrew Bible presented its readers with *literary art* that should be read synchronically *as* literary art. The second school of thought also rejects the evolutionary view of the origin of the Hebrew Bible and emphasizes its synchronous nature, but for quite different reasons. In this view the entire body of texts was created to serve the cultural and ideological needs of the postexilic 'Jewish' community. According to some (Carroll, Davies, Exum and Lemche) these texts date from the Persian era. According to others (Friis 1968; Diebner and

Schult 1975; Diebner 1992–93: 20-36) they should be read as anti-Hellenistic literature of the third to first centuries BCE.

Of these challenges we have to attend more closely to the view that the Hebrew Bible was a postexilic ideological fiction.[6] This view has important implications for involving 'culture' in the interpretation of the Hebrew Bible. If the complete Hebrew Bible had indeed originated in the Persian or Hellenistic eras, constructing its *discussed* cultural context would imply *only* that period. However, should this opinion not be tenable, the discussed cultural world of the biblical text may presuppose *changing* cultural patterns, also of pre-exilic times. To involve these contexts in the interpretation of biblical literature would then imply a complete cultural history of 'ancient Israel' (cf. Knierim 1985: 14; Dever 1997: 303).

The alternatives before us are so radical that researchers simply have to decide whose 'side' they are on. But 'choosing sides' is not always that easy, because, however much academia may parade itself as the rational instance *par excellence*, choosing between rival theories never is a purely rational exercise, because it mostly involves what Kuhn has called a 'conversion'. Like in all conversions, a conversion of an academic nature involves factors that are not strictly rational. A few remarks are called for in this context.

A first possible factor is the degree of frustration one experiences with a traditional theory. In this regard Gottwald (1985: 21) probably airs a fairly widespread sentiment, namely that the traditional religious and historical critical approaches to biblical interpretation have over the last few decades 'repetitiously reworked [certain classical problems] without much benefit of new evidence or fresh angles of approach' and have increasingly 'lost explanatory power'. 'In short,' Gottwald (1985: 21) says, 'religious and historical critical schemes of biblical interpretation are widely perceived to have reached the limits of their own turf and to be inappropriate to clarifying major aspects of the Hebrew Bible that excite curiosity and imagination.' However salient the insights gained via the religious and historical-critical approaches might be, the mere fact that they have become 'uninteresting' may form part of one's

---

6. Even though subscribers to the historical critical paradigm presently date much of the Hebrew Bible fairly late, they, like the 'final text approach' still accept the existence of earlier sources. In relation to the third challenge we have already dealt with the problematic lack of a cultural awareness in 'synchronic' interpretation.

1. Culture and Interpretation 59

(subconscious) motivation to convert to something more exciting.

Secondly, dissatisfaction with the side effects of a particular paradigm may result in the implicit abandoning of its methodological backbone. The present realization of the centuries-long ideological abuse of the Bible in political and ecclesiastical circles, even with the assistance of biblical scholars, may serve as an illustration here. In assessing the research programme of a scholar as eminent as William F. Albright, Long (1997: 91), for instance, finds that Albright's research constructed 'a Bible that was congenial to the values of a secular and scientific America'. In assessing the use of the Bible in the Roman Catholic Church, Keel (1997) documents the suffering the notion of the Bible as 'God's Work' has caused ordinary people and points out similar politically exploitable trends in the work of a scholar like Rainer Albertz (Keel 1997: 105-106). The effects of the Reformed tradition in, for example, South Africa, has been equally detrimental (Deist 1994, 1995), while Bible translations have not been innocent at all (Carroll 1996; Deist 1993b). Even (biblical) archaeological research, for long paraded as an 'objective' discipline, has apparently not escaped the ideological trap (Silberman 1997) and has tamed the past into something 'mytho-allegorical or utilizable' (Shavit 1997: 51). It stands to reason that a realization of this history of the Bible and biblical interpretation has contributed a great deal towards a growing scepticism over the Bible itself. The methodological spin-off of this development has been that, in comparison with the traditional hermeneutics of trust presupposed by, for example, existential (or ecclesiastical) interpretation and its companion historical exegesis, the hermeneutics of suspicion and its companion, ideology-critical biblical interpretation, have steadily gained in academic stature.

A third factor that may influence one's decision whether or not to switch allegiances is the relevance of the cultural contexts of and belief systems implied by alternative paradigms. One is, for example, intuitively more attracted by an approach that satisfies one's cultural orientation and ideological convictions (cf. Kessler 1994). After two centuries of (empiricist) analysis and (positivist) atomism, the present *cultural need* seems, for example, to favour intellectual approaches emphasizing connectedness and wholeness rather than analysis and detail. More than that, rationalism, empiricism, positivism and materialism have over the last century effected in (at least) the intellectual life of First World Western academia a thoroughly naturalist world view, looking upon religious sentiment and literature (including the Bible) with scepsis *a priori*. In such an environment the biblical text will naturally be 'guilty' until it has proved its innocence.

In the fourth place, if the philosophical implications of a theory tally with one's own experience of society or can assist in obtaining set goals that theory becomes a strong contender in the bid for acceptance. For instance, since the Enlightenment an unbridled optimism over what the rationalist-naturalistic world view (also underlying historical criticism) could achieve and, especially, the role of intellectuals in that achievement had permeated the academic world. This optimism has been shattered, though, by the horrors of two world wars, the detrimental effects of colonialization, and the global deterioration of the environment and quality of life. What has been won is not a world of reason and democracy but rather a world colonialized by bureaucracies, economic forces and money, in which intellectuals have a limited, if any, role to play. Even universities are nowadays run like businesses in which 'managers' rather than intellectuals, and student numbers rather than quality in education are valued. As Grimshaw and Hart (1996: 43) put it, '[F]or more than a decade now...academics have been forced to learn that their hard-won membership of the state-made elite no longer carries any guarantees of privilege.' In such an environment social theories voicing academics' dismay over the bureaucratic *coup d'état* (or with the potential of capturing the imagination of great numbers of prospective students) intuitively become attractive options.

Finally, quite apart from cultural-historical factors in the dying and rising of paradigms and methodologies, the mere natural succession of generations may effect one's choice of theory. As the 'great names' of a dominant (older) paradigm start losing their 'grip' on educational programmes, conferences, editorial boards, tea room discussions, and so forth, and finally disappear from the academic scene, they are replaced by a new generation with a different needs and objectives and subscribing to new (culturally created) plausibility structures. Even though the old theory or paradigm might not have been seriously flawed from a *rational* point of view, it may simply wither away and die. After all, subscribing to the views of a 'dead generation' simply does not make anyone look 'informed' at any conference.

Cultural, historical, political and generational factors, assisting a choice between theories, are not in themselves 'rational' or 'irrational'. They do, however, in creating an alternative environment of experience, over time restructure current 'common sense' to answer to new plausibility structures, with reference to which the 'rationality' of one's choice is then intuitively judged. 'Rational' decisions are therefore really contextual decisions. That is why something that has for a long time seemed quite 'rational' may come to be *intuitively* judged simply non-rational or non-sensical. In view of the cultural and philosophical shifts referred to above, Davies (1994: 32) may well be right that, whether or not his *argument* for a Persian-Hellenistic origin of the entire Hebrew Bible fiction is 'accepted at the moment' it will 'soon appear inevitable'. It may even soon seem 'obviously rational' for academics sharing or educated in the same cultural and historical context. The problem is, of course, that not everybody shares the same cultural and historical context. What seems obviously right for some may therefore still seem obviously wrong for other scholars. That is, after all, how scholars divide into camps and schools that often have little to say to each other.

In spite of this near-to-hopeless situation, one widely acknowledged scholarly criterion may perhaps assist a 'cross-cultural' debate, namely of accepting the *most elegant* explanation for a series of observations. *Elegant* here means 'the most simple explanation that can, with the aid of the fewest auxiliary hypotheses, account for the maximum of observed phenomena'. It is from this perspective, rather than with an appeal to 'obviously right/wrong', that I shall debate the Persian fiction theory. Even if the discussion can assist the (disputed) theory to become more elegant, it would have served a useful purpose.

The strategy that I shall adopt for the purpose of the debate is that of qualitative probabalism, proposed by Buksinski (1985): whenever a desired insight cannot be obtained through direct observation of 'facts' (e.g. the meaning of a written text or a historical event), one may make use of 'indicators', that is, observable things that 'indicate' the presence of something invisible. Such indicators are of the type 'If phenomena A, B, C, then explanation X or Y'. Experience and analogies tell what, under particular circumstances, the probability would be of A, B, C producing X or Y. Since the probability of A, B, C producing X or Y cannot, because of a lack or information, be calculated statistically, it is expressed in qualitative terms, such as, 'If A, B, C, then [always/often/sometimes/seldom] X'). What has to be ascertained, then, is the qualitative probability of the Persian fiction theory's explanation for the origin of the Hebrew Bible. The structure of the argument follows the excellent suggestion by Routledge (1995) for deciding on the best explanation for excavated architectural structures.

After these remarks we may turn to the Persian fiction theory. Not everybody promoting the theory puts all the cards on the table.[7] Even though presented at some levels as experimental, the most comprehensive presentation of this view is perhaps that by Davies (1992, 1994). For that reason, and not because he is the most radical representative of the trend, I choose him as a sparring partner. What Davies suggests, is (a) that, if not the entire Hebrew Bible, then by far the largest portion of it was of postexilic *origin*, so that the whole body of literature *implied a fairly synchronous postexilic cultural environment* and (b) that, if not the entire body of literature, then by far the largest portion of it was *fiction* (i.e. without any serious link with the sociopolitical world of the preexilic kingdoms of Israel and Judah) (Davies 1992: 81, 129; cf. Lemche 1995).

Even though Davies explicitly accepts that the responsible scribes could perhaps have made use of existing material, this concession seems more like a nod in the direction of the 'majority consensus'.

The prophetic books *may* well, for example, 'have a basis in collections of archived materials remaining from the Iron Age' (Davies 1992: 112); the scrolls of Genesis to Kings are the product of 'rewriting, emending, patching together, *sometimes* from discrete sources which with *some* plausibility can be reconstructed' (1992: 120); while Second Temple scribes had at their disposal '*some* individual prophetic oracles...wisdom sayings, psalms, perhaps even *some scraps* of official archives of the kingdom of Judah...a list of reigns, including *one or two* incidents' (1992: 122, emphasis added). The rhetoric of this concession is clearly minimalist, especially as far as *historical* material is concerned. The humorously invented 'Albright scribal college' (the imagined group responsible for writing up the 'history of Israel') merely had at their disposal 'scraps' of archive material, since the 'official archives

---

7. In view of the preceding discussion of the cultural context of changing paradigms of thought, I am intrigued by the kind of question Long (1997: 85) puts with reference to Albright: 'What was at stake in this encompassing gesture of historical construction?' The whole movement for a Persian-Hellenistic dating of the entire Hebrew Bible also seems to have an undeclared 'stake'. And one sometimes finds in these writings a disconcerting 'Albrightean' rhetoric and style that, according to Long (1997: 86), reflect 'a privileged place to empirical and rationalistic thought'.

1. Culture and Interpretation 63

of the Judaean monarchy *will have been either confiscated to Babylon, or, more probably, left in Judah*', so that the Judaean deportees would 'fairly certainly' not have had further access to it (1992: 79). The Hebrew Bible consequently is by and large an *ideological fiction* produced by various scribal schools, operating from the confinements of stone chambers in the palace or temple in Persian Yehud (Davies 1994: 28). And the purpose of their activity was to create an identity for an insulated group (or even a caste) (1992: 108, 116) of city dwelling elite repatriates, who did not necessarily have any ethnic or historical link with the original deportees (1992: 81-87). This means that there is 'no *necessity* to assign *any* part of the formation of *any* biblical book to the period of the historical kingdoms of Judah and Israel' (Davies 1992: 99).

With Davies I accept, very much for the reasons he puts forward,

(a) that the literary world presented in the Hebrew Bible should not, at least not without further argument (see Halpern 1997; Smelik 1992), be taken as a 'reflection' of the 'real world' of the first millennium BCE (Davies 1994: 23);

(b) that, given the thin spread of literates in the ancient Near East up to at least the seventh to sixth centuries BCE (see Goody and Watt 1968: 37-42), all *textual* material from anywhere in the ancient Near East, especially that of a non-commercial nature, is of necessity the product of the 2–5 per cent literate elite;

(c) that, at least in its stylized grammar, the Hebrew of the Hebrew Bible (but see also Margulies 1974: 58) is a late artificial linguistic construct—perhaps even a product of the Common Era (Davies 1992: 102-105);

(d) that the *literary shape* of the Hebrew Bible is a product of the period between the Second Temple and (at least) Bar Kochba (Diebner 1992–93: 23, 31);

(e) that the 'all Israel perspective', or the notion of an inclusive 'Israelite' identity, permeating the 'final form' of the Hebrew Bible most probably is a religious and politico-ideological literary creation by Second Temple scribes (see Hesse and Wapnish 1997: 263; but also Kallai 1993);

(f) that any historical construction of 'Israelite' history (or of any history, for that matter) requires a good deal of historical imagination (Davies 1992: 120).

I would, however, hold that imaginative historical construction is not a licence for free fantasy. The historical imagination, linking observations to form a coherent story about the past (Deist 1993a), should account for *all* available historical indicators, and also such indicators that may contradict the construction (cf. Diebner 1992–93: 22, 34; Halpern 1997: 331).

Following Routledge (1995), attention will be given to (a) a critique of the warrants connecting observation with explanation, (b) the absence of positive indicators implied by the explanation, and (c) indicators not accounted for by the theory.

The construct rests on the salient observation that a clear distinction should be drawn between the world *in the text*, presenting the periods of the patriarchs, the exodus, judges, kings, exile, etc. as having involved *all Israel*, and the world *of the scribes* who produced the text. However, the indicators presented to *warrant* the logical cohesion between observation (the unhistorical 'all Israel perspective' permeating Hebrew Bible literature) and explanation (the *entire* literary world was a deliberate ideological *fiction* created by an insulated and exclusive postexilic Yehud elite most probably *unrelated* to the erstwhile deportees) are either debatable or wanting.

Indicator 1. *There was little if any continuity between the Judaean and Yehud elite.* Although Davies (1992: 94) does allow for some continuity between pre-exilic Judah and postexilic Yehud, the question of whether or not the repatriates had descended from the deportees is not as immaterial to the theory as he (Davies 1992: 117) seems to suggest. It stands to reason that, had the repatriates indeed descended from the deportees (of a mere two generations earlier), their *historical* link with Judah would put the 'fiction' theory under strain. The theory would certainly be better served by repatriates who had nothing in common with the original deportees. It is precisely this logic that leads Davies (1992: 116-17) to erect hard borders between the people who had stayed in the land and the repatriates, and to view the latter as aliens and immigrants:

> The society is constituted by a fundamental contradiction: its élite is aware of its alien origin and culture, but its *raison d'être* implies indigenization: the Persians want the immigrants to accept their new land as their own... This new society generated its own identity, via literature... (Davies 1992: 117).

1. Culture and Interpretation   65

As evidence to indicate the repatriates' 'alien' origin Davies refers to Hoglund's study of Persian Yehud (Hoglund 1991: 65-68), according to which 'mixed repatriation' and 'deliberate ruralization' constituted Persian policy. It is, however, doubtful whether (a) mixed repatriation had in fact been Persian *policy* and (b) that, if such a policy existed, it was applied in the case of *Yehud*. Hoglund bases his views on (a) Kuhrt's debatable reading of the Cyrus cylinder (Kuhrt 1983), and (b) *biblical* references to earlier mixed ethnic deportation by the Assyrian and Babylonian states. Apart from the question of whether Mesopotamian examples are admissible here, and even if one granted (a) Kuhrt's interpretation of the Cyrus cylinder *and* (b) accepted that the Persians, like the Inka, Asteke and Tarascan states (Small 1997: 278, 280), practised enforced resettlement as a matter of policy (see, however, Weippert 1988: 690), there is no *material evidence* in Persian Yehud that such a mixed group of foreigners had in fact settled there. The Yehud objects of Egyptian, Arabian, Greek and Cyprian origin dating from Persian times are more readily explained with reference to lively trade within the borders of the Persian state than with reference to mixed ethnic settlers (see Weippert 1988: 706-18). On the contrary, the material evidence from Persian Yehud leads Carter (1994: 121-22) to suggest that the first period of Persian rule in Yehud should rather be reckoned as part of the Iron Age. A clear cultural break is only visibly indicated round about the fifth–fourth centuries BCE (and not in the sixth century as Hoglund [1991: 58] contends).

More than that, if one granted the presence of these traceless 'alien' repatriates in Persian Yehud, the mystery of the origin of the Hebrew Bible would deepen rather than be solved. If mixed repatriation had in fact been Persian *policy*, there must have been various other repatriated aggregate populations without identity in the empire. Why then would *only* the Yehud repatriates, without any historical thrust to inspire it, have devised *a disinformation programme as elaborate as the Hebrew Bible* to create a fictitious identity for themselves?

In the absence of material evidence warranting the (auxiliary) hypothesis of mixed repatriation, and in view of the new intricacies it causes, accepting the hypothesis that the returnees or repatriates had in fact been descendants from the sixth-century deportees from Judah would more elegantly explain (a) the *drive* for the establishment of a social identity as well as (b) the choice of that identity, namely *Israel* (see Horsley 1991:70).

Indicator 2. *The sociopolitical machinery that facilitated the birth of the fiction was a civic-temple-community.* The theory proposes as the engine of the Persian fiction a *civic-temple-community* governed by an exclusive, self-interested elite group of temple personnel.[8] Davies (1992: 116) says, '...the consensus view sees the immigrants as forming a temple-and-Jerusalem-centred exclusive cultic society which controlled in the name of its law the economic and political life of the province.'

The only evidence that, if admissible (see Bedford 1991: 161-62; Jobling 1991: 180), really indicates the existence of a civic-temple-community in Yehud is Ezra–Nehemiah's reference to a variety of temple functionaries typical of this kind of system (Blenkinsopp 1991: 31). But for the 'back-bone' of the system, namely *a temple owning land and managing production and distribution*, there is no evidence (Bedford 1991: 156-57). The picture Schaper (1995) draws of the economical and political situation in Persian Yehud is quite different. In his analysis the temple administration acted both as (a) a self-governing *religious* body and (b) a branch of the central government's *fiscal* administration, which had merely been a slightly adapted Babylonian administrative system introduced by Nabonidus. In this system, he says (Schaper 1995: 535) that 'cultural and political divides were of no importance at all. Solely the need for high revenues and administrative efficiency determined the course of action.' Also the material remains of the period, rather than reflecting the thriving elite community necessary to warrant the presence of a civic-temple-elite, indicate a poor and fairly backward community (Carter 1994; see also Weippert 1988).

To fit the evidence, the model of the civic-temple-community would have to be adapted to such an extent (cf. Blenkinsopp 1991: 29-30, 33; Bedford 1991: 155-59) that it would render *Yehud*'s civic-temple-community a *casus sui generis*, which would argue against a civic-temple-community rather than for it. On the basis of the available indicators one has to conclude with Horsley (1991: 170) that the idea of a civic-temple-community under Persian sponsorship is 'inappropriate as well as unnecessary'. The little there is in the *literary* sources to indicate a civic-temple-community could, if necessary, more easily be explained as an effort by the elite, challenged by the other Palestinian communities, to *picture* themselves as a civic-temple-community to gain in (lit-

---

8. To which may be compared the function of the temple in Heitzman's description of a 'ritual polity' (Heitzman 1991).

erary) stature—very much like pre-exilic praise singers had pictured the tiny Jerusalem as the mighty city of God.

The Persian fiction theory is, of course, not sold on the civic-temple idea. But if Yehud did not sport a civic-temple-community, what alternative sociopolitical organization could then have been in place that would have possessed the power and means to have produced the Hebrew Bible as *a fictitious ideology of identity*? In (cautiously) answering the question of how a miserably poor and small Yehud community could possibly have created the postexilic literature ascribed to them, Carter (1994: 137) only refers to those sections of the Hebrew Bible traditionally assigned to this era by *conservative historical critics*. If his construction of postexilic Yehud is anything to go by, the theory that the *entire* Hebrew Bible had originated from *that* community (and its successors in Hellenistic times) seems quite implausible.

Indicator 3. *The scribes of Persian Yehud had very little if any material from pre-exilic times on the basis of which they could have constructed the past.* The theory suggests that the Yehud scribes, in writing the 'history of Israel', had to revert to fiction because they would have had very little if any older material to work with. Since such material might have been available in the form of folk memory and written sources, the theory has to discredit both. Of course, if the repatriates were 'aliens' there could have been no 'oral memory' to work with. Since we have already dealt with the improbability of 'alien repatriates' we must now look into the theory's supposition that folk literature, rather than transmitting information about the past, merely reflects the conditions at the time of its production (Davies 1994: 25). *Ergo*, the stories the Yehud scribes told about the 'past' cannot reflect anything but Persian conditions.

This assumption, first articulated in biblical scholarship by Wellhausen (1905: 316), has ever since been repeated as a fact and without qualification in scholarly literature (cf. Lemche 1991: 14; Thompson 1991: 65-66; Gelinas 1995: 232; Whitelam 1995: 158). Davies (1992: 119), for example, views the story of the exodus as possibly 'reflecting' the returning of fugitives from Egypt in the Persian period, Gelinas (1995: 232) interprets the story of the 'division of the Davidic kingdom' as a reflection of 'the turbulent years at the close of the 8th beginning of the 7th century'. Others have seen the tension between Jews and Samaritans as the generator of Hebrew Bible literature or even the Hebrew Bible tradition about the kings as reflecting Jewish resistance against the Herodian dynasty. This appreciation of folklore rests on an disputable evolutionist anthropological notion of 'the primitive mind' no longer accepted *as a matter of fact* by anthropologists and folklorists. Freedman (1978: 83), for example, says

> In functional studies...a persuasive doctrine was developed according to which all statements made by informants which purported to be about the past were to be taken as statements about the present, in the sense that they were justificatory of present social arrangements... It is now, at a later stage of scholarship, clear that the scepticism was too widely applied.

Although one has to concede that this scepticism still has its supporters among anthropologists (cf. Law 1997), this is by far not a consensus opinion (cf. also Tonkin 1995; Vansina 1985).

To claim for folklore a capacity for memory is not to revert to an 'Albrightean' plea for 'accuracy' in the transmission of folklore. It would be as wrong to ascribe 'accuracy' to transmitted folklore *in general* (Goody and Watt 1968: 30-31; Finnegan 1970: 8-12) as it is to deny folklore any historical memory *in principle*. The remark merely questions, in the light of recent research into folklore, the matter-of-factness with which the Persian fiction theory assumes that folklore *of necessity* cannot 'remember' and accepts, therefore, that the caesura of Zion songs by the rivers of Babylon (Ps. 137) indicates amnesia on the side of the deportees. Whether or not folklore 'remembers' depends on the kind of orature (oral literature) and the social group involved. Finnegan (1970: 8), for example, distinguishes between the freedom exercised by traditional tellers of tales among the Chopi and Limba people and certain poets in Rwanda, 'where there is interest in the accuracy and authenticity of the wording (at least in outline) and where memorization rather than creation is the expected role of the performer'. And Goody and Watt (1963: 31) refer to 'formalized patterns of speech, recital under ritual conditions, the use of drums and other musical instruments, the employment of professional remembrancers' that may 'shield at least part of the content of memory from the transmuting influence of the immediate pressures of the present'. The claim of 'memory' for certain kinds of orature does not imply that memory is of necessity 'historically reliable'. The point rather is that folk memory (even elite returnee or local Judaean memory of earlier *fiction*) cannot as a matter of principle be ruled out as a possible source that Yehud scribes could have accessed.

1. *Culture and Interpretation* 69

The second supposition, namely that the returnee (or repatriated) scribes had virtually no written material from pre-exilic times to work from, also seems implausible. One might, of course, argue that a 'Chronicles of the Kings of Judah' has up to now not been found in Jerusalem. It is, however, difficult to imagine the absence of such 'chronicles' (see Millard 1985: 306-308). That (perishable) papyrus and leather had most probably been the medium for keeping records and writing letters in palace and temple is indicated by the presence of a great number of bullae—perhaps even from an early seventh century Jerusalemite chancellery (Shiloh 1983: 131)—which evidently once sealed papyrus and leather documents (Millard 1985: 304; Weippert 1988: 583), the eighth-century Barley Letter, the seventh-century Yavne Yam letter and Murabba'at papyrus (Cross 1962), etc.

Extra-biblical evidence shows that by the middle of the eighth century BCE both Israel and Judah had developed into real states (Jamieson-Drake 1991: 144). Had these royal courts not kept chronicles of some sort they would have been singular in the ancient Near East. Already Middle and Late Bronze Canaanite monarchs had scribes in their service (Ben-Tor 1997: 109, 124-26; Shiloh 1983: 131), as is also indicated by the Amarna correspondence of Palestinian origin (cf. Rainey 1983: 4-5). The later Moabite Stela, Tel Dan (Biran and Naveh 1993; see, however, Thompson 1994; Cryer 1995) and Siloam inscriptions, building inscriptions, etc. (cf. Weippert 1988: 586-87) also indicate the presence of scribes and recorders in various Iron Age Palestinian (city) states.

The book-keeping systems of eighth-century Samaria and Beth Shean (Mazar 1996: 163), the royal emergency planning evidenced by the *lmlk* jar handles (Rainey 1982) and the measure of planning that went into the lay-out of towns and the construction of buildings and city gates all indicate a fair level of secular scholastic training, even on town level (Isserlin 1984), while eighth–sixth-century graffiti and inscriptions like those from Khirbet el-Qôm and Kuntillet 'Ajrud indicate that literacy was not confined to the palace and administrative quarters, as Jamieson-Drake (1991: 148) assumes (see Weippert 1988: 583). Even if the evidence is ever so tiny, the early sixth-century Ketef Hinnom plaques at least show that a liturgical formula like the Priestly Blessing, also appearing in the Hebrew Bible, had been in written form prior to the exile (Yardeni 1991).

There are thus a variety of indicators to warrant the assumption that scribes had been fairly busy in pre-exilic Judah and its surroundings and that royal and temple archives would have existed. The practice in ancient Near Eastern warfare was not to destroy or confiscate royal archives, so that 'Chronicles of the Kings of Judah' might in fact have survived the fall of Jerusalem. If such archive material had indeed survived the destruction of Jerusalem, as Davies (1992: 79) also holds is possible, any party *that had remained in the land* could have exploited that material for their purpose. Seeing that the story of the monarchy relates events in Judah *after* the fall of Jerusalem, the authors of the book of Kings must have been among those who had *not* been deported.

In the drive to divorce Hebrew Bible literature from pre-exilic Judah, the Persian fiction theory might just be making too much of the *returnees'* fiction of the 'exilic empty land' (Carroll 1992) at the expense of those who had remained in the land. Barstad (1996: 80) concludes, perhaps a little sweepingly and overconfidently, that the 'archaeological evidence once and for all has made any claim that "the centre of gravity was moved from Judah to Babylonia" preposterous'. The fact is that Judah had not been a wasteland after the fall of Jerusalem until it was 'repopulated' in Persian times, and that much could still have been going on there in the absence of the former elite. Some of the sharp anti-elite prophetic literature could, for example, have been continued or composed by a 'second tier' elite who had remained in the land and gained power after the removal of the 'real elite'.

Such possibilities certainly have to be seriously entertained to avoid the overall theory of the postexilic *origin* of the Hebrew Bible from unconsciously becoming an ideological *fact* with which all information *has* to accord.

Indicator 4. *The Yehud scribes, working in seclusion, wrote what they were told to write, yet also criticized their masters.* Turning to the Yehud fiction writers themselves, the role and social location assigned to them by the Persian fiction theory are difficult to imagine. The models of scribal schools with reference to which Davies (1992: 120-23) constructs the (frankly admitted) imaginary postexilic scribal 'colleges' in Yehud mostly come from Mesopotamia and Egypt. Quite apart from the problematic use made here of Mesopotamian and Egyptian scribal schools as models for understanding Israelite and Judaean scribal practice (Jamieson-Drake 1991: 152-54), its consequence is that one has to assume that Yehud's (problematic) civic-temple-community was a 'state' and the scribal activity aimed at creating a 'national' identity (e.g. Davies 1992: 114, 130).

1. Culture and Interpretation 71

The supposed role of the Yehud scribes does indeed fit the environment of a *royal court* and *national temple* (with the accompanying scribal activities). Provincial Yehud could not, however, by any stretch of imagination be viewed as a *state* and its inhabitants as a 'nation' (see Carter 1994). On the contrary, books like Nehemiah and Ezra indicate that the adversaries of the 'returnees', having interpreted the rebuilding of Jerusalem's city walls and temple as acts of state formation, and therefore of open rebellion (Neh. 6.5-7), promptly reported the programme to the Persian king (Ezra 4.6-17; cf. Hoglund 1991: 64). Archaeological evidence also seems to indicate that no major refortification of earlier cities had been undertaken (or was allowed!) in the Persian period (Weippert 1988: 699-703). The Persians were not against the re-erecting of local sanctuaries and resuscitation of local religions (Weippert 1988: 690), but would not have allowed *state formation* in the empire. It would therefore seem that, if the scribal activities that brought about major sections of the Hebrew Bible have to be situated in a royal court and national temple, pre-exilic Judah rather than postexilic Yehud would be indicated.

The way in which the supposed scribal colleges are supposed to have functioned is equally problematical. On the one hand, the scribes are said to have meticulously written down what their paymasters told or allowed them to (Davies 1992: 107, 113, 124). On the other hand, in the theory's explanation for the origins of prophetic literature, they are also said to have criticized these same paymasters (Davies 1992: 107, 124). One has to keep in mind here that 'prophetic' criticism of important functionaries, like kings, court prophets, priests and other bureaucrats, are not mere (joking) admonitions but *shaming rebukes* (see Deist 1996a). Consider, for example, 'all tables are full of vomit, no place is without filthiness...[they] reel with wine and stagger with strong drink; the priest and the prophet reel with strong drink, they are confused with wine, they stagger with strong drink...' (Isa. 28.8, 10 RSV; cf. 5.11; Jer. 48.26). Some Sumerian and Babylonian texts do contain examples of such ridiculing and defaming speech, but these texts most probably reflect school exercises in rhetoric rather than serious 'literature'. Also, in Egypt important people were sometimes ridiculed. Consider, for instance, the Egyptian tomb painting depicting a finely dressed lady vomiting after having had too much to drink (Foster 1995: 2460). But these pictures do not represent public literature, while, according to the Persian fiction theory, the biblical texts had specifically been produced *for elite consumption* (Davies 1992: 108). Babylonian literature also provides examples of priests being ridiculed, but the ridiculer there is a court buffoon with the social license to do so (Foster 1995: 2462-64) and not an employee of an elite community in search of identity. The picture of the Yehud scribes both praising and ridiculing their paymasters therefore seems somewhat schizophrenic.

Finally, the idea of the hermetic isolation of city (scribal elite) from country (people) mediated at the most by the merchant class and perhaps the occasional storyteller (Davies 1992: 108, 114-17) seems anthropologically peculiar. Such isolation is atypical of any kind of a redistribution economy, which seems to have been in place in Yehud (Carter 1994: 138).

Even if one would, in spite of the lack of positive indicators for the theory's sociopolitical suppositions, accept the existence of the religio-political structures that could have produced the 'great fiction' there would still be a lack of evidence regarding the circumstances and mechanisms that would have made the ideology stick to the diversified groups of aspiring Yehudim.

That it is indeed possible to create fictitious 'ethnic' identities may be indicated by various historical examples. Small (1997), although problematically equating 'ethnicity' with social class, quotes examples from the Inka, Asteke and Tarascan states. South African experience may perhaps supply a more suitable model. The case in point is the formation of 'Afrikaner identity', the history of which also makes clear the conditions and mechanisms necessary for the formation and acceptance of a fictitious identity.

By the end of nineteenth century by far the majority of *white Afrikaans-speaking people* in South Africa had been subsistence farmers with a fairly low level of literacy, and therefore to a large extent dependent upon folk memory in respect of their own past. A large segment of these people had been crippled by the effects of the Anglo-Boer War, while most of them were plagued by poverty, crop failures and livestock diseases, and had by the early 1930s been living through a deadly influenza epidemic, two major financial depressions and were experiencing the culturally alienating influence of rapid urbanization. These circumstances created a golden opportunity for the elite ideologues, aspiring to self-government and eventual liberation from British colonialism, to forge a new and powerful ethnic group out of *historically different groups*. Hebrew Bible sources like Haggai, Zechariah,

1. *Culture and Interpretation*

Nehemiah and Malachi present an equally dismal picture of the returnees' situation. If one accepted these sources as reflecting something of the historical circumstances of the Yehud community, they could perhaps warrant the idea that the postexilic ideologues could have seized similar opportunities to forge the fictitious 'all Israel' identity among the returnees. But circumstances alone cannot sufficiently warrant the theory. What must also be in place to make a fictitious identity stick are certain *mechanisms*.

The mechanisms that assisted the formation of 'Afrikaner identity' had been varied. They included the reinterpretation of folk tradition and history, a ritual reinforcement of the ideology, the formation of secretive elite decision-making bodies and a massive investment in indoctrination.

Events experienced by or that were living in the memories of diverse sections of the 'target group' were firstly reinterpreted as events with 'national' meaning.[9] This 'national perspective' on historically isolated events was then symbolically supported by the introduction of national festive days,[10] the erection of a series of monuments[11] and ritual visits to them on festive occasions, and focused by a prolonged struggle for the acknowledgment of Afrikaans as an official language (which finally succeeded in 1924). Furthermore, leaders in the fields of business, politics, religion and education organized themselves into an exclusive 'covenant of brothers' that could plan, steer and even manipulate the

---

9. E.g. the landing on 6 April 1652 of a minute Dutch task group at the present Cape Town, the arrival of a group of French Huguenots in 1688, a series of late seventeenth- and early eighteenth-century border skirmishes between black and white settlers in the Eastern Cape, the departure between 1834 and 1838 of several small groups of frontier farmers from the Eastern Cape to non-British-controlled regions further north, various ensuing isolated battles, like the Battle of Blood River of 1838, and later more inclusive liberation struggles, like the Anglo-Boer War of 1899–1902.

10. Like the annual Founders' Day on 6 April, Hero's Day on 10 October and the Day of the Covenant on 16 December with its heavy *religious* overtones.

11. Such as the Huguenot monument in Franschhoek (Western Cape), the Voortrekker Monument in Pretoria (commemorating the Great Trek), the Blood River Monument in Natal, and the Women's Memorial in Bloemfontein (commemorating the thousands of women and children who had died in British concentration camps during the Anglo-Boer War). In 1938 a massive 'symbolic ox wagon trek', starting at various points throughout South Africa and converging at the Voortrekker monument in Pretoria, was also organized.

complete cultural life of white Afrikaans-speaking people. Finally, the 'all-Afrikaner' perspective on history and identity was taught in schools and universities and preached from pulpits. After a concerted effort of about 60 years the fiction of an 'all-Afrikanerdom' became an (ideological) reality that then 'stuck' for about half a century.

This history shows that it is indeed possible for an elite community to (at least temporarily) forge a fictitious identity for groups with different histories. But it also shows that (a) the conditions must be right, (b) that certain prerequisites must be indicated, and (c) that certain mechanisms are called for. First, the aggregate of people who in the end accepted the ethnic label of 'Afrikaner' had in any case shared the same (broad) *culture* and *language*. Secondly, the isolated events that were reinterpreted as 'national events' had (a) in fact *occurred* and (b) formed *part of the tradition* of the various sections of white Afrikaans-speaking people. It was by reinterpreting and distorting the oral and written *memory* of those events that the ideology of 'all-Afrikanerdom' could be presented as plausible and accepted as credible. *A complete fiction would not have done the job.* Thirdly, new symbols and rituals had to be devised to support and 'warrant' the distorted historical picture. Fourthly, the political, economic, academic and religious elite had to organize themselves and massively invest in persuading the common people. Finally, it was only after at least two generations of religiously supported indoctrination that most Afrikaans-speaking people started to forget that such an *ethnic* entity as an 'all-Afrikanerdom' had never really existed, and that the elite (politicians and ministers of religion) could effectively start appealing to 'Afrikaner identity'.

If the analogy holds, the model seriously questions the suppositions of the Persian fiction theory. According to the theory the Yehud aggregate most probably lacked *ethnic/cultural/linguistic* coherence as well as *continuity* with pre-exilic Judah (Davies 1992: 81). There is, further, no *historical basis* whatsoever on which the fiction could be plausibly constructed. Finally, other than the supposed use of power, there is no indication of the necessary *mechanisms* that could have turned the 'all Israel' fiction into a reality in people's minds. In the light of the available evidence and the model presented above, it would seem more plausible to explain the *success* of the 'all Israel ideology' among Yehudim by accepting, first, a fair degree of (ethnic/cultural) continuity between the populations of Judah and Yehud; secondly, a fair deal of shared memory; and, thirdly, objects such as traditional monuments as

1. Culture and Interpretation

the scenes and agricultural and religious festivals as the occasions of the 'publication' of the reinterpreted history.[12]

Apart from insufficient and lacking evidence to warrant the Persian fiction theory as an acceptable *explanation* of the origin of the Hebrew Bible there are also a number of counterindications that are worth mentioning, that is, texts and portions of texts that seem to make more sense in a social context of real ancient Near Eastern royal courts and temples than behind the walls of isolated scriptoriums in provincial Yehud. A few examples may illustrate the point.

Consider, for example, first, the 'royal' and 'Zion' psalms preoccupied with the glory, safety and prosperity of the king, his household and the royal city. It seems far more plausible to view the hyperbolic language of these psalms as actual praise songs in a real royal palace or temple than as creations of what must otherwise be a pathological messianic imagination.

Consider, secondly, the ethnocentric trend in so-called 'Deuteronomistic' literature. Davies (1992: 74, cf. 85) argues that, since the emphasis on 'ethnic identity' in Hebrew Bible literature would have been redundant in a monarchic state, it must have originated after the monarchy. However, in anthropological opinion exactly *state formation* (such as occurred in eighth century Israel and Judah) leads to a more pronounced 'ethnic differentiation and ethnocentrism', and to a dramatic increase in the 'potential for social conflict' (Haviland 1996: 336; see also Small 1997: 272-78). The 'ethnic' indicator thus seems to favour a pre-exilic date for the origin of 'ethnocentric' literature in the Hebrew Bible. Existing ethnocentric literature could, of course, later have served as a model for thinking about 'Israel'.

One could, thirdly, think of texts with forms, motifs, or wording borrowed from neighbouring literatures, such as the Egyptian Hymn to the

---

12. Consider, for example, the repeated reference to monuments (e.g. Gen. 35.20; Josh. 4.9; 8.29; 1 Sam. 6.18; 2 Sam. 18.18; 1 Kgs 8.8), place names, ethnic groups, customs, and phenomena (e.g. Gen. 22.14; 26.33; 32.32; 47.26; Deut. 2.22; 3.14; Josh. 5.9; 6.25; 7.26; 8.28; 9.27; 13.13; 14.14; 15.36; 16.10; Judg. 1.21, 26; 6.24; 10.14; 15.19; 18.12; 1 Sam. 5.5; 30.25; 2 Sam. 4.3; 6.8; 1 Kgs 9.13; 12.19; 2 Kgs 2.22; 8.22; 10.27; 14.7; 16.6; 17.34, 41; 2 Chron. 35.25) that 'are there up to this day'. Etiological narratives (often employing or implying the 'until this day' formula) are actually *justified* by the reference to concrete phenomena, rather than explaining their existence. In other words, the objectivity of the phenomenon rhetorically guarantees the 'truth' of the preceding narrative.

Sun (Ps. 104), the Ba'al epic (Ps. 29), the Wisdom of Amenemope (Prov. 22.17–24.33), the Babylonian Gilgamesh epic (Gen. 6–9) and motifs from the 'Canaanite' myths dealing with the divine court, such as occur in Psalm 82 and Deut. 32.8-9. Reference could, fourthly, be made to the structural parallel between Deuteronomy and Assyrian law codes pointed out by Weinfeld (1972). Recently, Otto, in a lecture before an *Oberseminar* in Stellenbosch, even argued that sections of Deuteronomy might be (polemic) *translations* of Neo-Assyrian legal texts. Such 'borrowings' make more sense in pre-exilic times, when international cultural exchange had not only been possible and unavoidable but sometimes also enforced, than they would in postexilic times, when the survival of the community depended on the drawing of clear *boundaries* between 'us' and 'them'.

Fifthly, to view the religious polemic against a fairly classical picture of 'Baalism' as a creation of the Yehud elite seems unfitting. The sixth–fifth centuries BCE saw the demise or radical reinterpretation of most of the older ancient Near Eastern religions and the birth of new ones—including perhaps also monotheistic Judaism (that would, of course, have *necessitated* the radical revision of older documents reflecting the 'old' religion). On the theory's assumption that literature merely reflects its time of origin, one would not expect the Yehud religious elite to have busied themselves with a dead religion like classical Baalism but rather to have paid attention to Zoroastrian and Hellenistic patterns of religious thinking. As Qumran literature (e.g. the Habakkuk commentary) shows, images and concepts that had in time become irrelevant or 'unseeming' were reinterpreted via the method of *pesher* to fit later situations. It would therefore be more obvious to explain the *retention* and reinterpretation of earlier concepts in later literature than to explain their *novel introduction* into a body of literature that had to address completely different issues.

A sixth contra-indicator has to do with various kinds of synchronisms between biblical and ancient Near Eastern sources from the ninth to the seventh centuries BCE. Such synchronisms concern, for example, references to institutions like the 'house of Israel' and 'the house of David' (on the Tel Dan Stele), various Assyrian military campaigns (Laato 1995), individuals like Omri, Hezekiah and Hazael (Eph'al and Naveh 1989), or even something as minute as a change in calendar ordered by Jeroboam I that may explain several inconsistencies in later texts (Talmon 1958), or a difference between the earlier Canaanite and later

1. Culture and Interpretation

Babylonian calendars that may explain differences between the set dates in Jubilees and 11QT for the feast of the first Fruits of Wine (Reeves 1992). Also such historical 'coincidences' like the socio-economic conditions presupposed by a book like Amos and the archaeology of eighth-century Samaria, or the polemic of a book like Hosea and the eighth-century belief in a bovine Yahweh of Samaria and his consort, witnessed to by the Kuntillet 'Ajrud inscription (Margalit 1990: 274-84).

These examples, which may be multiplied considerably, seem to suggest more than just a few scraps of information carried over from ancient Judah to the Yehud scribes and have to be accounted for by the Persian fiction theory.

The preceding critical notes do not seek to bolster the historical reliability of Hebrew Bible 'historiography' or to deny a late postexilic recasting of earlier material into a body of ideological literature. All indications are that the Hebrew text *we read today* dates (language and all) from the Persian to Roman times and is highly biased in favour of an ideological 'all-Israelite' identity. Indications also are that these texts had not been intended as a 'history of Israel'. Like 2 Maccabees, the books of Kings and Chronicles refer the reader interested in that kind of information to the relevant sources.

What the preceding discussion does do is supply arguments for the judgment that the historical probability of a tiny, dislocated, poor Yehud elite community, even lacking a common historical background, fabricating a massive block of identity-creating propaganda like the Hebrew Bible is not much higher than tenth-century BCE royal scribes in Jerusalem having produced a body of literature as extensive as the Yahwist source. In the light of the presently available evidence, one would therefore probably do better by accepting that, even though the present text had been compiled and tuned to *address* postexilic situations, its authors had access to quite substantial Judaean oral and written sources that had originated between the eighth and sixth centuries BCE.

Chapter 2

WHAT DO WE MEAN BY 'CULTURE'?

Chapter 1 argued for the incorporation of cultural information in interpreting biblical texts, and in the process made much of the 'cognitive world' of ancient speakers and hearers. Allesandro Duranti (1993: 236) says in this regard, 'The process whereby members of a given society produce acceptable versions of reality is embedded in local theories of what constitutes an acceptable account and who is entitled to tell the facts and assess their value and consequences.' But how is one to (re)construct the local theories of what constituted acceptable versions of reality in biblical times?

Scholars have over the centuries collected a vast amount of facts about ancient Israelite custom and way of life. In this connection, but in another context, Stephen Jay Gould (1989: 226) aptly remarks, 'The greatest impediment to scientific innovation is usually a conceptual lock, not a factual lock.' To (re)construct successfully the local versions of reality of biblical times one has to organize the available facts and observations in the form of a coherent story that may assign *meaning* to the facts. To spin out such a coherent story one needs more than a mere vague definition of culture (like the one presented in the introduction to this book). One needs a theory of culture, which is more easily asked for than done.

By the 1950s Kroeber and Kluckhohn had already collected over a hundred definitions of 'culture' in the literature (Haviland 1996: 32). The sheer variety of concepts of and approaches to culture may cause a conceptual lock in the discussion of biblical literature as a 'cultural' product. For this reason this chapter and the next intend clearing the ground somewhat in order to facilitate a further discussion.

After a few introductory remarks on renewed interest in culture over the last few decades, this chapter deals, first, with various approaches to the study of culture; secondly, with selecting a model for understanding

2. *What Do we Mean by 'Culture'?*

Israelite culture; and, thirdly, with some pitfalls in the description of especially ancient Israelite culture. Chapter 3 then briefly discusses the approach to culture presupposed by this study.

1. *Renewed Interest in Culture*

The study of culture has, over the past three decades, received increasing attention, not only in ancient Near Eastern and biblical studies, but on a more general scale.

While evolutionist models of thinking about the history of the ancient Near East dominated the scene for quite some time, the 1960s witnessed a marked shift in methodology. For instance, the anthropologically based theory on the process of early urbanization in Mesopotamia by Robert Adams published in 1966 signalled a clear departure from the then established views. Adams showed that, even though the organizational needs of irrigation could have enhanced the goals of the despotic state *once it had emerged*, the organization of labour in irrigation systems had *not* been the direct cause of the rise of despotic states, as had generally been assumed at the time. This kind of study made it clear that knowledge of cultural systems that had emerged much later or elsewhere under similar conditions could serve as handy models for the construction of a more reliable picture of the history of the ancient Near East, and encouraged scholars to take more serious note of anthropological theory.

Similar shifts took place in Syro-Palestinian historiography. Although already nineteenth century studies took note of anthropological theory of the time (Rogerson 1978: 12-21), theories on, for example, Israelite history, that had virtually dominated Hebrew Bible scholarship since the 1940s combined models from historical evolution and sociology. In this view, Israel had gradually developed from a nomadic or semi-nomadic existence into a sedentary community, at which stage they came into direct and prolonged contact with the Canaanite city dwellers. Hereafter they gradually adapted to the new circumstances, and in the process 'degenerated' in the field of religion from monotheism to polytheism, only to have been called back to their 'roots' by the writing prophets cherishing 'nomadic ideals'.

Anthropological studies on sedentarization, however, showed that the kind of gradual transition from nomadism to sedentarization, presupposed by the grand theory, had no real precedent (see Rogerson 1978: 17-22). Moreover, the dominant theory could no longer integrate and explain the contradictory information provided by Syro-Palestinian archaeology.

Also the sharp distinctions drawn earlier on between 'Israelites' and 'Canaanites', and between city dwellers and country dwellers became increasingly problematic in the light of anthropological studies. Even the long-standing conviction that the Hebrew terms משפחה, בית אב and שבט neatly fitted the categories 'extended family', 'clan' and 'tribe', respectively, became more than just suspect (Lemche 1985: 248-70). After a long period of fair certainty or 'normal science' as Kuhn would have called the earlier consensus, early Israelite history was once again up for grabs.

While broad-scaled sociological theories dominated the earlier scene (Mayes 1989), the change of mind in Hebrew Bible scholarship since roughly the mid 1970s was more than to anything else due to the introduction into especially Israelite historiography and history of religion of anthropological theory and know-how. What is necessary now, is to expand the benefit of these insights to the field of biblical interpretation. And, as will be shown in Chapter 4, this is already happening.

These developments in ancient Near Eastern and biblical studies form part of a much wider and general renewed interest in 'culture'. For quite some time the (academic) study of culture had not enjoyed enthusiastic support from all circles, especially not from those who had been the 'objects' of earlier ethnological research. The hurtful nature and persistence of the speculative descriptions and stereotypes travellers and administrators of colonial times gave of the 'primitive savages' living in far-away exotic regions, where 'civilization' had, in that view, not yet set foot, has contributed a great deal to these negative feelings (Grimshaw and Hart 1996: 16-18, 28-34). The use to which colonial powers had put cultural knowledge in formulating and enforcing oppressive administrative policies enhanced these negative feelings.

Even though political colonialism had already collapsed in the early 1960s, the painful experience of colonial times would not easily be erased. For example, the persistent practice in some academic organizations in the West of referring to non-First World citizens or minority cultures in First World states as 'ethnic'[1]—as if only 'they' were ethnic, while 'we' were normal and normative—keeps reminding individuals from these regions and groups of the erstwhile colonial superiority

---

1. Even though 'ethnic' has practically disappeared from scholarly writings (Banks 1996: 1).

2. What Do we Mean by 'Culture'?   81

complex and reinforces their reluctance to accept 'difference' and 'culture' as valid thought categories. Economic globalization, which, in many Third World countries, often boils down to economic hegemony, enhances this inherited mistrust.

However, two circumstances have, to some extent, contributed to overcoming entrenched suspicions. On the one hand, resistance in former colonies to colonial hegemony that had often been accompanied by protracted liberation struggles tended to foster among 'local' populations a strong sense of identity. 'Culture' steadily became something not to be ashamed but proud of. Also, *in* some Western countries, especially the USA and the UK, minority groups gradually came to resist 'melting pot' assimilationist and integrationist majority policies and to press for the recognition of 'local' identities and cultures (Turner 1994: 419). As Goldberg (1994: 12) puts it, 'Hegemonic or dominant identities and the exclusions they purport to licence have been challenged in terms of difference, or local or particular identities.' Even though 'culture' underwent a major shift of meaning in the multiculturalism and cultural studies debate (Turner 1994: 420; Collini 1994: 3) this debate stimulated interest in people's *locality*.

At the same time cultural and social anthropologists, whose studies had earlier on focused exclusively on extinct and 'exotic' cultures, have come to study their own heritage with the instruments developed for the description of 'foreign' cultures. Moreover, applied anthropology in such fields as business and medicine also contributed to a change in the definition of 'culture' to something that is not exclusively 'ethnic'.

The renewed emphasis on 'cultural identity' has advantages as well as disadvantages. On the positive side, it has replaced hierarchy with equality in intercultural communication. The liberal appeal to a 'common humanity' and the consequent disregard for cultural difference often showed itself in the past to be oppressive, because what was viewed as 'common' or 'universal' more often than not turned out to be nothing else but *Western* cultural assumptions paraded as normative (Banks 1996: 69-78, 109). The acknowledgment of difference as *difference in equality*, even though this is often more of an ideal than a reality, assisted in making at least some people aware of the cultural assumptions informing their 'way of thinking' and to accept the relative validity of other ways of looking at the world. It is in this, more positive sense of the term that we would like to speak of biblical cultures in terms of 'difference'.

On the negative side, the appeal to identity and difference has in the twentieth century caused immense human suffering in those countries where 'cultural identity' was assigned ontological status. One only has to think of the horrors of Nazi policies, the South African apartheid ordeal from 1948 to 1990, and the journalistically euphemized 'ethnic cleansings' in central Africa[2] and the Balkans (Banks 1996: 161-78) to realise the real dangers of overestimating, ontologizing and, especially, politicizing 'difference'.

Handled with the necessary care and respect, though, the concept of cultural identity and the honest search for 'the other' in the pages and original environment of the Bible may considerably enhance, and perhaps fundamentally change, our understanding of biblical literature and of ourselves.

2. *Anthropological Approaches to the Study of Culture*

In what follows a very broad overview is presented of various approaches Western scholars have invented to explain and understand the habitual ways in which particular groups of humans relate to their environment, organize themselves socially and politically, and so on.

Depending on the purpose and the desired degree of abstraction in such an overview, one may proceed in a number of ways. For example, one could divide the various approaches according to their focuses of study. Based on this criterion one could, for instance, distinguish between the traditionally British social anthropological and the traditionally North American cultural anthropological approaches. In the first approach the social organization, for example, kinship structure of a particular culture, forms the focal point of investigation. Other elements of the relevant culture are then interpreted as supportive of the particular society. In the second approach the societal structure of a community is viewed as a prerequisite for the existence of its particular culture, but social organization is not treated as a 'focal point' of investigation. The focus rather is on the way the cultural system as a whole interacts. In present-day anthropological research these two lines of approach have grown together to such an extent, though, that it would hardly be profitable for the purpose of this study to distinguish between the two.

---

2. For an appraisal of the events in Rwanda and Burundi, see Haviland 1996.

2. What Do we Mean by 'Culture'?

Classifying schools of thought according to their views on the relationship between 'fact' and 'theory' could be another way of looking at anthropological theories. From this perspective one could probably come up with a tripartite division of 'realist' (or 'deductive'), 'nominalist' (or 'inductive') and 'critical' (or 'retroductive') approaches (Gudeman and Penn 1982: 89-90). The first group (e.g. structural anthropology) would view a theoretical model as very powerful explanatory device with an autonomous existence, that is, existing apart from the actual culture 'facts'. The second group (that could include some forms of functional anthropology) would hold that explanatory models or theories have to be constructed inductively from the observation of actual behaviour. The third group (that may also find support in functionalist circles) would take a position in between the first two and view their theories as explanatory tools that establish relationships among observations, but which have to be continuously revised and amended to fit the facts. Even though these distinctions are of immense importance in deciding which procedures to adopt in the study of culture and for the status of the knowledge produced, they are still too abstract for the purpose of this study.

Based on the relationship between 'theory' and 'practice', or between approaches favouring general or universal theory formation and those favouring the description of one local culture, one could also distinguish between 'etic' and 'emic' approaches to the study of culture. This distinction draws an analogy between linguistics and anthropological research. In linguistics a distinction is made between describing linguistic phenomena with reference to language itself or with reference to something other than language. In phon*emics*, for example, phonemes are isolated by applying a semantic criterion (a phoneme is a minimal linguistic unit making a difference in meaning). Research along these lines identifies and describes the phonemes of a *specific* language. In phon*etics*, however, the sounds of a language are described with reference to biological features (such as a speaker's lips, teeth, tongue, nose, cheeks), and physical features (such as the way air passes through the trachea, lips or nose). Categories constructed along these lines, for example, bilabials, glottals, fricatives, etc. may be used to describe the sounds of *any* language or compare the pronunciation of sounds in *different* languages. Goodenough (1981: 16) explains the analogical approaches to anthropology as follows:

[W]hen we describe any socially meaningful behavioral system, the description is an emic one to the extent that it is based on elements that are already components of that system; and the description is an etic one to the extent that it is based on conceptual elements that are not components of that system.

Just as phonemics seeks to isolate the smallest meaningful linguistic units and to describe the way they operate as the building blocks in the linguistic structure of a language, 'emics' seeks to arrive at the most uncomplex cultural 'units' of a particular culture, while aetics' provides the 'frame of reference, the conceptual constants, through which to examine similarities and differences among specific behavioral systems of that type' (Goodenough 1981: 17). Although some anthropologists, for example Marvin Harris, prefer the 'etic' approach and others, like E.E. Evans-Pritchard and Mary Douglas, the 'emic' approach, the scarcity of 'emic' information on ancient Israel virtually forces biblical scholars to make use of existing 'etic' cultural theories to understand and explain the little they have in terms of 'emics'.

Related to the 'etic' versus 'emic' debate is the question of whether culture should be viewed as something concrete and empirical, or as something abstract and 'of the mind'. Some (more scientifically oriented) anthropologists prefer to take culture as something concrete and merely to describe what members of a culture do, manufacture, believe, etc. An emic approach suits this view best. Other (more historically or humanistically inclined) anthropologists prefer to see culture as something not directly observable, that is, as something 'of the mind'. An etic approach that would allow the *interpretation* of things people do, manufacture, believe, and so on in terms of abstract (psychological) notions best fits this approach.

For the purpose of this study it would perhaps be most profitable to simply look into the various ways in which scholars *explain* the existence and, especially, the workings of (a) culture. Taking this angle we shall briefly look at evolutionist, structuralist, functionalist, configurationalist and ethnohistorical approaches to 'culture'.

Evolutionist Approaches to Culture
In evolutionist approaches the interest lies in the *origins* of human culture and the mechanisms that caused its forward thrust. Several such forces have been suggested, ranging from biological and environmental to technological and ideological. The main characteristics of evolution-

ary explanations of human culture are naturalism and determinism. That is, the forces that caused culture to evolve and change are natural rather than spiritual and operate in a law-like fashion. The proponents of this model of explanation vary from sociobiologists to Marxists.

Sociobiologists study the group behaviour of all animals, including humans. Some of them, like Wilson, see genetics (and consequently mating systems) as the true driving force behind the evolution of human cultural. Wilson (quoted by Dennett 1995: 488), for instance, says, 'The similarities between the early civilizations of Egypt, Mesopotamia, India, China, and Central and South America...are remarkably close. They cannot be explained away as the products of chance or cultural cross-fertilization.' There must be a common cause, and that cause lies in human genetics. If you really want to get a grip on culture you should study genetics.

Other biologists, like the earlier Dawkins, without denying genetic base for the evolution of culture, draw a sharper distinction between animal and human culture. In this distinction human language and its spin-offs play an all-important role. Only human beings have the capability of using language to transmit knowledge, calculate possible outcomes of actions, 'dream up' solutions to problems, argue in a logical fashion, etc. Given that capability the similarities among ancient cultures to which Wilson refers may have another explanation. There is something like 'reinvention'. 'If a trick is good,' Dennett (1995: 487) says, 'then it will be routinely rediscovered by every culture, without need of either genetic descent of cultural transmission of the particulars.' Some of these 'softer' sociobiological explanations postulate a gene-like 'entity', called 'memes', to explain the speed of cultural evolution among humans. Memes are constituted by anything non-biological that is intentionally or unintentionally transmitted from one person to another. It can be a tune, a phrase, a design, a custom, a story, an epic. Culture, they claim, is a medium of design preservation and communication. What makes culture culture is its 'transmitability', its ability to form traditions and perpetuate habits that are not genetically enforced. If you want to understand culture you have to isolate and study the evolution of 'memes'.

Other evolutionists take the human capacity for culture for granted and set out to explain its evolution over time from 'primitive' to 'complex' or 'primitive' to 'modern'. In his *Evolution of Culture* Leslie White, for example, took technological development to be the cause of cultural change, and studied the relationship between the efficiency with which individuals in a social group spent energy on the completion of tasks and their level of advancement. The less energy individuals spend on attaining a certain goal (e.g. securing food), the more advanced the relevant group is on the ladder of evolution. What is interesting to note here is that, apart from its problematic equation of evolution with progress, the theory takes change in one sector of human activity (technological invention) to effect change in other areas of cultural activity (e.g. social organization and ideology). Even though the causation is conceived of as unilineal and fairly mechanistic, the idea of culture as something that can be explained in its own terms is evident.

Another line of explanation was taken by Julian Steward, who proposed a cultural ecological model. For him, culture was propelled by two main forces: the use made of the natural environment and the technologies invented to assist survival. To describe a particular culture attention should be paid to three questions. First, how efficient is the group's use of its natural environment for providing its basic needs, like food and shelter? Secondly, what technologies do they devise to ensure survival? Thirdly, how do the answers to these two questions explain the rest of the culture, for example, social and political organization, beliefs, etc. In this model, then, the physical environment and means of survival form the culture core from which the remainder of a culture evolves. Once more the causation is fairly unilineal, but the focus is on *relationships* among various cultural activities, such as getting food, devising plans to ease tasks, getting organized, etc.

In Marxist circles another approach to the evolution of culture is adopted. According to Marxist theory particular techno-environmental surroundings exert a variety of pressures on humans and cause a particular type of organizational structure to come into existence. Once a particular structure succeeds in surviving, mental structures (ideologies) are devised to protect that system. Up to this point Marxism shares ideas with other evolutionary theories of culture. It is, however, further postulated that all existing social structures derived from one original structure, namely a gens, in which collective property was the norm. Marriages were not contracted between individuals, but devised to create social bonds between groups. This (utopian) system gradually decayed into one in which transient systems, like private property, monogamy, patrilinear filiation, class and the state, evolved under historically conditioned circumstances. Marxist analyses have argued strongly for a fairly direct, albeit unilineal causal, relationship between physical environment, economic practice and social structures on the one hand and mental activity on the other.

Structuralist Approaches to Culture
The structuralist approach to culture that was introduced into cultural studies round about the middle of the twentieth century was in a sense a counter-reaction to, especially, French existentialism, that denied any 'meaning' in life. Viewed from this angle one may say that French structuralism, with Claude Lévi-Strauss as its founder, had more to do with the construction of meaning in culture than with social structures and the way in which culture 'works'.

However, the *theoretical basis* of structuralism has everything in common with structural linguistics and folkloristics. As indicated earlier on, de Saussure distinguished between language usage (*parole*) and language as an abstract system of rules (*langue*), the latter of which may be described as a system of relations among elements and without reference to the history of the system's evolvement. The Russian formalists and Prague structuralists followed a similar approach in describing folklore. In their view certain literary genres, such a fairy tales, only differed from each other on the surface. On a 'deeper' level they all exhibited a distinctive pattern or structure of related elements or 'functions'.

Following in these footsteps, structuralist studies of culture view observable human behaviour, which is normally taken for 'culture', as the mere local surface structure of 'culture' itself. Viewed on the level of surface structures, individual cultures differ quite considerably. Those differences are, however, not of an 'essential' nature. They are caused by physical, social and historical factors. On a 'deeper' level, though, they all share one (mental) structure, constituted by oppositional pairs, such as 'nature–culture', 'raw–cooked', 'good–evil', 'light–darkness'. Basic to all these oppositions is that of 'self–others', on which not only all human communication depends, but also certain social practices and rules are founded. For example, the pair 'self–others' lies at the root of the exchange of goods, marriage and incest taboos. This basic mental structure of human culture may now on the 'surface' take on various forms of economic activity, marriage practices, incest laws, etc.

It is clear that 'surface level culture' is here only appreciated as an instance of 'deep level culture', and 'deep level culture' is taken to be completely self-propelled and unaffected by outside forces. One major gain that has been achieved by this approach is the idea of culture as a structured system. Another gain was that, in stressing the common ground among various cultures, it counteracted the relativist tendency in many earlier anthropological studies that threatened to enclose various cultures each in its own unique cultural garden.

Structural-Functionalist Approaches to Culture
In discussing evolutionist and structuralist approaches to the study of culture, it was remarked that both acknowledged something of a *relatedness* between various elements of human culture. In the structural-functionalist view, mostly simply referred to as 'functionalism', culture exhibits not only a certain structuredness but also a dynamic interactive relationship among elements of that structure.

In this case (evolutionary) biology supplied the model of explanation. In this view an organism consists of a number of 'parts' interacting with each other according to certain natural laws. In employing the concept of a biological organism into an analogy or model for explaining the workings of culture, some also import the idea of a 'mechanism' into the explanatory framework for social data. Other anthropologists do not go as far as that and rather speak of culture as a dynamic interrelationship between various areas of human activity.

On the one hand there are then those who tend to take the model fairly literally and seek to explain the relationships among the structural elements of culture in a causal manner. In this view the causal nexus normally operates, as in materialism, 'upwards'. For example, the constraints of the environment cause a particular economic and social system and challenge technological innovation. Malinowski, for example, explained the workings of culture in terms of the satisfaction of a variety of human *needs*. The satisfaction of these needs 'causes' various sectors of culture to evolve and change. He distinguished primary, derived and synthetic needs. Primary, or biological, needs comprise things like procreation, nutrition, shelter and defence. Derived, or instrumental, needs are mostly of an organizational or conservational sort, like economic, legal and educational habits. Synthetic, or integrative, needs are those that have to do with knowledge, magic, religion, art, etc.

One may graphically represent this view as follows:

2. What Do we Mean by 'Culture'?

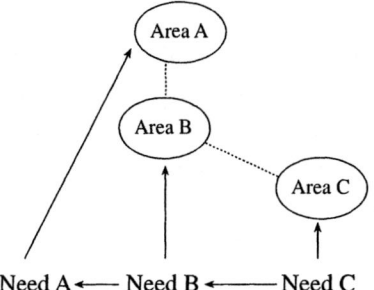

While the areas of cultural activity are related, their existence is *caused* by different needs. There may, of course, exist a causal relationship or hierarchy among the various *kinds* of needs.

On the other hand there are those who rather take the biological model as a kind of an analogy serving a hermeneutical goal. For them the idea of an 'organism' merely suggests that its different parts could be understood in terms of the whole and the whole in terms of its parts. Social values should, for example, and to put it rather crudely, not necessarily be understood as 'caused' by, for instance, environmental factors, but as capable of also affecting other, 'lower' cultural domains, like the environment. The relationships among the elements constituting culture are thus not viewed in terms of unilineal causation but as reciprocally effective, so that culture is seen as an interactive system. Radcliffe-Brown, for example, argued that the main function of culture was social integration, without which the group would not survive. In striving towards an equilibrium, culture is capable of adapting itself to various sorts of circumstances by rearranging elements making up a particular area of cultural activity (e.g. in the economic system), or by altering the relationships between two or more areas of cultural activity, (e.g. politics and religion). One may visualize this approach with the aid of the following diagram:

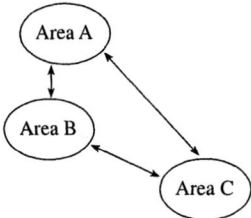

The two approaches do not exclude each other, though. In some instances the one seems more applicable and in other instances the other view seems more appropriate. The common denominator remains the view that culture could be viewed as an organism whose component parts should be studied in their relation to the system as a whole.

While a structuralist approach is not really interested in cultural difference, and is rather tuned to finding common denominators among cultures, and evolutionist explanations, accepting equal potential among cultures, put differing cultures on a scale of development, functionalist explanations of cultural difference tend to look at the different ways in which cultures 'organize' themselves. But whereas evolutionism views cultures as ever-changing and therefore as historical, functionalism tends to view cultures as stable, unchanging and static entities (Grimshaw and Hart 1996: 17, 25, 29-30).

Configurationalist Approaches to Culture
Not necessarily building on the insights of structuralism (interested in meaning) and functionalism (interested in coherence), but nevertheless similar to these interests, is an approach concerning itself with the unifying role of meaning in cultural systems.

In this view, all cultural behaviour is of a *symbolic* nature, that is, carries *meaning* that is shared by the group and abstracted by the individual from the social system through participatory interaction. Each human act thus has meaning. All such meanings tend to 'cluster' around central or core values, premises or goals. Culture is looked upon as an integrative configurational symbolic system to which a cultural group ascribes. Cultures do not differ from each other because of superficial 'traits', but because of the difference in the structure of their configuration of meaning. It was, and is sometimes still, suggested that each culture exhibits a unique configuration of meaning constituting the group's 'genius', 'distinctive soul' or 'unique spirit'. Such types of culture may then be fitted into a typological grid.

Since symbols and meaning have a strong psychological basis, typologies have been constructed on the basis of cognitive, affective and conative characteristics. A typology emphasizing cognitive, or ideational, characteristics of cultures focuses on distinctive ideas, master symbols, premises and unstated assumptions underlying actions or decisions. A typology stressing affective, or emotional, characteristics focuses on things like cultural values, attitudes and interests directing actions and choices. And a typology accentuating conative, or action-related, characteristics focuses on the ideals, goals, orientations and purposes of actions.

Kluckhohn, for example, described the Navaho Indian culture with reference to abstract cognitive assumptions like 'knowledge is power', 'harmony is essential', 'the universe is personal', 'evil and good are complementary', 'morality is situational', and so on.

Even though the idea of a typology of cultural geniuses has been heavily criticized, and has to a large degree been abandoned, the configurational approach has had three important spin-offs, the one in the region of *ethnolinguistics*, the other in the area of *cognitive* anthropology, and the third in the field of *value studies*.

Language had for a very long time been the playing field of linguists only. They successfully studied the internal phonological, syntactic and semantic features and structures of various languages. However, since the publication of studies by Edward Sapir and his student Benjamin Lee Whorf in the 1930s and 1940s, the study of language in the form of ethnolinguistics has become a specialist branch in anthropology as well.

When it was discovered that particular cultures used different systems of classifying things around them, for example colour, it was hypothesized by some that language actually 'mirrors' the mental world people live in and consequently gives one direct access to their view of the world. Others, like Whorf, argued even more boldly that, since language was their only means of thinking and talking about reality, it not only mirrored but *shaped* people's outlook on the world. Although the latter theory has long been practically discarded, the close connection between language and culture has ever since intrigued anthropologists.

Ethnolinguistics, which grew out of, and surpassed, Sapir's and Whorf's work, studies various facets of language in its relation to culture, for example, the way cultures classify reality, name their relatives, the way in which various strata of society use language or in which language is used in different social situations, the areas from which metaphors are drawn in a particular language, the ideological import of linguistic structures, etc. These studies have provided valuable insights into the way people see themselves, their bodies, social relations, environment, etc., form metaphors, think about problems and the unseen, etc., as well as into the intriguing relation between language and culture.

Cognitive anthropology focuses more on the psychological characteristics of culture and studies the ways in which individuals of a particular culture conceptualize and explain their environment, what kind of logic they apply to solve problems, etc. Of special interest is the 'world view' to which people of a particular culture subscribe and with reference to which they explain and understand phenomena and events in reality, reason about right and wrong and take decisions. In spite of all kinds of problems and dangers lurking in this kind of study, it remains valuable.

Value studies normally seek to explain the choices individuals of a particular culture make with reference to what they deem as desirable. It therefore deals with the normative side of a culture. To obtain knowledge of a culture's value system is as important as it is difficult. It is even difficult to reach a consensus of some sort of what is to be understood under cultural or social values. After having discussed twenty-five notions of the concept 'value', Joubert (1992: 23) decides that it may perhaps be best defined as 'notions of the good and desirable in personal dispositions, social conduct, societal arrangements, and cultural resources'. Notions of 'the good and desirable' are—of course never explicitly stated—not even in aphorisms and proverbs—but are always implied whenever humans have to exercise a choice. The values implied in a particular choice have to be discerned and named by the researcher. Even though value studies presents the researcher with a number of methodological and philosophical problems, it has been sufficiently shown that a study of a culture's values may afford researchers a handy hermeneutical tool for understanding (and even predicting) the actions of individuals socialized in a particular culture.

Ethnohistorical Approaches to Culture
Although anthropology normally interests itself in the description of a particular culture at a specific point in time, it has always been concerned with the history of human culture. Archaeological anthropology has always dealt with the earliest remains of culture (of a region) and historical anthropology studies *cultural change* that had occurred in the history of a particular group. The demise of colonialism has, however, stimulated the interest in what has become known as 'ethnohistory', that is, the history of a people with little or no historical records other than what archaeology and folklore can provide.

Of special interest here is the role of folklore in ethnohistory. Just as the study of language had for a long time been the domain of linguistics

2. What Do we Mean by 'Culture'? 93

so the study of folklore had been the domain of literary studies. Like language, folklore has, however, come to play an increasingly significant role in anthropology. The earliest anthropological studies of folklore, like Sir James George Frazer's *The Golden Bough*, sought to identify universal themes appearing in different folklores, and to establish possible borrowings by one group from another. In time, however, the interest shifted to studying a particular literature (whether oral or written) for other purposes. In structural anthropology, for instance, the study of mythology plays a significant role in establishing the recurrence of universal functions and in ethnohistory the stories, myths and poems of a group are scrutinized for possible clues to the history of the people under investigation.

In the process of using folklore and written (literary) texts as sources for the construction of the history of a group, anthropologists have established a valuable critical framework for working with these sources, a framework that is of particular interest for the present study. Two examples may illustrate the point.

Anthropologists are particularly adamant that the researcher interpreting folkloristic sources should for at least two reasons have an intimate knowledge of the culture that has produced the literature. First, because the researcher has to be able to distinguish among various kinds of oral and literary documents and their respective social locations and functions. Literature is here not studied for the sake of literature, *but as an integral part of the culture to which it belongs*. Secondly, because the researcher has to be acutely aware of the type of society that produced the literature. Freedman (1978: 83) explains why: '[T]he threat to ethnohistory from history is that the historian may too easily transfer to exotic societies the assumptions they make about their own.' The colonization of biblical literature by assumptions quite foreign to the cultural texture of these texts has always been and remains to be one of the major problems in biblical interpretation.

The second example may perhaps best be given by way of a quotation from Freedman (1978: 83),

> In functional studies...a persuasive doctrine was developed according to which all statements made by informants which purported to be about the past were to be taken as statements about the present, in the sense that they were justificatory of present social arrangements... It is now, at a later stage of scholarship, clear that the scepticism was too widely applied.

In Hebrew Bible studies this same doctrine is still widely applied to especially ancient Israelite literature, and it is perhaps high time that note is taken in this field of study of what is happening in ethnohistory.

3. *Choosing a Model for the Study of Biblical Literature*

Since it is the aim of this study to argue for the inclusion of cultural information in biblical interpretation, one has to be clear about what approach to 'culture' would be the most rewarding for this purpose. We have argued earlier that interpretation is an act of *communication*, and that communication, at least in the perspective of relevance theory, has much to do with the *cognitive worlds* of the (original) speakers and hearers. Viewed from this angle the anthropological approach that would best enhance biblical interpretation would be one that focuses on the *cognitive side* of culture. This singles out the configurational or ideational approach as the most suitable for the purpose.

However, by merely zooming in on an ideational approach one runs the risk of reducing culture to ideas in people's minds. Such a reduction would hamper interpretation in more than one way. First, as will be pointed out in the next section, the view that culture is 'located' in people's hearts or minds might result in viewing the 'other' as exotic and enclosed in a walled cultural garden does not allow for intercultural *communication*, which is what biblical interpretation is about. Secondly, culture is more than mere ideas in people's heads. In most approaches to culture the *interrelatedness* of people with their environment their (technological, social, political, religious, etc.) artefacts are seen as constitutive of culture. This relationship is, however, of a dynamic nature. That is, culture is not a mere 'system' working like a clock, as might be deduced from, for example, a structural functionalist approach. One will have to look for a model that can accommodate and explain cultural *change* without losing sight of the interrelatedness of *all* cultural spheres. This means that one has to supplement an ideational or configurational approach with some evolutionary approach. An evolutionary model would best answer in this facet of culture. The problem with evolutionary models is, however, that they tend to view cultural evolution as *determined* by environmental forces. In this way ideas might be reduced to ideological by-products of material forces. If this were true, it would have been impossible for someone to have novel ideas or for ideals to change society as well.

2. What Do we Mean by 'Culture'?

It would therefore seem that, for the purpose of this study, one has to be eclectic. While the focus must be on the *cognitive* side of Israelite culture (configurationalism), one has to take serious note of *evolutionary forces* pressing for change in the system (ecological anthropology) without losing sight of the fact that culture is constituted by a dynamic interaction among all cultural domains.

In sum, one may elucidate the theoretical and practical choices underlying this study with reference to a diagram devised by Johnson *et al.* (1984: 14-19) to explain different scholarly definitions of and approaches to 'social reality'.

	Nominalist	*Realist*
Materialism	Empiricism	Substantialism
Idealism	Subjectivism	Rationalism

Empiricism combines a nominalist view of social reality (or culture) with a materialist methodology. That is, in this view culture is not an 'entity' (e.g. an underlying set of principles) that exists apart from what people do, think, believe, etc. Culture is what people, living under particular physical and economic conditions, are in a sense forced to do, think and believe. Therefore, a culture may be described by observing people and describing their behaviour. Combining nominalism and idealism, *subjectivism*, like materialism, does not view culture as 'existing' apart from the things people do, think and believe, but unlike materialism it views human behaviour in an idealist way as a matter of personal or group choice. For this reason culture cannot be 'observed' directly. A group's culture (e.g. its motivations for making particular choices) has to be inferred from their actions. The *rationalist* position combines realism and idealism in viewing culture as real abstract structures existing apart from the things people do, think and believe, as structures of the mind 'instructing' them, as it were, to act, think and believe the way they do. Since culture 'exists' in a group's categories of the mind, it cannot be 'observed'. Their actions have to be explained deductively with reference to those categories. *Substantialism* shares the empiricist view that culture is expressed in the concrete things people do, think and believe, and therefore makes much of empirical observation of human behaviour. But it does not share the view that these acts, thoughts and beliefs may be adequately explained with reference to material forces alone. With rationalism it accepts that culture is something more than personal or group choice—like in subjectivism—and views culture as something 'of the mind'. While the only access to a culture's 'mind' is through observation of culture enacted, one needs a theoretical 'grid' with reference to which the 'real' cultural assumptions may be explained and described.

These positions do, of course, not represent watertight compartments. The diagram merely serves to describe various ideal views. In practice scholars go about their job in a somewhat eclectic manner. Nevertheless, the position that most properly describes the approach adopted in this study would be substantialism. This implies that Israelite culture will be 'observed' in their literature and other cultural remains and interpreted from the perspective of configurationalist theories. In making these choices one has to be aware of several looming pitfalls, though.

4. Pitfalls in the Study of Culture

It is fairly obvious that anthropological theories and insights will enhance our understanding of 'ancient Israelite culture'. Such a cross-fertilization is, however, not without its problems. Without suggesting that the following remarks provide an exhaustive list of such problems, they may serve to caution against too much optimism and too-high expectations.

In the first place an extended first-hand exposure to the culture under investigation has always been a prerequisite for sound anthropological work. This opportunity does not exist for biblical scholars, who, like cultural archaeologists, only have the meagre remains of a bygone culture to work with. There will consequently always be huge gaps in our knowledge. The situation is, however, not altogether desperate. Although not produced from an anthropological point of view and not always done with the necessary critical care, earlier scholars like Carl Friedrich Keil and Franz Delitzsch, I. Benzinger, F. Nötscher, A.G. Barrois, A. Bertholet, Johannes Pedersen and Roland de Vaux had collected a vast amount of cultural information from the Hebrew Bible and archaeology that may be sifted and reinterpreted from another theoretical angle. More recently a number of studies based on a variety of anthropological and sociological theories and treating specific areas or institutions of Israelite culture were published. These publications

2. What Do we Mean by 'Culture'?   97

showed that anthropological theory may contribute a great deal towards a coherent explanation of elements of Israelite culture. Syro-Palestinian archaeology, specifically regional archaeology in that area, has over the last three decades contributed enormously to a better understanding of the physical environment and living conditions in Bronze and Iron Age Palestine, and afforded better insight into the social and political organization in the region in those times. It has shown that anthropological theories may provide one with a tested framework with reference to which the available data may be coherently interpreted.

The practice of employing anthropological theories or models in interpreting ancient Israelite culture has, however, confronted biblical scholars with at least two problems. First, as has been indicated by the foregoing discussion, there is the problem of the variety of theoretical options to choose from. Some of these theories show an idealist and others a materialist bias. Some assign realistic value to their constructed theories, while others see theories as valuable fictions and still others take a critical realist stand. Choosing a theory by definition determines the kind of explanations that will be offered for phenomena and their relationships. Gottwald, for example, chose a materialistic theory of culture and a revolutionary theory of cultural change and came up with a picture of early Israelite history that differs widely from the picture Lemche arrived at through a more inductive and evolutionary approach. Boman, employing the Sapir–Whorf theory, constructed a picture of the Israelite mind that had hardly any window in the direction of the Aegean world.

Secondly, to use a description of another, comparable, culture as a model for describing Israelite culture (e.g. using an African model to explain Israelite culture) may equally disturb the picture. Earlier on some scholars, for example, classified ancient Israel as a 'primitive' society and consequently mistakenly explained Israelite religion almost exclusively in terms of magic and mysticism. Others modelled their picture of early Israel on descriptions of nomad and semi-nomad cultures. They now seem to have chosen an inappropriate model.

Schopman (1986) points out a number of negative results of interdisciplinary cross-fertilization. For instance, concepts carried over from one field of research to another may initially contribute to the generation of new insight, but after a while prove to be a hindrance rather than a help. This has been the case with the description of early Israelite society in terms of 'families', 'clans' and 'tribes'. Schopman also gives examples of the havoc the transfer of methodologies and tools from one field to another may cause. One therefore has to be extremely careful in simply looking upon anthropological theories as 'take-away' methodologies. One has to be quite clear about the exact nature of one's problem and ensure that enough suitable information is available for the model to be applied successfully.

A third problem area concerns pluralism in cultures, and cultural change. A culture seldom has but one face. It often consists of a variety of subcultures of, for example, social class, age or gender. This situation renders talk of 'the cognitive world' of a particular culture *as a whole* problematic. Karl Marx, for example, even though he recognized oppressed classes as constituting a kind of subculture, reasoned that those classes all suffered from a false consciousness. This implies that all oppressed groups are fooled into *sharing* the outlook of their oppressors, and, consequently, also the social and economic reasoning prescribed by the powerful class. Recently, however, James Scott (1990) has argued convincingly that oppressed groups only seemingly 'share' the outlook of the ruling class, but that they in actual fact share among themselves a 'hidden transcript' of reality that differs considerably from the 'public transcript' shared by the powerful. Marx's theory on the cognitive side of the culture of the oppressed may thus be completely wrong. In the light of the existence of subcultures it would most probably be wrong to speak of 'Israelite culture' as if it had but one face to show.

On the other hand, the existence of subcultures within broader cultures might entice one to postulate a subculture as an explanatory mechanism, while such a subculture never existed. This might, for example, be the case with the distinction 'urban–rural', which had for some time been a popular way of explaining Israelite culture but is now seriously questioned.

The same pitfall lurks in view of cultural change. Israelite history (if one for a moment excludes early Judaism from the picture) can be followed for roughly five hundred years. During that time many things normally effecting cultural change occurred. For example, at some stage a form of centralized government was instated, only to be divided soon afterwards into two political entities who lived in animosity for quite some time. Pressure exerted by imperial powers forced these two 'states' into various alliances with local kingdoms and other imperial powers. For some time ownership of land equalled work force. Then

2. What Do we Mean by 'Culture'?

followed a period during which some landowners lived elsewhere while others tended their holdings on a sharecropping basis. At times the land experienced sharp population increases. At other times it suffered prolonged droughts and famines. In the light of such events it is extremely problematic, if not impossible, to speak of 'Israelite' culture as a stable entity. One has to reckon with cultural change.

A fourth problem area lies in the anthropological construction of the 'other', which has been a hotly debated issue in anthropological discourse. What Banks (1996: 182-87) says about the ways in which anthropologists view 'ethnicity' is of importance in respect of constructing the other as cultural being as well. He distinguishes three approaches which he illustrates with the following diagram:

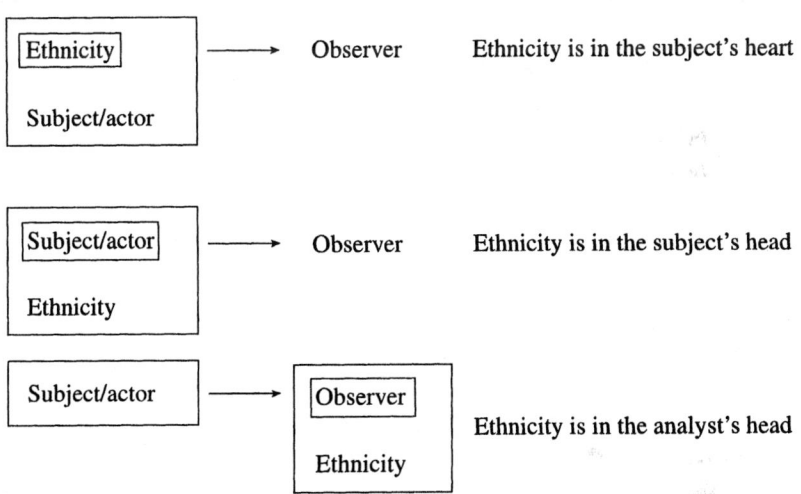

The first line illustrates the view of some anthropologists (mostly Soviet ethno-theorists) that ethnicity is a fundamental constitution of being human. Ethnicity therefore is 'something' in the heart of a person, something characteristic, real and permanent of which a person is conscious. The middle line illustrates the position of those anthropologists (mostly structural functionalists) who view ethnicity as something instrumental. In other words, people *learn* the culture they have been born into and to act it out for their own good. In this way culture, although not something inherent 'in the heart' of a person or group, is something 'of the mind'. The third line views ethnicity not as something that 'belongs' to the other, but as a device used by the analyst 'to make sense of or explain the actions and feelings of the people studied'

(Banks 1996: 186). This view does not suggest that people do not differ in the ways they see the world and do things, but that the *construction* an analyst makes of the other is *his* construction. It is *his* way of seeing the other from the perspective of how *he* sees the world and does things. Given the choice for a substantialist approach to culture, this is an important point to remember.

Even though one may view culture in a substantialist way as something learned and 'of the mind', any description of that 'mind', for example, of Israelite culture or of the cognitive world of that culture, should not be looked upon as a *re*construction of 'how ancient Israelites really thought', but as a systematic *con*struction from the perspective of a present-day analyst on the basis of a particular anthropological theory. Such a description remains a *present-day* endeavour to understand the other.

An observation by Wagner (1996: 52-53) referred to in Chapter 1 is to the point here. According to him we in a sense 'invent' the culture we are studying. In that sense the other's culture becomes something in the head of the analyst. But since our description rests on (perspectivist) observation that invention is not a free fantasy. Studying a culture implies the development of a reciprocal relationship between subject and object: in constructing the other one is also constructing oneself, since it is only in confrontation with 'the other' that one becomes aware of oneself and 'receives' a culture. In constructing or inventing the other one may therefore not set oneself up as the norm from which the other deviates. Neither may one view the other *person* as 'locked up' in an enclosed, windowless cultural garden. Culture is not something essential in a person's heart. It is at the most the product of enculturation into ways of doing things and looking at the world. In that sense it is something of the mind, but the mind *as seen from my perspective*.

Certainly, one of the most difficult hurdles in getting acquainted with a culture, especially so in the case of a 'dead' culture, is to gather some form of an understanding of the cognitive world of the 'other' that would enable one to understand actions as *intentional*, that is, to ascribe *meaning* to the subject's actions not merely from the point of view of, for instance, functional theory, but *from the perspective of the subject himself*. To be sure, if a culture must in the end make sense to an outsider then answering 'why' questions becomes more important than answering 'how' questions. Answering 'why' questions is, of course, extremely difficult, and not only because nobody can look into someone

2. What Do we Mean by 'Culture'?

else's head, and not only because even members of a culture do not always know why they do things the way they do, but also because the answers to 'why' questions, in the words of Duranti (1993: 216), 'emerge as interactive properties of complex systems that include, or must interface with, socioeconomic as well as cultural (e.g. ethical) dimensions of human action'.

In mainstream Western philosophy intentionality is, for example, a 'product' of 'the individual's mind as the meaning-making organism' (Duranti 1993: 221). This view becomes extremely problematic as soon as one takes a cross-cultural perspective, since the limitations and constraints placed on individual choice in some societies fashion the individuals' intentionality, while interpretative strategies also differ cross-culturally. In interpreting and evaluating actions some cultures emphasize the subjective state of the speaker's mind (his motivation), while others are more concerned with the consequences of a person's talk and actions (Duranti 1993: 222-23). In like manner certain utterances may in one language mirror emotion (as a state of mind), while comparable reactions in another culture may express social relationships (values). However difficult, assigning (constructing or inventing) meaning is what understanding a culture is about. If we would like to understand Israelite culture in order to understand its literature, there is no way other than taking these risks.

An awareness of the problematic nature of constructing the culture(s) of ancient Israel is in itself no insurance against committing mistakes, even serious ones. Being aware of these problems, and trying to avoid them as best one can, is, however, already a substantial improvement on *not* being aware of or not even caring about them. It is as oppressive to lock up 'the other' in a cultural garden as it is to deny him or her the right to be different.

Chapter 3

CULTURE, LANGUAGE AND MEANING

Chapter 1 argued that acquaintance with a text's cultural world is indispensable for successful communication between text and reader, for validating exegetical hypotheses and for creating a critical self-awareness in the exegete. Chapter 2 suggested that a mixture of configurational and evolutionary approaches to culture would best serve the study of the place of literature in culture. This chapter now takes a broad look at the contribution insight into Israelite culture, studied from these angles, can make to biblical interpretation. The next six chapters will then look in a more focused way into the contribution knowledge of the various cultural domains may make to the understanding of Hebrew Bible texts.

1. Cultural Domains, Function and Meaning

Cultural anthropology distinguishes a variety of interactive 'domains' through which a culture may be studied and described, such as the interaction between humans and their environment, the technologies they apply, their economic system (or system of production and distribution), their social and political organization, forms of social control, language (and literature), religion, art and world view. These distinctions are, of course, made from a *modern* perspectives and they are of a *theoretical* nature. It is only since the Industrial Revolution and the introduction of the modern state that such activities as economy, politics, religion, etc., have to a certain extent become compartmentalized. In subsistence societies things are much more involved and integrated. Moreover, a person never acts in, for example, a purely economic, political or religious way. While acting economically he may, for instance, also involve the social or political structures, the values of the community, and so on. In reality a culture is therefore constituted by the constant *interaction* of a variety of human activities that cannot be

3. *Culture, Language and Meaning*

separated in watertight compartments. The theoretical demarcated 'domains' merely enables an observer to focus more clearly on one *kind* of activity at a time and to investigate its interrelationship with the rest of the cultural system, and is *our* way of constructing the other.

The following schematic representation may assist the ensuing discussion:

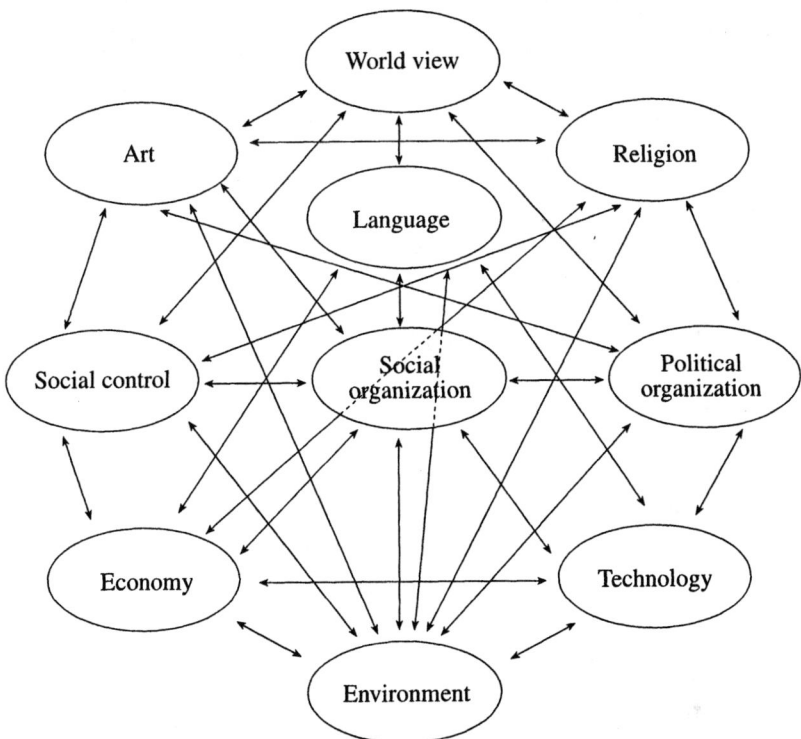

The diagram may be misleading in two ways. On the one hand it might create the impression of culture as a static entity, which no culture is. The double-headed arrows are supposed to indicate that the cultural 'system' is in fact a dynamic 'organism' in that *every* sphere of culture interacts with *all* other spheres. An activity in one 'domain' may involve a variety of other cultural spheres, and change in one sphere may trigger change in various other spheres.

On the other hand the implication that 'below is fundamental' and 'above is derived', as well as two-dimensionality of the representation may seem to imply the vulgar Marxist view that the environment and economy are the 'cause' of, for instance, mental concepts, and that ideas therefore necessarily are the *products* of environmental and economic factors. This is not the idea. The double-headed arrows suggest that the relationships between various cultural domains are *reciprocally* effective, so that a particular religious view or cultural value (derived from any cultural domain) may, for instance, also effect the environment. To forestall possible misconceptions one could think of the diagram above as a two-dimensional representation of a flexible, transparent object with a number of flat surfaces, each flat surface representing a cultural domain:

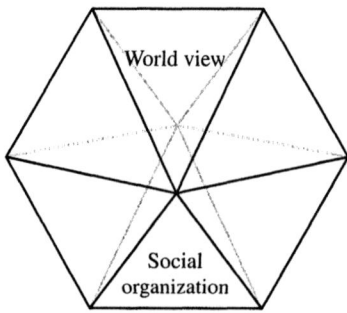

'Tilting' the solid in various directions enables one to look at culture from different *perspectives* (or interests) without reducing it to any one perspective (e.g. 'culture is environment/technology/economics/language/world view') or implying a materialist or idealist explanatory framework. In the illustration above, culture is, for example, viewed *from the perspective of language*. From this perspective certain cultural domains come directly in sight, while the others, visible *through* the sphere (e.g. environment, technology, economy, etc.) are, although not in direct sight, *always* implied. Any one of these domains may consequently act as a 'prime move?' of cultural change.

Furthermore, one has constantly to keep in mind that, even with the above emendations to the diagram above, the reciprocal influences suggested to be exerted among the various domains do not represent 'reality'. They are the theoretical constructs of the 'omniscient' observer. To say that, under certain circumstances, economic factors 'caused' a shift in cultural values, or that, under certain circumstances, a religious belief 'effected' a change in people's attitude towards the environment, is not to say that the people *of* that culture view things in the same way. They may see a quite different relationship between things. We shall therefore refer to theoretical relationships between cultural phenomena as

3. Culture, Language and Meaning   105

(cultural) *functions*. How members of a culture view things, the explanations they provide for their existence and the values they attach to them will be referred to as the *meaning* of such phenomena. Had this study been intended as a theoretical *description* of Israelite culture its focus would have been on function rather than on meaning. Given the perspective of this study, though, the emphasis is more on the meaning of Israelite views, customs, institutions, etc.

Any attempt at capturing the *meaning* of things automatically brings the linguistic domain into focus, since it is through language that people express their interpretation of life. We shall, therefore, first, deal with the function of language and custom as meaning-constituting devices in culture. The next six chapters will then provide examples of how knowledge of the various cultural domains may assist a (literary) interpretation of Hebrew Bible literature.

2. *Language and Meaning*

'[I]f we are today to try and understand the Israelite mind,' Winton Thomas (1960: 427) wrote, 'we must try our best to discover...the living and lively language of the people. The undertaking is in a sense a kind of archaeological operation which involves digging deep into the layers of speech used throughout countless generations.' Even though Winton Thomas was merely talking about recovering the meaning of the idiomatic use of biblical Hebrew his proposition implies that the language of a group may somehow serve as a window into its culture.

Voluminous books have been written on the relation between language and culture. The few remarks on the topic that follow are mere examples illustrating the role of language in culture. The examples are drawn from four fields, namely the role of language in classifying reality, the relations a language may establish among linguistic categories, the role of metaphor and the role of language in literary representation.

Language plays a pivotal role in a culture's 'picture' of reality. While the number of natural- and human-made 'objects', relations among these objects, the potential variety of experiences individuals may have in dealing with such objects etc. are, for all practical purposes, infinite, the vocabulary of a language, like its capacity for expressing relations, is finite. For that reason, and because of the limited capacity of the human brain to perceive, sort and store information, language has to opt for some form of economy. One way of linguistic economizing is coded categorization.

Every language classifies observable objects and experiences in hierarchically organized categories. In some instances a diversity of objects or experiences are lumped together under one term. In other instances a variety of terms may be used to point to aspects of a single phenomenon. At a certain stage speakers of ancient Hebrew, for example, used to lump together all foreign peoples under the term גויים. At the same time, however, they used various terms to distinguish different kinds of rain, for example, גשם, מטר, זרם, יורה, סגריר, טל, מלקוש, and רביבים, normally translated by 'shower', 'rain', 'rain-storm', 'early rains', 'steady, persistent rain', 'dew', 'late rains' (or 'spring rain') and 'copious showers', respectively. Some of these terms carry a more generic meaning, while others refer to a specific *type* (or time) of rain.

The criteria for classifying natural objects or phenomena are varied. Consider the following two examples. In Genesis 1 both the domains created by divisions, and also the created inhabitants of those domains are described, as the following table shows:

Day	Division	Creation	Day
1	Light/darkness	Light sources	4
2	Heaven/water	Inhabitants of air/water	5
3	Water/ land	Inhabitants of water/land	6
	Creation of plants		
	Domains (immobile)	*Contents (mobile)*	

To find an act of *creation* (plants) in the column containing acts of *division* seems logically inconsistent with the 'division–creation scheme' classifying the divine acts. This kind of 'inconsistency' has led some scholars to postulate two 'sources' in the history of the text. Without denying the possibility of sources underlying Genesis 1, the 'awkward' position of the creation of plants in the scheme does not count in favour of the source theory. There is a very good reason for the 'inconsistency': the author was forced by his cultural classification system of objects to distinguish between 'mobile' and 'immobile' entities. Unlike the sun, animals, fish and people, heaven, earth, water, and plants are not mobile. To have mentioned 'plants' together with mobile entities would have violated the accepted classification system for objects, and would consequently have yielded an implausible story.

Not all classification systems rely on observable criteria, though.

3. *Culture, Language and Meaning*

Some criteria are informed by religious beliefs, which may be so strong that they may override 'empirical' criteria. The ancients normally distinguished four kinds of animals. As a zoologist of name, Solomon is said to have spoken of beasts/cattle, birds, reptiles and fish (1 Kgs 4.33; cf. Deut. 4.16-18; Ps. 148.10). The first and the last of these categories live either on land and in water, respectively. The other two are anomalies. Birds fly in heaven *and* nest on earth, while (amphibian) reptiles live in water *and* on land. Ergo, there are *four* categories of animals. Not so in Gen. 1.28 and Ezek. 38.20, as Clark (1968) observes. Humankind's dominion is there said to be over '*fish* of the sea and over the *birds* of the air and over every living thing *that moves upon the earth*'. Reptiles and beasts are here lumped together in one class. This classification is an innovation by the Priestly writer. The reason for this 'reclassification', Clark (1968: 447) argues, is not cosmological but is 'directed towards such concerns as which animals are proper for sacrifice, are clean and can be eaten. P wants to say that these cultically determined divisions are part of the established order or creation'. This extra *meaning*, then, is the 'reward' for investing extra processing effort to recover the intended meaning of the 'anomaly'. But to be able to do so one has to know that the four-category system was the normal one and that Genesis 1 deviates from it.

Another type of linguistic categorization is the use of what linguists call 'marked' and 'unmarked' categories. In Hebrew, for example, reality is classified with the aid of masculine and feminine forms, where the masculine form most frequently is the unmarked form. Consider, for example, עברי 'a Hebrew' but עבריה 'a Hebrewess', חבר 'husband' but חברת 'wife', יהודי 'a Jew' but יהודית 'a Jewess' etc., where the endings ה– and ת– *mark* the feminine gender. The fact that the masculine form is the 'normal' (i.e. unmarked) form, says something about the position of 'male' relative to 'female' in this culture. But there is more to gender in Hebrew.

The language shows a tendency (not a rule) to classify abstracts, uncontrollable (natural) forces, parts of wholes, limited areas and utensils as feminine, while actors, wholes and a variety of limiting forces are classified as male. Consider, for example:

	Masculine	Feminine
Concrete/abstract	cf. עבד 'labourer'; גבר 'strong man'; רשע 'evil doer'	עבודה 'labour'; גבורה 'strength'; רשעה 'evil'
Natural forces		שמש 'sun'; רוח 'wind'; אש 'fire'; אור 'light'
Whole/parts	אני 'fleet'; שער 'hair'; שיר collection of poems or songs	אצבע 'finger'; יד 'hand'; כתף 'shoulder'; אניה 'ship'; שערה 'a hair'; שירה 'a song'
Limiting/limited	נהר 'river'; הר 'mountain'	עיר 'city'; ארץ 'country'; שאול 'netherworld'; באר 'well'
Utensils		חרב 'sword'; בד 'bucket'; נעל 'shoe'

This 'view' of masculinity as active, setting boundaries, representing wholeness, etc. is also extended into Hebrew syntax. For example, whenever the subject of a sentence refers to masculine *and* feminine actors the verb of the sentence is constructed in the *masculine* plural form.

Although it cannot be said that languages 'reflect' social reality or 'determine' the way people think about the world, examples like these may indicate a linguistic community with a masculinity-slanted value system that, in the case of the Hebrew Bible, is confirmed by the *social* system it presupposes and prescribes. The 'manner of speaking about reality' provided by linguistic categories not only comes in time to stand *for* reality but, given the slow pace of change in linguistic forms, also serves as a conservative factor in culture.

Languages not only categorize reality and in that way ascribe value to such categories, they also express a wide variety of relations among terms and categories of terms. Such relations may be expressed as spatial, temporal, semantic and symbolic or denote inclusion, exclusion, complementarity, instrumentality, comparison, causation, etc. (Goodenough 1981: 68). Even though all languages have the ability to express

3. Culture, Language and Meaning 109

such relations, the relations that are in fact established in a particular language are dependent upon such things as the relevant culture's view of time and space, its rules of inference, its value system (e.g. including and excluding) and its capacity to bear with contradiction, etc.[1]

Some of the expressed relations may be physically observable, while others may represent postulated relationships between the seen and the unseen. People may, for instance, ascribe the death of a person to poisoned food (see 2 Kgs 4.38-41), but death might also, for example, be attributed to an act of God (see 1 Kgs 22.19-23; 2 Sam. 6.67). Since causality forms part of a culture's *system of meaning*, causal relations accepted in one culture to exist between events or phenomena may not impress people from another culture. It would, for example, have been as nonsensical for an eighth-century BCE Ephraimite farmer to have listened to weather forecasts referring to high and low pressure systems as it would be for a secularized farmer of the twentieth century CE to act out painful rituals in order to secure rain (cf. 1 Kgs 18.25-29). Neither would a modern army general rely on the outcome of a threefold omen to decide which target to attack next. Yet, according to Ezek. 21.21-22 this is exactly what the king of Babylon would do to decide whether to attack Jerusalem or Rabbah first:

> at the fork in the two roads...he *shakes the arrows*, he *consults the teraphim*, he *inspects the liver*. Into his right hand comes the lot for Jerusalem, to set battering rams, to call out for slaughter, for raising the battle cry, to set battering rams against the gates, to cast up ramps, to build siege towers.

Relations among objects, events, visible and invisible forces may be explained with reference to empirical observation (e.g. mobile versus immobile), custom (e.g. clean versus unclean), accepted forms of inferential logic, experienced emotion, etc. While certain cultures, for example, those subscribing to naturalism and empiricism, prefer all explanations to employ one set of (observable) criteria only, others, like Israelite culture, find it necessary to explain events with reference to various criteria, so that even the same event may (under the same or differing conditions) be explained with reference to *different* kinds of relations. A certain event may, for instance, be explained as caused by divine *and* human factors, or divine/evil *and* chance factors. The exodus narrative, for example, ascribes the pharaoh's refusal to let the

---

1. See Chapter 8.

Hebrew slaves go both to him and to a divine intervention (cf. Exod. 8.15; 9.12; cf. Deist 1986, 1989), while Saul's first meeting with Samuel was due to both chance and divine intervention (1 Sam. 9.5-10, 14-15; cf. Deist 1993c). A character in a biblical story therefore always has to reckon with *various* forces that may influence his decisions and acts. Going to the battle-field may, for example, require intelligent preparation *and* planning of strategy *and* divination *as well* as carrying out certain rituals. In this context Goodenough (1981: 70) says, 'The more people segregate their experiences into independent domains, the greater the corresponding number of strategies for action they must develop.' It is perhaps for this reason that, in Israelite culture, 'intention' in human action was less valued than its *outcome*, and that the plots of stories hinge more on the consequences of actions but seldom, if ever, on the inner deliberations of actors. The *outcome* shows whether the character was shrewd/wise enough to take into consideration *everything* that a wise and intelligent person would have taken into account to effect a positive result. In this perspective the 'externalized' morality often found in the Hebrew Bible, according to which a person is not judged by his intentions but by the consequences of his acts also becomes intelligible. Being unaware of the acceptability in Israelite culture of multiple causality (that may result in logical paradoxes) might lead a present-day reader to view as inconsistent or contradictory what the writer had considered perfectly coherent.

Multiple causality may perhaps even be more complicated. For post-enlightenment thinkers logical consistency and coherence are products of the brain. Biblical Hebrew, however, has no word for 'brain' or 'nervous system'. 'Thinking' is done in the upper part of the torso, in the chest—'heart' is probably not a correct translation of the Hebrew לב—while 'emotions' originate from the lower part of the torso (the kidneys, liver and stomach). Thinking and feeling involve the *body*.[2] But to what extent are thinking, feeling and acting necessarily 'coherent'? It is often said that a *hand* stole or murdered (see Deut. 2.7), *feet* chose the wrong path (see Prov. 6.18; 7.11), *eyes* that do not see right (Prov. 10.10; 28.7; 30.17), etc. Consequently, one has to be watchful of their behaviour (cf. Prov. 18.21; 21.23; 26.28; 30.32; Eccl. 5.1-2). The frequent attribution of (wilful) action to limbs is often regarded as instances of metonymy, but this opinion might just as well

---

2. See further Chapter 8.

be a mistaken cross-cultural interpretation. Only a thorough investigation into the Israelite conception of the self will tell whether or not this way of speaking presents instances of metonymy. If the organs and limbs had in fact been ascribed independent action, it may explain such punitive practices as blinding the eye (1 Sam. 11.2; 2 Kgs 25.7), cutting off the hand (see Deut. 25.11) and laming the feet (see Judg. 1.6-7) of perpetrators.

Apart from assisting classification and establishing relations among categorial objects, a language also assists people in understanding new things in the light of the known. This is the function of, among other things, comparison, simile, metaphor and parable. Consider for example metaphor. Studying the metaphors people live by (to twist the title of Lakoff and Johnson [1980]) makes one aware of the intricate relationship between language and the other cultural domains.

Lakoff and Johnson (1980: 7-8), for example, show that industrialized capitalist societies often depict *time* metaphorically in terms of money, resources and valuable commodities (thus in economic terms). People say things like, 'You're *wasting* my time'; 'This gadget will *save* you hours'; 'You need to *budget* your time'; 'He's living on *borrowed* time'.³ Such metaphors not only explain an object or event in one domain with reference to an object or event in another domain, but also betray a particular system of values. Lakoff and Johnson (1980: 22) say, 'The most fundamental values in a culture will be coherent with the metaphorical structure of the most fundamental concepts in the culture.'

'Ontological metaphors' may again reveal the degree to which certain forces are looked upon by a culture as entities or substances (that may, consequently, affect relations among objects, events, and so on). If a person says, 'Inflation is *lowering* our standard of living,' or 'We

---

3. In the Hebrew Bible 'time' is, for example, viewed quite differently from 'time is money'. Rather than an economic 'commodity' time is a religious entity. Human 'time' is but a vague category, like the time to let animals drink (Gen. 29.7) or the time for the harvest (Prov. 25.13), or the time of old age (Ps. 71.9). All time belongs to God (Ps. 10.5; 106.3) and he fixes the 'dates' of occurrences. Human beings have to wait on this time (Ps. 31.16). To secure success one has to find out the divinely planned time (Ps. 102.14; 32.6; Isa. 13.22). Not following the divine plan may cause one's 'time' to become 'not-one's-time' (Job 15.32; 22.16). Time, then, is not something one can 'create' or take advantage of, but something that one has to wait for and for which one has to trust in God.

need to *combat* inflation,' he views 'inflation' as an entity that can be referred to, acted against, etc. (Lakoff and Johnson 1980: 26). In the Hebrew Bible 'sin' (חטאת; חטאה) is looked upon as such an 'entity' that may lurk at the door (Gen. 4.7), affect the health of one's 'bones' (Ps. 38.3), can be gained and increased (Prov. 10.16; Isa. 30.1), hauled in with ropes (Isa. 5.18), hidden (Hos. 13.12) or blotted out (Ps. 109.14) and that has cords that can bind a person (Prov. 5.22). In similar fashion 'steadfast love' (חסד) can be given (Mic. 7.20), kept/saved (Exod. 34.7), withheld (Job 6.14), established (Ps. 89.3), remembered (Jer. 2.2), desired (Hos. 6.6), reaped (Hos. 10.12), held on to (Hos. 12.7) and loved (Mic. 6.8), while it can actively surround, preserve or forsake people (Ps. 32.10; Prov. 20.28; 3.3), fill the earth (Ps. 33.5), form a foundation (Ps. 89.15), or be a crown (Ps. 103.4).

These examples suffice to illustrate that metaphor analysis has more to it than merely 'grasping the point'. Metaphors are, in a sense, betrayers of, among other things, human conceptions, orientations and values. Although not much has been done along these lines in analysing Israelite culture—and although the texts containing these metaphors date from different times—it is clear that metaphors can assist in analysing Israelite cultural values. It is also clear, though, that, since metaphors may draw analogies between *any* two cultural domains, the interpretation of metaphor (and simile) requires a sound knowledge of the whole cultural system. Consider the following example from Lamentations 1 in which imagery is drawn from *the environment and subsistence* ('deer' and 'hunter' [vv. 6, 13], 'famine' [v. 11]); *the social world* ('widow' [v. 1], 'lovers' and 'friends' [vv. 2, 19]; 'elite' [vv. 15, 19]); *economy* ('labour' and 'rest' [v. 3], 'bartering' [v. 11], 'ploughing' [v. 14], 'wine-press' [v. 15]); *values* ('nakedness' and 'shame' [v. 8], 'illness' [vv. 13, 20]); *view of self* ('identity' [v. 10], 'entrails' and 'heart' [v. 20]); *religion* ('[ritual] impurity' [v. 9]); *safety and security* ('warriors' and 'army' [v. 15]); *law and justice* ('seeking asylum' [v. 17], 'revenge' [v. 22]). To read this text not merely from a religious point of view but from the perspective of cultural disruption makes it clear that, beyond—or perhaps the basis of—the distress of faith, it pictures a total cultural collapse.

Finally, language does not only categorize reality, establish relations among categorial objects and betray in its metaphors cultural orientations, values and beliefs. It also interprets the world and represents reality in story form. The narrative and poetic worlds picture, interpret and explain the world people live in with reference to the implied linguistic categories, logical links, metaphors, cosmological orientation, social values, religious convictions, political, social and economic preferences. To understand the world presented in language necessitates an intimate knowledge of the categories, values, convictions, orientations and preferences of the relevant culture. An example may illustrate the possible influence of a cosmological orientation in Hebrew literary representation.

In a recent study, Marais (1998), building on insights of Exum and Bal, found that one of the basic strategies of representation in the book of Judges is what could be called perspectivist juxtaposition. The (cycles of) stories in the book are not linked in a logically or temporally *sequential* manner, but are merely juxtaposed so as to provide the reader with a variety of *perspectives* on the related events. The story of the judges presents the reader with military, historical, religious and individual perspectives, each perspective adding to the picture by complementing the others. In the story of Samson, for instance, Samson's father did not *see* Yahweh, his parents did not *see* Yahweh's plan with the Philistines, while Samson ended up by losing his sight altogether. Immediately following on this story about 'the loss of sight' are the last chapters of the book in which everybody does 'what is good in his own eyes'. By merely juxtaposing the story of Samson to the subsequent stories in the book, the narrator invites the reader to view the one in the light of the other and to derive *meaning* from the juxtaposition. Marais further argues that perspectivist juxtaposition is not a mere literary strategy but permeates Hebrew syntax as well. One could perhaps go a step further by arguing that complementary juxtaposition had at the time been a popular way of explaining the way life 'worked'. To motivate this suggestion a short detour is necessary.

Even though the Ugaritic myths cannot be used as typical of 'Syro-Palestinian' religion, the construction of the Ugaritic pantheon seems to suggest just this kind of complementary juxtaposition. Consider the following section from 'divine genealogy' and the functions of some of the gods in the pantheon:

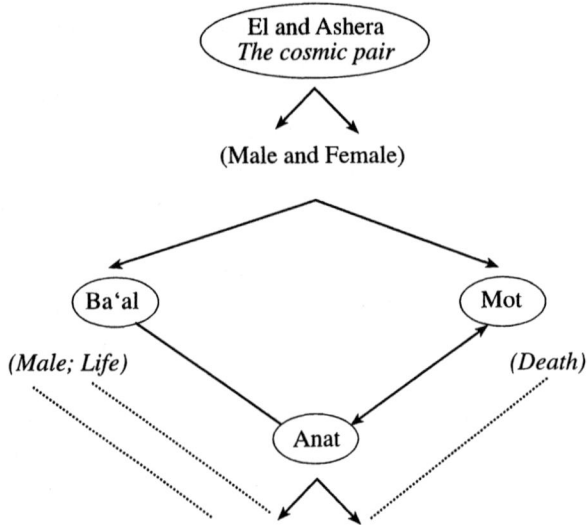

A pantheon may be said to present an abbreviated cosmic philosophy. Viewed from this perspective, the construction of the Ugaritic pantheon seems to suggest that *oppositional* or *paradoxical pairing* was seen as one of the basic constructional principles of the cosmos. But oppositions, such as male–female; life–death; love–war, were not viewed as contradictions, since they were all 'children' of the *one* (dual) cosmic principle, and therefore at the most complementary forces. This cognitive scheme seems to have (and in a sense still seems to be) a constitutive element of oriental cosmology and philosophy (see R. Harris 1991; Lelyveld 1994; Stetkevytch 1989).

Underneath the Deuteronomistic battle for monotheism in many Hebrew Bible narratives there are sufficient indications that a comparable cosmology enjoyed widespread support among Israelites. The failure of the Deuteronomist's 'prophetic movement' to secure monotheism in pre-exilic times may perhaps have resulted from its failure to convince people to substitute one (male) cosmic principle for the popular dual and paradoxical principle. Where this substitution had, in fact, taken place, it seems to have caused serious conceptual problems. It was now no longer possible to explain chaos and evil as paradoxical yet *complementing* forces. In monotheism chaos and order, evil and justice became *contradictions*. Some sought to alleviate the contradiction by ascribing good and evil to Yahweh (cf. Isa. 45.7) and to use male *and female* metaphors when speaking of him. Other groups, probably inspired by the Persian cosmology, later reverted to a dua*listic*

3. *Culture, Language and Meaning* 115

cosmology in which God and Satan, each with elaborate 'armies', opposed each other on the 'battlefield' of human experience.

If the majority of Israelites had in fact subscribed to a world view in which paradox and complementarity had been operative principles it would explain the tendency in biblical literature to *represent* reality accordingly. And if this is true, present-day readers should be rather careful not to regard literature in which opposing views are juxtaposed as 'inconsistent' or 'contradictory', but rather understand such oppositions as a feature of literary representation giving expression to the 'logic of the world of the biblical text' (Davies 1992: 34).

There is, of course, no such thing as every individual in a society subscribing to *exactly* the same cosmology. 'Israelite' cosmology can therefore be nothing more than a broad generalization. Within such a broad framework there is room for private interpretations and applications. However, the degree to which an individual may publicly represent the world differently from the culture's dominant view depends upon various factors, like his role in society, the public expectations coupled to that position, the degree to which his culture allows for dissidents, whether he is seen as an insider or an outsider, a conformist or nonconformist, etc. The picture the prophetic books paint of the values of Israelite society would, for example, most definitely not have tallied with the view the upper classes had of society—hence the stories of their public ridiculing and prosecution. But then the prophets' picture of their society seems to have been deliberately ironic and consciously distorted for rhetorical purposes. To say this with any degree of confidence, though, *implies* knowledge of the dominant picture society at the time had of itself, which, in turn, implies an anthropological description of the society in those times. Until such a description is produced present-day readers should at least be aware of the linguistic strategies involved in world-making, such as categorization, establishing relations between objects, phenomena and events, the use of metaphor and irony, and the relevant literary custom of representation.

This short excursion into language as a cultural phenomenon illustrates at least two things. First, the fact that there is more to language than mere phonology, syntax and semantics, that 'meaning' is a complicated terrain and that valid interpretation of texts ideally implies a full knowledge of the relevant culture as well as of the cultural world constructed by the relevant language. Secondly, the undesirability of severing a language from its culture and interpreting texts in that language *as if* they were written in the reader's own language, which is, of course, a major temptation for readers using a translation of the Bible into their languages.

3. *Custom and Meaning*

In an effort to satisfy their needs or to maintain their group's equilibrium people devise plans. Their goals may vary, such as securing sufficient food, supplying safe shelters, obtaining the goodwill of an influential person or a god, getting rid of a tyrant. Those plans that yield the best results for a specific purpose tend to become 'recipes' for action, for example, a detailed plan for securing the right materials, availing oneself of appropriate skills, choosing the right time, ensuring that the necessary organizational structures are in place, etc.

Not all human needs can be catered for simultaneously, though. While some may be satisfied concurrently, others imply the use of the same material, instruments, skills or experts and can therefore only receive attention successively. Such needs require prioritizing and scheduling (as illustrated by the Gezer calendar), or a different way of organizing the community. Tasks that need to be carried out concurrently may, for example, be divided among different sections of the community (e.g. between men, women, children and the elderly) or assigned to different specialists (such as elders, metal workers, shepherds, farm hands, priests, etc.). Once a satisfactory recipe for attaining a particular goal has been found it becomes a routine that reduces the burden of individual improvisation.

Different groups (e.g. families) may, however, develop different routines of attaining particular goals, so that different routines may be followed in different places. But once a specific routine has, for some reason, been accepted by a cultural community as the *right* way of obtaining a specific goal, such a routine becomes a *custom.* A custom typically is 'our' way of achieving our goals. The patriarchal stories, for example, seem to imply a custom of young men marrying a cousin (consider Isaac's marriage to the daughter of his father's brother and Jacob's marriage to the daughters of his mother's brother). The reasons for a routine becoming a custom may vary. One criterion would be that a routine fits in with the *values* shared by the group.

The value system of a culture in its turn, consists of a number of goal-oriented 'rules' prescribing the rights, privileges and duties of

3. Culture, Language and Meaning 117

each member of the group. A routine that fits 'the rules' will be more acceptable than one that violates them. The rules stating the rights, privileges and duties of community members are, however, not explicitly verbalized. They are rather implied in all actions that have the sanction of the group. Inculturation means, among other things, getting acquainted with the customs and, especially, the values and rules of the group. Novices become inculturated by being instructed, carefully observing customs being acted out, listening to proverbs, stories about the past, fables and myths, watching rituals being carried out, paying attention to what is sanctioned and what is not, etc. This is also the route biblical scholars should take in order to be able to validate their hypotheses on the *meaning* of cultural symbols, the actions of characters, their gestures, and so on.

For the valid interpretation of a biblical text it is, for example, necessary to know whether a character in a story acts according to custom, according to a local routine, or whether he or she improvises on the spot, and whether or not such improvisation would be acceptable from the point of view of the group's values. Without such knowledge it is near to impossible to understand the characterization going on in a story, or to decide whether or not a character's actions complicate the plot of the story. Put differently, in the absence of readers' knowledge of the customs implied a story will only with difficulty, have an adequate contextual effect on the reader's cognitive world. On the other hand, since these are biblical texts that are *supposed* to communicate, a reader, finding the story 'irrelevant', may be tempted to put in extra processing effort and be 'rewarded' with extra meaning that is not part of the intended meaning. This happens, for example, when preachers resort to allegorical interpretation or readers, driven by their own sense of logic, 'harmonize' seemingly contradictory reports or biblical with present-day knowledge of chemistry, physics, palaeontology, ethics, and so forth. Against this background, one may concur with Sternberg (1992: 469): 'The emptier the requirements of competence...the fuller the divorce of the so-called reading method from the subject on which it operates...'

Chapter 4

ENVIRONMENT AND MEANING

Ecological anthropology has shown that the environment (soil type, climate, topography, vegetation, etc.) has a major influence on the kind of culture that may evolve in a particular region. The relative availability of arable land, for example, puts a constraint on the number of people that can be sustained in an area, and thereby in a sense determines the size of sustainable families and villages. For the purposes of demographic estimates of the Iron Age population of Palestine, archaeologists, for example, use different averages for different regions. For the desert fringe they count 9.9 people per built-up hectare, for the smaller villages 14.0, and for the larger villages 18.9 (Finkelstein 1990: 50). The size of a community and its economic activity again determines to a great extent the type of social organization necessary to ensure survival, while the topography of the area determines the lay-out of a village and the shapes and sizes of its houses (Weippert 1988: 401-407). The ancients were acutely aware of the power of environmental forces to shape their lives. With the little technology at their disposal they were, as a matter of fact, extremely vulnerable in the face of wind and weather. Not only with regard to stormy weather but also when the seasonal rains did not come in time, or not at all. This realization certainly had consequences for the way they viewed and spoke of environmental forces and for the development of patterns of behaviour and custom.

Despite the constraints the environment puts on the kind of culture that may develop in a region and the challenge it presents to human creativity, it would be reductionist to think of culture merely in terms of environmental determinism (Kent and Vierich 1987), because human activities and values also influence the environment. For example, when trees are felled for fuel or for the erection of shelters it may negatively affect the vegetation of a region. This effect may be aggravated by the

4. Environment and Meaning

clearing of wooded areas for agricultural purposes, the practice of slash-burning and overgrazing—especially by goats. On the other hand the building of terraces along slopes may prevent normal erosion, while controlled grazing on such terraces may increase the fertility of the soil. Technological development may also affect the environment. For instance, the manufacturing of charcoal, pitch, tannin (used for tanning and dying) and lime is dependent upon a sufficient supply of wood (Currid 1984: 6-7). When and as the demand for such products grows, the vegetation may suffer and soil erosion increase. Demographic factors may further negatively affect the environment. Long periods of stability and peace often lead to a marked increase in the population, which must be fed. Famines and wars, on the other hand, often cause great numbers of refugees to migrate to better or safer areas. From the second half of the eighth to the early seventh centuries, Jerusalem, for example, experienced an influx of refugees from the north, causing the city to more than triple in size (Weippert 1988: 589-91). Politico-economic measures like over-taxation may equally lead to the over-exploitation of the natural resources and excessive deforestation. Finally, certain social values, like cattle numbers as a status symbol (cf. Gen. 24.35; 26.14; 32.5; 2 Sam. 12.2; Job 42.12), may lead to overgrazing and soil erosion.

The ancients were not unaware of the effects of human conduct on the environment, and expressed this relationship in religious terms. These beliefs reflect something of the *meaning* the environment obtained in the Hebrew language. The Priestly document, for example, pictures the *land* as an active agent that, responding to human conduct, could 'vomit out' those who 'defile' it (Lev. 18.25, 28; 20.22). In the prophetic view the consequences of human sin is the 'withering' (אבל) of the land (ארץ, אדמה) (Isa. 24.2; 33.9; Jer. 4.28; 12.4, 11; 23.10; Hos. 4.3; cf. Amos 1.2). And in apocalyptic thought nature and natural forces are deeply involved in the foreseen cataclysm (Amos 8.8; Isa. 24.4; Joel 1.12).

1. *Heavenly Bodies*

As in the rest of the ancient Near East, where the sun blazed down for most of the year, the moon marked the festive seasons and the stars served as important navigational points of reference, the Israelites stood in awe before the (moving) heavenly bodies. Eternity, time, and space were spoken of with reference to them. The expression 'May he live *while the sun endures*, and as *long as the moon*' (Ps. 72.5) stands for 'eternity', while the eclipse of the sun, moon and stars marks 'end of time' (Isa. 13.10; Amos 8.9). Until such time, however, 'sunrise' and 'sunset' mark morning and night (cf. Gen. 32.31; Exod. 17.12; Judg. 9.33), and 'when the sun grows hot' midday (Exod. 16.21; 1 Sam. 11.9). The expression 'from the rising of the sun to its setting' (Ps. 113.3; Mal. 1.11) again simply means 'the whole earth, everywhere'. In metaphorical speech *light* means 'prosperity, safety, well-being', while *darkness* implied 'danger, doom' (cf. Ps. 18.28; 139.11-12; Prov. 4.18; Isa. 5.20; 30.16; Amos 5.18; Job 3.3-10).

If the sun is an entity with reference to which ultimate time and space may be expressed and whose light symbolized the good, it is understandable that the omniscient and omnipresent Father-God could also be called 'sun' (Ps. 84.11). But indications are that the sun meant more to the ancients than a mere source of light and a marker of time and space (cf. Ezek. 8.16). Consider, for example, the presence of sun symbols in the temple and palace (2 Kgs 23.11), the fact that the sun played a role in omens (cf. Isa. 38.8), and the many eighth-century BCE stamp seals and seal impressions with the winged sun as emblem (Weippert 1988: 605-607). In this context a formulation in Nathan's rebuke of David after his extra-marital rendezvous with Bathsheba becomes interesting.

> Thus says the Lord: ...I will take your wives before your eyes, and give them to your neighbour, and he shall lie with your wives in the sight *of this very sun* (לעיני השמש הזאת). For you did it secretly; but I will do this thing before all Israel, *and before the sun* (ונגד השמש) (2 Sam. 12.11-12).

The expression 'in the sight of this very sun' implies that Nathan is pointing to something *in the palace* (note that he 'entered' a room in 12.1). The implication is clear that the author of the narrative, who lived and worked a few centuries after the time of David, accepted as a matter of fact that David's throne hall would have contained a sun disk. Moreover, there are many indications in the Hebrew Bible that not only the ordinary people but also the elite practised astral worship (cf. 2 Kgs 17.16; 21.3; Jer. 7.18; 8.2; 44.17-25).

The Deuteronomic-Deuteronomistic literature, of course, condemned the practising of astral worship (e.g. Deut. 4.19; 2 Kgs 23.5) and later literature seems to indicate that at least *authors* took the trend seriously. In declaring his innocence Job, for example, says:

4. *Environment and Meaning* 121

> If I have looked at the sun when it shone, or the moon moving in splendour, and my heart has been secretly enticed, and my mouth has kissed my hand; this also would be an iniquity to be punished by the judges, for I should have been false to God above (Job 31.26-27).

The expression '(if) my mouth has kissed my hand (ותשק ידי לפי)' probably means as much as '(if) I blew a kiss (to them)', which was one of the gestures of adoration or worship of the heavenly bodies.

Another interesting case involving heavenly bodies is Joshua's well-known 'prayer' in Josh. 10.12, usually translated by, 'Sun, stand still at Gibeon, and Moon, in the valley of Aijalon,' which probably is not a very accurate translation of the Hebrew. The text says that it quotes the poetic phrasing of the 'prayer' שמש בגבעון דום ירח בעמק אילון from the old 'Book of Jashar'. The verb דום does not really mean 'stand still', but 'keep quite'. What the Book of Jashar said was that Joshua uttered a incantation to ensure that the sun god and the moon god, supporting the enemy, would not provide them with oracles on that day. Asking and receiving oracles were, of course, part and parcel of ancient Near Eastern warfare (cf. Judg. 20.18; 1 Kgs 20.14; 22.6, 15; Ezek. 21.21). If the sun god and moon god would keep quiet Joshua would win the war. And so the Book of Jashar continues, '[T]he sun did keep quite (וידם), and the moon remained inactive (עמד), until the nation took vengeance on their enemies.' The Deuteronomistic editors could, of course, not allow such a blatant recognition of the sun god, especially not by a heroic figure like Joshua (who still has to conclude a decisive covenant in ch. 24). By ignoring the address to the moon and applying its inactivity (עמד) to the sun, they turned the incantation into a prayer to *Yahweh*, and commented, 'The sun stopped (ויעמד) in mid heaven, and did not hurry to set for about a whole day. There has been no day like it before or since, when the Lord heeded a human voice; for the Lord fought for Israel.'

Here is thus a clear instance of later editing of older material that has all but erased the culture discussed in the text.

2. *Natural Forces and Climate*

Natural elements like the wind, snow, hail and rain, were believed to have been stored up in heavenly store rooms (Deut. 28.12; Ps. 135.7; Jer. 10.13; Job 38.22-23) with divinely operated gates (Mal. 3.10). Psalm 147.16-18 says, 'He gives snow like wool; he scatters frost like ashes. He hurls down hail like crumbs—who can stand before his cold?

He sends out his word, and melts them; he makes his wind blow, and the waters flow.' Because of humankind's helplessness before the forces of nature they were often looked upon as theophanies. Consider, for example, Ps. 50.3, 'Our God comes and does not keep silence, before him is a devouring fire, and a mighty tempest all around him.' Or Isa. 29.6, 'You will be visited by the Lord of hosts with thunder and earthquake and great noise, with whirlwind and tempest, and the flame of a devouring fire.' It therefore comes as a (polemic) surprise to read in 1 Kgs 19.11-12 that, in visiting Elijah, Yahweh was not in the strong wind, the earthquake, or the fire but in 'a sound of sheer silence'.

Accompanying the summer rains were fast-moving clouds, thunder and lightning, whose mysterious movement and sound so impressed the ancients that they took them for divine activities. Consider, for example Job 36.29, 'Can anyone understand the spreading of the clouds, the thunderings of his pavilion?' and Job 37.1-5:

> At this also my heart trembles, and leaps out of its place. Listen, listen to the thunder of his voice and the rumbling that comes from his mouth. Under the whole heaven he lets it loose, and his lightning to the corners of the earth. After it his voice roars; he thunders with his majestic voice and he does not restrain the lightnings when his voice is heard. God thunders wondrously with his voice; he does great things that we cannot comprehend.

Given the importance of rain in this dry country and the mystery of the accompanying phenomena, it comes as no surprise that a battle would ensue between Ba'al, the weather god *par excellence*, and Yahweh, of whom it was also claimed that he controlled weather. For Ba'al was widely acknowledged as the 'rider of the clouds', the god of thunder and lightning who impregnated the earth through gushes of rain to give birth to vegetation and food. The idea is still retained in Ps. 77.17 'The clouds poured out water; the skies thundered; your arrows flashed on every side.' The term translated here with 'poured out' (זרמו) is also used for the male emission (cf. Ezek. 23.20) during sexual intercourse. In the book of Hosea the battle between Yahweh and Ba'al is clear. Consider, for example, Yahweh's accusation against 'mother' Israel:

> their mother has played the whore; she who conceived them has acted shamefully. For she said, I will go after my lovers; they give me my bread and my water, my wool and my flax, my oil and my drink (Hos. 2.5).

4. *Environment and Meaning*

Consider also the way in which the ancient poets pictured Yahweh in terms that normally described Ba'al:

> The voice of the Lord is over the waters; the God of glory thunders, the Lord, over mighty waters. The voice of the Lord is powerful; the voice of the Lord is full of majesty. The voice of the Lord breaks the cedars; the Lord breaks the cedars of Lebanon. He makes Lebanon skip like a calf, and Sirion like a young wild ox. The voice of the Lord flashes forth flames of fire. The voice of the Lord shakes the wilderness; the Lord shakes the wilderness of Kadesh. The voice of the Lord causes the oaks to whirl, and strips the forest bare; and in his temple all say, 'Glory!' The Lord sits enthroned over the flood; the Lord sits enthroned as king forever (Ps. 29.3-10).

Or Ps. 104.3, 'You [Yahweh], make the clouds your chariot, you ride on the wings of the wind' (cf. also Pss. 18.10; 104.3). Against this background it is also to be expected that the literature would picture a showdown between Yahweh and Ba'al as a contest in controlling the weather, as it is narrated in the Carmel scene (1 Kgs 17).

The climate of the land is harsh. To emphasize the hardships he endured in Laban's service, Jacob says, 'It was like this with me: by day the heat consumed me, and the cold by night, and my sleep fled from my eyes' (Gen. 31.40). The feared hot eastern wind from the desert dries out the grass (Ps. 103.16), blights the ears of wheat (Gen. 46.6), carries locusts to the land (Exod. 10.13) and destroys ships (Ps. 48.8), so that the expression 'the day of the east wind' became a metaphor for disaster (Isa. 41.16; Jer. 4.11).

Given the climatic conditions and the severity of the weather it is only natural that *shade* and *shelter*, essential for human survival, became symbols for 'refuge' and 'deliverance' (Judg. 9.15; Isa. 4.6), even a metaphor for 'mercy' (Isa. 16.3). Consider, for example, the picture of the just princes' rule in Isa. 32.2, 'Each will be like a hiding place from the wind, a covert from the tempest...like the shade of a great rock in a weary land.' Also the imagery in the vision of the restoration of Jerusalem after God's judgment. At that time God will erect a canopy over the city that will serve 'as a pavilion, a shade by day from the heat, and a refuge and a shelter from the storm and rain' (Isa. 4.6). Here is the poet's praise of Yahweh in Isa. 25.4-5:

> For you have been a refuge to the poor, a refuge to the needy in their distress, a shelter from the rainstorm and a shade from the heat. When the blast of the ruthless was like a winter rainstorm, the noise of aliens

like heat in a dry place, you subdued the heat with the shade of clouds;
the song of the ruthless was stilled.

Shade might even have acquired a religious dimension to its meaning. Hos. 4.13 accuses the Israelites of sacrificing under oak, poplar, and terebinth, 'because their *shade* is good'.

3. *Water Sources*

The Deuteronomists picture Palestine as 'a land with flowing streams, with springs and underground waters welling up in valleys and hills' (Deut. 8.7-9). By contrast Egypt was for them a place 'where you sow your seed and irrigate by foot like a vegetable garden' (Deut. 11.10). Other sources refer to the Nile valley as a well-watered place that is like a divine garden (Gen. 13.10) and to Palestine as a land that 'devours its inhabitants' (Num. 13.32). According to these sources at least the region 'in the direction of Zoar' also used to be like a divine garden, but that was '*before* the Lord had destroyed Sodom and Gomorrah' (Gen. 13.10). In its present shape that region can only stand as a symbol of divine destruction (Deut. 29.23; Isa. 13.19; Jer. 49.18). Measured against reality the Deuteronomists' view can only be idealistic, if not ideological.

The scarcity of water in the region explains the variety of terms for 'rain' to which I referred in the previous chapter, namely זרם, מטר, גשם, מלקוש, טל, סגריר, יורה and רביבים. Some of these terms, we said, carry a more generic meaning, while others refer to a specific type (or time) of rain, as the following diagram illustrates:

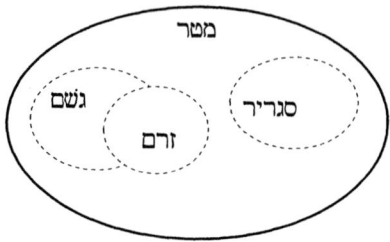

Even though an English translation of the Hebrew terms may give some impression of their *referents*, the translations do not necessarily allow access to their *meaning*. Words are *symbols* pointing to life experience, in this case of the hardships caused by the particular environment and climate in which rain, as well the *kind* and *time* of rain,

4. Environment and Meaning 125

were of ultimate concern, as several proverbs indicate. Consider, for example, 'Like clouds and wind without rain is one who boasts of a gift never given' (Prov. 25.14), 'Like snow in summer or rain in harvest, so honour is not fitting for a fool' (26.1); 'A ruler who oppresses the poor is a beating rain that leaves no food' (28.3).

For an Israelite subsistence farmer without sufficient and effective storing facilities for food, little or no rain meant misery and famine (Deut. 11.17; 28.24; 1 Kgs 17), which meant a loss of independence, as Neh. 5.3 indicates, 'We are having to pledge our fields, our vineyards, and our houses in order to get grain during the famine.' That famine struck with regular intervals is indicated by several stories with famine as their setting. Examples are the stories of Abram's sojourn in Egypt (Gen. 12.10-20); Isaac's sojourn in Gerar (Gen. 26.1-15); Joseph and his brothers (Gen. 41–45); Ruth, and of the two women who had to cook their sons to survive (2 Kgs 6.24-32; cf. also 2 Sam. 21.1; 1 Kgs 8.2; 4.38; 2 Kgs 25.3). On the other hand, too much rain meant destruction (Gen. 7.4; Exod. 9.33). But the right kind of rain at the right time (Deut. 32.2) meant freedom from creditors (Deut. 11.14; 28.12) and independence. Access to the *meaning* of the terms for 'rain' assists a reader in choosing the interpretation that complies with the principle of relevance. Consider, for example, the rain similes in Deut. 32.2: 'May my teaching *drop* like the rain (כמטר), my speech condense *like* the dew (כטל); *like* gentle rain (כשעירם) on grass, *like* showers (כרביבים) on new growth.' Without the 'feel' of the *meaning* of the various categories of rain for a subsistence farmer the similes become a monotonous repetition and the communication about the nature of the *torah*, assisting the obedient from 'planting time' till 'full growth', fairly pointless.

The importance of water is further reflected by the terms used to refer to various water sources. Different kinds of rivers were, for example, distinguished, such as נהר, פלג, נחל and אפיק. Some of these were mostly dry river beds, others seasonal rivers (wadis), others perennial. Given the topography of the land wadis tend to be dry in the dry season but to flow rapidly in the rainy season. In the narrative about the drought in Elijah's time, it is said, 'But after a while the wadi dried up, because there was no rain in the land' (1 Kgs 17.7). That is why David could easily pick up his five smooth stones in the wadi (1 Sam. 17.40), while on another occasion two-thirds of his men could not complete the pursuit of the Amalekites, because they were 'too exhausted to cross the Wadi Beso' (1 Sam. 30.10). When Amos admonishes his audience to 'let justice roll down like waters, and righteousness like an ever-flowing stream (wadi)' (Amos 5.24), he makes sure that his reference to a wadi (נחל) is not misunderstood as an intermittently flowing stream by adding an adjective (איתן). In doing so he implies that righteousness should *continuously* come thundering down like a wadi after a thunderstorm. But when Trito-Isaiah speaks of Yahweh's once and for all return to Zion, he is precisely thinking of the finality with which water gushes down the steep wadis: '[H]e will come like a pent-up stream (כנהר צר) that the wind of the Lord drives on'.

Whether one has to think of a פלג as an underground source of water,[1] a point where two streams flow together to form a river, or just as another kind of stream is not certain. The idea of a 'flowing together' may be suggested by the frequent occurrence of the term in the plural (or dual) and by two images in which this term occurs. The first is Lam. 3.48, where it says, 'My eyes flow with rivers of tears (פלגי־מים) (at both sides of my nose?) because of the destruction of my people.' The other is Prov. 21.1, which reads, 'The king's heart is streams of water (פלגי מים) in the hand of the Lord; he turns them wherever he will.' It seems as if there is a choice in the direction the royal streams might flow. Whatever the case may be, פלגי מים were certainly thought of as a kind of perennial source of water. A tree planted at פלגי מים is evergreen and bears its fruit on time, and so became an image for the wise and righteous (Ps. 1.3).

If the people were merely dependent upon rain and rivers, Palestine would really have 'devoured' its inhabitants. But there are also other sources of water. One may think of pools or marshes (אגמ־מים), fountains (מקור מבוע), springs (מעין, באר מים החיים, מקור חיים), wells (באר, בור), old quarries with standing water or consciously hewn cisterns (ביר, בור), etc. Fountains and springs played an important role in the life of villagers, and their locations were commonly known to travellers, as the location of stories at this or that well or specific directions given with reference to them indicate (cf. 1 Sam. 19.22; 2 Sam. 3.26; 1 Kgs 18.5; Jer. 41.9). But fountains, wells and springs were more than mere 'sources' where one could find water. Numbers 21.17-18 indicates that the digging of a well was accompanied by a ritual, while other texts suggest that fountains and wells had often been specifically and cere-

---

1. Interestingly enough the hollow of a bone containing the bone marrow is also referred to as פלג.

4. *Environment and Meaning*

moniously named (cf. Gen. 26.19-22). Moreover, various narratives indicate that they were believed to have been locations where events might reach a turning point (cf. Gen. 24.11-18; 29.2-10; 37.24-28; Exod. 2.15-20; 1 Sam. 9.10-13). When Yahweh thus sends Isaiah to meet King Ahaz precisely 'at the end of the conduit of the upper pool' (Isa. 7.4), this would have been the ideal place where the king would have expected to receive a divine revelation.

To have been without water in that region was to face a life-threatening situation (cf. Gen. 21.15-16). During a drought of three years Ahab commissioned Obadiah to go through the land 'to all the springs of water and to all the wadis' to see whether there would perhaps be some grass to keep the horses and mules alive (1 Kgs 18.5). This is why a threat like Hos. 13.15 was a death threat: '...the east wind shall come, a blast from the Lord, rising from the wilderness; and his fountain shall dry up, his spring shall be parched.' In Isa. 30.14 the situation is different—and more frustrating—because the prophecy says that, although there would be water to drink, 'not a sherd is found for...tipping water out of the cistern'.

The scarcity of water and the effort to secure enough of it often lead to disputes over ownership and right of access. Such disputes form the background to some stories (e.g. Gen. 21.14-21, 30; 26.19-32). It was therefore desirable to possess one's own undisputed water sources and not to be dependent upon someone else's. In the Assyrian general's speech before the walls of Jerusalem, he, among other things, promised the soldiers who would surrender that 'everyone of you will...drink water from your own cistern' (Isa. 36.16). To have drunk from someone else's cistern or fountain gave the owner power over the dependent one. It is against this background that Prov. 5.15-20, warning men against relationships with 'foreign women' and exploiting *fountain* as a metaphor for a woman or wife (Lev. 20.18), uses nearly all the terms for water sources:

> Drink water from your own cistern (מבורך), and fresh water from your own well (בארך). Should your springs (מעינתיך) be dispersed abroad, streams of water in the streets? Let them be yours alone, and not for strangers with you. Let your fountain (מקורך) be blessed, and rejoice in the wife of your youth... For why should you, my son, be exhilarated with an adulteress, and embrace the bosom of a foreigner?

The value attached to water and its beneficial effects finds, apart from Psalm 104, perhaps its most eloquent expression in Ps. 65.9-13:

You visit the earth and *water* it, you greatly enrich it; the *river* of God is full of *water*, you provide the people with grain, for so you have prepared it. You *water* its furrows abundantly, settling its ridges, softening it with *showers*, and blessing its growth. You crown the year with your bounty; your wagon tracks overflow with richness. The pastures of the wilderness overflow, the hills gird themselves with joy, the meadows clothe themselves with flocks, the valleys deck themselves with grain, they shout and sing together for joy.

Against this background various sayings, similes and metaphors with 'water' as their theme or point of comparison become transparent. Consider, for example, Jeremiah's lament over his fatal relationship with Yahweh, 'Truly, you are to me like a deceitful brook (אכזב מים), like waters that fail' (Jer. 15.18) or, 'Like a muddied spring or a polluted fountain are the righteous who give way before the wicked' (Prov. 25.26). Consider also the prophecies of restoration, as in Isa. 41.18: 'I will make the wilderness a pool of water, and the dry land springs of water,' or Ezekiel's vision of the water flowing from below the threshold of the temple, becoming a mighty river flowing into the Dead Sea, causing its water to become fresh, so that people can fish from En-gedi to En-eglaim. On the banks of the river all kinds of evergreen trees good for food and healing will grow (Ezek. 47.1-12; cf. Zech. 14.8).

4. *Fauna*

Building upon the customary division of 'animals' in four groups referred to earlier, one may distinguish the following 'types' in the animal kingdom:

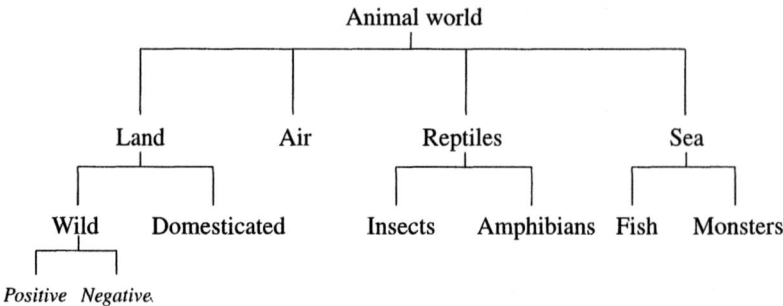

A variety of animal life is mentioned in the Hebrew Bible, including dangerous animals, such as the jackal (תן), wolf (זאב), hyena (אי), bear

4. *Environment and Meaning*

(דב), leopard (נמר) and lion (כפיר, לביא, ארי, אריה), several kinds of snakes (נחש, שפיפן, אפעה, שרף, פתן, צפעני, עכשוב), variously translated by 'snake', 'adder', 'viper', etc.), the deer (צבי), gazelle (איל), and quite a number of birds, to which we shall return. (Domesticated animals will be discussed in Chapter 5.)

Lions and bears were of the pastoralists' greatest enemies, and from time to time shepherds had to fight them off their flocks (1 Sam. 17.34-36). Sometimes a whole party of men had to hunt down a lion (Isa. 31.4). It stands to reason that a person who could single-handedly kill 'a lion in a pit on a day when snow had fallen' (2 Sam. 23.20) would be remembered as a hero. Given the threat of the wild to people and their possessions, it is natural that a time of perfect peace would be pictured as a time when

> the wolf shall live with the lamb, the leopard shall lie down with the kid, the calf and the lion and the fatling together, and a little child shall lead them. The cow and the bear shall graze, their young shall lie down together; and the lion shall eat straw like the ox. The nursing child shall play over the hole of the asp, and the weaned child shall put its hand on the adder's den (Isa. 11.6-8; cf. 35.9; 65.25; Ps. 91.13).

The nature and behaviour of Palestinian wild life was a rich source of figurative language. The lion, 'which is mightiest among wild animals and does not turn back before any' (Prov. 30.30) was a favourite, and some of the term's symbolic usages depend upon the class of people employing the symbol. Most generally the lion symbolized majesty and power. Consider, for example, 'They shall go after the Lord, who roars like a lion; when he roars, his children shall come trembling from the west' (Hos. 11.10), or 'The lion has roared; who will not fear? The Lord God has spoken; who can but prophesy?' In the world of the elite the lion also symbolized power. Solomon's throne is said to have been flanked by two lion figures and the steps leading to the throne by twelve more (1 Kgs 10.19-20). But for them the lion figure also had an apotropaic function. The lion figures flanking Solomon's throne, like the lion figures that decorated the beds of the Samarian elite (Amos 3.12; Mittmann 1976) and many city, temple and palace gates (Amiran 1976) looked away from the object it symbolically guarded. Against this background Amos's words, 'As the shepherd rescues from the mouth of the lion two legs, or a piece of an ear, so shall be rescued the people of Israel sitting in Samaria on their divans and on their cushions from Damascus' (my translation) have an ironical twist to them. The elite, sitting on chairs whose armrests are decorated with lion heads protecting them, will be devoured by a wild lion from the bush (Weippert 1985b: 15-16). A second general lion image symbolizes bravery. A person could be said to have a 'heart like the heart of a lion' (2 Sam. 17.10; cf. Prov. 28.1; 30.30; Isa. 31.4; Job 10.16). The lion was also looked upon as self-assured and without natural enemies. Nineveh, for example, is said to have been a 'lions' den, the cave of the young lions, where the lion goes, and the lion's cubs, with no one to disturb them' (Nah. 2.11). It is this meaning of 'lion' that makes the lion parable of Ezek. 19.1-9 ironic.

> What a lioness was your mother among lions! She lay down among young lions, rearing her cubs. She raised up one of her cubs; he became a young lion, and he learned to catch prey; he devoured humans. The nations sounded an alarm against him; *he was caught in their pit; and they brought him with hooks to the land of Egypt*... [S]he took another of her cubs and...he became a young lion, and he learned to catch prey; he devoured people. And he ravaged their strongholds, and laid waste their towns; the land was appalled, and all in it, at the sound of his roaring. The nations...spread their net over him; *he was caught in their pit. With hooks they put him in a cage*, and brought him to the king of Babylon; they brought him into custody, *so that his voice should be heard no more on the mountains* of Israel.

Perhaps more in line with the experience of common people, the lion also stood for fear or awe-inspiring phenomena and events. Consider 'I will become like a lion to them, like a leopard I will lurk beside the way' (Hos. 13.7), or Jer. 49.19 in which Yahweh is pictured as a lion 'coming up from the thickets of the Jordan against a perennial pasture, I will suddenly chase Edom away from it... Who is the shepherd who can stand before me?'

It is this dangerous nature of the lion that inspired soldiers of the time to decorate the handles of their swords with the image of a lion's head from whose opened mouth the blade of the sword protruded (Meek 1951). Expressions like 'the sword devours' (Deut. 32.42) and 'to put into the mouth of the sword' (הכה לפי חרב) have thus to be understood quite literally. A sword or dagger with two such lion heads (שני פיות), like the one Ehud had himself made, was meant to be twice as 'devouring'.

Although it could be said of a wicked ruler that he was like 'a roaring lion or a charging bear' (Prov. 28.15), imagery for negative phenomena tends to employ other animals. Bad people are rather said to be 'like

4. *Environment and Meaning*   131

jackals among ruins' (Ezek. 13.4) or like 'evening wolves that leave nothing until the morning' (Prov. 28.15; Zeph. 3.3). Utter destruction could be pictured with, '[I]ts strongholds...shall be the haunt of jackals, an abode for ostriches. Wildcats shall meet with hyenas, goat-demons shall call to each other; there too Lilith shall repose, and find a place to rest' (Isa. 34.13-14; cf. Job 30.29; Jer. 9.1; 10.22). Even utter sorrow was pictured with animal imagery: 'I will make lamentation like the jackals, and mourning like the ostriches' (Mic. 1.8).

When thinking of a dog, modern readers are readily reminded of 'man's best friend'. When dogs were domesticated in Palestine is not certain, but an expression like 'your dogs' (Ps. 68.23) and the presupposed presence of dogs in Samaria (1 Kgs 21) indicate that they were. References to dogs in Hebrew Bible literature are, however, never favourable. They are either licking blood (1 Kgs 14.11; 16.4; 21, etc.) howling around cities (Ps. 59.6), eating their own vomit (Prov. 26.11) or serve as image of threatening life situations (Ps. 22.16). The same negative image of the dog is indicated by the metaphorical usage of the term 'dog' in self-abating or insulting speech. In his argument with Saul David says, 'Against whom has the king of Israel come out? Whom do you pursue? A dead dog? A single flea?' (1 Sam. 24.14), and in his humble acceptance of David's generosity Mephibosheth says, ' "What is your servant, that you should look upon a dead dog such as I?" ' (2 Sam. 9.8). The use of 'dog' in these cases is proverbial (1 Sam. 24.14) and customary (cf. 2 Sam. 3.8; 16.9; 2 Kgs 8.13; several Lachish ostraca, and some Amarna letters [Thomas 1960: 414-15, 417]). The one instance in which 'dog' may be used in a positive (although still humble) sense is in the expression 'hire of a harlot' (מחיר זונה) paralleled in Deut. 23.9 by 'price of a dog' (מחיר כלב). In this case *dog* is probably used in the sense of the Phoenician expression 'dogs-of-god' and the Neo-Babylonian *kalbu*, which both refer to a certain kind of priest and in which case Thomas argues that the term does not carry with it 'any sense of dishonour' but refers to the humble and devoted nature of the priest's service to the god. The other instance is the expression 'Am I a dog's head?' (ראש כלב) used by Abner in 2 Sam. 3.8. In this case the reference probably is not to a dog at all, but to a 'dog-faced baboon', also known for its viciousness (Thomas 1960: 421). If this is correct, Abner is not using self-abasing language, but provides a 'fiercely aggressive justification of his standing' (Thomas

1960: 421). But, vile and unclean as a dog may be, a living dog is still better than a dead lion (Eccl. 9.2)!

Even though antelope is, apart from in the dietary laws (Lev. 11; Deut. 14), not mentioned often, the gazelle and deer were looked upon much more favourably than the animals of prey. The deer, for example, occurs in images of speed (2 Sam. 2.24; Isa. 35.6) and the gazelle in similes of speed, beauty and grace (2 Sam. 2.18; Cant. 2.9, 17; 4.15; 7.3). But deer, gazelles and other smaller animals were, of course, also a source of food and were hunted or caught in traps and snares. The fate and behaviour of these animals during the hunt provided the ancients with images of close encounters and afforded them with figurative expressions like 'Save yourself like a gazelle from the hunter' (Prov. 6.5), or 'The wicked have laid a snare for me, but I do not stray from your precepts' (Ps. 119.110). A man who heeds the call of the 'foreign woman' goes 'like an ox to the slaughter, or bounds like a stag toward the trap' (Prov. 7.22).

Outside the exodus narrative and in poems recollecting these events (e.g. Ps. 78.45; 105.31) amphibians, like frogs, and insects, like flies and gnats, are not often referred to in the Hebrew Bible. The most frequently mentioned are the various stages of development of locusts (ארבה). Consider, for example, the picture of utter ruin painted in Joel 1.4, 'What the cutting locust (הגזם) left, the swarming locust (הארבה) has eaten. What the swarming locust left, the hopping locust (הילק) has eaten, and what the hopping locust left, the destroying locust (החסיל) has eaten.' In Solomon's prayer locusts are mentioned together with disasters like famine, plague, blight, mildew and the siege of cities by enemies (1 Kgs 8.37). Like any major disaster locust swarms were looked upon as divine punishment for moral transgression. Amos 4.9 accuses the audience, 'the locust devoured your fig trees and your olive trees; yet you did not return to me, says the Lord'. Because of their ability to multiply, the speed at which they can devour plant growth, the size of their swarms and the devastation they cause, locusts often served as a point of comparison in military similes, such as when the size of an army is compared to that of a locust swarm (cf. Judg. 6.5; Jer. 46.23; 51.14, 27). In the Assyria speech in Nahum 3 it is said:

> The sword...will devour you *like the locust*. Multiply yourselves *like the locust*, multiply *like the grasshopper*!... *The locust* sheds its skin and flies away. Your guards are *like grasshoppers*, your scribes like *swarms of locusts* settling on the fences on a cold day—when the sun rises, they fly away; no one knows where they have gone (Nah. 3.15-17).

4. Environment and Meaning

Sometimes, as in Joel 1–2 *locust* simply becomes a metaphor for 'an invading army' (Deist 1988).

An interesting member of the Palestinian fauna is the bee. Honey is often referred to in the Hebrew Bible as a source of nourishment or valuable gift (cf. Gen. 43.11). It forms part of the formulaic reference to Palestine as 'a land of milk and honey' (e.g. Exod. 3.8) and occurs in the description in Deut. 8.8 of Canaan as 'a land of wheat and barley, of vines and fig trees and pomegranates, a land of olive trees and honey'. Yet the bee itself is referred to only three times in the Hebrew Bible (Deut. 1.44; Ps. 118.12; Isa. 7.18), and always in a negative sense. Moreover, like leaven, it was forbidden as an offering (Lev. 2.11). This really is strange. Should one deduce from this that, although the Israelites valued honey, they despised a bee? In a fairly extensive study Margulies (1974) investigated this oddity and found that the bee (and the 'social organization' in a bee's nest) played an important role in Philistine female-dominated mythology. While the ancient Israelites probably had nothing against bees, the editors of the biblical text took exception against the Philistine opinion of this little creature. This is indicated by the fact that certain manuscripts of the LXX add to the eulogy on the ant in Proverbs 6 also a eulogy on the bee (Margulies 1974: 71), not any longer to be found in the Hebrew Bible. Margulies (1974: 58) refers in this connection to the 'Massoretic tendency towards purification', in accordance with which words that were found offensive or with unwelcome associations were systematically removed, covered up or reinterpreted in such a manner that their original meaning became faded. References to bees, let alone a eulogy on bees, reminding of the religious practices of the 'uncircumcised' Philistines, were consequently also removed or 'faded'. Three interesting conclusions may be drawn from this discussion. First, that Samson's riddle about honey from a lion carcass is particularly fitting. On the one hand, because bees and Philistines belong together, and on the other hand, because of the wrong, but therefore purposely chosen, setting of a beehive in a carcass, which indicates impurity. Secondly, because we have here an example of editorial work on the Hebrew text that rendered the present text a not too trustworthy guide to the culture of ancient Israel, not even always to the culture discussed in the text. Thirdly, it not only demonstrates how extra effort invested in processing the textual information rewarded Thomas with extra meaning, but also that a great deal of cultural information is sometimes presupposed by a text to form part of the reader's encyclopaedic memory.

In its dietary laws the Hebrew Bible distinguishes a large variety of birds (cf. Lev. 11) that are not mentioned again or do not function in Hebrew imagery. Yet birds played such important role in the diet of ancient Israel that, in order to ensure their survival in the area, a rule had to be made at some stage that would prohibit nest snatchers from killing the mother bird with the young (Deut. 22.6-7). Images of bird catching consequently frequently occur in the Hebrew Bible. Consider, for example, the image in Hos. 7.12, 'I will cast my net over them; I will bring them down like birds of the air,' or the image of a narrow escape in Ps. 124.7, 'We have escaped like a bird from the snare of the fowlers; the snare is broken, and we have escaped.' Or the even narrower escape expressed as 'save yourself like...a bird from the hand of the fowler' (Prov. 6.5). Consider also the image of panic borrowed from bird-catching in Isa. 16.2, 'Like fluttering birds, like scattered nestlings, so are the daughters of Moab at the fords of the Arnon.' Or the image of a person who is not on his or her guard and not thinking before doing, who is 'like a bird rushing into a snare, not knowing that it will cost him his life' (Prov. 7.23), or like a gullible dove (Hos. 7.11). But even though birds may be gullible, they are not stupid, because 'in vain is the net baited while the bird is looking on' (Prov. 1.17).

Moreover, even though birds are easily caught and therefore not very intelligent, they obey the set times for migration. This behaviour created the opportunity for the author of Jer. 8.7 to coin the comparison, 'Even the stork in the heavens knows its times; and the turtledove, swallow, and crane observe the time of their coming; but my people do not know the ordinance of the Lord.' Moreover, up in the air they can see everything. 'Do not curse the king, even in your thoughts, or curse the rich, even in your bedroom; for a bird of the air may carry your voice, or some winged creature tell the matter', Eccl. 10.20 warns. Something hidden even from the bird's eye view is, consequently, mysterious. So is wisdom, which is 'hidden from the eyes of all living, and concealed from the birds of the air' (Job 28.21).

Observing the behaviour of birds in flight also provided Hebrew speakers with a rich source of imagery. The seemingly aimless flying done by birds like the sparrow and the swallow gave birth to the saying, 'Like a sparrow in its flitting, like a swallow in its flying, an undeserved curse goes nowhere' (Prov. 26.2). Compared to these birds the eagle,

4. *Environment and Meaning*

swooping down on its prey, is direct and swift. The eagle soaring high and diving towards the earth without clapping its wings fascinated the ancients (Prov. 30.19). Anything that happened suddenly and unexpectedly, especially disastrous events, could be compared to the swiftness of an eagle (cf. Deut. 28.49; Jer. 48.40; 49.22; Hab. 1.8). But what disappeared suddenly could also be compared to an eagle taking off (e.g. Prov. 23.5). An eagle soaring in heaven or sitting high in the mountains on a nest became the image of self-assurance and pride (Obad. 1.4; Jer. 49.16). There even seems to have been a belief that the eagle had the capacity to perpetually renew its strength (cf. Ps. 103.5; Isa. 40.31).

The bird imagery discussed up to this point is, apart from certain images based on the eagle's behaviour, fairly negative, at least from the perspective of intelligence and vigilance. Birds of prey and the ostrich were looked upon even more negatively. To indicate the desolation of a place it is often pictured as inhabited by the hawk, owl, raven and the ostrich. Thus 'the hawk and the hedgehog shall possess it; the owl and the raven shall live in it' (Isa. 34.11), or 'wild animals will lie down there, and its houses will be full of howling creatures; there ostriches will live, and there goat-demons will dance' (Isa. 13.21). Also the sounds birds make became a source of negative imagery. Consider, for example, 'I will make lamentation like the jackals, and mourning like the ostriches' (Mic. 1.8), or the image of exiled women 'moaning like doves' (Nah. 2.7; also Isa. 38.14; 59.11).

There is, however, one bird that was viewed in a positive light—perhaps because of its vulnerability and gullibility: that is the dove. Male lovers call their female friends 'dove' (Cant. 2.14; 5.21; 6.9), and even people, often pictured in the Hebrew Bible as female in relation to Yahweh, speak of themselves as Yahweh's 'dove' (Ps. 74.19). Also, in ancient Palestinian iconography the dove plays an important role in love scenes. A typical scene shows a female lover releasing a dove from her hands to fly to her lover, indicating her acceptance of and readiness for him. From this visual imagery stems the expression 'Your eyes are doves' (Cant. 1.15; 4.1) or 'his eyes are like doves' (5.2), meaning so much as, 'I can see that she/he is ready for me'. On this expression follows invariably a eulogy on the partner's naked body. Consider Cant. 4.1-6, where the male lover, after having described his lover's hair, teeth, lips, mouth, cheeks, neck and breasts, proceeds, 'Until the day breathes and the shadows flee, I will hasten to the mountain of myrrh and the hill of frankincense', whereby the female pubic area is indicated. Similarly, the female lover describes her lover's cheeks, lips, arms, body and thighs (also suggestive of the sexual organ), and adds 'he is altogether desirable'.

Compared to the distinctions made in Hebrew between various kinds of land animals, fish are always spoken of as a collective entity without differentiation. This indicates that fish did not play an important part in the ancient Palestinian diet or day-to-day experience. Yet there are references to fishing (Jer. 16.16) and fishing implements (cf. Job 41.1, 7). Jerusalem—at least in later times—even had a gate called the 'Fish Gate' (cf. Zeph. 1.10; 2 Chron. 33.14). And in the imagery of restoration Ezek. 47.10 promises, 'People will stand fishing beside the sea from En-gedi to En-eglaim; it will be a place for the spreading of nets; its fish will be of a great many kinds, like the fish of the Great Sea'.

Of greater importance from the point of view of cultural interpretation is the conception that the sea was inhabited by enormous underwater creatures that caused it to be always moving. These were the Leviathan (לויתן), the fleeing and twisting serpent (נחש) and the dragon (תנין) (Isa. 27.1), sometimes called Rahab (Isa. 51.9). As in the Babylonian cosmogonic myths, these creatures represent negative forces that have been subdued in the process of creation. Praising the creative power of Yahweh, Ps. 74.13-14 says 'You divided the sea by your might; you broke the heads of the dragons in the waters; you crushed the heads of Leviathan; you gave him as food for the creatures of the wilderness.' Even though these mighty monsters have been subdued, they have not been wiped out and still threaten created order. Some texts play down their power (e.g. Ps. 104.26-29), others see their final annihilation in the future (Isa. 27.1).

An interesting use of sea monster imagery is its application to the Egyptian pharaoh and the deliverance from Egypt. Ezekiel 29.3 speaks of the pharoah as the 'dragon sprawling in the midst of its channels, saying, "My Nile is my own; I made it for myself" ', while Ezek. 32.2 says of him, 'You consider yourself a lion among the nations, but you are like a dragon in the seas; you thrash about in your streams, trouble the water with your feet, and foul your streams.' Instead of earning respect and creating order the pharaoh is a figure of disorder and fear. Finally, Isa. 51.9, employing dragon imagery, reinterprets the deliverance from Egypt as a creative act by Yahweh: when he cleft the waters of the sea he killed Rahab, the sea monster.

5. *Flora*

The Palestinian region has no less than 718 plant species spread over its three climatic regions, namely the Mediterranean area, with an annual rainfall of over 350 mm, a narrow strip west of the Hebron–Jerusalem–Shechem–Tiberias watershed, with an annual rainfall of 150–350 mm, and the huge area in the south of the region with an annual rainfall of 25–150 mm. In prehistoric times much of the first two regions had been overgrown with wood and shrubs, which was over time destroyed by natural disasters, human and animal activity (Mulder 1982: 778). In the Iron Age woods were only to be found on the higher mountains and in the Jordan valley, although 'wood' (יער) should be understood here as an area with some high trees and a thick undergrowth of shrubs, herbs and grass (Mulder 1982: 784), also indicated by Hebrew terms like חרש ('forest'), סבך or עבים ('thicket'). It is in these areas where animals like the lion, wolf, bear and wild pig held sway that 'wood' became a negative symbol. Consider Yahweh's rebuke to Jeremiah, when he complains that he has no strength left to continue the divine mission, '...if in a safe land you fall down, how will you fare in the thickets of the Jordan (בגאון הירדן)?' Because the wooded areas were difficult to negotiate, people in trouble would, in spite of the lurking danger of wild animals, take to the woods (cf. 1 Sam. 22.5). But to wage in war in such an area could spell disaster. 1 Samuel 18.8 says that, in the battle of Absalom and his followers against David's forces, 'the forest claimed more victims...than the sword'.

The Hebrew Bible distinguishes a wide variety of plant life. Among the most frequently mentioned trees one finds the acacia (שטה), almond (לח), broom (רתם), cedar (ארז), cypress (ברוש), fig (תאנה), fir (ברושים), holm (תרזה), myrtle (הדס), oak (אלון, אלה), olive (זית, עץ, שמן), palm (תמר), pine (תאשור), plane (לוז, תדהר), pomegranate (רמון), poplar (לבנה), sycamore (שקמה), tamarisk (אשל) and willow (צפצפה). Solomon's botanical knowledge is said to have covered the whole range, from 'the cedar that is in the Lebanon to the hyssop that grows in the wall' (1 Kgs 4.33). This remark already gives an impression of the way in which plant life was organized in the wisdom lists, namely from large to small. Leaving fragrant plants aside for the moment and considering the mentioning of groups of plants and the imagery involving trees and shrubs, one may construct the following alternative 'classification':

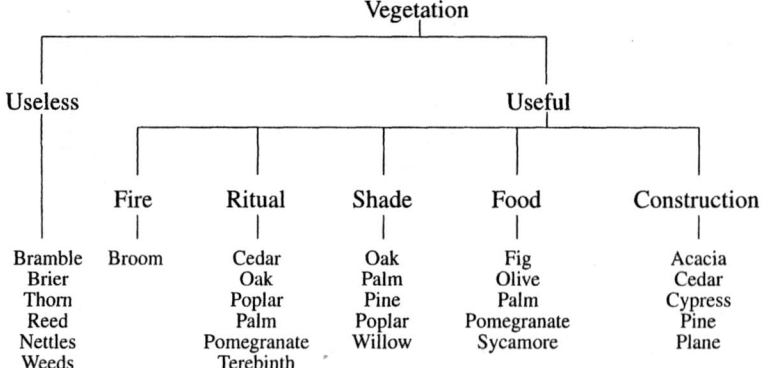

For people who mostly travelled on foot or on the back of a donkey a thick growth of thorn or bramble bushes or brier made progress difficult, if not impossible. Proverbs 15.19 uses this experience to contrast the progress in life made by the lazy and the righteous, 'The way of the lazy is overgrown with thorns, but the path of the upright is a level highway.' A place overgrown with these plants is useless. This is the sense of the often-recurring curse in the Hebrew Bible involving thorns, thistles and brier, for example,

> Where there used to be a thousand vines, worth a thousand shekels of silver, will become briers and thorns. With bow and arrows one will go there, for all the land will be briers and thorns; and as for all the hills that used to be hoed with a hoe, you will not go there for fear of briers and thorns (Isa. 7.23-24; cf. 5.6; 34.13).

To live among thorns and thistles may, however, indicate 'safety', because of the difficulty for an enemy to enter the area (Ezek. 2.6). Experience with these plants gave rise to their symbolizing 'difficulty' (cf. Nah. 1.10; Prov. 15.19; 22.5). Thorns, thistles and brier, finally,[2] are useless plants. So are the godless: 'like thorns that are thrown away' (2 Sam. 23.6). And of the bureaucrats and priests of Micah's time it is said, 'The best of them is like a brier, the most upright of them a thorn hedge' (Mic. 7.4).

As indicated earlier on, shade, shelter and the supply of wood was vital for survival in the region[3] as well as for the application of certain

---

2. For a further discussion, see 'Farming' in Chapter 5.
3. For a discussion of domesticated trees (e.g. olive, palm, vine, etc.), see 'Farming' in Chapter 5.

4. Environment and Meaning

technologies. For general construction purposes the cypress, holm and acacia seem to have been popular. But where endurance and luxury was necessary other woods were used. Describing the ships of Tyre, Ezek. 27.5-7 says,

> They made all your planks of fir trees from Senir; they took a cedar from Lebanon to make a mast for you. From oaks of Bashan they made your oars; they made your deck of pines from the coasts of Cyprus, inlaid with ivory.

Each one of these trees was selected for some or other inherent quality that would suit a specific purpose in shipbuilding. It was precisely the qualities, quantities and status value of the trees of the region that supplied speakers and writers with points of comparison or metaphor. Consider in this regard the following examples.

Symbol	*Text*	*Reference*
Beauty	The encampment of Jacob is 'like palm groves that stretch far away…like aloes that the LORD has planted, like cedar trees beside the waters'.	Num. 26.6
Solidity	The Behemoth makes its tail 'stiff like a cedar'	Job 40.17
Height	'I destroyed the Amorite before them, whose height was like the height of cedars'	Amos 2.9
Strength	'[I destroyed the Amorite] who was as strong as oaks'	Amos 2.9
Power	'I have seen the wicked…towering like a cedar of Lebanon'	Ps. 37.35-36
	'the Lord of hosts has a day against…all the cedars of Lebanon, lofty and lifted up; and against all the oaks of Bashan'	Isa. 2.12-13
Prosperity	'The righteous flourish like the palm tree, and grow like a cedar in Lebanon'	Ps. 92.2
	'[Solomon]…made cedars as numerous [in Jerusalem] as the sycamores of the Shephelah'	1 Kgs 10.27; 2 Chron. 1.15; 9.27
Luxury	'David said to the prophet Nathan, 'I am living in a house of cedar, but the ark of the covenant of the Lord is under a tent'	2 Sam. 7.2
	'Are you a king because you compete in cedar?'	Jer. 22.15; cf. Zeph. 2.14

Symbol	Text	Reference
Restoration	'the sycamores have been cut down, but we will put cedars in their place'	Isa. 9.10
	'I will put in the wilderness the cedar, the acacia, the myrtle, and the olive; I will set in the desert the cypress, the plane and the pine together'	Isa. 41.19
Change	'I bring low the high tree, I make high the low tree; I dry up the green tree and make the dry tree flourish'	Ezek. 17.24
Endurance/ old age	'like the days of a tree shall the days of my people be'	Isa. 56.3
Hope/hope lessness	'if [a tree] is cut down, ...it will sprout again, and...its shoots will not cease. Though its root grows old in the earth, and its stump dies in the ground, yet at the scent of water it will bud and put forth branches like a young plant. But mortals die, and are laid low; humans expire, and where are they?'	Job 14.7-10
	The eunuch says, 'I am just a dry tree'	Isa. 56.3

Some trees had a more pertinent magic or religious connotation. These are the oak, terebinth and poplar, while the images of other sorts, like the palm and pomegranate were popular in sculpturing of a religious nature (Nielsen 1989: 290-92). To work his magic on Laban's herds Jacob cuts himself rods of poplar, almond and plane (Gen. 30.37). Together with the oak and the terebinth, the poplar is also associated with fertility (Hos. 4.13), while almond or almond blossoms are mentioned in contexts of magic or visions (cf. Num. 17.23; Jer. 1.11) and appear on the tabernacle's lampstand (Exod. 25.33; 37.20), which itself took the form of the 'tree of life'. Cedar wood was used in certain purification rituals (Lev. 14.4; Num. 19.6). For sculpting an idol artisans chose cedar, holm or oak (Isa. 44.14). But most conspicuously religious connotations were attached to the oak (אלה, sometimes translated as 'terebinth') and the tamarisk (אשל). The oaks of Moreh (Gen. 12.6; Deut. 11.30), near Shechem (Gen. 35.4; cf. Judg. 9.6), near Bethel (Gen. 35.8), in Zaanannim (Josh. 19.33), at Oprah (Judg. 6.11), Tabor (1 Sam. 10.3), and Jabesh (1 Chron. 10.12) all carry religious value. The shade of an oak was a popular location for fertility ceremonies (Ezek. 6.13; Hos. 4.13), and there even is reference to an oak 'in the

4. *Environment and Meaning* 141

sanctuary of the Lord' (Josh. 24.26). It is also under an oak that Gideon brings his offering (Judg. 6.19) and where the 'man of God' could be found (1 Kgs 10.12). Whether one should read more into the story is not certain, but it remains interesting to note that, on the day the trees 'ate' more of Absalom's men (וירב היער לאכל בעם) than were 'eaten' by the sword (מאשר אכלה החרב), Absalom himself was expressly caught by 'the huge oak tree' (האלה הגדולה, 2 Sam. 18.8-9). In Gen. 21.33 Abraham plants a tamarisk and names it; in 1 Sam. 22.6 Saul, not knowing where to find David, sits under a tamarisk; and in 31.13 he and Jonathan are buried under a tamarisk.

Given the religious connotations attached to various tree types and the relationship between Ashera and trees comes as a surprise to read in Hos. 14.8 (Heb. v. 9) after a hefty polemic against Ba'al and Ashera worship, '[Yahweh] am like an evergreen cypress; your faithfulness (פריך, literally 'your fruit') comes from me.'

Like in the rest of the ancient Orient, tree fables were also told in Israel. These fables can, of course, only communicate effectively if the hearer has access to the *meaning* the various kinds of trees obtained in the language. When King Amaziah challenged King Jehoash of Israel, the latter replied through a letter, 'A thornbush on Lebanon sent to a cedar on Lebanon, saying, "Give your daughter to my son for a wife"; but a wild animal of Lebanon passed by and trampled down the thornbush.' The point of this little fable is that kind should mix with kind, and that a person overestimating his stature will be ruined. The letter then continues, 'You have indeed defeated Edom, and your heart has lifted you up. Be content with your glory, and stay at home; for why should you provoke trouble so that you fall, you and Judah with you?' A more extended fable is the well-known one in Judg. 9.8-15, in which the trees are looking for a king. Each tree replies with reference to its function in the human world. The olive tree answered, 'Shall I stop producing my rich oil, by which gods and mortals are honoured, and go to rule over the trees?' The fig tree replied, 'Shall I stop producing my sweetness and my delicious fruit, and go to rule over the trees?' The vine said, 'Shall I stop producing my wine that cheers gods and mortals, and go to rule over the trees?' But the bramble (or thorn bush) declared himself willing: 'If in good faith you are anointing me king over you, then come and take refuge in my shade; but if not, let fire come out of the bramble and devour the cedars of Lebanon'. The irony of a fig, olive or vine tree taking refuge in the shade of a little thorn bush is obvious. On the other hand, it is also ironically true that a fire starting in the undergrowth of a plantation or forest can, in fact, ruin the trees.

That trees had to be chopped down to supply humans with fuel and building material was accepted as normal (cf. 1 Kgs 5.8-10). During military campaigns the area around the city was cleared of trees to make flight from the city difficult and to obtain fuel to set fires against the besieged city's walls. Consequently tree felling obtained a military flavour. In an oracle delivered to Joram before his encounter with Moab, Elisha says, 'You shall conquer every fortified city and every choice city; every good tree you shall fell, all springs of water you shall stop up, and every good piece of land you shall ruin with stones' (2 Kgs 3.19). In this context chopping down became a metaphor for conquering a city or country. Jeremiah 22.7 uses this imagery in a threat against the king of Jerusalem, 'I will prepare destroyers against you, all with their weapons; they shall cut down your choicest cedars and cast them into the fire.' 2 Kings 19.23 describes the Assyrian king's pride over his military successes as, 'With my many chariots I have gone up the heights of the mountains, to the far recesses of Lebanon; I felled its tallest cedars, its choicest cypresses; I entered its farthest retreat, its densest forest.' And at the fall of Babylon the trees rejoice: 'The cypresses exult over you, the cedars of Lebanon, saying, "Since you were laid low, no one comes to cut us down"' (Isa. 14.8).

The chapter has merely scratched the surface of the meaning Hebrew speakers attached to the environment and environmental phenomena, and of the rich imagery they drew from their environment. It did, however, illustrate that its environment had a profound influence on the language and literature of the Bible. Also, that the *meaning* of a term in the Bible may differ from its mere referent. As a matter of fact, we are fairly uncertain about the exact referents of, for example, Hebrew fauna and flora terminology. A comparison of a text like Lev. 11.13-19 in various translations will provide enough proof of that. What is therefore necessary is that readers of the Bible should invest in establishing the *meaning* the various terms obtain in the cultural world discussed in the text. This kind of knowledge can then function as an encyclopaedic 'memory' with reference to which a reader may, in accordance with the principle of relevance, choose that interpretation of a term (e.g. 'lightning', 'early rain', 'eagle', 'lion', 'thorn', 'cedar', 'oak') in an expression, phrase or text that can be called the 'intended meaning'.

Chapter 5

ECONOMY AND MEANING

To speak of 'economy' in the context of subsistence communities or communities without a currency system, is to invite misunderstanding on the side of present-day readers. One could limit the meaning of the term to its etymological meaning by saying economy is 'the management of a household'. That would to an extent be true in the case of ancient Israel, where the household had indeed been the backbone of the economic system. But to limit the Israelite economy to that of households would be reductionist. The best option is perhaps to follow Haviland (1996: 186) in defining an 'economic system' as any system by which 'goods are produced, distributed and consumed'. The specific *system* applicable to a community then depends on the pattern of subsistence in the relevant region, like hunting and gathering, agriculture, pastoralism, etc.

1. *Property*

The basic productive unit reflected in the Hebrew Bible is the farm. Artisanship was a side line, so to speak (Weippert 1988: 635). Even though some farmers were mostly occupied as agriculturalists and others mostly as pastoralists, by the eighth century BCE, when the first portions of the biblical texts seem to have been written, agriculture and animal breeding were joint ventures on most farms (cf. Dar 1986: 6). This is already indicated by the general term for 'farm land', namely שדה, or נחלת שדה, on which different kinds of farming could be practised (compare Gen. 29.2; 34.5; Exod. 9.3 with Gen. 37.7; Judg. 19.16; Ruth 2.3).

These farms were not privately owned but belonged to the whole community. Hence the expression שדי מגרש referring to the 'common land' belonging to villages and cities (cf. Josh. 21.12; Neh. 5.3). In some or other way, for example, by casting the lot, the common land was distributed among households for cultivation and often marked out by boundary stones.[1] Once the boundaries of each allotment had been settled, no one had the right ever to enlarge his property by shifting or removing the markers. 'You must not move your neighbour's boundary marker, set up by former generations', Deut. 19.14 admonishes. Deut. 27.17 goes even further: 'Cursed be anyone who moves a neighbour's boundary marker'.

People sharing the same allotted area are, of course, bound by fate. They belong to each other and stick to each other. The expression, 'we do not share with you' is therefore a strong expression of dissociation denying any bond, common fate or responsibility. When David suffers a setback and has to flee Jerusalem, one Sheba son of Bichri sounds the trumpet and cries out, 'We have no portion in David, no share in the son of Jesse! Everyone to your tents, O Israel!' (1 Sam. 20.1). The same happens when Rehoboam takes over the reins from his father (1 Kgs 12.16).

Since the property allotted to each household was determined by chance, some properties would have been better than others. It is this background that provided the psalmist with a metaphor to describe his life experience as a believer: because Yahweh holds his 'lot' (גורל) in his hands, 'the boundary lines (חבלים) have fallen for me in pleasant places; I have a goodly heritage' (Ps. 16.6). The same background accounts for the opposite metaphor of 'bad luck' that meets the ungodly (Job 20.29).

Although allotted to it, the piece of land did not 'belong' to the household. As an 'inheritance from the fathers' (נחלת אבות, cf. Num. 36.3, 8; 1 Kgs 21.3, 4; Prov. 19.14) it could be inherited from generation to generation, but never sold (Lev. 25.34). Interestingly enough 'to inherit' and 'to possess' are both expressed by the single verb נחל. It was only in Persian–Hellenistic times that property could be sold by deed and for money (cf. Jer. 32.44). What had in earlier times been allotted to a household became its 'share, allotment' (חלק), 'holding' (אחזה) or 'inheritance' (נחלה). It was this custom of property rights that provided Hebrew writers with two significant metaphors. The first con-

---

1. On the basis of his survey of Samaria, Dar (1986: 7) is of the opinion that boundary markings were not in use in the Iron Age, a conclusion of which we might be perhaps rightly sceptical. Whatever the case might have been previously, at some stage this had become customary.

cerns the ideology of ownership of the land, and the second the relationship between Yahweh and his people.

On the one hand Joshua 13–22 tells how the land had initially been distributed among the Israelite tribes through the casting of the lot. That this had been the way the land historically came in Israelite possession is extremely improbable. Nevertheless, this is how the Deuteronomists *represented* the past. The authors chose to employ an economic custom ('allotment assures perpetual rights') as model to express Israel's *eternal right* to the land, which, as allotted inheritance, was inalienable (consider Deut. 4.21; 15.4; 19.10; Jer. 12.14). On the other hand, there are the religious metaphors of Israel being Yahweh's 'inheritance' or 'allotted share', and Yahweh being the believers' 'share'. Picturing the supreme god El sharing out the nations among the gods and Israel to Yahweh, Deut. 32.9 says, 'the Lord's own portion was his people, Jacob his allotted share'. The people here 'are' a piece of land apportioned to Yahweh. To Aaron, who receives no land, Yahweh says, 'I am your share and your possession among the Israelites' (Num. 18.20) and Jer. 10.16 calls Yahweh 'the portion of Jacob', while various psalms speak of Yahweh as 'my portion' (Pss. 16.5; 119.57; 142.6). Here Yahweh 'is' the apportioned land. These metaphors establish a close relationship between Yahweh and his people. It might have been a relationship that started off by chance, but precisely for that reason it was unbreakable. It is against the background of the inalienability of an 'inheritance' that the idea of Yahweh 'selling' his inheritance, Israel, came as such a shock (Ps. 44.13; Ezek. 30.12).

A household's 'share' or 'inheritance' was its livelihood. The expression 'allotment and inheritance' therefore came to mean '(means of) subsistence' or 'sustenance' (cf. Deut. 14.27). To be driven from one's inheritance means to be deprived of sustenance, as the song of lament in Mic. 2.4 explicitly states, 'We are utterly ruined; the Lord alters the inheritance of my people; how he removes it from me! Among our captors he parcels out our fields.'

Because the land belonged to the villages and nobody had title to it, it was there for the sustenance of the whole village. Some Hebrew Bible texts speak of a custom of allowing the poor and needy, without the permission of the 'owner', to sustain themselves by picking up ears and collecting grapes left behind by the harvesters (cf. Deut. 23.24-25; 24.19-21; Lev. 19.9-10). Other, especially Deuteronom(ist)ic, texts reflecting other mores prescribe that a portion of the income of the temple, that had initially been meant for the sustenance of the religious specialists, be distributed among the poor and vulnerable people, and include in their lists of vulnerables a section of the religious specialists that had for some reason at some time lost their privileged status (e.g. Deut. 12.1-19; 14.22-29; 16.11-14; 26.11-12). The custom of allowing the poor to glean has interesting consequences for the interpretation of the book of Ruth. First, does the expression 'Let me go to the field and glean among the ears of grain, behind someone *in whose sight I may find favour* (אחר אשר אמצא־חן בעיניו)' (Ruth 2.2) mean that she had to ask the owner's permission to glean? If so, since nothing of the sort is implied by the 'law', does the narrative reflect a changed custom of later times? In Dar's view (Dar 1986: 7) property rights in Persian times did indeed differ from those of early Iron Age II. Secondly, her actual request to Boaz's overseer, 'Please, let me glean and gather *among the sheaves* [בעמרים] behind the reapers' (2.7) differs from her earlier declaration of intention, namely to glean among the *ears* (בשבלים), which is also what the 'law' implies when it urges owners not to cut the fringes of grain fields. Ruth's expression 'to glean *behind* someone' seems to imply that the poor were also allowed to pick up the ears that fell in the process of cutting, gathering and binding. But Ruth expressly asks permission to glean among the bound *sheaves*. It would seem that the overseer could not on his own authority grant such a request and that Ruth simply and stubbornly stood there, waiting for the owner to arrive. It is perhaps a misunderstanding of this fine nuance of the story or editorial dismay about such an assertive female Moabite alien that in the end rendered Ruth 2.7b's ותבוא ותעמוד מאז הבקר ועד־עתה זה שבתה הבית מעט unintelligible.

2. *Labour*

If the Samaritan farms of pre-exilic times can be taken as a norm, one could say that farms were on average 10 hectares in size, of which 40–50 per cent was cleared of stones and shrubs for agricultural purposes (Dar 1986: 4-6). In Iron Age IIA each farm had a central structure that could house between 20 and 30 persons (Dar 1986: 7), but in the later Iron Age hamlets were also erected the fringe of farms, probably indicating the settlement of secondary patriarchal kinships and families (Dar 1986: 8). In these homesteads lived the major source of labour: the farmer and his family.

5. Economy and Meaning

Labour conditions were hard, especially in view of the climate and topography of the country. Properly clearing and preparing a piece of land for agricultural purposes involved the removal of the original plant growth, often including thorn bushes and weeds, clearing the area of stones, building terraces and, in the case of certain types of agriculture, ensuring a sufficient water supply. Then there were the tasks of ploughing, sowing, weeding, pruning, harvesting and getting the produce in a storable form. In view of the possibility of a crop failure, which could happen as many times as three out of ten (Matthews and Benjamin 1993: 38) the farmers used to practise staggered sowing, which meant a longer sowing as well as a longer harvesting season. Apart from these tasks, there were also the farm animals to look after: sheep, goats and cattle, as well as those animals that assisted the labourers in their work, namely donkeys and oxen.

Clearing an area of thorns, thistles and brier was, for obvious reasons, essential. Warning the people of Judah to get their lives in order, Jer. 4.3 uses the metaphor 'Break up your fallow ground, and do not sow among thorns'. In removing thorn bush and brier, workers' hands and bodies got continuously pricked and scratched. This experience became a metaphor for 'irritation'. If Israel would not properly 'clear out' the promised land of its former inhabitants, they would remain as barbs in their eyes and thorns in their sides; 'they shall trouble you in the land where you are settling' (Num. 33.55; cf. Josh. 23.13). By contrast Ezek. 28.24 sees the future of Israel as one in which 'The house of Israel shall no longer find a pricking brier or a piercing thorn among all their neighbours who have treated them with contempt.'

After hacking out thorns, thistles and brier, the farmer made a heap of them and set it alight. Also, this process became a source for figurative speech: 'The godless are all like thorns that are thrown away; for they cannot be picked up with the hand; to touch them one uses an iron bar or the shaft of a spear. And they are entirely consumed in fire on the spot' (2 Sam. 23.6-7; cf. Isa. 33.12). Instead of clearing an area by axe and saw, a farmer could use the slash-burning method to remove unwanted vegetation from his field. It is possible that the imagery in Isa. 10.1-19 plays on these two methods. Assyria, so the text says, was used by Yahweh as an axe and a saw to clear overgrown areas, among which also counted Samaria and Jerusalem. But then the axe, Assyria, began to think of itself as the hand that swung it, that is, Assyria became proud of its achievements. Therefore, Assyria also had now to be 'cleared', but this time not by axe and saw. 'The light of Israel will become a fire, and his Holy One a flame; and it will burn and devour his thorns and briers in one day' (Isa. 10.16). Then the fire will get out of hand: '[T]he glory of his forest and his fruitful land the Lord will destroy... The remnant of the trees of his forest will be so few that a child can write them down' (10.17-18).

Also, the intense heat, however short-lived, of a burning heap of thorn bushes provided an image for trouble. The enemy, says Ps. 118.12 'blazed like a fire of thorns'. Sometimes such fires were used to cook food. Because this kind of fire is short-lived and barely leaves coals, the cooking pot had to be hung or put near to the flames. The rapidness with which the prayer in Psalm 58 expects Yahweh's interference in the present situation is aptly expressed by the metaphor, 'Sooner than your pots (i.e. the righteous) can feel the heat of thorns...may he sweep them (i.e. the godless as the fuel) away' (Ps. 58.9). Even the sound of a thorn fire was used in a simile: 'Like the crackling of thorns under a pot, so is the laughter of fools' (Eccl. 7.6), that is, intense and short-lived.

When the bushes had been cleared away, it was time to collect the stones from the surface. This kind of work was of course reserved for a time of the year when there was no other urgent work to be done. Hence Ecclesiastes's assertion that there is a specific time for gathering stones (Eccl. 3.5). Palestine had many surface stones, especially in its hill regions, as the biblical text also suggests. Whenever stones had for some reason to be piled up or thrown they were always at hand (cf. Josh. 7.25-26; 2 Sam. 18.17; 16.6; 2 Kgs 3.19). The stones were collected in heaps. During the night fog condensed on them to provide a natural drip irrigation system for plants in their vicinity. Job 8.17 pictures the godless as a vine with its roots twined around such a heap and spreading its shoots over the garden. These stones could, of course, also come in handy should the farmer decide to build terraces (שדמות) on his property (cf. Isa. 16.8; Hab. 3.17). Terrace building along the slopes of hills, an ancient skill still practised in the Middle East today, is an effective way of stemming soil erosion and of securing run-off water (Dar 1986: 6), but extremely hard work.

Only after all these preparatory works could the labourers start cultivating the soil by digging it up, ploughing, harrowing and sowing it with all kinds of grain (Turkowski 1969: 25-33). The custom in these regions is first to dig up the virgin soil by hoe and then to plough it. The

5. *Economy and Meaning* 149

cleared area is divided into two parts. The first part is planted while the second lies fallow and serves as a pasture for animals, whose droppings also fertilize the soil. The next year (or whenever the first part turns infertile) the fallow land is broken up by ploughing it. What is important is that the breaking up of the soil is done at the start of the first winter rains (December–January). These rains soften the soil to allow for ploughing and the ploughing allows the soil to take up more of the rain later on. Apart from sowing, Hebrew Bible literature also refers to 'planting', for example, vineyards (Deut. 28.30), an olive yard (Josh. 24.13), fruit trees (Lev. 19.23), etc.

These activities also became metaphors and parables in the writers' minds. Soil that can be hoed is useful because it is deep enough for agricultural purposes (see Turkowski 1969: 25). In predicting calamity for Jerusalem, Isa. 7.25 says that 'all the hills that used to be hoed with a hoe, you will not go there for fear of briers and thorns', that is, everything useful for subsistence will be gone. When Jer. 4.3 (cf. Hos. 10.12) urges the audience to 'break up your [rather: "for yourselves"] fallow ground [ניר], and do not sow among thorns', the text urges the people to do two things: first, to not use the 'tired' soil of the past couple of years, but to change their attitude as one would turn from infertile to more fertile soil, but, secondly, to do the necessary preparations, for 'fallow ground' itself is normally overgrown with weeds, and to prepare for the 'sowing season'. For people for whom the soil was not a dead, but a living entity that could even become sad (Isa. 24.4; Jer. 23.10; Joel 1.10; 2.21), ploughing naturally became an image of suffering. The poet of Ps. 129.3 says, 'The ploughers ploughed on my back; they made their furrows long.' Predicting suffering for Judah, Micah of Moresheth said, 'Zion shall be ploughed as a field' (Jer. 26.18), and, in a somewhat difficult text, Hos. 10.11 predicts hard days for Ephraim (and Judah?): 'I will make Ephraim break the ground (ארכיב); [Judah?] must plough (יחרוש); Jacob must harrow (ישׂדד) [for?] himself.' Here people become the oxen before the plough and the harrow. The same process gave occasion to an extended metaphor (perhaps a parable) in Isa. 28.23-25 in which divine punishment is announced, but also temperance, on the part of Yahweh:

> Do those who plough for sowing plough continually? Do they continually open and harrow their ground? When they have levelled its surface, do they not scatter dill, sow cumin, and plant wheat in rows and barley in its proper place, and spelt as the border?

There will be an end to Yahweh's punishment (ploughing and harrowing) and in its stead will come restoration (sowing).

To break up the hard soil and prepare the fallow lands for sowing, one had to wait for the early rains to soften the soil. But when the rains stayed away one had to take the chance of dry sowing. Hence the proverb, 'Whoever observes the wind will not sow; and whoever regards the clouds will not reap' (Eccl. 11.4). To have sown grain in the soil meant to *leave* it there permanently. Hence the metaphor, 'I will sow her [i.e. Ephraim] for myself in the land' (Hos. 2.23—Heb. v. 25). Having sown the seed in the ploughed lands was, however, not the end of the farmer's trouble. In the same furrows weeds came up spontaneously. Turning this experience into a simile Hos. 10.4 accuses the people of Israel, 'litigation springs up like poisonous weeds in the furrows of the field', that is, the people are the field that Yahweh ploughed and sowed, but nothing but weeds came up. If not pulled up, weeds could spoil the harvest. The weeds were therefore carefully uprooted and used for fodder (Turkowski 1969: 101) or thrown away. In Jer. 12.12 Yahweh says of the 'evil neighbours', 'I am about to pluck them up from their land (נתשם מעל אדמתם).' While a property overgrown with thorns and nettles quickly identified a lazy farmer (Prov. 24.30-31), such a farm could also serve as an image of desolation in prophetic speech: 'As for all the hills that used to be hoed with a hoe, you will not go there for fear of briers and thorns' (Isa. 7.25).

While attending to the wheat and barley fields, farmers also had to look after their vines. Leviticus 25.3 reminds the farmer, 'Six years you shall sow your field, and six years you shall prune your vineyard.' Also pruning became a metaphor. Consider: '[Yahweh] will cut off the shoots with pruning hooks, and the spreading branches he will hew away' (Isa. 18.5). The vine here is the people and the farmer Yahweh. What sounds like a positive 'correction' to the people is, however, completely negative, because the season Yahweh chooses for pruning is wrong. He does not do it during the winter, as he should have, but 'before the harvest, when the blossom is over and the flower becomes a ripening grape'. Especially since the ancient farmers did not bind up the shoots of their vines but left them to grow flat along the surface, a vineyard that was not regularly pruned and cared for soon became a wilderness. In the Parable of the Vineyard (Isa. 5) the owner finally gave up his vineyard. 'I will make it a waste,' he says (Isa. 5.6), 'it shall not be pruned or hoed, and it shall be overgrown with briers and thorns.' For a

5. *Economy and Meaning*

farmer to come to such a decision, the vineyard must have been pretty bad (cf. Isa. 7.23).

Whoever sows something can only expect to reap what was sown. Common sense would therefore have dictated the proverbs of sowing and reaping, like, 'Those who plough iniquity and sow trouble reap the same' (Job 4.2), or, 'Those who sow righteousness get a true reward' (Prov. 11.18). But sowing has to do with the hope of gain. A good year could deliver as much as fifteen times the input. Common sense would therefore also have convinced the first audience of Hosea that, if they would sow the wind, they could only expect to reap a whirlwind (Hos. 8.7), but also that, if they would sow righteousness, they could expect to harvest steadfast love (Hos. 10.12). So Yahweh, the farmer, also expected a gain after all the trouble he took with his vineyard:

> He dug it and cleared it of stones, and planted it with choice vines; he built a watchtower in the midst of it, and hewed out a wine vat in it. He expected it to yield grapes, but it yielded wild grapes (Isa. 5.2).

The people must have been equally disappointed when they were told that Yahweh was going to turn their expectations into nothing:

> They have sown wheat and have reaped thorns, they have tired themselves out but profit nothing. They shall be ashamed of their harvests (Jer. 12.13).

The harvest was three out of ten times a failure, but seven out of ten times a success, and 'those who sow in tears reap with shouts of joy' (Ps. 126.5). Then it was time to harvest wheat (חטין) and barley (שערים), beans (פול) and lentils (עדשים), millet (דחן) and spelt (כסמים), dill (קצח) and cumin (כמן), flax (פשתה), olives (זית) and grapes (ענבים). In the case of wheat and barley the plants were cut by sickle, gathered and stacked in sheaves, then transported to the threshing floor, where they were spread and threshed. Depending upon the kind of grain or the purpose for which it had to be threshed, the threshing was done by beating (חבט) the plants with a stick (מטה) or a rod (שבט), if it was something like dill, cumin (Isa. 28.27) or a small amount was needed (Judg. 6.11; Ruth 2.17), while in the case of wheat and barley, cattle or donkeys trampled them and wagons or sledges were driven over them. The custom of muzzling threshing animals to prevent them from eating from the grain (Turkowski 1969: 101-106) is rejected by Deut. 25.4. In Ps. 39.1 the poet reverses the function of the muzzle. In the presence of the godless he puts a muzzle on his mouth 'that I may not sin with my tongue', that is, that no wrong word gets *out*.

The subsistence farmer could not afford to lose any material that was possibly usable, so the chaff resulting from the treading was divided into two types. The thickest fragments of straw, plant roots and the lower parts of the stalks were separated from the rest to be used as fuel or (mixed with clay) as building material. The finer and better chaff was collected and stored for fodder. Only then could the winnowing process start (Isa. 30.24), during which only the finest, non-usable chaff pieces were blown away by the wind (Turkowski 1969: 108). Once the chaff pieces had been separated from the kernels, the process of sieving would begin. First, a coarse sieve was used that would hold back the larger pebbles, pieces of thorn bush or other waste. Then the fine sieve was used, which again let through the kernels but held back thorns, tiny pebbles and coarse sand kernels (Turkowski 1969: 108; Weippert 1985a: 21-22). What remained behind in the coarse sieve and fell through the fine sieve was thrown away. Among both sets of waste there were, of course, always grain kernels. As an image of utter calamity for the godless, Job 5.5 pictures hungry people consuming not only the harvest of the godless, but even the little that remained among the waste, so that there was absolutely nothing left for the godless. In spite of the winnowing and double sieving process it was never possible to remove all dirt and sand from the wheat or barley before it was ground, so that some small sand grains would inevitably get into the flour, and of course the bread baked from it. Biting on a sand grain is an awful experience. 'Bread gained by deceit is sweet,' Prov. 20.17 says, 'but afterward the mouth will be full of gravel.' And Lam. 3.16: 'He [Yahweh] has made my teeth grind on gravel, and made me cower in ashes.'

While the sheaves were normally transported to where the threshing floor was, the grape harvest was processed in the vineyards. The grapes were collected in small cisterns and trodden by foot to release the juice, which flowed via one or more pipes into a somewhat deeper rock tank or into earthen vases (Weippert 1988: 636). The olive harvest took place in October. The fruits were beaten off the trees with sticks (Deut. 24.20), collected and taken to the farmstead where the olives were pressed. For the production of small quantities of olive oil they would put the olives on a flattish stone surface, with a sunken outlet leading to a clay pot, and crush the fruits with another flat stone. For larger quantities of oil labourers would put crushed olives in a basket with a weight on top. At some installations a wooden beam fixed to a wall at one end

5. *Economy and Meaning* 153

would be used to exert extra pressure on the weight in the basket (Weippert 1988: 636).

Harvesting, the joy of harvesting and the subsequent processing of the natural products provided Hebrew speakers with a rich variety of images, similes and metaphors, of which the following table gives some impression.

Procedure	*Text*	*Comment*
Harvesting	A little while and the time of her [Babylon's] harvest will come (Jer. 51.33)	A time of reckoning is a harvest
Reaping	Human corpses shall fall...like sheaves behind the reaper, and no one shall gather them (Jer. 9.22)	Dead bodies are like sheaves
	Put in the sickle, for the harvest is ripe (Joel 3.13)	Judgment is cutting grain
Binding sheaves	Let them be like the grass on the housetops that withers before it grows up, with which reapers do not fill their hands or binders of sheaves their arms (Ps. 129.6)	A person of value is a sheaf
Transporting sheaves	So, I will press you down in your place, just as a cart presses down when it is full of sheaves (Amos 2.13)	Judgment is the weight of sheaves
Spreading wheat on the threshing floor	But they do not...understand...that he [Yahweh] has gathered them as sheaves to the threshing floor (Mic. 4.12)	Judgment/discipline is to be put on the threshing floor
	You shall come to your grave in ripe old age, as a shock of grain comes up to the threshing floor in its season (Job 5.26)	Fulfilment is a sheaf/To die is to go to the threshing floor
Threshing floor	Babylon is like a threshing floor at the time when it is trodden (Jer. 51.33)	The scene of punishment is a threshing floor
Threshing	I will not revoke the punishment; because they [Damascus] have threshed Gilead with threshing sledges of iron (Amos 1.3)	Killing people is threshing

Procedure	Text	Comment
	The king of Aram had destroyed them and made them like the dust at threshing (2 Kgs 13.7)	Killing people is thoroughly to thresh them
	On that day the Lord will thresh [beat with a stick] from the channel of the Euphrates to the Wadi of Egypt, and you will be gathered one by one, O people of Israel (Isa. 27.12)	Only a few people are concerned
	Dill is not threshed with a threshing sledge, nor is a cart wheel rolled over cumin; but dill is beaten out with a stick, and cumin with a rod. Grain is crushed for bread, but one does not thresh it forever; one drives the cart wheel and horses over it, but does not pulverize it (Isa. 28.26-28)	Following the right procedure of threshing is measuring out appropriate punishment
Winnowing	A king who sits on the throne of judgment winnows all evil with his eyes (Prov. 20.8)	Discriminating/judging is to winnow
	A wise king winnows the wicked, and drives the wheel over them (Prov. 20.26)	Discriminating/judging is to winnow; to punish is to thresh
	You shall winnow them and the wind shall carry them away, and the tempest shall scatter them (Isa. 41.16)	To conquer/destroy is to winnow
	And I will send winnowers to Babylon, and they shall winnow her (Jer. 51.2)	To conquer is to winnow
	Therefore they shall be...like chaff that swirls from the threshing floor (Hos. 13.3)	To be sentenced is to be declared chaff
	The multitude of tyrants [shall be] like flying chaff (Isa. 29.5); How often are they [the wicked] like... chaff that the storm carries away? (Job 21.18)	To be destroyed is to be made chaff

Procedure	Text	Comment
	When a sieve is shaken, the refuse appears; so do a person's faults when he speaks (Sir. 27.3); I will...shake the house of Israel... as one shakes with a sieve, but no pebble shall fall to the ground (Amos 9.9)	To discriminate is to sieve
Beating off olives/harvesting grapes	Gleanings will be left in it, as when an olive tree is beaten—two or three berries in the top of the highest bough, four or five on the branches of a fruit tree, says the Lord God of Israel (Isa. 17.6); For thus it shall be on the earth and among the nations, as when an olive tree is beaten, as at the gleaning when the grape harvest is ended (Isa. 24.13)	A remnant of people are olives left after the beating of the trees
Harvesting grapes	Joy and gladness are taken away from the fruitful field; and in the vineyards no songs are sung, no shouts are raised; no treader treads out wine in the presses; the vintage-shout is hushed (Isa. 16.10)	Judgment means no harvest
Treading	Go in, tread, for the wine press is fun. The vats overflow (Joel 3.13; cf. Jer. 25.30; Lam. 1.15)	Judgment is treading grapes
Enjoying the produce of the harvest	You shall sow, but not reap; you shall tread olives, but not anoint yourselves with oil; you shall tread grapes, but not drink wine (Mic. 6.15; cf. Deut. 28.40)	Judgment is to be deprived of the produce of the harvest

In view of Ps. 126.5, 'Those who sow in tears will reap with shouts of joy' (my translation), and of the references in the examples above to joyous shouting during harvest time, it is ironic that by far the most popular use of harvest images is for picturing *judgment*. But it is precisely the difference between the common association of harvest and joy that is twisted to achieve an ironic effect. The intention of these images is to shock.

The opposite of harvesting is, of course, planting—also in the field of metaphor and simile. And although one sows in tears (Ps. 26.5), 'sowing' and 'planting' always have positive connotations (cf. Ps. 107.37; Jer. 1.10; 12.2; 18.9; 24.6; 42.10; Hos. 2.23). To continue the daily routine is 'to build houses and plant vineyards' (Jer. 29.5; Ezek. 28.6), and to be restored is to be planted (Jer. 31.5, 28; 32.41; Hos. 2.25; Amos 9.14-15).

In spite of this negative imagery the biblical text provides ample evidence of a high appreciation of wheat and barley, the palm, olive and fig tree, and vines. They are actually looked upon as divinely bestowed gifts (Ps. 104.14-15). The palm, olive and vine stood for prosperity (Pss. 52.8; 92.12; 128.3), beauty (Cant. 7.7-8; Hos. 14.6) and good prospects (Hos. 9.13). Believers even called themselves Yahweh's vine (Ps. 80.14; cf. Jer. 2.21; Hos. 10.1) or olive tree (Jer. 11.16). Likewise the products of these trees were highly valued.

Against the background of the Palestinian climate and landscape and the hard labour required for subsistence it is quite understandable that a lusty garden would seem the ideal environment to an ancient Israelite. 'A garden,' Werner Berg (1988) quotes from a prospectus distributed at an international gardening exhibition, 'is humankind's picture of the ideal world, and since most people are conditioned by the society of which they form part, the garden of each society and each epoch reflects the dream-world of a society...' (my translation). This is also true of ancient Israel. In Berg's terminology the literary picturing of Palestine as a beautiful and fertile garden with sufficient water supplies (cf. Deut. 8.7-9; 33.13-14, 16; Num. 13.23; 24.5-7, etc.) not only sounds like a commercial, but was indeed intended as propaganda. Some writers of Hebrew Bible 'garden texts', aware of the fact that the garden image did not fit the reality of the region, situated the divine garden in the mythological past, before the cataclysmic destruction of Sodom and Gomorrah (Gen. 13.10), spiritualized the image or postponed it to the eschatological future. Genesis 2, situating the garden in the mythological past, summarizes the dreams of an Israelite peasant: the dry soil is watered to produce a garden with perennial streams, full of beautiful, shady and fruit bearing trees, but no thorns or thistles. There is no hard labour but minerals galore, peace between humankind and animals, and the man with his wife are in charge of everything. Other writers spiritualized the garden symbol and applied it to the people of Israel. Consider, for example, Exod. 15.17: 'You brought

5. *Economy and Meaning* 157

them in and planted them on the mountain of your own possession.' Still other writers picture this garden in the future, when everybody would sit under his or her vine and fig trees, with nothing to frighten them (Mic. 4.4; Zech. 3.10), or at a time with plenty of water and tree species. In Ezekiel's vision of the new land, for example, he saw

> on the bank of the river a great many trees on the one side and on the other. He said to me, This water flows toward the eastern region and goes down into the Arabah; and when it enters the sea, the sea of stagnant waters, the water will become fresh. Wherever the river goes, every living creature that swarms will live, and there will be very many fish, once these waters reach there. It will become fresh; and everything will live where the river goes. People will stand fishing beside the sea from Engedi to En-eglaim... On the banks, on both sides of the river, there will grow all kinds of trees for food. Their leaves will not wither nor their fruit fail, but they will bear fresh fruit every month, because the water for them flows from the sanctuary. Their fruit will be for food, and their leaves for healing (Ezek. 47.7-12).

Of this land people would say, 'This land that was desolate has become like the garden of Eden' (Ezek. 36.35).

In view of the background of the Palestinian climate and landscape and the hard labour required for subsistence it is also understandable that 'philosophers' viewed farm labour and social relations on the farm as a curse. Having pictured the lusty original Garden of Eden in Genesis 2, the narrator goes on to relate that picture in Gen. 3.15-19 to the harsh reality of a cursed ground from which one could only eat by continuously battling against thorn and thistle growth. Even to get enough hands on the farm is only possible through the painful pangs of childbearing. Moreover, it would have been a much more pleasant place if man and wife could have been each other's equals instead of the husband ruling over his wife and she dancing to his tunes.

Activity	*Example*	*Hebrew term*
Farmers	2 Chronicles 26.10	אכרים
Ploughers	Psalm 129.3	חרשים
Planters	Jeremiah 31.5	נטעים
Sowers	Psalm 126.5	זרעים
Reapers	Ruth 2.3	קצרים
Winnowers	Jeremiah 51.21	זרים
Shearers	1 Samuel 25.7	גזזים
Wine treaders	Amos 9.13	דרך ענבים

An interesting feature of the Hebrew vocabulary concerning farm labour is that, depending on their main activity at specific times of the year, the same labourers are referred to by different terms (cf. Turkowski 1969: 108), as is shown by the table above.

Given this way of speaking it is worth considering whether one should necessarily deduce from Amos's assertion that he was a herdsman (בוקר) and a dresser of sycamore trees/picker of sycamore fruit (שקמים בולס) (Amos 7.14), that those terms refer to his full-time occupation. His statement may, in the light of conventional speech, also be translated with:

> I am no/have never been a prophet or a son of a prophet. To the contrary, *while I was busy herding and picking sycamore fruits* [i.e. attending to my farming business of the season] Yahweh took me away from behind the sheep [i.e. I am a sheep farmer, you know] and said to me, 'Go, prophesy!' Therefore now, listen...

In this case the superscript of the book, which identifies Amos as אשר־היה בנקדים מתקוע, could be taken to simply indicate that he was from among the Tekoan pastoralists and not an agriculturalist like, for example Elisha, who is taken from behind the plough (1 Kgs 19.19).

Of the animals on a farm, the most frequently mentioned in the Hebrew Bible are sheep and goats, the donkey (חמר), and cattle (בקר). Also mentioned are the mule (פרד), the horse (סוס) and the camel (גמל). Even though, according to archaeological evidence, pigs (חזיר) did form part of the Israelite diet (Hesse and Wapnish 1997), they have been edited out of the Hebrew Bible's narrative world, which once again illustrates the problematic relationship between the culture in and of the text.

In summaries of possessions, cattle, donkeys, and mostly also sheep, form the core (cf. Exod. 22.9; 23.4; 1 Sam. 22.19; 27.9; Job 1.3). Apart from in stereotyped formulas of wealth (Gen. 12.16; 30.43; 32.7) or possession (Exod. 9.3; Job 1.3; Ezra 2.67), the camel is only mentioned in connection with long-distance travelling (Gen. 24 *passim*; 31.17; 1 Kgs 10.2) and with foreign (desert) nations like the Amalekites (1 Sam. 15.3; 30.17; Isa. 60.6), Aramaeans (2 Kgs 8.9), Ishmaelites and Midianites (Gen. 37.25; Judg. 6.5; 7.12), Kushites (2 Chron. 14.15), Medians (Isa. 21.7), Arabs (Jer. 49.29) and others (1 Chron. 12.40; Zech. 14.15). According to 1 Chron. 27.30 David even had to appoint an Ishmaelite as his camel handler. Likewise, horses are, except for Isa.

5. *Economy and Meaning* 159

28.28, always mentioned in a military or royal context, while 'mule' also carries a royal connotation (cf. 2 Sam. 13.29; 18.9).

The donkey (חמר; אחון [fem.]; עיר [masc.]) was generally used for transport, whether of people or goods (cf. Gen. 42.26; Exod. 4.20; 1 Sam. 16.20; 25.20, 42; 1 Kgs 13.29). In the narrative world of the Hebrew Bible the expression 'to saddle a donkey' indicated preparation for something, that is, it means so much as 'to set out on a journey' (cf. Gen. 22.3; Num. 22.21; 1 Sam. 17.23; 2 Sam. 17.23; 19.26; 1 Kgs 2.40; 13.13, 27; 2 Kgs 4.24) and to dismount from a donkey 'to have reached the goal of the journey' (cf. Josh. 15.18). To own enough donkeys to transport one's family seems to be a status symbol (cf. Judg. 10.4; 12.14), while the number of donkeys one owns co-defines one's wealth (cf. Gen. 12.16; 24.35; 30.43; 32.5; Job 1.3).

Next to the donkey, cattle and flock were of importance for the subsistence farmer. This importance is indicated by, for example, the different terms used to distinguish the different age groups, sexes and functions of cattle. According to Koenen (1994) בקר is the generic concept for 'cattle' in distinguishing domesticated cattle from the wild species (ראם). It can therefore be used instead of any of the more specific terms. The meaning of שור comes close to that of בקר, but שור is the generic term for *farmyard* cattle in general, that is, without reference to age or sex (Koenen 1994: 543). When Jacob says to Esau, 'I have שור, donkeys, flocks, male and female slaves' (Gen. 32.5), he therefore does *not* refer to 'oxen', which is how most translations take the term, but to 'farm cattle' generally. Its usage differs from that of בקר in that it does not distinguish domesticated from wild, and also in that, while one cannot speak of 'a' בקר in Hebrew (unless by using the formula בן־בקר) one can speak of 'a' שור (cf. Num. 7.3). While שור refers to cattle on a farm generally, אלף refers to cattle from the exclusive perspective of agriculture, that is, with the exclusion of sacrificial or legal contexts (in which case שור is used; see Koenen 1994: 545). As a specialized (though not completely exclusive) term for the sacrificial context פר is used (Koenen 1994: 541). In by far the most instances פר refers to a sacrificial bull. The feminine form פרה is, however, not the 'opposite sex' of the sacrificial פר. It merely refers to any 'cow' in general. עגל/ עגלה denotes an age category and indicates an animal of up to about three years old (Gen. 15.9), that is, including a young calf. On the other end of the spectrum stands the אביר, possibly the 'breeding bull'. One may summarize the discussion on cattle as follows:

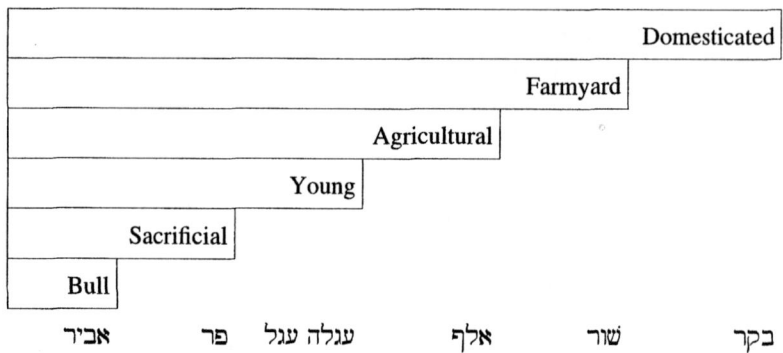

The importance of cattle and donkeys for the farmer is expressed by the proverb, 'Where there are no 'oxen' (אֲלָפִים) there is no grain; abundant crops come by the strength of the 'ox' (שׁוֹר)' (Prov. 14.4) and indicated by the reference in Isa. 30.24 to 'the 'oxen' (אֲלָפִים) and donkeys that till the ground'. Their importance for subsistence farmers explains their inclusion in the ten commandments among the 'farm hands' deserving a rest on the sabbath, and finally the 'law' urging neighbours to return strayed cattle and donkeys to their rightful owners (Exod. 23.4). Given the explicit 'laws' on muzzling, days of rest, strayed animals and yoking cattle and donkeys together (Deut. 22.10), one gets the impression that the life of an 'ox' and donkey in the real world of a poor subsistence farmstead was far less pleasant than that of their literary counterparts—otherwise there would not have been such 'laws'.

Hebrew Bible literature bases quite a few comparisons and metaphors on domesticated cattle. Some images come from the natural behaviour of these animals. Calves and young cattle were known for their liveliness, vitality and inexperience in handling the tasks they had to accomplish on a farm. In promising the returned exiles a time of prosperity under the wings of the Sun of Righteousness, Mal. 4.2 (Heb. 3.20) pictures them as 'leaping like calves from the stall'. The rain Yahweh gives on the mountains 'makes Lebanon skip like a calf' (Ps. 29.6). Like Canaanite religion, popular Israelite religion personified 'vitality' through an image of a young bull. And in admitting guilt Ephraim aptly says, 'I was like a calf untrained' (Jer. 31.8). As in many cultures, among the Israelites the full-grown bull was also renowned for aggressiveness and power. Employing this characteristic of the bull, Isa. 10.13 says that 'like a bull' Yahweh has brought down the Assyrian power. Particularly, the horns of the bull and his wild counterpart, the wildebeest, came to symbolize strength and power. To symbolize his

5. *Economy and Meaning* 161

fighting power, Zedekiah 'made for himself horns of iron, and he said, "Thus says the Lord: With these you shall gore the Arameans until they are destroyed"' (1 Kgs 22.11; cf. Deut. 33.17). When his horns are kept high the bull is ready to fight, but if they lie in the dust, the bull is done for. Equally with people. Psalm 92.10 says of God, 'You have exalted my horn like that of the wild ox.' And Job 16.15 literally says that his 'horn has been severely beaten into the dust'. The sexual behaviour and make-up of domesticated animals become part of Hebrew imagery. So, for example, negatively, the female camel on heat (בכרה, Jer. 2.23), or the sexual physiology of donkeys, horses and bulls. Judah's political flirting with Babylonia and Egypt is pictured as a whore lusting after sweethearts with members like those of donkeys and an emission like that of stallions (Ezek. 23.20). And describing the fortune of the godless, Job 21.10 says, 'Their bull breeds (עבר) goes over/impregnates, without fail; their cow calves and never miscarries.'

Other images play on the relationship between owner and cattle, for example, in answering his friends' accusations that he should rather speak to God about his afflictions, Job says, 'Does the wild ass bray over its grass, or the ox (שור) low over its fodder?' (Job 6.5): if there were fodder in my crib (that is, had God looked after me), I would not have complained. Also employing the crib and fodder image is Isa. 1.3 'The ox (שור) knows its owner, and the donkey its master's crib; but Israel does not know, my people do not understand.' Some images appeal to common sense, as in Amos 6.12, where the rhetorical question implies a negative answer: 'Do horses run on rocks? Does one plough the sea with oxen?' Some appeal to the reader's knowledge of the location of good pastures. In Amos 4.1 the elite of Samaria is addressed as 'cows of Bashan', to which is then added the contradictory phrase 'who are on Mount Samaria'. But then this contradiction is exactly the point: cows get fat on the hills of Bashan (Ps. 22.13; Deut. 32.14), not on the hill of Samaria. Ergo, they could only have got fat (rich) by robbing the others on that hill of their sustenance (Weippert 1985a: 10). Others require knowledge of the behaviour of farm animals and the way this behaviour is technically overcome. Proverbs 26.3 says, 'A whip for the horse, a bridle for the donkey, and a rod for the back of fools': also a fool cannot be 'talked' into the right behaviour and has to be contained in another manner.

Flocks consisted of sheep and goats—perhaps fewer sheep and more goats than one would gather from existing English translations of the

Hebrew Bible. Translations normally render both the terms צאן and שׂה with 'sheep'. But these two terms refer to 'flock' and 'an individual from a flock' respectively. Such a flock may consist of sheep or goats, or of a mixture of the two, so that an individual (שׂה) may be either a sheep or a goat. This is clear from Deut. 14.4, which speaks of an individual sheep and goat as שׂה כשׂבים and שׂה עזים respectively. Consider also Jacob's wages, namely 'every speckled and spotted individual (כל־שׂה נקד וטלוא), that is, every black individual among the sheep (וכל־שׂה־חום בכשׂבים) and every spotted and speckled among the goats (וטלוא ונקד בעזים)' (Gen. 30.32; cf. also Exod. 12.5). The terms explicitly denoting 'sheep' and 'goat' are כשׂב and עז.

Sheep and goats are subdivided into masculine and feminine, while goats may either be ordinary goats (עזים) or hairy goats (שׂעיר עזים, the genitive qualification distinguishing the domesticated goat from the wild goat, the שׂעיר). One thus arrives at the following picture:

Collection	Flock צאן		
Individual	Sheep/goat שׂה		
Type	Sheep כשׂב	Goats	
		Ordinary goat עז	Hairy goat שׂעיר עזים
Masculine	איל	עתוד; תישׁ	שׂעיר עזים
Feminine	רחל; כשׂבה	בת עז	שׂעירת עזים
Child	טלה	גדי (גדי־עזים)	עדי

Most farms had a dimorphic economic basis, that is, practised agriculture as well as herding. In a dimorphic economy, planning was essential, especially since the mixed agricultural side of it with its practice of staggered sowing involved different planting, weeding, pruning and harvesting calendars. In order always to have enough hands for the agricultural side of the economy, smaller children of a household would be responsible for pasturing the flocks. But flocks needed more attention than that. Since goats are roaming animals (the גרים of Isa. 5.17) and sheep normally follow them, they could easily got lost or fall prey

5. *Economy and Meaning*

to predators. Given the character of the landscape they could also fall into ravines or hurt themselves. Especially during the lambing season more specialized knowledge was called for. Moreover, when the grazing in the immediate vicinity of the village got sparse the flocks had to be taken elsewhere. To avoid losing hands on the farm at critical stages, farmers would therefore (collectively) contract part-time or full-time shepherds to attend to their flocks (Matthews and Benjamin 1993: 53-58) and would take over the responsibility for leading the flocks to pastures and water, protecting them against predators, taking care of sick animals, looking after the lambs and kids and finding safe places where the flocks could stay overnight. These people were responsible for the owners' flocks, and, when one of them was caught by a predator, the hired hand had to produce evidence of that fact by showing the owner a piece of the animal left behind by the lion, bear or hyena (Exod. 22.9-12; Amos 3.12—see Weippert 1985a: 15).

Herds, flocks, meadows, grazing and shepherding all provided Hebrew writers with a source of simile and metaphor. While watered and green pastures symbolized prosperity and care (Ps. 65.12; Heb. v. 13; Isa. 30.23), a built-up area that becomes a pasture (Isa. 5.17; 27.10; Zeph. 2.6), withered and dry pastures (Ps. 37.20; Jer. 9.10; 23.10; Amos 1.2), a kraal where flocks have trodden the dust to powder (Isa. 7.25), the image of a lion amid a flock (Mic. 5.8; Heb. v. 7). 'Judgment', like 'hardship', is also symbolized by a sheep or goat chosen, fattened or led away to be slaughtered (Ps. 49.15; Heb. v. 15; 44.11; Heb. v. 12; Jer. 12.3). 'To be endangered' is expressed as a stray sheep or goat with nobody to look for it (Num. 27.17; 1 Kgs 22.17; Ps. 119.176; Isa. 13.14; Zech. 10.2). By contrast, 'safety' is a flock led (Ps. 78.52; 80.1; Heb. v. 2), gathered (Mic. 2.12), led to pastures (Isa. 40.11; Mic. 7.14) and taken to a safe place to lie down (Lev. 26.6; Job 11.19; Isa. 17.2; Ps. 23.2; Isa. 14.30; 65.10; Hos. 2.18; Zeph. 2.7; 3.13). While, as mentioned earlier, a built-up area that becomes a pasture is a symbol of judgment and disaster, an even greater disaster is pictured by the image of a shepherd too scared by the place to let his flock *lie down* in that area (Isa. 13.20). Total peace, on the other hand, is when flocks and predators lie down in the same pasture (Isa. 11.6-7).

That the shepherd image was popular among Hebrew Bible writers is well-known. There are two shepherd images, the first of the owner-shepherd and the second of the hired or contracted shepherd. The first always stands for Yahweh, who guides the individual (Gen. 48.15) or the group (Gen. 49.24; Ps. 80.1; Heb. v. 2) to pastures and water (Ps. 23.1; and (unless we follow cf., however, Matthews and Benjamin 1993: 63-66), carries the sick animals or lambs (Ps. 28.9; Isa. 40.11), as well as protects his flock against predators and other dangers (Jer. 31.10). The hired hands (i.e. the kings and bureaucrats) are contracted (קום Hif.) by Yahweh (2 Sam. 7.7; Ps. 78.71; Isa. 44.28) to protect his flock (Jer. 23.2-4). However, the hired hands do not look after Yahweh's flock (Jer. 23.2-4) and act unsympathetically, like those looking after the animals selected for slaughtering (Zech. 11.4), and will therefore be dealt with accordingly.

Apart from shorter similes and metaphors adding meaning to and brightening up Hebrew Bible literature, some paragraphs consist of extended pastoral and agricultural metaphors. Consider, for example, Ezekiel 34, in the first part of which (vv. 2-6) the contracting owner, Yahweh, confronts the hired hands (royal court, bureaucrats) for not having fulfilled their contract:

> Ah, you shepherds of Israel who have been feeding yourselves! Should not shepherds feed the sheep (הצאן)? You eat the fat, you clothe yourselves with the wool, you slaughter the fatlings; but you do not feed the sheep. You have not strengthened the weak, you have not healed the sick, you have not bound up the injured, you have not brought back the strayed, you have not sought the lost, but with force and harshness you have ruled them. So they were scattered, because there was no shepherd; and scattered, they became food for all the wild animals. My sheep were scattered, they wandered over all the mountains and on every high hill; my sheep were scattered over all the face of the earth, with no one to search or seek for them.

Like Yahweh, any farmer would have fired and punished such hired hands (Ezek. 34.10) and personally taken over the care of the flock from them (34.11-16). The second part of the chapter (34.17-24) shifts the attention from the hired hands to the flock itself. Within Yahweh's flock there are those (the rich and non-bureaucratic elite), who, typical of some rams and he-goats, 'pushed with flank and shoulder, and butted at all the weak animals' until they were scattered far and wide. Not only did these animals feed on the best pastures; they also trod down with their feet the rest of the field. And when they came to water pools, they drank of clear water, whereafter they fouled the rest with their feet. In this way they got fat while the rest of the flock starved. Therefore, the shepherd is going to 'judge between sheep and sheep, between rams and goats' and catch out all the fat ones for slaughtering and save his flock, so that they will no longer be ravaged. Only then will he appoint another (trusted) hired hand over them, namely David, who shall feed them and be their shepherd.

Given the importance of agricultural produce and the well-being of the herds and flocks to a subsistence farmer, it is understandable that complete catastrophe is pictured as the collapse of the economic basis of a community. Consider Joel 1.19-20:

> The seed shrivels under the clods, the storehouses are desolate; the granaries are ruined because the grain has failed. How the animals groan! The herds of cattle wander about because there is no pasture for them; even the flocks of sheep are dazed... For fire has devoured the pastures of the wilderness, and flames have burned all the trees of the field.

The same catastrophe is also pictured poetically when 'the fig tree does not blossom, and no fruit is on the vines;...the produce of the olive fails, and the fields yield no food;...the flock is cut off from the fold, and there is no herd in the stalls' (Hab. 3.17). Complete restoration, on the other hand, is expressed by the exact opposite of these images. Then Yahweh gives rain for the seed with which one sows the ground (אדמה) so that the produce of the ground is rich and plenteous. Cattle graze in broad pastures and oxen (אלפים) and donkeys (עירים) till the ground. While threshing, they are not muzzled, but allowed to eat not only of the straw on the threshing floor but *winnowed* silage—which is quite unheard of, because farmers would perhaps mix a little barley or vetch into the cattle's fodder only in cases of emergency (Turkowski 1969: 108). Furthermore, on every mountain and every hill there are brooks running with water. Also, the light of the moon is like the light of the sun, and the light of the sun like the light of seven days. And Yahweh binds up the injuries of his people and heals their wounds (Isa. 30.23-26).

3. *Distribution*

One or more basic economic systems may be operative in subsistence economies. Following Haviland (1996: 196-97) one may distinguish the following types:

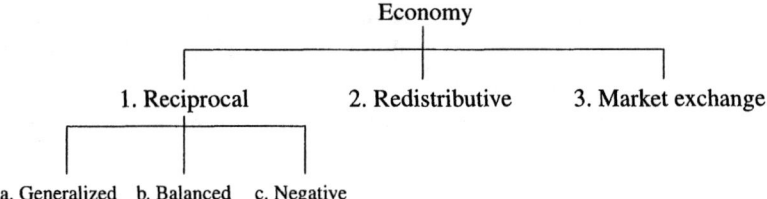

In a *generalized reciprocal economic system* (1a) goods of roughly equal value are regularly exchanged between households in a community. The exchange is a ritualized token of good neighbourliness and prestige. When Abraham sends out his servant to fetch Isaac a wife from among Abraham's relatives, he sends his family 'all kinds of choice gifts' (מתנת, Gen. 14.10) to express his friendly attitude towards them. When Jacob returns from Mesopotamia and encounters Esau, he sends him a gift comprising 200 female goats, 20 male goats, 200 ewes and 20 rams, 30 milch camels and their colts, 40 cows and 10 bulls, 20 female donkeys and 10 male donkeys (Gen. 32.14-15). This gift must at once establish good relations and express Jacob's status. Expressing his benevolence towards the Joseph clans, Yahweh also gives them gifts (Deut. 33.13-16). As an expression of their attachment to him people are urged to present Yahweh with gifts (Lev. 7.14; Ps. 76.12). Apart from constantly reinforcing social relations and expressing status, gift-giving is a way of sustaining a household experiencing shortages and therefore provides a form of social security for the needy. If they maintain good relations with Yahweh, Deut. 28.12 promises the faithful, 'The Lord will open for you his rich storehouse, the heavens, to give the rain of your land in its season and to bless all your undertakings. You will lend to many nations, but you will not borrow.'

Balanced reciprocity (1b) is a system of more sporadic gift-giving, but with 'strings attached', in that receiving a gift from a person means to be expected to respond promptly with a gift or service of equal value, or risk disturbed social relations. When Saul and his servant decide to call in the help of the diviner to help them find strayed donkeys Saul worries: '...what can we bring the man? For the bread in our sacks is gone, and there is no present to bring to the man of God. What have we?' (1 Sam. 9.7). It is in this context that Prov. 18.16 asserts, 'A gift opens doors; it gives access to the great', but also says, 'Like clouds and wind without rain is one who boasts of a gift never given' (Prov. 25.14). Such a person risks social sanctioning. That is why one finds

5. *Economy and Meaning*

Abigail, whose husband refused David and his men a gift after David protected his Nabal's workmen (1 Sam. 25.15-16), loading her donkeys and hurrying behind David's party (1 Sam. 25.3-21).

The importance of gift-giving in the economic system discussed in and presupposed by the Hebrew Bible is indicated by the variety of terms referring to various sorts of gifts, such as ברכה (Gen. 33.11; Josh. 15.19; 1 Sam. 15.27; 2 Kgs 5.15);[2] מנחה (Gen. 33.11; 43.11-26 *passim*; Judg. 6.18; 1 Sam. 10.27; 2 Kgs 8.8, 9); משאת (Jer. 40.5; Amos 5.11; Est. 2.18); מתן (Prov. 18.16); מתנה (Gen. 25.6; Ezek. 46.16, 17); מתת (1 Kgs 13.7; Prov. 25.14; Ezek. 46.5, 11); שחד (1 Kgs 15.19; 2 Kgs 16.8; 20.12); and תשורה (1 Sam. 9.7). To understand these terms attention should be paid to the implied economic or social function of the actions they denote. ברכה, מתן and מתנה fall in the sphere of generalized reciprocity. These terms denote the kind of gift a father gives to his children or a friend to friends (Josh. 15.19; 1 Sam. 30.23-31; Ezek. 46.16-17; 2 Chron. 21.3). Compare also the expressions נפש ברכה (Prov. 11.25) and איש מתן (Prov. 19.6) for 'a generous person'. But as general terms they may sometimes include some of the more specialized meanings of the other terms, such as a gift of honour (2 Kgs 5.15). שחד, תשורה and מנחה fall in the category of balanced reciprocity. Although both שחד and מנחה have in time developed specialized meanings, one can still detect something of their general usage. מנחה denotes something that a socially inferior person gives to a social superior in exchange for, for example, advice (2 Kgs 8.8) or protection (2 Sam. 8.2). If the gift is not forthcoming, social sanction follows. This term, often cast into the phrase נשא מנחה ('to carry a gift') is especially used in the context of tribute paying (Judg. 3.17). The מנחה brought to Yahweh, and sometimes also expressed as 'tribute bringing' (cf. 1 Chron. 16.29) also falls into the category of balanced reciprocity. If the offering is not brought, Yahweh may retaliate through natural catastrophes. Even though he cannot accept the tribute like a king he can smell it. In

---

2. Although further investigation is necessary to confirm this supposition, it would seem that, in quite a few instances in the Hebrew Bible where it is normally translated with the abstract 'blessing', '(reciprocal) gift' would have been a more appropriate translation (e.g. Lev. 25.21; Ezek. 44.30; Joel 2.13-14; Mal. 3.10). Consider also Esau's question to Isaac in Gen. 37.36: 'He [Jacob] took away my birthright [בכרתי]; and look, now he has taken away my blessing [ברכתי]. Then he said, Have you not [at least] reserved a gift [ברכה] for me?' to which Isaac replies, '...with grain and wine I have sustained him. What then can I do, my son?' (27.37).

expressing his innocence before Saul David says, 'If it is the Lord who has stirred you up against me, may he accept ['smell'] an offering [ירח מנחה]' (1 Sam. 26.19). In the ritual texts, however, the term seems to have simply taken on the meaning of 'offering'. The meaning of שחד took an opposite direction. It seems to have had the simple meaning of a balanced reciprocal gift which could open important doors for the donor (1 Kgs 15.19; 2 Kgs 16.8), but since this kind of gift was always brought by a social inferior to a superior it was, different from the משאת, sometimes also brought in secret (Prov. 21.14) and could urge the receiver to do what he would not normally have done (Prov. 17.23). Hence in most cases the term now simply means 'bribe'. A משאת could be donated by a social superior to an inferior (2 Sam. 11.8; Est. 2.18; Ps. 141.2), but was more generally a gift by a social inferior as an expression of the donor's appreciation of the receiver's social status. This term in the end simply came to mean 'tax' (2 Chron. 24.6).

Negative reciprocity (1c), normally operating between people belonging to different communities, is a system through which one secures for oneself desirable goods belonging to someone else. Bartering in a market place is such a form of negative reciprocity. Since giver and receiver do not necessarily share the same goal, it is a form of competition, which opens the door to intense bargaining, battles of wits and cunning. Bargaining often occurs in narrative scenes. Abraham bargains not only with Ephron to secure for himself a piece of land (Gen. 23) but also with Yahweh (Gen. 15.1-4; 18.23-33). Ehud bargains with the elders of his city (Judg. 11.5-11) and Yahweh (11.30-32), and petitioners praying for divine assistance often have recourse to the same strategy (e.g. Ps. 22.2-22; 80.2-8). Folklore positively evaluates cunning in situations of negative reciprocity. Through cunning Jacob ensured for himself the majority share in the company he shared with his father-in-law (Gen. 30.37-43), and through the same cunning and double talk Ehud became a national hero (Judg. 3.19-22). The point in this kind of economy is to get the better deal for oneself by outwitting the other and by winning the competition. But the same strategy is frowned upon when the 'opponent' is actually a 'neighbour', in which case one would expect the norms of at least balanced reciprocity to apply. 'A scoundrel (אדם בליעל) and a villain (איש און)', Prov. 6.12-13 says, 'goes around with crooked speech, winking the eyes, shuffling the feet, pointing the fingers,' that is, pretending to be honest while giving secret signs to his partner (cf. 10.10; 16.30). 'Morality' has a socio-economic context.

5. Economy and Meaning 169

When certain occupations, like trading, become specialized the buyer becomes 'the other' and the rules of negative reciprocity apply. In the absence of standardized weights and measures a seller, if not watched carefully, might use one (heavier) set of weight stones when weighing what the client offered, but another (lighter) set of weights when measuring the goods provided in exchange. For some observers (with a more 'all-Israel' perspective) this practice was a deterioration of morals. Whether buyer or seller, if one was an Israelite one should treat all other Israelites as 'brothers' (cf. Lev. 19.35-36; Hos. 12.7; Amos 8.5; Prov. 20.23).

The third pattern, market exchange, presupposes allocated places to which producers bring their goods and exchange them for things they need. In subsistence economies the market is the place for bartering, and therefore for negative reciprocity, and trade. The market place is, however, not merely a place for the exchange of goods, but also for the exchange of ideas and news, and to socialize. In ancient Israel the grounds of a sanctuary, where people would go for ritual purposes, often also provided a market place. It could have been on such 'market days' that Amos delivered his 'state of the nation' speeches, which got him into trouble with the palace officials (Amos 7.10-17).

Whatever kind of reciprocal system may be in use in a particular culture, production in this system is not geared for surplus, but merely to supply in the needs of a household, gift-giving of various sorts and for bartering, and is planned accordingly. Not so in a *redistribution system*, which presupposes some form of (central) government (e.g. a chiefdom, hierocracy or monarchy) to operate. The people in authority (a chief, priest or monarch) collect produce or demand services from the members of the group and distribute the collection according to a customary pattern. It is obvious that this system cannot work unless the producers produce more than is necessary for their own subsistence. They have to produce according to the demand of the redistributer.

Owing to a variety of circumstances, a class of people not making a living from agriculture but who nevertheless have to be fed, sheltered and clothed, emerge in many subsistence societies. They are priests, the king or chief, administrators, army personnel, royal servants and artisans. Apart from the artisans this class does not produce anything. But because of their social status and political power they have the authority and means to extract their livelihood from the produce of the farming community. The logic behind a redistribution economy is that centralized control over the distribution of goods and services will ensure that everybody can make a living and will be safe even in times of shortages. For the system to function effectively, planning and administration are of crucial importance. The 'distributors' have to know how many contributors to the system there are and what they are capable of producing. They have to keep record of what comes in and goes out and to provide places of safe storage for incoming goods and to devise plans for wise distribution of the contents of the store houses. They also have to devise plans (strategies of coercion) to ensure that what is due to come in does indeed come in, and so on. They also have to ensure that the administration has a large enough labour force to provide the necessary physical infrastructure for the system to, for example, build storehouses, and to see that these structures are indeed erected. A redistribution economy thus presupposes a fairly extensive administration and the ability to keep records that can be stored for longer periods of time and are easily retrievable (e.g. in some sort of archive).

Although evaluated negatively—probably from the point of view of a reciprocal economy—the picture Samuel paints for his people of the 'ways of a king' (1 Sam. 8.11-17) contains various elements of the process by which a redistribution economy may accumulate goods and obtain services for redistribution. The texts says the king will conscript from among the ordinary folk militia, artisans and labour, levy taxes and make land grants by dispossessing some and benefiting others.

Even though a monarchy with a centralized economy probably only emerged in Israel and Judah round about the eighth century BCE, the biblical text 'dates' the addition of a full-fledged redistribution economy to the traditional reciprocal economies to the times of David and, especially, Solomon and is fairly positive about the novelty: 'Judah and Israel were as numerous as the sand by the sea; they ate and drank and were happy...and lived in safety, from Dan even to Beersheba, all of them under their vines and fig trees' (1 Kgs 4.20-25). But the authors are quick to add 'during Solomon's lifetime', since they are, with a very few exceptions, fairly negative about the kings after David and Solomon. For them, with their 'all Israel' interest, the time of David and Solomon is the 'Golden Age'. But reading their narratives carefully one detects in their discussed or presupposed culture quite a few traits typical of a redistribution economy. To start with there are the lists of bureaucrats:

5. Economy and Meaning

Office	David: 2 Sam. 8.16-18	David: 2 Sam. 20.23-26	Solomon: 1 Kgs 4.1-19
General (על־הצבא)	Joab	Joab	Benaiah
Recorder (מזכיר)	Jehoshaphat	Jehoshaphat	Jehoshaphat
Chief priests (כהנים)	Zadok and Ahimelech	Zadok and Abiathar	Azariah son of Zadok
Secretary (סופר)	Seraiah	Sheva	Elihoreph and Ahijah
Chief of the guard (הכרתי והפלתי)	Benaiah	Benaiah	
Priests (כהנים)	David's sons	Ira the Jairite	Zadok and Abiathar
Minister of serf labour (על־המס)		Adoram	Adoniram
Minister of state administration (על־הנצבים)			Azariah
The king's friend (רעה המלך)			Zabud
Minister of public works (על־הבית)			Ahishar
Directors (נצבים)			Ben-hur, Ben-deker, Ben-hesed, Ben-abinadab, Baana of Ahilud; Ben-geber, Ahinadab, Ahimaaz, Baana son of Hushai; Jehoshaphat; Shimei; Geber, one official in the land of Judah

From this table there emerges a picture of growing centralization, the prerequisite for a redistribution economy. In the first Davidic list there are, apart from the priests, a chief of the military staff, a chief of the armed guard, a record keeper and a scribe. The second list contains an extra official, namely one overseeing serf labour. Dropping the chief of the armed guard but retaining the overseer of forced labour, the Solomonic list adds 'the king's friend' (to which we shall return in Chapter 7), a chief palace official (על־הבית) and 13 officials overseen by a senior official (על־הנצבים). These officials are said to be tax collectors in 12 newly created 'districts', each of which has to supply the palace for one month in a year. Since the moon-based calendar sometimes had to add an extra month to bring that calendar in tune with the sun calendar, a thirteenth official is also appointed. The thirteenth district, while benefiting all the time, only had to contribute to the central pool every few years. This district is Judah, simply called 'the land' (הארץ). Thus, in spite of its assertion that 'all Israel' lived in happiness and quiet, it is clear from the list that Judah enjoys privileged status and that some nepotism, often a trade mark of early and simple redistribution economies, is involved.

In the absence of a monetary system the contributions made to the central pool of a redistribution economy are in kind and therefore have to be weighed and measured. In the case of the biblical text this would have been the task of the officials answering to the record keeper (מזכיר). But there is a snag: in the absence of uniform weights and measures (see Weippert 1988: 584) the royal house has its own standards, the 'royal' cubit, ephah and *bath* (cf. 2 Sam. 14.26), all being about 13 per cent in excess of the normally accepted measures (Yeivin 1969). This means that what was due to the central pool would always be roughly 13 per cent more than one would have been bargained and planned for.

What is contributed to the central pool is kept in 'storehouses' erected in the capital and at various other places. A central storehouse could be referred to by various terms. בית האספים seems to have been a fairly generic term for 'storehouse', while other terms differentiate between בית האוצר 'a treasury' (e.g. 2 Kgs 20.13); מסכנות 'storerooms for agricultural products' (e.g. 2 Chron. 32.28); בית נכאת 'storeroom for spices and fragrant oils' (e.g. 2 Kgs 20.13) and בית הכלי 'arsenal' (e.g. 2 Kgs 20.13). In later times there were also store rooms at the city gate (אספי השערים) (Neh. 12.25). Cities for the storage of agricultural products are called ערי המסכנות (e.g. 1 Kgs 9.19; 2 Chron. 17.12). This linguistic differentiation between the various kinds and locations of storing facilities indicates a fairly well-organized redistribution economy, which, in its turn, indicates the need for a large number of royal bookkeepers and administrators. Because these centrally stored supplies were so crucial for survival in times of war, storage cities were one of the chief targets of invading armies (cf. 2 Chron. 16.4). This explains the folly of Hezekiah's showing *all* his storehouses to a Babylonian

5. *Economy and Meaning*

diplomatic delegation (2 Kgs 20.12-18). Also, in times of famine the secret of the content of storehouses had to be carefully kept, especially in the presence of foreigners. It is this circumstance that provides Joseph, in charge of the Egyptian storehouses, with the golden opportunity of plausibly accusing his brothers (coming from a foreign country) of being spies (Gen. 42.9).

In a simple redistribution economy the first beneficiaries of 'state income' are, apart from the chief or king, the officials administering and defending the income. For loyal service in this regard the reward was to be exempted from certain duties or taxes (cf. Ezra 7.24), to be promoted (with more privileges attached to the new post), or to be granted land. Consider in this regard David's advice to Solomon on his accession to the throne: 'Deal loyally, however, with the sons of Barzillai the Gileadite, and let them be among those *who eat at your table*; for with such loyalty they met me when I fled from your brother Absalom' (1 Kgs 2.7). Making the recipient economically dependent upon the central authority is also a way of ensuring the recipient's future loyalty (Postgate 1971: 74). This is the reason for David's allowing Meribaal to 'eat at the king's table' (2 Sam. 9.11), by which he not only makes Meribaal indebted to him but also creates the opportunity for putting this possible aspirer to the throne under the close surveillance of the other officials 'at the king's table' (cf. 1 Kgs 10.5; Jer. 52.33). The consequences of disloyalty involved the reverse, as when Solomon sacked Joab as chief of the army and appointed Benaiah, the former head of the armed guard, in his place (1 Kgs 2.28-35).

Although in a redistributive economy the chief or king does not own the land, he has the (delegated) authority to donate (redistribute) to persons of his choice crown land, holdings without heirs and abandoned or dispossessed land. Land could be dispossessed if a person could be shown to have been unable or negligent in performing certain agreed upon obligations towards the crown, or if a person was found guilty of treason (Postgate 1971: 74, 82, 85). This take-and-give practice, called *našû-nadanu* after Assyrian sources, was well known in the ancient Near East. In the biblical text the authority to redistribute land only gradually accrues to the chief or king. In 1 Sam. 22.7-8 Saul rebukes his officials (הנצבים עליו) for not having told him about the friendship between David and Jonathan: '...will the son of Jesse give every one of you fields and vineyards, will he make you all commanders of thousands and commanders of hundreds? Is that why all of you have conspired against me?' Saul suspects David of having promised his officials a redistribution economy, which implies that Saul himself is still practising some form of reciprocal economy. And, indeed, soon we find David changing the system when he donates land to Meribaal, the son of Jonathan (2 Sam. 9.7). And when Meribaal's servant cunningly convinces David that Meribaal has been plotting against him, David promptly dispossesses him and donates the land to Ziba (2 Sam. 16.1-4), only to share the same land between Meribaal and Ziba a little later (2 Sam. 19.25-31). These texts suggest a fundamental departure from the property rights (inalienable allotted land) obtaining in a reciprocal subsistence economy, a departure which provides the outline for the plot of the Naboth narrative (1 Kgs 21).

The logic of a redistribution economy is that of ensuring the just redistribution of services and goods among the population and, especially, combating utter pauperization in times of crisis, when the central storehouses can provide. This is the logic of the measures Joseph takes in Gen. 41.53-57. When, during the Aramaean siege of Samaria, a famine broke out in the city and two women approached the king asking for help, he thought that they were begging for food from the royal stores. Hence his reply, 'No! Let the Lord help you. How can I help you? From the threshing floor or from the wine press?' (2 Kgs 6.26-27), that is, the stores are empty and you know it well; you also know that there is no new harvest forthcoming.

As long as a group has some way of negatively sanctioning an incompetent or unjust central authority ordinary people have some safeguard against corruption. But when the central authority is a monarch whose continuity is guaranteed by lineal succession, common people are extremely vulnerable. The only way to get rid of an unwanted central government then is by the assassination of the symbol of central authority, the king. This is one of the reasons for the many assassinations of royalty related in the Hebrew Bible (e.g. 1 Kgs 15.27-29; 16.9-11, 17-23; 2 Kgs 9–10; 11.13-16). But royalty, of course, knows this and ensures through *unequal* distribution that a crowd of well-to-do elite, standing to lose too much to turn against the monarch, surrounds the throne. Even the queen of Sheba, says 1 Kgs 10.5-6, was flabbergasted at the sight of the food on Solomon's table, 'the *seating of his officials*, and the attendance of his servants'. Of course, the elite around the monarch would envy the persons in higher positioned seats at the 'king's table'. That is why Prov. 15.17 says, 'Better is a dinner of

5. Economy and Meaning

vegetables where love is than a fatted ox and hatred with it' (וְשִׂנְאָה־בוֹ, quite literally 'with hatred in it': that is, the hatred of the hand that passes the meat contaminates it).

Apart from providing security in times of trouble, a redistributive economy also enables the provision of effective protection. Because tasks can be centrally planned, funded and executed, a much better and strategically planned safety network can be set up. Of Solomon 2 Chron. 8.4-6 says that he built Tadmor, Baalath, Upper and Lower Beth-horon, storage towns, fortified cities with walls, gates and bars, and towns for chariots and cavalry in all the land of his dominion. The labour to construct such places of safety and the provision of militia are, of course, at least partly the beneficiaries, the ordinary folk. That is why censuses had to be held (to get information for the purpose of planning—the task of the overseer of the palace; cf. 2 Sam. 24) and why one of the high officials at the king's table is the overseer of forced labour. The narrators tell of conscripted forced labour, 30,000 men in total, who worked in shifts of 10,000 a month in the Lebanon. To these are added 70,000 labourers and 80,000 stonecutters in the hill country. And these labourers were overseen by 3,300 supervisors (1 Kgs 5.13-16; cf. 1 Kgs 9.15-19). Although the narrator states that none of these conscripts was an 'Israelite' (מִבְּנֵי יִשְׂרָאֵל, 1 Kgs 9.20-22), in an earlier statement on conscript labour it is said that these labourers were indeed recruited out of 'all Israel' (מִכָּל־יִשְׂרָאֵל, 1 Kgs 5.13).[3]

The burden such a centre of a redistribution can become is indicated by the lavishness of the list of items said to have been daily consumed in Solomon's palace (1 Kgs 4.22-23, 26-28). This list is, of course, inflated and reminds one of the ironic Sumerian letter by a fictitious King Gilgamesh commanding a vassal immediately to send him '70,000 black horses with white stripes, 100,000 mares whose hides have markings like wild tree roots, 40,000 continually gambolling miniature calves, 50,000 teams of dappled mules, 50,000 fine calves with well-turned hooves and horns intact' (Foster 1995: 2463). The Solomonic list is, however, not meant to be laughed at but to exhibit the prestige of the king (cf. 1 Kgs 4.24-25). And that is not even all. There was also the straw and barley for his thousands of horses (1 Kgs 4.26-

---

3. In Shea's interpretation of some of the Samaria ostraca (Shea 1985) the Samarian officials, apart from keeping record of the incoming levies of agricultural produce, also recorded the names of ordinary people who had been conscripted to render services to the king.

28), and, so the narrative continues, apart from the donation of a number of Galilean villages, Solomon's annual payment to Hiram for goods delivered consisted of 20,000 *cors* of wheat as food for his household, and 20 *cors* of fine oil (1 Kgs 5.11). Just how expensive this was will become clear when, in the next section, we shall pay attention to the value of the consumption of wheat and barley.

Somebody had to foot the enormous bill. Even though their contribution would have been substantial, not everything was supplied by the peasant farmers. There were other means of securing income and labour, such as, first, tolls from passing caravans, taking booty from conquered nations (1 Chron. 26.27; 2 Chron. 14.13; 20.25; 28.8—not mentioned in the book of Kings), forcing them to pay annual tributes (2 Kgs 3.4) and making slaves out of prisoners of war (2 Sam. 12.31; Gelb 1973). Secondly, since the central power in a redistributive economy owns the entire land and has the authority to grant and redistribute it as the need arises, it normally has land at its disposal to utilize for the production of additional supplies and combating budget deficits. Thirdly, international trade also secured (with an inbuilt system of negative reciprocity) goods not produced or manufactured in one's own area of jurisdiction. The authorities featuring in Hebrew Bible narratives exploit all three possibilities.

Of King Uzziah of Judah, for example, it is said that he made war against the Philistines, Arabs and Meunites and made the Ammonites pay tribute, that he built defensive towers in Jerusalem and in the wilderness, hewed out many cisterns for his large herds, both in the Shephelah and in the plain, and that he had farmers and vine-dressers in the hills and in the fertile lands (2 Chron. 26.6-10; cf. Rainey 1982; and compare the reference to the royal wine-press in Zech. 14.10). Such royal pastoral and agricultural holdings were sometimes huge concerns that could contribute quite substantially to the redistributable income of the land (Dar 1986: 12-16). The large numbers of jar fragments discovered in the Judaean area carrying the *lmlk* ('belonging to the king') inscription, or the royal winged sun and rosette emblems (Weippert 1988: 577, 606-607) bear witness to this contribution to the often mentioned royal treasuries (cf. 1 Kgs 14.26; 15.18; 2 Kgs 16.8; 18.15).

International trade also plays a role in the narratives. While international traders are said to have traversed Palestine since the days of Jacob (Gen. 37.25), it is again King Solomon who is said to have been a keen player in international trade:

5. *Economy and Meaning* 177

> The weight of gold that came to Solomon in one year was six hundred sixty-six talents of gold, besides that which came from the traders and from the business of the merchants, and from all the kings of Arabia and the governors of the land (1 Kgs 10.14).

Of him it is said that he had a harbour built at Ezion-geber (1 Kgs 9.26) in which he had a fleet that functioned jointly with the Phoenician fleet (renowned for its international trafficking [Ezek. 27]) and that ensured a regular supply of gold, silver, ivory, apes, and peacocks (1 Kgs 10.21-22). Also that he was the middle-man organizing horse trade between the Egyptians and the Hittites and Aramaeans (1 Kgs 10.28-29). Apart from Solomon, and quite in general, the Persian king discovers in his records that 'Jerusalem has had mighty kings who ruled over the whole province Beyond the River, to whom tribute, custom, and toll were paid' (Ezra 4.20).

At least in picturing the 'Golden Age', the authors represent the introduction of a redistributive economy and of its agent, the court and elite, in a positive manner. It is this age that is held up as an example of prosperity and glamour. What is said in a negative sense about this age is said from a purely cultic point of view. For the rest the palace is a place of splendour. This is also the picture in the so-called prophetic books, only this time the evaluation of the palace is different. The criterion here is not status and prestige, typical of a redistribution economy, but economic justice from the point of view of reciprocity, as we shall show shortly.

Disposing of income in a redistributive economy may be variously motivated (Haviland 1996: 200): to ensure loyalty on the side of the agent's supporters by securing for them an adequate standard of living, to establish alliances outside the agent's territory, or simply to maintain a position of superiority by a display of wealth. As examples of the first motivation one may refer to David's treatment of Meribaal and Achish's donation of the town of Ziklag to David in exchange for services rendered (1 Sam. 27.1-6). As an example of the second motivation one may refer to Solomon's donation of 20 villages in Galilee to Hiram (1 Kgs 9.11; cf. also 1 Sam. 18.22-27). In a society in which *accumulation* of goods does not symbolize prestige, ceremonious distribution becomes the only means of demonstrating status. This is the economic background for the spendthrift royalty and elite that one encounters in the pages of the Hebrew Bible. Esther 1.7 says of the king's feast, 'drinks were served in golden goblets, goblets of different kinds, and the royal wine was lavished according to the bounty of the king (המלך כיד)'. The parties thrown at the palace even became a criterion for display; hence the expression 'a feast like a king's feast' (2 Sam. 13.27—LXX). This public display of economic status forms the backdrop of the parties thrown by the rich, to which Amos 6.1-6 refers:

> those who lie on beds of ivory, and lounge on their couches, and eat lambs from the flock, and calves from the stall; who sing idle songs to the sound of the harp, and like David improvise on instruments of music; who drink wine from bowls, and anoint themselves with the finest oils (cf. Isa. 5.12).

The need for public display of status is the backdrop for the wardrobes of the women of Jerusalem stacked with anklets, headbands, crescents, pendants, bracelets, scarfs; headdresses, armlets, sashes, perfume boxes, amulets; signet rings and nose rings, festal robes, mantles, cloaks, handbags, garments of gauze, linen garments, turbans, and veils (Isa. 3.18-23). As a sign of their changed status after the judgment they will display stench instead of perfume, a rope instead of a sash, baldness instead of well-set hair, a binding of sackcloth instead of rich robe, shame instead of beauty (Isa. 3.24).

If public display is a means of expressing status and one has to keep up with the Joneses, it is obvious that the elite's demand for goods will, in this kind of economic system, constantly increase, and that the pressure on those who have to supply the redistributable goods will increase accordingly. This is the context of Amos's accusation against the notables of Samaria of living in houses of hewn stone while trampling on the poor and taking from them levies of grain (Amos 5.11). And Mic. 2.1-2 again castigates the elite of Jerusalem for oppressing proprietor and household (גבר וביתו), owner and inheritance (איש ונחלתו). Because of an increased demand on the side of the distributing agent and/or because of a crop failure, suppliers may fall behind in paying their due. For such people there are not many options. They may try getting a loan from the agent, for which they have to pledge something (e.g. a gown, a head of cattle or their farm), or they may offer to work off the debt. Interest on loans had always been high in the ancient Near East, so that, depending on the success of the next harvest, a debtor might get into still deeper economic trouble. Where there is no 'public' check on the redistributing authority and the measures it may resort to in order to secure its due, all sorts of malpractice may easily develop. Job 24.3 says of the godless, 'They drive away the donkey of the orphan; they

5. *Economy and Meaning*

take the widow's ox for a pledge.' Amos 2.8 accuses the elite of Samaria of laying down on 'garments taken in pledge'. And Hab. 2.6 addresses the Assyrian tyrants with, 'You who heap up what is not your own! How long will you load yourselves with goods taken in pledge'. In Neh. 5.3 some desperate people protest, 'We are having to pledge our fields, our vineyards, and our houses in order to get grain during the famine' while others complain, '...we are forcing our sons and daughters to be slaves, and some of our daughters have been ravished; we are powerless, and our fields and vineyards now belong to others' (Neh. 5.5). It is in an effort to check such malpractice that Deuteronomy stipulates:

> No one shall take a mill or an upper millstone in pledge, for that would be taking a life in pledge. When you make your neighbour a loan of any kind, you shall not go into the house to take the pledge. You shall wait outside, while the person to whom you are making the loan brings the pledge out to you. If the person is poor, you shall not sleep in the garment given you as the pledge. You shall give the pledge back by sunset, so that your neighbor may sleep in the cloak and bless you; and it will be to your credit before the Lord your God. You shall not take a widow's garment in pledge (Deut. 24.10-13, 17).

It is this kind of *economic* situation that forms the context of Amos's plea to 'let justice roll down like waters, and righteousness like an everflowing stream' (Amos 5.24), and that led to the insistence in the later laws that at least fellow 'Israelites' should not be charged interest (Exod. 22.25; Lev. 25.36-37; Deut. 23.19-20) and their debts be written off after seven years (Exod. 21.2; Deut. 15.12, 18).

In the light of the foregoing discussion one may say that the cultural world in the text of the Hebrew Bible displays a mixed economy, namely of reciprocity and redistribution. Customs operative in one system do not easily translate into those of another system, and may even obtain a completely different function if 'transplanted'. For instance, the practice of ritual gift giving in a reciprocal economy may become ritual bribing in a redistribution economy. In a redistribution economy a gift from a social inferior to a superior neither functions as a public form of social security, nor does it symbolize good neighbourliness or express the prestige of the donor. In the distributive context a gift indicates the donor's degree of *dependence* on the recipient. The more important the request or the person to whom it is addressed the bigger the bribe. The Hebrew Bible, whose ethics is closely linked with a reciprocal economy, frequently mentions and condemns bribery (cf. Exod. 18.21, 23.8; Deut. 16.19; 1 Sam. 8.3; 12.3; Pss. 15.5; 26.10; Prov. 15.27; 17.8, 23; Isa. 1.23; 5.23; Ezek. 22.12; Amos 5.12; Mic. 3.11; 7.3).

The situation unfolding in the pages of the Hebrew Bible gets even worse when foreign creditors come on the scene, that is, foreign conquerers demanding a tribute from the existing redistributive agents in Samaria and Jerusalem, especially because of the negative sanctioning following the suppliers' inability to collect the demanded tribute or efforts to shed the foreign parasite. Consider 2 Kgs 17.3-4: Shalmaneser of Assyria makes Hoshea of Israel his vassal, who then pays him tribute. But then

> the king of Assyria found treachery in Hoshea; for he had sent messengers to King So of Egypt, and offered no tribute to the king of Assyria, as he had done year by year; therefore the king of Assyria confined him and imprisoned him. Then the king of Assyria invaded all the land and came to Samaria; for three years he besieged it.

This, says the narrator, was the beginning of the end of the kingdom of Israel. Except for a few notes on the devastating effects of the tributes extracted by the Assyrian and Babyonian overlords on the treasury in Jerusalem, very little is said on how these tributes and gifts were collected (cf. 1 Kgs 14.25-26; 2 Kgs 16.6-8; 18.14-16). The texts do, however, give some impression of the Persian system. They mention three kinds of taxes due by conquered nations, namely the *mandattu* (Persian: *midda*; מנדה, Ezra 4.13, or מדה, Ezra 4.20), the *biltu* (בלו, Ezra 4.13), and the *ilku* (הלך, Ezra 4.13). The *mandattu*, temporarily stored in the temple treasury, was paid in silver or in kind and later transported to the Persian capital (Ezra 7.24). The *biltu* was a kind of poll tax 'paid' by rendering services as required, while the *ilku* was a property tax (Schaper 1995: 537-38). The revenue of the latter two taxes seems to have partly accrued to the king and to have been partly redistributed among the local officials. These officials consisted of the temple hierarchy, overseen by two Persian officials and their personnel, who would have cashed in most of these redistributed goods. The senior Persian overseer was what the Babylonians called the *reš šarri bel piqitti*, 'the one in charge of the king's chest'. The second figure carried the Akkadian title of *gitepatu(m)*, an Iranian loan word, originally referring to the overseer of the royal livestock, but in the Persian empire to the person responsible for assessing and melting the metal contributions to the

5. *Economy and Meaning* 181

king's chest (Schaper 1995: 533). All three taxes had to be paid by all the citizens, while the temple personnel, typical of a redistribution economy, were exempted from some (Ezra 7.24). But the royal tax was not all that was extracted from the peasants. In addition they had to pay the תרומה (Neh. 10.39; Heb. v. 40), a 10 per cent tax imposed by the temple officials for their own sustenance. Of this tax, consisting of fruit, grain, wine, and oil, the firstlings of cattle and flock, 90 per cent accrued to the temple personnel themselves. And on top of that there were also services to be rendered, such as supplying the temple with firewood (Neh. 10.34-39; Heb. vv. 35-40). Given the poor agricultural conditions described in the book of Malachi it is no wonder to hear the people complain:

> We are having to pledge our fields, our vineyards, and our houses in order to get grain during the famine... We have to borrow money on our fields and vineyards to pay the king's tax... And we are forcing our sons and daughters to be slaves, and some of our daughters have been ravished; we are powerless, and our fields and vineyards now belong to others (Neh. 5.1-5).

The priests and other religious functionaries were all but happy with their share. In Zechariah 11 the 'shepherd' of God's flock gives up his task by symbolically breaking his staff. On this the flock acknowledged his worth and paid him his wages: 30 pieces of silver. Unhappy with their evaluation of his worth the shepherd casts the silver to the 'melter' (יוצר), that is, the *gitepatu(m)* (11.13), indicating that the amount could just as well have been added to the king's taxes (see Schaper 1995: 530).

The economic system of redistribution is also reflected in the concepts and metaphors employed in the religious language of the Hebrew Bible. Yahweh is, first, pictured as the one who owns a heavenly storehouse (אוצר, Deut. 28.12), in which he stores wind (Ps. 135.7), rain (Deut. 28.12) snow, hail (Job 38.22) for distribution. He is, secondly, a land granter. The whole territory of 'Israel' belongs to him, and he has the authority to dispossess present 'owners' and redistribute the land among his favourites. Consider Deut 9.5, 'because of the wickedness of these nations the Lord your God is dispossessing (מורישם) them before you' (cf. also Deut. 7.1; 12.29). He is, thirdly, a redistributer of booty. Thus, in the oracle against Tyre, 'Her merchandise and her wages will be dedicated to the Lord; her profits will not be stored or hoarded, but her merchandise will supply abundant food and fine clothing for those who live in the presence of the Lord' (Isa. 23.18). Fourthly, because Yahweh is Israel's only 'true' king (Judg. 8.23) and the priests his officials, a 10 per cent levy is to be brought to his 'storehouse' (בית האוצר) to sustain the temple service (cf. Lev. 2.30-32). But not only the officials benefit from his redistribution of goods. In his kingdom redistribution is practised according to the true logic of the system, namely to feed the hungry and vulnerable (cf. Deut. 14.28-29; 26.12-15). Fifthly, when this levy is not delivered he may resort to all sorts of coercion (cf. Mal. 3.10). Finally, as a just redistributer, bribery plays no role in his kingdom (Deut. 10.17; cf. 1 Chron. 19.7).

4. Consumption

As we have already pointed out, while the biblical text pictures cattle and donkeys as a source of labour and transport, goats, sheep and cattle serve as providers of milk, meat, fat, skin, hair and wool, all of which are either consumable or useful for the manufacturing of clothing, curtains and mats. Animals were, of course, worth more living than dead. While grazing in the fields or on the terraces their dung fertilized the soil. But in spite of this positive function, dung on the field came to stand for 'judgment' (2 Kgs 9.37; Ps. 83.12; Jer. 8.2; 9.22). Flocks also were a form of 'banking'. Farmers traded some of their agricultural products for sheep and goats, which could be kept for longer than wheat, barley and wine. As the necessity arose they could then trade some of this 'banked capital' for other products, such as farming implements. In later days, when land could be bought, cattle, sheep and goats also provided the 'capital' to acquire land. Proverbs 27.25-27 urges the hearers to look well after their flocks, because

> When the grass is gone, and new growth appears, and the herbage of the mountains is gathered, the lambs (כבשׂים) will provide your clothing, and the goats the price of a field (מחיר שׂדה); there will be enough goats' milk (חלב עזים) for your food, for the food of your household and nourishment for your servant-girls.

Milk, mostly sheep's milk and goat's milk, and its products, curds and cheese, formed part of the Palestinian peasant's daily diet and were for that reason highly valued. Milk (חלב) and/or curds (חמאה) taken without or together with honey (דבשׁ) or honeycomb (יער, צוף־דבשׁ, צוף) occurs as a sought-after (cf. Job 20.17), nourishing and tasty (Cant. 4.11) dish put before guests (Gen. 18.8; 2 Sam. 17.29). Like the frequently mentioned combined drink of 'milk and honey', eating curds with honey symbolizes prosperity and well-being (Isa. 7.15, 22). When Deut. 32.13-14 says that Yahweh fed Israel with 'produce of the field...nursed him with honey from the crags, with oil from flinty rock; curds from the herd, and milk from the flock, with fat of lambs and rams; Bashan bulls and goats, together with the choicest wheat' it implies therefore that Yahweh not only looked well after them but that he treated them like guests of honour. To indicate a time of prosperity one could say that you get milk for free (Isa. 55.1), or sip milk from the udder (Isa. 60.16). Or you may use the image of udders dripping with milk and cisterns filled with wine to the extent that the meadows in the hills flow with milk and mountains drip with wine (Joel 3.18; Heb. 4.18).

But milk does not only feature as a drink. It is also used in comparisons for whiteness (e.g. Gen 49.12; Lam. 4.7) as well as in sexual metaphors. Contemplating the process by which he was created (Job 10.8-12), Job uses a milk-and-curd-cheese metaphor to describe how he was conceived and became a foetus, 'Did you [Yahweh] not pour me out (תתיכני, that is, *let me be poured out* in the form of semen) like milk (וכגבנה תקפיאני) and curdle me (i.e. into a foetus) like cheese (לחלב תתיכני)?' In 21.22-26 Job describes the fortune of some people compared to the misfortune of others. The fortunate man's 'buckets' (עטיניו, 'testicles') are 'full of milk' (חלב) (i.e. he is virile) and 'the marrow of his bones moist' (i.e. he has vitality), while the other man dies without having 'eaten' (cf. Prov. 30.20) of what is good (ולא־אכל בטובה; note the ב plus *feminine* of טוב, only occurring here). One is reminded here of the idealized he-man of Ezek. 23.20, whose 'members were like those of donkeys, and whose emission was like that of stallions', referred to earlier. Somewhat more problematic, but not less informative, is the metaphor for sexual intercourse in Job 29.6. Having just described the good times (autumn weather) he knew when (a) God had still been on his side and (b) his *children* were still around him (29.45), he continues, '[W]hen my steps (הליכי, a *hapax*) were washed (רחץ) with milk, and the rock poured out for/toward me (עמדי, cf. LXX ὄρη μου, 'my rock') streams of oil' (29.6). For the metaphor of a rock for a wife/ woman, on which Eliade has written extensively, compare Isa. 51.1. Job thinks of the times when he and his wife still had a healthy sexual life. Finally, in Cant. 5.12 the girl says to her lover, 'His eyes are like doves beside springs of water, washed in milk (בחלב רחצות), waiting for the right time (?) (יְשָׁבוֹת־מִלֵּאת)' (Cant. 5.12). Although the meaning of the second half of the sentence is not clear, the idea of 'washing in milk' of Job 29.6 also occurs here. Since eyes that are '(like) doves' symbolize readiness for the sexual partner the extension of the metaphor of 'washing in milk' for the sexual act is logical.

Although animals were valued for their labour and produce they were also slaughtered for their meat (cf. 1 Sam. 16.20; 25.11; 2 Sam. 6.19; Isa. 22.13). Even though the skins of slaughtered animals are said to have been processed for building material (Exod. 25.5), bags for the storage and transport of water (Gen. 21.14), milk (Judg. 4.19) and wine (1 Sam. 1.24), and into clothes (Lev. 11.32) and leather articles, like sandals (Ezek. 16.10) and girdles (2 Kgs 1.8), as a raw product they do not feature in biblical imagery. With meat the picture is, however, different.

The expression 'bread and meat' means 'nourishment' (1 Kgs 17.6; Ps. 78.20). In hard times even donkey's meat could serve as food. 2 Kgs 6.25 says, 'As the siege continued, famine in Samaria became so great that a donkey's head was sold for eighty shekels of silver...' nearly three times the price of a slave (Exod. 21.32). The meat of fattened animals symbolizes status and wealth (1 Kgs 1.19; Prov. 15.17). To serve a guest with fattened meat is therefore a token of hospitality and of the host's appreciation of the guest (1 Sam. 28.22-25). The meat of young animals also features as a delicacy (Gen. 27.9; Amos 6.4). In Weippert's interpretation of the reference to עגלים מתוך מרבק in Amos 6.4 (Weippert 1985a: 7-9) she argues that the Hebrew expression means 'a calf tied to its mother' and refers to the ancient custom of tying a calf to the mother's front leg, where it could still be with the mother but unable to reach the udder. If this interpretation is correct, the wealthy people of Samaria are accused of slaughtering a calf that is still being weaned. All in all the symbolism of meat is favourable and positive.

In spite of this positive attitude towards meat the slaughtering of an animal is looked upon as brutal. Hence the metaphoric use of 'slaughtering' for acts of particularly brutal and cold-blooded killing (e.g. Judg. 12.6; 2 Kgs 10.7, 14; Jer. 41.7; 52.10; Ezek. 16.21). Micah 3.3 also uses this image to picture the brutality of the Judaean elite. They 'eat the flesh of my people, flay their skin off them, break their bones in pieces, and chop them up like meat in a kettle, like flesh in a cauldron'. The image of a kettle of meat may serve to symbolize negative or positive experiences. A walled city may be said to be a 'pot'. To say 'this

5. *Economy and Meaning* 185

city is the pot, and we are the meat' (Ezek. 11.3) is to say that it will be only a matter of time before it will get too hot in the 'pot'. But to put choice meat in a kettle, kindle a fire and let it simmer (Ezek. 24.3-5) is to invest a lot. To then find out that the kettle (the city of Jerusalem) was rusty (impure) is to have wasted a costly and highly valued commodity (Ezek. 23.6). Not to spoil the meat, it has to be taken out and the kettle put over a huge fire to cook off the rust (Ezek. 23.9-12).

The importance of grain, wine and oil is already indicated by the frequently occurring sequence of grain, fresh wine and fresh oil (דגן תירוש ויצהר), e.g. Deut. 28.51; 2 Chron. 32.28; Neh. 5.11; 10.39; 13.5; 13.12; Jer. 31.12; Joel 2.19) or simply grain and new wine (e.g. Deut. 33.28, 2 Kgs 18.32, 2 Chron. 32.28, Isa. 36.17, Hos. 7.14; Joel 1.10; Zech. 9.17). 'Wine, oil and grain' came to be a shorthand for, or symbol of, 'sustenance' (so also in the Samaria and Arad ostraca [Weippert 1988: 635]). To have stored up enough 'wine, oil, and grain' for all eventualities was not only wise (Prov. 10.5; 30.25), but could even save one's life. A mere sentence, 'Do not kill us, for we have stores of wheat, barley, oil, and honey hidden in the fields' (Jer. 41.8) convinced Ishmael not to kill the speakers.

The importance or scarcity of a particular resource or the amount of effort that goes into securing it often causes people to assign symbolic status value to it. Already the fact that wheat flour, oil and wine constitute an offering pleasing to Yahweh (Lev. 23.13) is an indication of their symbolic value. Their symbolic and status value are confirmed by the contexts in which these commodities are mentioned.

While דגן (sometimes also שבר) refers to 'grain' in general, wheat (חטים) and wheat flour (קמח) were, and still are among present-day Palestinian peasants, the ideal grain type for baking bread. The value attached to wheat is indicated by the fact that it constituted a popular currency in trade (cf. 1 Kgs 5.11; Heb. v. 25) and for tribute (2 Chron. 27.5). Barley (שערה) took second place and would only be used for baking bread when the wheat crops failed or when too little was left after trade and tax to feed the household (Turkowski 1969: 110). This preference is reflected by lists of commodities in which wheat always takes precedence over barley (cf. Deut. 8.8, 2 Sam. 17.28, 2 Chron. 2.10, 15; Isa. 28.25; Jer. 41.8; Ezek. 4.9; etc.), as well as by the price of these commodities (2 Kgs 7.1). But more than that, references to wheat (and wheat flour) always imply status, while references to the eating of barley imply poverty. Thus, Yahweh supplies the faithful with wheat

(Ps. 81.17); humans offer wheat to Yahweh (Exod. 29.2; Judg. 6.19; 1 Sam. 28.24); hosts present bread made of wheat flour to important guests (Gen. 18.6; 1 Sam. 28.24); and to have little wheat flour left is to be on the brink of poverty (1 Kgs 17.12). By contrast, in times of need people eat bread baked from barley flour. It is during a famine that a man brings Elisha and his followers some barley bread (2 Kgs 4.38-44). When the Midianite raids have completely impoverished Israel (Judg. 6.6) and Gideon confronts them with his 300 men, one of his men dreams of a barley bread that tumbled into the Midianite camp (7.13). It is therefore significant that the impoverished widow Naomi arrives in Bethlehem at the beginning of the *barley* harvest (Ruth 1.22), while the plot of the story reaches its climax directly after the *wheat* harvest (2.23). It is, moreover, only during the threshing and winnowing of the wheat harvest that miracles or important things happen, or God appears to people (1 Sam. 6.13; 1 Chron. 21.20; cf. 1 Sam. 12.17; Judg. 15.1). What exactly the relationship is between barley and sexuality is not clear, but there seems to be a connection (cf. Ezek. 13.19; Hos. 3.2), which might also be part of the background of Boaz's gift to Ruth after her visit to him on the threshing floor and everything that happened there (Ruth 3.15).

Since olive oil, in spite of, or perhaps because of, the effort needed to manufacture it (Weippert 1988: 636), became a sought-after export product (Ezek. 27.17) and had a high symbolic value. Ezekiel 16.13, reminding Israel in metaphorical language of Yahweh's care for her, mentions olive oil together with other sought-after commodities, 'You were adorned with *gold* and *silver*, while your clothing was of *fine linen*, rich fabric, and *embroidered* cloth. You had *choice flour* and *honey* and *oil* for food.' And when Hezekiah wants to show off his status to his Babylonian visitors (so Isa. 39.2), he shows them 'his treasure house, the *silver*, the *gold*, the *spices*, the *precious oil*, his whole *armoury*, all that was found in his storehouses'.

The case with wine is somewhat different. It was valued in a positive as well as in a negative way. On the negative side is the experience expressed in Prov. 23.29-31:

> Who has woe? Who has sorrow? Who has strife? Who has complaining? Who has wounds without cause? Who has redness of eyes? Those who linger late over wine, those who keep trying mixed wines. Do not look at wine when it is red, when it sparkles in the cup and goes down smoothly. At the last it bites like a serpent, and stings like an adder.

Using this (literal) experience as a metaphor for suffering Ps. 60.3 says, 'You [Yahweh] have made your people suffer hard things; you have given us wine to drink that made us reel'. And to describe the confusion and anarchy in the ranks of the Jerusalemite religious elite Isa. 28.7 says, 'These also reel with wine and stagger with strong drink; the priest and the prophet reel with strong drink, they are confused with wine, they stagger with strong drink; they err in vision, they stumble in giving judgment.'

More common is the association between wine and judgment. Because the ancient farmers did not have sophisticated filtering equipment, stored wine naturally formed a sediment. When such a wine jar was not handled carefully or when a jug was emptied too quickly and completely, the sediment got mixed with the wine. To picture a thorough punishment Ps. 75.8 says, 'In the hand of the Lord there is a cup with foaming wine, well mixed; he will pour a draught from it, and all the wicked of the earth shall drain it down to the dregs.' There is a suggestion of deceit in this image. 'Mixed wine', that is, spiced wines and not wine mixed with water (cf. Isa. 1.22), was valued as something special (Ps. 75.8; Prov. 9.2, 5; Cant. 5.1; 8.2). The wicked will therefore be very pleased to be offered this wine. But when they turn the cup upside down to gulp the last of the tasty stuff they will swallow the sediment as well.

On the positive side, when 'the wine dries up, the vine languishes, all the merry-hearted sigh' (Isa. 24.7), or when grain, new wine and oil lack (Hag. 1.11), or the harvest fails (Jer. 8.20; Joel 1.10), things have taken a turn for the worse. But prosperity is when 'your barns [are] filled with plenty, and your vats...bursting with wine' (Prov. 3.10), when the threshing floors are full of grain and the vats overflow with wine and oil (Joel 2.24), or when the one who ploughs 'overtakes the one who reaps, and the treader of grapes the one who sows the seed, when the mountains drip sweet wine, and the hills flow with it' (Amos 9.13; cf. Lev. 26.5). Consequently the shorthand for merry-making is 'wine and oil' (Prov. 21.17; cf. Amos 6.6) or meat and mixed wine (Prov. 9.2). To live a good life is to be wine that has been handled with care. Hence the saying, 'Moab has been at ease from his youth, settled like wine on its dregs; he has not been emptied from vessel to vessel, nor has he gone into exile; therefore his flavor has remained and his aroma is unspoiled' (Jer. 48.11). Even lovers employ wine imagery.

Love is better than wine (Cant. 1.2; 4.10) and sexual pleasure is wine taken with milk (5.1) or spiced wine (8.2; cf. 7.2).

5. Conclusion

The tour through the economic world of the biblical text, which could certainly have been extended considerably, shows that the biblical text is deeply embedded into *specific* economic contexts of production, distribution and consumption. Knowledge of these discussed or implied economic and value contexts of terms, expressions, or customs may, first, assist the reader in understanding particular texts as expressions of economic functions. Such knowledge may, secondly, assist her in finding the involved cultural *meaning* of terms, and, thirdly, in interpreting metaphors involving the economic systems implied by the text.

To isolate 'economy' for the purpose of discussion should, however, not lead to an atomistic perspective. The reciprocal economic systems discussed in the chapter are deeply involved with particular social systems (see Chapter 7) while the redistributive economy presupposes the existence of particular political systems (Chapter 8). At the same time we have referred to certain social sanctions implied by the various economic systems. Moreover, we have shown that similes and metaphors derived from the various economic systems *functioned* in domains like social organization and religion. Always to remind oneself of the interrelatedness of the various domains that make up the particular culture is, therefore, of the utmost importance.

Chapter 6

TECHNOLOGY AND MEANING

The discussion of the economic domain of biblical culture has reminded readers of the integrated and dynamic nature of a complete cultural system. This reminder is even more necessary in a discussion of technology as part of culture. Technology, human inventiveness in coping with the problems encountered in making a living and making life more bearable, predictable and safe, is closely integrated with the economic, social and political facets of culture, and also involves art and religion, while it has a notable effect on cosmological views. That technology is treated here as a separate 'domain' is merely for the sake of convenience, namely to afford the opportunity of focusing on certain techniques, crafts, tools and other manufactured goods. In this way the function of technological development as well as the *meaning* of some manufactured items may be foregrounded. Even though there are texts dealing specifically with 'technology' they are few. To facilitate a discussion on the topic we have for that reason to rely more on extra-biblical knowledge of the times between the Iron and the Roman ages.

1. *Agricultural Technology*

A farm measured between 10 and 16 hectares, of which roughly 10–20 per cent was cultivated, depending on the soil type and the availability of water (Dar 1986: 4-6). On such farmsteads archaeologists have found evidence that the farmers had mastered several kinds of technology. Apart from the know-how of quarrying stone for building purposes, they had tools and equipment to assist them in their labour, such as chisels for stone dressing, ploughs, harrows, ropes, hoes, sickles, shovels, forks, brooms, threshing beaters, pruning knives, stretchers that fitted on the backs of donkeys, bridles and bits for steering donkeys, mules (and horses), wagons, yokes, goads and oil and wine presses (cf. Turkowski 1969: 25-27, 28-32; 103-108; Dar 1986: 4). For the manufacturing and repair of most of their more sophisticated equipment farmers had to turn to some 'specialist' in the area (Turkowski 1969: 28, 101), normally one of the farmers in the vicinity. They also had various human-made storing facilities, like silos for grain (Turkowski 1969: 109), jars for wine and oil, and rock-hewn cisterns for water. Apart from terracing, farmers also had knowledge of the damming of streams and the construction of canals for irrigation purposes and for diverting flood water to cisterns and dams (Dar 1986: 57). What holds true for the small subsistence farmer is also true of larger holdings and especially the state farms, for the methods of production and the tools used on these farms did not differ from those of the smaller households. The difference between the small farmer and the bigger holdings lies in the size of things. On one of the larger farms of the Persian period Dar (1986: 11), for example, found an oil press over two metres in diameter and the press beam nearly six metres long. A farm at Ḥirbet Shehadah in Samaria had no less than three threshing floors, while a nearby farm at el-Marah sported threshing floors with a total surface of 500 square metres (Dar 1986: 19). It is also clear that, whereas one of the farmers in the area normally had special knowledge of some facet of farming, especially on the technical side of it, in later days trained artisans were appointed on the royal farms for various tasks. Nevertheless, the technologies involved remained basically the same until the Roman period. A few examples may illustrate the role of technology in linguistic expressions and literary imagery.

The animal most commonly used for transport was the donkey, while the upper classes and military also employed the mule and the horse. To steer these animals a bridle (רסן) and a bit (מתג) were used. A very practical application of this custom, likening Yawheh's instructions to a bridle and bit and playing on the common experience of breaking in mules and horses, occurs in a simile in Ps. 32.9, 'Do not be like a horse or a mule, without understanding, whose temper must be curbed with bit and bridle, else it will not stay near you.' The same circumstances forms the background of a pregnant metaphor indicating Yawheh's power over the Assyrian king: 'Because you have raged against me and your arrogance has come to my ears, I will put my hook in your nose (cf. Ezek. 19.4, 9; 29.4; 38.4) and my bit in your mouth; I will turn you back on the way by which you came' (2 Kgs 19.28). Also, in Prov. 26.3 the bridle functions in the context of discipline: 'A whip for the horse, a bridle for the donkey, and a rod for the back of fools.' If a donkey,

6. *Technology and Meaning* 191

mule or horse could get rid of the bridle, it could not be restrained. Casting off the bridle therefore became a metaphor for being out of control or beyond restraint. Hence, 'Because God has loosed my bowstring and humbled me, they [i.e. the rabble formerly restrained by Job's status as an honoured member of the community] have cast off restraint in my presence' (Job 30.11).

Quite a few agricultural implements are mentioned in 1 Sam. 13.19-20,

> Now there was no smith (חרש) to be found throughout all the land of Israel...so all the Israelites went down to the Philistines to sharpen their ploughshares (מחרשתו), mattocks (את), 'pickaxe'), axes (קרדמו) or sickles [following the LXX τὸ δρέπανον αὐτοῦ instead of the Hebrew 'ploughshare' (מחרשתו)].

The pickaxe was a sturdy instrument used both as a hoe and an axe. With it the roots of trees on new land were cut and the surface of virgin soil or fallow fields broken (Turkowski 1969: 25) *before* ploughing could begin. It is therefore significant that Isa. 2.4 sees the people beating their swords into pickaxes (לאתים, not מחרשות 'ploughshares'): these people are preparing to *break new land*, to start over again. When, in Joel 3.10 (Heb. 4.10) they beat their pickaxes into swords the dangers facing the farmers in the image are so great that they willingly forfeit the possibility of breaking new ground. Such action would put an end to the two-field system of sowing, since nobody would have been able to hoe fallow land. Crops would have had to be grown over and over on the same soil, which would inevitably lead to poor crops and disaster. For ploughing the farmer used cattle yoked to the plough. The yoke (על) consisted of a strong wooden pole (מטה) of approximately 150 cm × 10 cm put over the napes (שכם) of the two animals. To prevent them from throwing off the yoke two sets of vertically installed pegs fitted the yoke over each animal's nape. Fitted to the lower ends of these pegs were two forelocks (מוסרות) of about 40 cm long, which were then tied round the animal's neck (cf. Turkowski 1969: 30). The farmer used either a stick (שבט) or his goad to urge on the animals. Picturing human beings as yoked cattle, the elders of Israel complain to Rehoboam over their plight under Solomon's taxes and forced labour, 'Your father made our yoke (עלנו) heavy' (1 Kgs 12.4). To symbolize the Judaeans' coming plight under the Babylonian conquerors, Jeremiah yoked himself, complete with bar, pegs and forelocks (Jer. 27.2). And to express Israel's liberation from Assyrian vassalship

Isa. 9.4 says Yahweh has broken the Assyrian king's burdensome yoke (על סבלו), his bar across the shoulders (מטה שכמו), and his driving stick (שבט הנגש). Depending on the identity of the owner implied in the imagery, to break the yoke's forelocks and shed the yoke either symbolizes liberation (Isa. 58.6; Nah. 1.13) or obstinate behaviour (Jer. 5.5). Instead of using a stick to urge on the animals the farmer could also use the goad (דרבן), which was a long stick with an iron tip fixed to one end (see 1 Sam. 13.21). The actual function of this instrument was quickly to clean the ploughshare in the process of ploughing and to break up the larger clods on newly ploughed land (Turkowski 1969: 30, 32). Picturing the students of a sage as cattle before a plough, Eccl. 12.11 says, 'The sayings of the wise are like goads (דרבנות)', that is, they not only urge the student on, they also prevent the plough from clogging up and assist by completing what the plough cannot do properly, that is, the advice of the sage also assists the student in the proper and efficient execution of his or her task in life.

The early sickle (גל) was a hook-shaped metal knife used for cutting grain, grass and even thin branches of trees and shrubs (Turkowski 1969: 101). As a harvesting instrument it was wielded with a rhythmic left-to-right waving movement. Hence 'harvesting' could be expressed as 'waving (נוף) the sickle' (Deut. 23.25; Heb. v. 26), and a grain harvester be called 'the wielder of the sickle' (תפש מגל, Jer. 50.16). The waving action with the sickle grew into an image of waging war with the sword (Jer. 50.16), while the expression 'to put in the sickle' (שלח מגל), linking up with the metaphorical use of 'harvest', came to serve as a metaphor for judgment (Joel 3.13) as well. The harvest of the sickle is transported to the threshing floor by a fairly primitive wagon or cart (עגלה), which provided the basis for a simile picturing hard times, as in Amos 2.13: 'I will press you down in your place, just as a cart presses down when it is full of sheaves.' At some stage the sledge (מורג הרוץ) was introduced as a more efficient threshing instrument than animal treading. The sledge not only separates the grain from the straw but it also cuts up the straw, making the winnowing process easier and the chaff less bulky and therefore more easy to store and more suitable for use as fodder and in clay mortar. The typical sledge consists of a few planks nailed together with holes bored through them and with potsherds or flintstones driven tightly into the holes. A later type of sledge (according to Turkowski [1969: 106] only in Roman times) had iron edges fastened to the bottom of the sledge. Describing the impenetrable

6. Technology and Meaning

protective covering of Leviathan, Job 41.30 (Heb. v. 22) uses the image of the older type of sledge: 'Its underparts are like sharp potsherds; it spreads itself like a threshing sledge (חרוץ) on the mire.' The way the sledge operates becomes an image of victory in war. Promising future fame for the Jewish community of Persian times, Isa. 41.15 says that Yahweh will make them a new threshing sledge with sharpened teeth (בעל פיפיות) that will thresh (cut up) the mountains and make the hills like chaff (i.e. they will conquer the whole world). In Amos 1.3, however, the *iron*-tipped sledge (חרצות הברזל) symbolizes *excessive* violence. To express a thoroughly executed winnowing process the instruments (Turkowski 1969: 106-108) used in the process are expressly mentioned, as in Isa. 30.24, 'the oxen and donkeys...will eat silage, which has been winnowed with shovel (רחת) and fork' (מזרה), that is, pure silage.

Unlike the technology involved in growing and harvesting grain, the *technology* employed in the making of wine or the manufacturing of oil does not feature in the Hebrew Bible, neither as a reference nor as an image. Even though the initial process of wine-making is metaphorically employed for 'suffering' (Lam. 1.15), the only 'tool' mentioned is the wine-press (גת, יקב) in which the grapes are trodden (דרך). Similarly with the production of oil. Even though there were olive presses in abundance in Palestine, either a mere verb is used to refer to 'oil pressing' (צהר Hif.) or reference is merely made to the 'treading' of olives (Mic. 6.15) or to the pounding of the fruits in a mortar (Exod. 27.20).

2. *The Technology of Subsistence*

Lashing out at families preparing offerings for 'the queen of heaven', Jer. 7.18 mentions children gathering wood, fathers kindling a fire and women kneading dough. Such activities would have been a daily scene on the 'profane' side of subsistence as well. To bake bread one needs flour, fire, an oven and a technique of baking. Saving 'fire' for later discussion, we highlight here the technologies of grinding and baking.

The mill itself is referred to as רחים (Exod. 11.15; Num. 11.8), the dual form indicating that the mill consists of two sections, namely the softer and smaller 'upper stone' (פלח רכב, Judg. 9.53; cf. Deut. 24.6) and the much larger and harder 'lower stone' (פלח תחתית, Job 41.24; Heb. v. 16). It was with the upper stone that the woman crushed Abimelech's skull (Judg. 9.53). The Hebrew Bible view of just how essential an instrument the mill was is clear from Deut. 24.6, which says, 'No one shall take a mill (רחים) or an upper millstone (רכב) in pledge, for that would be taking a *life* in pledge.' Seeing that רחים already implies the upper stone, its explicit mentioning here should perhaps be taken as an intensification of the statement, for example, 'a mill, not *even* the upper stone'. In Job 41.24 (Heb. v. 16) the lower stone provides a point of comparison for the unyielding attitude of Leviathan: 'Its heart is as hard as stone, as hard as the lower millstone.' Other texts utilize as imagery the dual *process* involved in grinding, namely first crushing the grain by pounding it with the upper stone and then grinding the broken kernels by rubbing the upper over the lower stone. Consider, for example, as a metaphor for 'oppression', 'What do you mean by crushing my people, by grinding the face of the poor?' (Isa. 3.15). That grinding was looked upon as a task not to be performed by people of status is indicated by two passages, the one descriptive, the other an image. Consider, 'Every firstborn in the land of Egypt shall die, from the firstborn of Pharaoh who sits on his throne to the firstborn of the female slave who is behind the handmill' (Exod. 11.5), and the judgment passed on 'the daughter of Babylon' in Isa. 47.2, 'Take the millstones and grind meal, remove your veil, strip off your robe, uncover your legs...' Yet when the sound of the millstones stops, it is a sign of gloom and doom to come, as in Jer. 25.10, 'I will banish from them the sound of mirth and the sound of gladness, the voice of the bridegroom and the voice of the bride, the sound of the millstones and the light of the lamp' (cf. Eccl. 12.4).

Before the dough is kneaded the fire has to be kindled in the clay oven (תנור). While the fire is burning in it, the oven is referred to as a 'burning oven' (תנור אש), which, because of its construction, gives off much heat at the front opening. It is this 'hotness' that becomes a metaphor for anxiousness (Ps. 21.10). Once the fire has been kindled, the dough may be kneaded and put aside to leaven. All the time an eye has to be kept on the fire. It has to be constantly stirred to ensure all the wood burns. When the wood has been burnt the resulting coals are either removed or moved to one side of the oven and the bread put in the hot oven. The oven is then sealed. This part of the process afforded the sages with the saying, 'For lack of wood the fire goes out, and where there is no whisperer, quarrelling ceases' (Prov. 26.20). After a set time the oven may be opened again and the baked bread taken out. The whole process forms the point of reference for Hosea's description of the deceitful elite of Samaria plotting against an unwitting king.

'They are...like a heated oven (כתנור בערה) whose baker does not need to stir the fire, from the kneading of the dough until it is leavened,' that is, they *seem* dependable enough to function without supervision. On the king's birthday they even go to the party and are accepted by him as friends. But they are treacherous ovens. Their unstirred wood does not burn out, so that, when the oven is closed, the remaining wood merely smoulders within (ישן אפהם, literally 'their baking sleeps'). Consequently, when the oven is opened in the expectation of finding a perfectly baked bread, the smouldering pieces of wood blaze up (בער כאש להבה) and devour the king. (Hos. 7.4-7). Certain kinds of bread were not baked in the oven but roasted over the coals. In this case the cakes have to be regularly turned over to prevent them from burning on one side, while being unbaked inside. This is the imagery of Hosea 7.8: 'Ephraim is a cake not turned.' The repeated use of the oven causes it to become pitch black from the soot of smoky and smouldering fires. It is this observation which led to the comparison, 'Our skin is black as an oven from the scorching heat of famine' (Lam. 5.10).

3. *Architectural Technology*

Here we have to distinguish between constructions erected by private people on farmsteads or in villages, towns or cities, and royal and administrative buildings, because contrary to 'private' dwellings, official buildings were mostly carefully planned, firmly constructed and situated in well-planned quarters of cities and towns. Since town planning is part and parcel of the construction business, which shows a marked change from about the middle of the tenth century BCE (Kempinski and Reich 1992: 191-92), and clearly distinguished between official and private residences (Herzog 1992b), it will also receive some attention here.

Farmhouses consisted of single- or double-storied constructions, (Weippert 1988: 394; Netzer 1992: 196). Farmhouses, built of partly tooled, dry-laid limestone (Dar 1986: 3) or sun-dried bricks of mud and straw, were constructed in the form of a rectangle between 400 and 1200 square metres (Dar 1986: 3, 6), of which approximately 45 per cent was built up, 25 per cent covered and 30 per cent an open courtyard (Weippert 1988: 395). The main room of the flat-roofed house was situated at the rear of the construction and could accommodate up to 30 persons (Dar 1986: 7). If the necessity arose (cf. 2 Kgs 4.9-10) an extra room could be added on top of the main room. The two-storied house would have been somewhat more convenient, in that the upper storey would provide more living and sleeping facilities. The owner of a 'household' (בעל־הבית, Exod. 22.7-8; Heb. vv. 6-7) thus was in charge of quite a few people and belongings.

This brief account of the layout and construction of a farmhouse can assist the cultural interpretation of some Hebrew Bible texts. Consider, for example, how the simile of a man narrowly escaping from a lion and bear only to be bitten by an adder when he reaches the safety of his house (Amos 5.19) gains in rhetorical power when one thinks of the credibility of a snake hiding among the dry-laid limestone chunks in the wall of a house. Or how the story of Ham laughing at the nakedness of his drunken father (Gen. 9.20-25) might have assisted in disciplining the younger members of a household in which different generations lived together in the same room. Or, finally, how, given the number of people who had to live together under one roof and share the same facilities, some folk sayings and other expressions gain in meaning. Consider, for example, 'A soft answer turns away wrath, but a harsh word stirs up anger' (Prov. 15.1), or 'To watch over mouth and tongue is to keep out of trouble' (Prov. 21.23), or the poet's exclamation, 'How very good and pleasant it is when kindred live together (and that) in unity!'—note the גם in the expression שבתו אחים גם־יהד (Ps. 133.1).

The courtyard was typically divided into two by a row of pillars. One half of the pillared area had a beaten earth surface and was the scene of domestic activities, such as grinding wheat, making pots, cooking food, baking bread, pressing oil, spinning and weaving (Netzer 1992: 196). If one was very lucky there could even have been a well in the courtyard (2 Sam. 17.18). The other half of the pillared area often had a stone paved surface where supplies and tools could be stored and/or domestic animals kept (Netzer 1992: 198; Weippert 1988: 395). Thus, the woman who, preparing a meal for King Saul, slaughtered the fatted calf which was 'in the house' (בבית, 1 Sam. 28.24). While the lower storey of a two-storied house normally served the same purposes as that of the pillared area of the one storey house, the upper storey provided more sleeping room and space for domestic activities. While smoke from cooking and baking was not a problem in the open courtyard of one-storied houses, it must have been a nuisance in badly ventilated two-storied buildings (Netzer 1992: 199). This experience seems to have been the background of imagery in which smoke plays a role. Hence, 'like smoke they [the wicked] vanish away' (Ps. 37.20), but 'they shall

6. Technology and Meaning

be like...smoke *from a window*' (Hos. 13.3), and 'Like vinegar to the teeth, and *smoke to the eyes*, so are the lazy to their employers' (Prov. 10.26). Everything in the vicinity of a smoky hearth becomes dirty and smelly. Given the association of a 'black skin' (cf. Job 30.30; Lam. 5.10) and 'a bad smell' (Job 19.17; Isa. 3.24) with suffering, the simile for hardship and suffering in Ps. 119.82-83 gains in meaning, 'My eyes fail with watching for your promise; I ask, 'When will you comfort me? For I have become like a wineskin in the smoke...'.".

The Hebrew Bible makes a clear distinction between ordinary village settlements (כפר הפרזי; מחנים) and fortified cities (עיר/קריה; המבצר, בצורה, ערי). What the origin and function of this difference is becomes clear from the findings of archaeology. Herzog (1992b: 232) distinguishes seven settlement patterns for Iron Age I, which may be summarized as follows:

Type	*Characteristics*
Huts and pits	A number of huts arranged in an oval with nearby ovens and pits serving as silos
Clusters of pens	Clusters of walled sheep pens enclosing the dwellings of the owners as well
Enclosed settlements	Adjacent dwellings mostly built against a slope but always in a circle to form a common courtyard in the middle, but with no public buildings among them
Israelite settlement villages	High density and unplanned built-up area without prominent buildings or allowing for a central courtyard. The settlement develops according to the agglutinative principle. Economy based on agriculture and crafts
Clusters of enclosures	Groups of houses built in a circle with doors facing outward joined together in a cluster
Planned cities	A city with an orthogonal network of streets dividing the settlement into insulae
Canaanite cities and Egyptian administrative centres	Acropolis with palace and administrative centre with simpler houses on the outskirts

Classifying Iron Age II cities and towns, Herzog (1992b) employs three criteria, namely layout models (peripheral, radial or orthogonal planning), the quantitative relationship between public structures and private dwellings, and streets and open areas in the urban system. In *peripheral* 'plans' it is (a) mostly only the city wall that follows the (oval) contour of the hill on which the city is situated, while houses are built at random. Sometimes, however, the plan involves (b) concentric streets (following the hill's contour) divided in the middle by a road emerging from the city gate. *Radial* plans utilize central points in the settlement with streets following the radii emanating from these central points. *Orthogonal* planning ignores the topography and plans the city along streets outlining square or rectangular areas. To build houses in these areas sometimes requires extensive levelling and quarrying. Applying these criteria to the excavated settlements, Herzog categorizes them in four types: capital cities, major administrative, secondary administrative cities, and provincial towns. The following table summarizes the typical features of each:

Category	*Plan*	*Relationship of public to private building*	*Streets and open areas*	*Other characteristics*
Capitals	Orthogonal	Public buildings separated from private dwellings	Public area has large open courtyards; private dwellings more densely grouped	Orthogonal planning creates monumental impression
Major administrative	Orthogonal units within radial plan combined with peripheral (b)	Public buildings cover the largest part	Large centre court in public area; private dwellings dense	Clear distinction between public and private areas; public areas monumental
Secondary administrative	Orthogonal units within radial plan	Public buildings cover the largest part	Streets of uniform width, space fairly evenly distributed	Whole city is planned (Lacish); public area monumental
Provincial	Mostly unplanned, agglutinative growth	Few distinguishable public structures	Streets are mere open spaces between houses; dense	Little distinction between public and private

6. *Technology and Meaning*

Comparing the data for Iron Age I and Iron Age II, it is clear that, in tandem with the change from a reciprocal to a mixed economy dominated by its redistributive section, Iron Age II saw marked distinction developing between 'private' and 'public', subject and authority, unmistakably symbolized by the planning of capital and administrative cities. In this context a few observations by Herzog are important from a cultural point of view: first, that orthogonally planned areas, preferred at 'settlements of social, political or military importance', stand out from their surroundings and effect a monumental impression (1992b: 247). Secondly, that in major administrative cities one may observe a contrast between the monumental planning of the public part and the poor, irregularly planned private residential quarters (1992b: 258). Thirdly, that in the event of a city changing its status (e.g. Tell en-Nasbeh being converted from a provincial town to an administrative city), such a city may double in size without its population significantly increasing (at Tell en-Nasbeh the population increased from 750 to 800 [1992b: 263]). What characterized the system were therefore *visible* boundaries of status, authority and wealth.

We shall return to this point in discussing social control and the challenge to it in Chapter 9, because there is a connection between the status expressed by the architecture and planning of cities and the challenge to status and authority one encounters in the so-called prophetic literature. What is important at this stage is to draw attention to the complementary nature of city planning and architecture. It is in the orthogonally planned areas that one also finds the *buildings* creating an impression of monumentality (authority/power) through their size (e.g. storehouses), their shape (e.g. the royal residence or temple) or the building material used (e.g. hewn stone).

Capitals, administrative and provincial cities all had walls around them (Weippert 1988: 608-12). A city wall is called חומה, which distinguishes it from the lowish, roughly erected wall enclosing a garden and courtyard (גדר) and the wall in a building (קיר). The city wall was, however, but one part of the defensive system of a fortified city. As important were the towers (מגדלים) on the wall, the city gate (שער) and the provision of accessible water and food for times of siege in war (cf. Shiloh 1992). The type of defensive structures erected for a settlement was decided by its role in the administration (cf. 2 Chron. 19.5), economy or strategic planning (cf. Jer. 4.5) of the monarchy (Herzog 1992b: 265). The more important the city the better its fortifications were.

Ordinary villages (חצרים) would have no fortification at all or would have an outer ring of houses facing inward to a common square as a protective measure. More important cities would be protected by any of three types of casemate walls: freestanding, integrated (i.e. where the first row of dwellings formed part of the wall), or filled (in which case the cavity between the walls was filled with earth) (Herzog 1992b: 269). The most important cities would be protected by massive walls (note 'the broad wall of Babylon' חמות בבל הרחבה Jer. 51.58). These walls might have been any of three types: the ordinary massive wall (with a toothed effect created by regular deviations of approximately half a metre pointing in the same direction), the offset-and-inset type, or the wall with projecting towers on top of it.

Any kind of wall was already an improvement on no wall at all. The Hebrew Bible pictures the times before the monarchy as a time of utter vulnerability, when nomads raided the Israelite settlements at will (Judg. 3.13; 6.1-5; 10.9, 12; 1 Sam. 13.1-2) and when the terrified people had to hide themselves in caves, holes, rocks, tombs and cisterns (Judg. 6.2; 1 Sam. 13.6). To have been in the vicinity of a fortified city was like having a mother nearby. This feeling of security gave rise to the expression the *daughters of the fortified city* (cf. Judg. 1.27) for 'surrounding villages'. Once fugitives from the outlying villages had succeeded in reaching a fortified city they could feel themselves safe (2 Sam. 20.6). For this reason 'wall' became a symbol of protection, safety and security. The security of Thebes, says Nah. 3.8, is that 'she sat by the Nile, with water around her, her rampart a sea, water her wall'. Nabal's workers say of David and his band that they have always been a wall (protection) to them while they were in the open with the sheep (1 Sam. 25.16), and Prov. 18.11 that rich people think of their wealth as their safety ('fortified city') and security/protection ('high wall'). Ultimate security is to have a wall of fire around one (Zech. 2.5), and to *be* a fortified copper wall (חומת נחשת בצורה) is to be unconquerable. Conversely, to have all one's fortified cities attacked at the same time is the ultimate symbol of insecurity (Isa. 2.15), because under such circumstances there is no 'mother' to which a 'daughter' can flee. Similarly, if there is a breach in the wall, it spells 'danger' and 'ruin' (e.g. Job 30.14). If there is an imminent threat and weak spots are discovered in the wall there is no time to transport stones from elsewhere or to manufacture clay bricks and leave them in the sun to dry (cf. Nah. 3.14). Under such circumstances the authorities would as an emergency measure simply tear down the first row of houses along the wall and use the material to repair the wall. In a moving scene Isaiah 22 pictures Yahweh as the 'weeping god' (22.4) who sees the hopelessness of his people's frantic emergency measures, 'You counted the houses of Jerusalem, and you broke down the houses to fortify the wall. You made a reservoir between the two walls for the water of the old pool' (22.10-11)—but everything is in vain. If, in such an emergency situation, someone can successfully defend a weak spot or breach, one is saved, albeit by the skin of one's teeth, as when Moses stood in the breach as God was on the brink of destroying Israel (Ps. 106.23; cf. Ezek. 22.30). If, however, a breach can be repaired in time, it means renewed safety, which is the meaning of the imagery in Isa. 58.12's repairs to a breach in the wall. On the other hand, if the defensive wall was not built correctly in the first place, it cannot guarantee safety for the inhabitants of the fortified city. Moreover, it may even fall over, and, apart from leaving the inhabitants unprotected, a lot of them might get killed in the process (1 Kgs 20.30). So much may be implied by the imagery of Amos 7.7 of Yahweh standing on the city wall with a plumb line in his hand, measuring the wall, which is Israel, which seemingly is about to fall over (cf. also Isa. 30.13).

This image links up with another, according to which the wall is the city and its inhabitants. Consider, for instance, Lam. 2.18 where the broken wall of Jerusalem symbolizes the dire circumstances of its inhabitants and is summoned, 'Cry aloud to the Lord, O wall of daughter Zion (חומת בת־ציון)! Let tears stream down like a torrent day and night! Give yourself no rest, your eyes no respite!' Finally, a wall, even though it symbolizes safety, still implies an enemy and lurking danger that might successfully breach it. Ultimate safety is when one *needs* no physical wall at all, as in Zech. 2.4, 'Jerusalem shall be inhabited like villages without walls (פרזות), because of the multitude of people and animals in it.' These people will be protected by their *faith* in Yahweh, who will be like a fiery wall around them (2.5).

The gate in the outer wall was, of course, a vulnerable spot in the defence of a city and its construction and reinforcements received special attention. According to 1 Chron. 22.3-4 David provided 'great stores of iron for nails for the doors of the gates and for clamps, as well as bronze in quantities beyond weighing, and cedar logs without number'. As long as the bar behind the two gates lasts the enemy cannot enter and the people are safe. In Ps. 147.13 'reinforcing (חזק) the gate's bars (בריחי שעריך)' is a metaphor for 'peace and blessing'. Pondering over Yahweh's care for his people, the poet says 'he strengthens the bars of your gates' (v. 13). Even though the 'gate bar' is suggested by the military context of a preceding reference to 'the strength of horses' (v. 10) and the subsequent reference to 'peace' (v. 14), the *means* by which Yahweh reinforces the bar (vv. 13-19) are *children, spiritual* guidance and *natural phenomena*, like wheat, snow, frost, hail, wind, water. To have no use for gate bars means to live in tranquillity. Jeremiah 49.31 (cf. Ezek. 38.11) speaks of a wealthy, peaceful nation (גוי שליו) that lives on its own (בדד) and in security (יושב לבטח), a nation that has no gate bars (ולא־בריח לו). If the gate gives way in an attack the enemy may enter. And so the gate became a metonym for the city and its inhabitants (cf. Isa. 3.26; 14.31), and 'to own the gate' (ירש את השער, Gen. 22.17) a metaphor for 'to be in charge of/rule over the *people* of the city'. As a symbolic gesture of 'owning the gate' after Jerusalem was taken, 'all the officials of the king of Babylon came and sat in the middle gate...with all the rest of the officials' (Jer. 39.3).

With a view to slowing down attackers at the gate the design of the older kind of gate allowed only indirect access to the city. But this design also made it difficult for the inhabitants to negotiate the bends with laden animals, chariots or wagons. For that reason later gates were designed to give direct access to the city and had to be fortified and defended in a different manner (Herzog 1992b: 272-74). It is, however, not the defensive side of the city gate that features in the imagery of the Hebrew Bible, but its economic, social, judicial and political function. Directly behind the gate were two 'chambers' into which the doors could swing open and in which the guard could take its place. Other types of gates provided a further set or even two sets of chambers behind the gate (referred to as four- and six-chambered gates, respectively). In these extra chambers benches were installed for the seating of various assemblies, like public meetings of the elders of the city and hearings of the court of justice. Even the king had his regular place there (1 Sam. 20.25). Some city gates also provided for certain cultic events (2 Kgs 23.8). Between the city gate and the first building of the city was the city's public square where people could be assembled for various purposes, as when Hezekiah assembles the combat commanders to encourage them after the disheartening address by the Assyrian officer (2 Chron. 32.6).

In biblical literature various events take place at the city gate. This is

6. *Technology and Meaning*

the place where public announcements are made. When Yahweh sends Jeremiah to the inner gate at the palace complex ('by which the kings of Judah enter and by which they go out', see below), as well as to 'all the gates of Jerusalem' (Jer. 17.12), the message he sends is not only official but also of public concern. And because the message of Lady Wisdom is in the public interest she announces it at the city gate (Prov. 1.21). The gate is also the place where people in the know discuss public affairs. To have a regular seat at the gate is to be an honoured and respected citizen. Reminiscing on his former status, Job says, 'When I went out to the gate of the city, when I took my seat in the square, the young men saw me and withdrew, and the aged rose up and stood' (Job 29.7-8; cf. Prov. 31.23). A person unable to follow these discussions or to make a contribution shows himself a fool (Prov. 24.7). 'Public affairs' include the conduct of individual citizens. To be 'whispered' about in the gate is to be humiliated ('I am the subject of gossip for those who sit in the gate'—Ps. 69.12; Heb. v. 13), but to be 'mentioned' is to be honoured ('let her works praise her in the city gates'— Prov. 31.31). The gate is also a place for negotiations of various sorts. This is where Abraham concludes a deal with Ephron (Gen. 23.17-18), where Boaz negotiates his complicated marriage (Ruth 4.1-12), and where the honourable man of Ps. 127.5 succeeds in challenging his opponent. The gate, finally, is a place where justice is meted out by the elders (or responsible officials) of the city (Deut. 17.5; Amos 5.10, 12, 15). Defending his upright past as a judge in the gates, Job says, 'If I have raised my hand against the orphan, because I saw I had supporters at the gate; then let my shoulder blade fall from my shoulder, and let my arm be broken from its socket' (Job 31.21-22; cf. Prov. 22.22).

Besides the wall around the city, capital and some administrative cities had an additional inner wall protecting the 'administrative officials from the civilian population' (Herzog 1992: 274). It is possible that this inner wall is the referent in the combination 'wall and palaces' (e.g. ארמנתיה...צר חומת in Amos 1.7, 10, etc.). Like the city walls these walls also had a guarded gate ('the gate of the guard', Neh. 12.39), which probably also served as a kind of prison (Jer. 37.14-21; Liid 1992). When Jeremiah thus delivers some of his speeches at this gate it signifies that they are intended for the 'official' ears of royalty and bureaucrats (cf. Jer. 7.2; 26.10; 36.10).

Depending on their proximity to the capital, the dwellings of the elite of monarchal times differed marginally to markedly from those of ordinary people. In this regard Reich (1992: 210) states as a rule of thumb: the greater the distance from the capital the smaller the architectural difference between the dwellings of the bureaucrats and the ordinary people. In the royal cities, for example, the 'courtyard houses' (Netzer 1992: 199) of bureaucrats are conspicuous. Apart from these houses, which often formed part of the larger administrative buildings, store rooms, treasuries (Herzog 1992b) and fortifications (Herzog 1992b; Meshel 1992) of the royal or secondary cities (Netzer 1992: 200), there were, of course, also the royal palaces (Reich 1992).

The 'courtyard houses' of officialdom, appearing on the scene from the middle of the tenth century BCE, are characterized by their better location in the cities, their size and the costlier material used in their construction (Reich 1992: 202). Compared to ordinary houses, they were erected around a larger courtyard flanked on three sides by rooms with thicker walls—in the royal cities even constructed from hewn stone. Hence the accusation against the Samarian elite, 'you trample on the poor and take from them levies of grain, you have built houses of hewn stone' (Amos 5.11). Playing on the comparative durability of stone-built houses, the same elite can say elsewhere, 'The [mud] bricks have fallen, but we will build with dressed stones...' (Isa. 9.10). But, emphasizing his comparative defencelessness before Yahweh, Job (4.18-19) says, 'Even in his servants he [Yahweh] puts no trust, and his angels he charges with error; how much more those who live in houses of clay (בתי־חמר) whose foundation is in the dust, who are crushed like a moth.'

Large administrative buildings dating from between the tenth and the seventh centuries BCE have been discovered at several places all over the territory of ancient Israel and Judah (Herzog 1992a: 223-25; Weippert 1988: 604-607, 698-703). Part of these buildings are the storehouses (מסכנות, 2 Chron. 32.28), built according to a fairly fixed plan (cf. Isserlin 1984: 174-78): a rectangular building divided into three by two rows of pillars. The floor of the two side sections are brick-paved, while the central section had a floor of beaten earth. It would seem that the paved areas were used as store rooms for various products—the paved floor protecting the products from damp—while the central area served as a loading zone for the delivery and collection of supplies (Herzog 1992a: 225-28). The cities in which these storehouses were situated were called ערי מסכנות (Exod. 1.11; 2 Chron. 16.4; 17.12). As a part of such an administrative complex there were also scribal cham-

6. Technology and Meaning

bers (שכת הספר, cf. Jer. 26.10, 12) and treasuries (אוצרות, 2 Chron. 32.27). Scribal chambers, found, for example, in Samaria, Megiddo and Hazor, were constructed in sets of four small rooms on both sides of a narrow corridor (Herzog 1992a: 229). The treasuries were for the storage of precious metals and stones, spices and fragrant oils. Seeing that the Samaria ostraca were found in the same kind of building that can be identified as treasuries, one has to assume that archives were also kept in them.

That the writers of the Bible had a Syrian *bit hilani* type (Reich 1992: 203) of palace in mind when they described Solomon's palace (1 Kgs 7.1-14), is fairly clear.[1] These palaces, which differed considerably from the Assyrian type also evidenced on Israelite and Judaean territory (Reich 1992: 214-22), had a particular lay-out. The entrance was between two pillars in proto-Aeolic style (Reich 1992: 212) leading to a portico, which served as a guard and waiting room. From there one entered the throne hall (אולם הכסא, 1 Kgs 7.7), which was surrounded an all sides by store, scribal and living rooms. The walls and roof of the central hall were higher than those of the surrounding rooms. To allow for light and air in the central throne hall, the part of its walls protruding above the flat roof of the surrounding rooms were equipped with rows of windows (חלנות, sing. חלון) on each side (1 Kgs 7.5). To allow the king to enjoy the fresh air coming through the upper windows, his private throne chamber was elevated on rows of pillars (עמודים) with a staircase (לולם) or מעלות 'steps') leading to it (1 Kgs 10.19-20). Hence this upper room (עליה) could be referred to as the 'cool upper room' (עלית המקרה). The pillars were mostly overlain with wood on which stylized palm trees were carved (cf. 1 Kgs 6.29, 32, 35).

From the portico a flight of stairs led to a second story, where the royal chambers were situated (1 Kgs 7.8). Adjoining the palace was an extensive walled-in and brick-paved courtyard (Stern 1992: 307-308) of over 3,000 square metres. Along the wall of the courtyard, to which a gatehouse gave access, numerous other rooms, for example, scribal chambers, were grouped (Reich 1992: 206). The courtyard itself was used for public ceremonies, the performance of the duties of horsemen and grooms, and household tasks of the palace personnel (Reich 1992: 210).

---

1. This supposition assists a great deal in interpreting the movements and motivations in the story of Ehud's assassination of the Moabite King Eglon (Deist 1996b).

Palaces were erected on foundations of 'carefully laid ashlar stones with marginal dressing' (Reich 1992: 205; Weippert 1988: 597-603; 1 Kgs 7.10), which at the entrances also served as thresholds, also between different sections of the palace complex, for example, between the palace and the temple. It is with reference to this kind of threshold that Ezek. 43.8 says with reference to the kings of Judah:

> When they placed their threshold by my threshold and their doorposts beside my doorposts, with only a wall between me and them, they were defiling my holy name by their abominations that they committed; therefore I have consumed them in my anger.

The walls were constructed from hewn stone (1 Kgs 7.11; אבן־שלמה, 1 Kgs 6.7; גזית, Isa. 9.10), sun-dried clay bricks (לבנים, Gen. 11.3; Reich 1992: 208-209), or with layers of stone or brick interspersed with layers of wooden poles (Reich 1992: 213; 1 Kgs 7.12). The inside of the walls was often covered by costly timber and sometimes decorated with ivory (Reich 1992: 206, 214; 1 Kgs 7.3; 22.39). Where the upper part of the walls met the ceilings the last layer of stone was crenellated, that is, 'stepped inward' (Stern 1992: 308).

The construction of these buildings and cities required skill and technical know-how, which must have led to occupational specialization, which, as we shall see shortly, is also part of the cultural world of the biblical text. Moreover, the erection of these cities and structures must have necessitated massive conscription of labour, which also constitutes a theme in biblical literature (see 2 Sam. 20.24; 1 Kgs 4.6; 5.13; 9.15, 20-21; 11.28; 12.18; 2 Chron. 8.8; Prov. 2.24; Jer. 22.13). According to 1 Kgs 5.15, Solomon had as many as 70,000 labourers and 80,000 stonecutters (חצב) for, as 2 Kgs 12.12 puts it, the production of quarried stone (אבני מחצב) for use by the masons (גדרים).

In the later (seventh century BCE), smarter type of palace constructed after Phoenician architectural style, windows and balconies received special attention. The windows were two to five 'stepped' openings (חלוני שקפים, 1 Kgs 6.4), each step recessing further back from the opening than the previous one (Stern 1992: 306). The window frames rested on a row of decorated balustrades, that is, small columns with a ring of drooping leaves in the middle and a double volute at the top (Stern 1992: 307). Given the luxurious nature of these palaces compared to the dwellings of the ordinary people, the formulation of the judgment over the king in Jer. 22.13-14 is quite understandable:

6. *Technology and Meaning*

> Woe to him who builds his house by unrighteousness...who makes his neighbours work for nothing, and does not give them their wages; who says, 'I will build myself a great house with spacious upper rooms,' and cuts out *windows* for it, *panelling* it with cedar, and *painting* it with *vermillion*.

The Assyrian type of palace built in Palestine topped the luxury of the Israelite royal dwellings in that it even sported bathrooms with a drainage system (Reich 1992: 218), cleverly constructed mudbrick vaults and floor paving of fired brick (Reich 1992: 221-22). It is with a quite biting irony that Hab. 2.9-11 announces the downfall of Assyria with the following words:

> Alas for you who get evil gain for your houses, setting your nest on high to be safe from the reach of harm! You have devised shame for your house by cutting off many peoples; you have forfeited your life. The very stones [with which your palaces have been built] will cry out from the wall, and the plaster will respond from the woodwork, 'Alas for you who build a town by bloodshed, and found a city on iniquity!'

Quarrying stone for the production of building material is as much of an art as stone-dressing. To remove a solid, dressable chunk of stone from a solid stone mass requires the skilled use of heat and chisels. Heating a rock (e.g. by making a fire on it) makes it crack. Once cracks appear chunks of stone may be loosened from the rock by carefully manipulating the cracks with chisels. Quarrying, cutting and dressing of stone was, consequently, looked upon as a special skill, and the imagery derived from this art symbolizes positive things. Thus, we read, for example, 'Listen to me, you that pursue righteousness, you that seek the Lord. Look to the rock from which you were hewn, and to the quarry from which you were dug' (Isa. 51.1). Here Yahweh is the stone-cutter working in the quarry, the matriarch Sarah. Even in oracles of doom one gets the impression that images of 'stone dressing' or of a hammer (פטיש) pounding a rock to pieces have a 'corrective' side to them. Consider, for example, 'I have hewn them [חצבתי] by the prophets, I have killed them by the words of my mouth, and my judgment goes forth as the light' (Hos. 6.5). Also 'Is not my word like fire...and like a hammer [כפטיש] that breaks a rock in pieces' (Jer. 23.29), an image not consisting of two comparisons, but referring to the two subsequent processes of one and the same act of quarrying stone.

The last type of defensive construction was the 'towers' (מגדלים; בירניות) situated on strategic hills outside the fortified cities (1 Chron.

27.25; 2 Chron. 26.10; Weippert 1988: 613-20). 'Strategic' here refers to two aspects of their location. First, to the suitability of their location as look-out points, for example, in places where the occupants of the towers could see fairly long stretches of major roads (cf. 2 Kgs 9.17). Secondly, to the visibility of one tower from another. Should a guard detect enemy movements in his area he would raise a flag (נס) or give a smoke signal to the next tower, which would pass the message on to the next until the message reached the fortified city and the capital. The towers were thus part of the technology of telecommunication (Weippert 1988: 615). Depending on the terrain on which they were built, these 'towers', or rather fortresses, mostly consisted of oval, round or rectangular casemate walls of 1.5–2.5 metres in width (Meshel 1992: 296). They were constructed from undressed locally quarried stone (Meshel 1992: 300), surrounded a courtyard of between 126 and 3,750 square metres (Meshel 1992: 295), and included a fortified gate. Some of the fortresses also had defensive towers on the wall (Meshel 1992: 298) and all of them had some form of water supply, mostly hewn cisterns. The living quarters of the guard were either in the wall or close to the fortress, where the inhabitants had animal pens and practised agriculture. Given the fact that such towers were erected from the far southern Negev to the north, these constructions also served as a refuge for civilians in the outlying areas far away from fortified cities.

To indicate an entire country Hebrew Bible writers sometimes use the phrase 'from watchtower (ממגדל נוצרים) to fortified city (מבצר עד־עיר)' (2 Kgs 17.9; 18.8; cf. Isa. 2.15). When used in an image it is not always possible to decide whether the 'tower' referred to is a tower on the wall of a fortified city, a fortification within a fortified city, or an outlying fortress. Proverbs 18.10 seems to have a field tower in mind when it says, 'The name of the Lord [i.e. Yahweh himself] is a strong tower; the righteous run into it and are safe.' Perhaps also Ps. 61.3, 'You are my refuge, a strong tower against the enemy.' In an even tighter metaphor, Yahweh is said to be 'a tower of salvation' (2 Sam. 22.51). More frequently the signalling function of these towers are employed as rhetorical strategies to indicate imminent danger. Consider, for example, 'Raise a standard toward Zion, flee for safety, do not delay, for I am bringing evil from the north' (Jer. 4.6), or the cry 'All you inhabitants of the world…when a signal is raised on the mountains, look! When a trumpet is blown, listen!' (Isa. 18.3) preceding an announcement of judgment. If, in times of war, fugitives saw the flags of a friendly fortress, it gave them a direction in which to flee. This experience inspired the poet to say of Yahweh, 'You have set up a banner for those who fear you, to rally to it out of bowshot' (Ps. 60.4; Heb. v. 6). The signalling system of the fortresses also served as a metaphor for 'broadcasting', often used in the context of making good news public. For example, 'Declare among the nations and proclaim, set up a banner and proclaim, do not conceal it, say: "Babylon is taken"' (Jer. 50.2), or, 'May we shout for joy over your victory, and in the name of our God set up our banners' (Ps. 20.5; Heb. v. 6).

Keeping in mind the planning, collection and delivery of supplies, the artisanship and labour that went into the establishment of a fortified city and its building complexes, certain short notes in the Hebrew Bible may be considered understatements that are packed with emotion and meaning. Consider, for example, 'Their father [Jehoshaphat] gave them [his six sons] many gifts, of silver, gold, and valuable possessions, *together with fortified cities in Judah...*' (2 Chron. 21.3). Or the dramatic statement, 'In the fourteenth year of King Hezekiah, King Sennacherib of Assyria came up against all the fortified cities of Judah and captured them' (2 Kgs 18.13). Or the pregnant phrase 'the city has fallen' (הכתה העיר, Ezek. 33.21).

4. *Mining Technology*

An ideal place, like the Garden of Eden, is not only a place of water, fruit trees, animals and peace, but also a place where precious metals and stones are in abundance, especially gold (Gen. 3.11-12). Describing the possessions of the King of Tyre, Ezekiel says, 'You were in Eden, the garden of God; every precious stone was your covering, carnelian, chrysolite, and moonstone, beryl, onyx, and jasper, sapphire, turquoise, and emerald; and worked in gold were your settings and your engravings' (Ezek. 28.13). In this perspective the land of milk and honey given to Israel was but halfway to Eden, for it is a land 'whose stones are iron (ברזל) and from whose hills you may mine copper (נחשת)' (Deut. 8.9), but not gold. In spite of the extensive simile employing as its point of comparison shaft mining in search of gold, silver, iron and copper (Job 28.1-19), only the latter two could be found in Israelite territory. Of these two the biblical text has it that (at least) early Israel had not managed the art of extracting iron from ore (1 Sam. 13.19-21). The authors rather present their readers with a picture of large-scale direct importation of chrysolite from Ethiopia (Job 28.19), gold from Ophir (1 Kgs 10.11) and Uphaz (Jer. 10.9), and silver from Tarshish (Jer. 10.9; cf. 1 Macc. 8.2), or of heavy trading with merchants of silver, iron, tin, lead (Ezek. 27.12) and precious stones (1 Kgs 10.11). When classified according to *value* the descending order of 'workable' substances is gold, silver, bronze, tin, iron, lead, wood and stone (Isa. 60.9; Ezek. 22.18). If the criterion is difficulty of working or hardness iron and bronze top the list (Job 6.12; Jer. 6.28; Mic. 4.13).

Because of their scarcity, it is especially silver and gold that were valued among the metals. Silver and gold were among the first things that invaders were after (Josh. 6.24; Nah. 2.9), and, the best to buy off a prospective invader (2 Kgs 12.18; 18.16). Therefore, gold and silver could become one's 'trust' (Job 31.24). But if one cannot buy off an invader with silver and gold, one's case is fairly hopeless (Isa. 13.17; Ezek. 7.19; Zeph. 1.18). Wearing gold is a sign of status and power (2 Sam. 12.30; Ps. 45.9). To describe a person as dressed in crimson, embroidered cloth and gold is to speak of royalty (2 Sam. 1.24; Jer. 4.30; Ezek. 16.13). This is why lovers, speaking of each other in royal imagery, also see each other as either adorned with silver and gold or *being* of silver and gold (Cant. 1.11; 3.10). To say that something is rarer than gold is to express *extreme* rarity or scarcity (Isa. 13.12), and to say that something, for example, a fitly spoken word (Prov. 25.11) or a wise rebuke (Prov. 25.12), is like gold is to point out its extreme desirability. Since silver, gold and precious stones can only be imported from afar and afforded by royalty and the extremely wealthy upper class, no metal or any other possession surpasses gold and silver in value, so that only spiritual things can be said to be *more* valuable than gold. And to make that comparison is to stress the *extremely* beneficial nature and desirability for society of such attitudes, behaviour or conduct. Such things are instruction (Ps. 19.10; 119. 72), wisdom (Job 28.15-17; Prov. 3.14), or a good name (Prov. 11.22). Against this background the contrasts in Lamentations between being/possessing gold and being earthenware/having lost one's glitter are especially striking:

> How the gold has grown dim, how the pure gold is changed! The sacred stones lie scattered at the head of every street. The precious children of Zion, worth their weight in fine gold—how they are reckoned as earthen pots, the work of a potter's hands! (Lam. 4.1-2).

6. *Technology and Meaning* 211

But to be promised gold instead of bronze, silver instead of iron, bronze instead of wood and iron instead of stones is to be promised complete restoration (Isa. 60.17; cf. 60.9).

5. *Manufacturing Technology*

Even though the biblical text does not make much of the mining industry, the refining of metals and the manufacturing of metal and other products receive ample attention and function in various images.

Raw metal first has to be refined before it can be moulded into some object. The melting process was the same for all metals (Ezek. 22.20): the unrefined metal was put in a melting pot (כור or מצרף; cf. Prov. 17.3) and melted over a charcoal (פחם) fire in a furnace fanned by a bellows (מפח; cf. Isa. 44.12; Jer. 6.29). While still in a liquid form the dross (סיגים)was removed. If a good quality metal was required, the process was repeated until the liquid contained no dross. Gold, but even more so silver, used to be refined several times before it could be used for manufacturing purposes. 'Take away the dross from the silver,' Prov. 25.4 says, 'and the smith has material for a vessel.' The refined (צרף) metal was then poured (נתך) into a mould (חרש) or container. The better the quality of the raw product the less dross it produces, so that the refining process (צרף) can be looked upon as a test of quality (בחן). Given the high prices metals reached and the hard labour invested in the refining process, it must have been a terrible disappointment for a refiner to have found that he had been cheated with a poor-quality raw metal.

In Hebrew Bible imagery God (once also his representative, Jer. 6.27) is often pictured as a smelter, his anger as the fire or bellows, adversary as a furnace, and people as raw metal in the melting pot, for example, 'As one gathers silver, bronze, iron, lead, and tin into a smelter, to blow the fire upon them in order to melt them; so I will gather you in my anger and in my wrath, and I will put you in and melt you' (Ezek. 22.20; cf. Isa. 1.25; Jer. 9.7). Sometimes, though, God is a deeply disappointed refiner cheated by a swindling merchant. Thus, for example, 'Israel has become dross to me; all of them, silver, bronze, tin, iron, and lead [i.e. all layers of society]. In the smelter [difficult times] they have become dross [they deserted him]' (Ezek. 22.18). Or, 'The bellows blow fiercely, the lead is consumed by the fire; in vain the refining goes on, for the wicked are not removed. They are called 'rejected silver,' for the Lord has rejected them' (Jer. 6.29-30). Specially hard times, whether in the past or in the future, are pictured as a process of repeated refining, as in refining silver or gold. For instance, 'For you, O God, have tested us; you have tried us as silver is tried' (Ps. 66.10); 'I will put this third into the fire, refine them as one refines silver, and test them as gold is tested' (Zech. 13.9). Consequently, a difficult though not trying experience is pictured as a refining process *unlike* that of silver, for example, 'See, I have refined you, but not like silver; I have tested you in the furnace of adversity' (Isa. 48.10). What emanates from God, however, needs no refining and testing, because it is the finished product, for example, 'The promises of the Lord are promises that are pure, silver refined in a furnace on the ground, purified seven times' (Ps. 12.6; Heb. v. 7).

The refining metaphor pictures difficult times positively. Like the agricultural metaphors of winnowing and sifting, smelting and refining are processes of *discrimination*: 'All the wicked of the earth you count as dross; therefore I love your decrees' (Ps. 119.119; cf. Isa. 1.25; Mal. 3.3). The onus of coming through such a time lies with the afflicted. People with a clean conscience therefore have nothing to fear from the refiner and may be (or are) confident. Consider Job's declaration, 'He [God] knows the way that I take; when he has tested me, I shall come out like gold' (Job 23.10). After the process the dross, like the fine chaff, is thrown away and forgotten.

What has been refined goes to various artisans. The Hebrew Bible looks upon artisans, and especially upon the instructors of artisans, as people with more than just skill. Like Bezalel son of Uri and Oholiab son of Ahisamach they have a divine gift of designing for (חשב) and working in (חרש) gold, silver, bronze, precious stones and wood, as well as of weaving (ארג), designing for and embroidering (רקם) fabric, and of teaching (להורת) their skills to other people (Exod. 35.30-35). All-rounders like them are technical instructors rather than artisans *practising* all these skills. This is also how the Chronicler, unlike the Deuteronomists, understood the task of the Phoenician Huram-abi contracted by King Solomon as a specialist (איש־חכם; cf. חרש חכם 'a specialist smith', Isa. 40.20) of working in gold, silver, bronze, iron, purple, crimson, and blue fabrics, and of engraving (ידע לפתח), to join his own specialists (החכמים אשר עמי) (2 Chron. 2.7). That such all-rounders were instructors rather than ordinary artisans is also indicated by the fact that ordinary workers in metal and fabric are normally pic-

6. Technology and Meaning

tured as people specialized in only one or two of these trades. In Deuteronomistic literature a collection of various kinds of metal workers are referred to as החרש והמסגר, 'artisans and the (lock)smiths' (2 Kgs 24.14, 16; Jer. 24.1; 29.2), and in their view the artisan King Hiram sends to Solomon is not an instructor but a specialist *bronze/copper* smith (וימלא את־החכמה ואת־התבונה ואת־הדעת לעשות כל־מלאכה בנחשת, 1 Kgs 7.14). Artisans of all kinds are indicated by the generic term חרש, and sometimes distinguished from each other by an added 'genitive', for example, חרשי עץ 'carpenters', חרשי אבן (also חצבים) 'stone-hewers/dressers', חרשי קיר (also גדרים or בנים) 'builders', etc. Often they are simply indicated by their job. Consider the titles of the artisans involved in creating an idol (Isa. 41.7), namely the overseeing (?) artisan (חרש), the smelter/refiner (צרף), the manufacturer of gold plate (מחליק פטיש), and the blacksmith (חולם פעם), and the distinction made in 2 Chron. 24.12 between iron and copper smiths (חרשי נחשת ברזל). The way in which Bezalel, Oholiab and Huram-abi are introduced indicates the high regard the writers had for such craftsmen. Yet in the writings of the ancient Near East upper-class people tended to look down upon them, as is clear from the Egyptian 'Satire of the Trades' and ben Sira 15.

The smiths heated the metals they had to mould over a charcoal fire (פחם) in a furnace, and hammered the hot metal with different kinds of hammers: iron with heavy hammers (מקבות) on an anvil (פעם), and gold or silver (that was required in plate form) with a smaller hammer (פטיש) that was also used for final stone dressing. In more complicated jobs different sections of an item were constructed or moulded separately and later put together by soldering, adhesive material (דבק) or nails (מסמרים) (cf. Isa. 4.7). The smiths also manufactured jewellery, such as armlets and bracelets, earrings, pendants, anklets, crescents and nose rings (Num. 31.50; Isa. 3.19-22), as well as more personal items like amulets, seals and signet rings (cf. Weippert 1988: 626-31, 652-71, 706-18). Engraving (פתח Pi.), mostly mentioned in cultic contexts, was done on stone, horn, gemstone and gold (cf. Exod. 28.9, 11, 36; 39.6; Jer. 17.11; Zech. 3.9) with an iron or specially hard-tipped (diamond?) stylus (עט). Job 19.24 even suggests engravings done on rock with an iron stylus and then filled with molten lead. Given the price of metals these artisans could only have been employed by elite society and would consequently have lived in the bigger cities.

Although the work of artisans of metal is frequently mentioned, the manufacturing of metal objects seldom plays a role in Hebrew Bible imagery, probably because of the later prohibition of the manufacturing of images, which forms the backdrop of the ironic descriptions of the manufacturing process of an idol (Isa. 41.6-7; 44.12-20; Jer. 10.3-16). However, some of the artisans' products function in narratives and literary imagery. So, for example, the Israelites' extraordinary contribution towards the manufacturing of the equipment of the tabernacle includes articles of gold, armlets and bracelets, signet rings, earrings and pendants (Exod. 35.22; Num 31.50). Towards the construction of Aaron's bull image everybody merely donated golden earrings (Exod. 32.2-4). But then notably golden earrings sometimes connote 'idolatry', as when they are specifically mentioned as one of the items Jacob buried under the oak near Shechem (Gen. 35.4). Their presence in a lady's cupboard may, however, merely indicate her elite or royal status, as in Isaiah's description of the ladies of Jerusalem's high society (Isa. 3.19-22). Even Yahweh presented his adoptive daughter, Israel, with all sorts of gold and silver jewellery (עדי): bracelets (עמידים), a neck chain (רביד), a nose ring (נזם), earrings (עגילים), and a beautiful crown (עטרת) (Ezek. 16.11-13). Wearing ornaments was, after all, such a 'woman's thing' that the custom even functions in a rhetorical question: 'Can a girl [בתולה] forget her ornaments, or a bride her attire? Yet my people have forgotten me, days without number' (Jer. 2.32). While one may accept that this custom applied to at least all younger women, the wearing of costly golden and silver jewellery served as a symbol of status, as in Isa. 3.19-22. Moreover, this expression of status could be used to impress menfolk. Picturing Israel in this role, Ezek. 23.40, for example, says that lady Israel, having sent messages of invitation to different men, bathed herself, painted her eyes and decked herself with ornaments (cf. Jer. 4.30). But exactly this trick is condemned in Ezekiel 16: by behaving herself in this way Israel belied her high status as the (adoptive) child of Yahweh. Of such a person the sages would say, 'Like a gold ring in a pig's snout is a beautiful woman without good sense' (or: void of discretion [פרת טעם], Prov. 11.22). While the wearing of jewellery symbolizes status and wealth, taking them off symbolizes sadness and mourning. When the Israelites heard of Yahweh's decision not to lead them to the promised land any more, 'they mourned, and no one put on ornaments' (Exod. 33.4).

Pottery was a very important component of the Israelite household and economy. Clay pottery was used as cooking pots and storage jars

6. Technology and Meaning

for commodities like water, grain, wine and oil. It also played a major role in the trading of agricultural products, and clay was used for ornaments (see Weippert 1988: 410-12). Since taxes were paid in kind and transported to the collection points in jars, potters would, after the introduction of a redistribution economy, have been in great demand, and the Hebrew Bible sometimes pictures them as royal employees (cf. 1 Chron. 4.23). Yet the filthiness of their work (they had to dig for and tread clay) caused important people to look down on them and their products (cf. Lam. 4.2). After having dug their clay, potters had to tread it until it had the right texture to be formed either by hand or on the potter's wheel. If an object on the wheel did not turn out right, the potter would lump the clay together, that is if it was still workable, and remould the object or alter the design. Pottery could have been sun-dried or oven-baked. Whichever way it was manufactured it remained very fragile. A broken jar was useless and was simply cast away. At the most such potsherds could be used to lift some water out of a cistern, handle coals in a fire (Isa. 30.14) or to scribble short notes on, uses for which they had not been made.

Potter's clay, the manufacturing of pottery, and pottery itself serve as points of comparison in various Hebrew Bible similes and metaphors. The treading process symbolizes rough handling, as in Isa. 41.25: 'He [Cyrus] shall trample on rulers as on mortar, as the potter treads clay.' The flexible nature of clay, allowing it to be formed into various shapes, and the way it yields to, for example, a seal impressed on it serves in Job 38.14 to picture the different patterns that the coming light of the morning creates on earth. Yahweh is often pictured in the role of a potter and the individual of the group as potter's clay. Consider the comparison between the process involved in the manufacturing of a clay object and God's forming a human being before birth (Job 10.9). Or 'You [Yahweh] are our Father; we are the clay, and you are our potter; we are all the work of your hand' (Isa. 64.8). It is the potter who decides what he wants to shape on his wheel. Ben Sira 15.6 says:

> A potter kneads the soft earth and laboriously molds each vessel for our service, fashioning out of the same clay both the vessels that serve clean uses and those for contrary uses, making all alike; but which shall be the use of each of them the worker in clay decides.

This view of the potter's right to decision afforded Hebrew Bible writers with two telling comparisons between Yahweh's work and that of a potter. The first is his 'moulding' evil on his wheel: 'Look, I

[Yahweh] am a potter shaping evil against you and devising a plan against you' (Jer. 18.11). The other is that the object on the wheel has no say in the shape it is taking on under the potter's hands: 'Woe to you who strive with your Maker, earthen vessels with the potter! Does the clay say to the one who fashions it, "What are you making"? or "Your work has no handles"?' (Isa. 45.9; cf. 26.9). The lumping together of reusable clay and the reshaping of the object on the wheel becomes the point of comparison in Jer. 18.1-6: ' "Can I not do with you, O house of Israel, just as this potter has done?' says the Lord' (v. 6). When the people remain unrepentant Jeremiah is sent to a city gate to smash symbolically a jar there (Jer. 19.1-2, 10-13) to indicate the impossibility of the Potter-god 'reshaping' his object (Judah). Finally, the finality of a broken jar serves as an image of final judgment: 'You [the King] shall break them [those who rebel against you] with a rod of iron, and dash them in pieces like a potter's vessel' (Ps. 2.9; cf. Isa. 30.14).

The manufacturing of fabric was another trade exercised in ordinary households or by a specialist weaver (רקם ארג). Depending on the product manufactured, various kinds of natural fibres were used, for example, straw, flax, wool and goat's hair, each of which underwent a different process before it could be woven into an object. Wool and goat's hair, for example, had first to be spun into a yarn on a spindle (Dalman 1937: 42-62). The spindle consisted of two parts, namely a head piece (פלך) with a wooden shaft protruding through a hole in the head piece. The head piece had a flat surface on the one side, was oval on top and was made of stone, bone, clay, or later also of wood, with a metal hook fixed to it to hold the spun yarn (Dalman 1937: 51). The second part (פישור) was a stick on which the unspun wool or flax was wound. While plucking and twisting a rough yarn from the raw material, the worker feeds the rough yarn into the spindle, of which she sets the headpiece in motion by rubbing the upper part against her thigh. It is with these two parts of the spindle that the ideal housewife of Prov. 31.19 busies herself. Spinning was the exclusive domain of women and a disgrace for adult men. That is why, in cursing Joab, David says, among other things, 'may the house of Joab never be without one...who holds a spindle' (2 Sam. 3.29).

Depending on the use the spun thread (חוט) would be put to, it could be strengthened by twining up to 12 threads into one cord or string. Consider the reference to the strength of a threefold cord (חוט משלש) in Eccl. 4.12 (Dalman 1937: 62-70). Depending on its function, the flax cord (פְּתִיל־פִּשְׁתִּים, Ezek. 40.3) was known by various names, such as יְתָרִים ('bow string', Judg. 16.7-9), מֵיתָרִים ('tent cord', Isa. 54.2), חֶבֶל ('rope', Josh. 2.15; Jer. 38.6). Various Hebrew Bible images derive from the characteristics of these objects. A single yarn stands for something insignificant (Gen. 14.23) and extreme weakness is like a flax thread smelling fire (פְּתִיל־הַנְּעֹרֶת בַּהֲרִיחוֹ אֵשׁ, Judg. 16.9). Depending on the reason for the application presupposed by the image, a broken cord can symbolize liberation (Ps. 129.4) or calamity, as in Jer. 10.20: 'My tent is destroyed, and all my cords are broken.' A strongly attractive force is a rope pulling one closer (Hos. 11.4), a bad conscience is dragging along a heavy weight on a rope (Isa. 5.18), and affliction and death are strong ropes binding one down (Job 36.8; 2 Sam. 22.6).

The poor would use just the natural fibre, while the rich could have their materials coloured. Except for blue, all coloured fabric mentioned in the Hebrew Bible would have been of wool (Bellinger 1962: 652). In the Hebrew Bible coloured clothes immediately identifies a person of status (cf. Isa. 63.1). To colour natural fibre, like wool, a bundle of the spun thread was first put in a trough and washed by treading, then the excess water was beaten out of the fibre by first hitting it on a flat stone or with a stick and then wringing the bundles of fibre (Dalman 1937: 71). The cords were separated from each other and the whole bundle went into another trough containing diluted colouring agents manufactured from different ingredients derived from plants or animals (Dalman 1937: 73-76). The darkest purple colours (תְּכֵלֶת) were prepared from the Phoenician mussel, of which 12,000 were needed to produce 1.5 g of colouring (Dalman 1937: 79). A slightly cheaper colouring agent that gave a somewhat lighter purple (אַרְגָּמָן) was obtained from the purple snail collected on the northern Palestinian shore. In Deut. 33.19 the tribe of Zebulon, sucking 'the affluence of the seas and the hidden treasures of the sand' (Deut. 33.19) is associated with the trade in this colouring agent (Dalman 1937: 78-83). Two still cheaper colouring agents, producing a deeper purple (שָׁנִים) and a bright red colour (תּוֹלָע) were obtained from a female insect and type of worm found in one of the oak types of the hill country, respectively (according to [Dalman 1937: 84-85] one and the same worm). Although their colouring agents were few in number, the characteristics of the material that was dyed added a rich variety of colour (see Bellinger 1962: 652). For other, for example, cosmetic (Isa. 3.16) or painting (Jer. 22.14; Ezek. 23.14), purposes different agents were used (Dalman 1937: 88).

Of these colours the expensive dark and lighter purple naturally symbolize divinity and royalty. Apart from the repeated instructions in Exodus 26–28 to manufacture all kinds of purple fabric for the Tent of Meeting and the clothes of the high priest, it is also said that people clothe idols in purple (Jer. 10.9). Consider also the references to the purple clothes of the Assyrian royalty (Ezek. 23.25-26) and Mordecai (Est. 8.15; cf. Dan. 5.7). When the ideal wife of Proverbs 31 thus ends up wearing purple (31.22) she has earned herself the highest possible status. Similarly, Lady Wisdom displays her royal status by decorating her couch with coloured coverings of Egyptian linen (Prov. 7.16). However, like Jezebel, who tried to save her life by dressing herself up and painting her eyes to impress Jehu (2 Kgs 9.30), Lady Jerusalem has also spent a fortune in vain:

> And you, O desolate one, what do you mean that you dress in crimson [שָׁנִי, 'red'], that you deck yourself with ornaments of gold [עֲדִי־זָהָב] that you enlarge your eyes with paint [פּוּךְ]? In vain you beautify yourself. Your lovers despise you; they seek your life (Jer. 4.30).

Even though scarlet, purple and red symbolize status and royalty they class *semantically* with black, which, as we have seen in discussing the meaning of 'night' versus 'day' has a negative meaning (cf. Exod. 10.15; Job 30.30; Jer. 4.20; Mic. 3.6). Using the semantic class of these darker (but cheaper) colours, Isa. 1.18 invites Judah: 'though your sins are like scarlet (שָׁנִים "dark red"), they shall be like snow; though they are red like crimson (תּוֹלָע "bright red"), they shall become like wool'. Once the thread was coloured it could be rolled up into a ball (דּוּר) or coil (צְנֵפָה) for use on the loom. Using the preparation of this ball as comparison, Isa. 22.17-18 warns Shebna, the officer in charge of palace affairs who has been climbing the bureaucratic ladder to the top: Yahweh will whirl him round and round on a coil (צָנוֹף יִצְנָפְךָ צְנֵפָה), and throw him like a ball (כַּדּוּר) into a wide land.

The loom itself (דַּלָּה) might have been one of several types, although the most commonly used types during the Iron Age were the horizontal and the Greek vertical. For all practical purposes these two apparatuses consisted of the same technical parts (Dalman 1937: 93-135; Bellinger 1962: 652-53), but the horizontal loom was the apparatus mostly used by women (אֹרְגוֹת, cf. 2 Kgs 23.7) This loom consisted of two beams (about 2–3 metres apart) held in place by four pegs driven into the ground. As a basis for the weaving process a dampened, thicker cord was strung over the loom to cover about 60 cm to form the warp, which was held in place at the weaver's end of the loom by a pole. The technical term for forming a warp is סכה (Dalman 1937: 93). Picturing God as a weaver and the mother's womb as a loom, the beginnings of human life in the womb are sometimes portrayed as setting up a warp (Job 11.10; Ps. 139.13). The warp itself is referred to as שתי, and since weaving work was mostly done by women, the preparers of the warp are called שתת (Isa. 19.10). The somewhat thinner weaving cord was tied to the end of an oval-shaped shuttle, which was then woven through the strings of the warp to form a web (מסכת). When Samson tells Delilah to weave (ארג) his hair into the web on the loom she not only does that, but also drives the end of his locks into the ground with one of the pegs (LXX, thinking of the vertical loom!) holding the loom in place. But when Samson wakes up he pulls away 'the pin, the loom, and the web' (Judg. 16.13-14). The shuttle had to go over the first cord of the warp, underneath the next, over the next, and so on. To allow the shuttle to follow this route more easily every second cord was first picked up and the different strands of the warp held apart by a wooden rod (ניר).[2] Once this trajectory has been cleared the shuttle may pass through faultlessly and quickly. It is in comparing his life span with the swift passage of the shuttle through the cords of the warp that Job 7.6 says, 'My days are swifter than a weaver's shuttle.'

Instead of lying flat on the ground the upper beam of the vertical loom might have leaned against a wall or tree, or the whole instrument might have been mounted on two poles of approximately 200 × 25 × 15 cm, which were then planted vertically into the ground. The lower beam, made of hard wood, was held in place by pegs driven into the ground. It is probably to this lower beam that Goliath's spear is compared (1 Sam. 17.7; cf. 2 Sam. 21.2; 1 Chron. 11.23; 20.5). The vertical loom was mostly operated by male weavers (ארגים, Dalman 1937: 107-108). Since it was more sturdy it could stand more tension, so that the fabric produced on it could be woven more tightly, e.g. for use in the fabrication of sleeping mats (משכב) and canvas for ship sails and tents. Among them were also the craftsmen specializing in weaving with differently coloured cords (מעשה רקם, Exod. 26.36) and those who wove

---

2. Even though this term is always translated with 'light' some contexts seem to rather favour 'guiding rod' as the referent. Consider, for example, 'Haughty eyes and a proud heart—the guiding rod of the wicked—are sin' (Prov. 21.4), or, 'His [David's] God gave him a guiding rod in Jerusalem, setting up (להקים אחריו) his son after him, and establishing Jerusalem' (1 Kgs 15.4).

patterns (מעשה חשב, Exod. 26.1), sometimes mistranslated by 'embroidered' and 'skilfully worked', respectively. To this craft also belonged the finishing of 'finely worked' (שׁרד) material, like the weaving into the finished cloth of a golden thread (Exod. 39.3; Dalman 1937: 126; Bellinger 1962: 654). For the manufacturing of many-coloured fabrics, the warp and the weaving thread obviously needed to be of different materials or colours. In descriptions of a mixed colour cloth the type or colour of the warp is always mentioned first (Bellinger 1962: 653). The specification for the curtains of the tabernacle ('of fine twisted linen, *and* blue, purple and crimson yarns' [Exod. 26.1]) thus prescribe that the warp has to be linen and the weaving material coloured wool. In the specifications for the screen of the courtyard ('blue, purple, and crimson yarns, *and* of fine twisted linen' [Exod. 27.17] the exact opposite is indicated. Once a cloth had reached the desired length the weaver would remove the fabric from the loom, rolling it up as he or she went, and cut the threading yarn. In Isa. 38.12 this procedure becomes a metaphor for the end of life and of dying: '...like a weaver I have rolled up my life; he cuts me off from the loom...' If a professional weaving was going on, it meant that there were elite who ordered the clothes and that business was good, but if weaving stopped, disaster had already struck the elite. This is the implication of the metaphor employed in Isa. 19.9:

> The workers in flax [עבדי פשתים, that is, those who produce raw material for the production of linen] will be in despair, and the carders [שׂריקות, preparing the flax to be spun and woven] and those at the loom [ארגים] will grow pale.

6. *The Technology of War*

The technology of war involved defensive and offensive systems. We have already mentioned the technology employed in the construction of fortified cities, city gates, towers and fortresses. What remains to be discussed is the technology of weaponry (שׁלח; נשק; כלי מלחמה) that had been used in actual battles. Fretz (1982) distinguishes four categories of weapons, which may be summarized as follows:

6. Technology and Meaning

Category	Terms	Referent
Projectiles	קלע	Sling
	סגר; שריה; כידון	Javelin
	שטט; מסע	Dart
	בן־קשת; חצי; חץ	Arrow
	(with אשפה קלי; and קשת)	(with bow and quiver)
Shock weapons (thrust, hack and strike weapons)	מכרה; חרב	Sword
	קון; צלצל; כידון; חנית	Spear
	רמח	Lance
	מקל יד	Handpike
	יתד	Peg
	קרדום; גרזן	Axe
	תותח; מפץ; מפיץ	Club
	שבט	Rod
Mobile weapons	כבול; כר	Battering ram
	מרכבה; מרכב; רכוב; רכב; גלגל; חצן; עגלה	Chariot
	סוס; פרשים	Cavalry
Protective gear (against shock weapons and projections)	סריון; שריון	Coat of mail
	סריון	Breastplate
	דבק	Scale armour
	מצחה	Greaves
	קובע; מעוז ראש; כובע	Helmet
	סחרה שלם; צנה; מגן	Shield, buckle

Aiding a siege war (צרים; מצור) was, of course, also the siege wall and other siege works, for example, the siege ramp (סללה), siege tower (בחון), siege-work (חיק) and battering ram, which is only mentioned in wars against Israel/Judah (Fretz 1982: 894), and rightly so, since the lighter, mobile battering ram was first introduced into ancient Near Eastern warfare in the eighth century by Tiglath-pileser III (Herzog 1992b: 265). Even though Fretz's categories have not been established from a semantic point of view, they seem to have much in common with how Hebrew speakers classified their weapons. In literary imagery in which implements of war play a role, one item from each of Fretz's categories normally *frequently* features, for example, among the projectiles the *arrow*, among the shock weapons the *sword*, among the mobile weapons the *chariot*, and among the protective gear the *shield*. In lists of war items, where the bow naturally replaces the arrow, the relative prominence of these items also emerges. In longer lists of implements of war the items are simply mentioned in the order of decreasing or increasing size, for example horse, chariot, shield, bow (Jer. 46.9; Zech. 9.10), or bow, sword, war horse and horseman (Hos. 1.7). In shorter lists, however, certain patterns emerge. If the *bow* is mentioned, it mostly takes precedence over other implements of war, for example, bow and shield (2 Chron. 17.17); bow, spear, shield (Ps. 46.10; Jer. 50.42); bow and javelin (Jer. 6.23); bow and coat of mail (Jer. 51.3); bow, infantry, horse (Amos 2.15). If the *sword* is part of the list it takes precedence, for example, sword, spear, javelin (1 Sam. 17.45); sword and spear (1 Sam. 13.22; 17.47; Nah. 3.3); while the *spear* has precedence over the javelin (1 Sam. 17.45; Job 39.23; Ps. 35.3). If, however, the *shield* forms part of the list, it tends to take precedence over other items, for example, shield and sword (Deut. 33.29; 1 Chron 5.18; Ps. 76.3); shield and spear (1 Chron. 12.8, 12, 34); shield and buckler (Ps. 35.2; 91.4; Ezek. 38.4, but cf. Jer. 46.3 and Ezek. 23.24). The indication of *soldiers* by expressions like 'those (able to) carrying shield and sword' (Jer. 46.9; 1 Chron. 5.18), or 'experts in shield and spear' (1 Chron. 12.8, 24, 34; cf. 2 Chron. 25.5), or 'able to draw the sword' (2 Sam. 24.9; 1 Chron. 5.18; 21.5) also indicates the relative significance of these items. It therefore is only logical that the arrow/bow, sword and shield would be most frequently used in stock literary imagery, with the first two symbolizing danger and the last safety. However, if greater calamities are pictured, other items in the offensive or defensive technology also feature. Consider the following table:

Meaning	Symbol	Examples
Hardship	City under siege; attacked by arrows	Job 6.4; 19.20; Pss. 7.12-13 (Heb. vv. 13-14); 31.21; 38.2 (Heb. v. 3)
Get ready (for attack)	Arrows in quiver; bent bow, drawn sword; prepare/oil/ uncover shield	Pss. 11.2; 37.14; Isa. 21.5, 15; 22.6; 49.2; Jer. 46.3
Danger	Arrows in quiver; arrow; sword; war club	Prov. 25.18; Jer. 5.16; Lam. 3.13; cf. Ezek. 23.24
Life-threatening situation	Hammer; battle cry; siege work/ wall; fire/breach in the wall; battering ram; collapsing wall; cavalry, archers, exile	Isa. 30.13; Jer. 4.29; 49.27; Ezek. 4.2; 21.22; 26.8; 38.4; Amos 4.3; Nah. 2.5

Meaning	Symbol	Examples
Defence, protection	Someone draws spear/ javelin on one's behalf; quiver full of arrows; shield; buckler; helmet; breastplate; fortress	Pss. 3.3; 5.12; 18.2, 35; 35.2; 127.5, etc.
Peace	Breaking the bow; shattering the spear; burning the shield, melting the sword	Ps. 46.9; Isa. 2.4

7. *The Technology of Measurement*

In monarchical Israel and Judah a great deal of planning went into cities and buildings, while the redistribution economy necessitated keeping record of quantities and to determine the value of products (Isserlin 1984). To understand texts referring to the measurement of length, surface, volume and weight it is necessary to be aware not only of the technology involved (e.g. measuring instruments) and its function in the cultural system, but also of the wider systems of calculation of which these measurements formed part (cf. Seybold 1982: 246-48).

The first important observation to be made in this regard is that the Hebrew Bible reflects a particularly confusing system of measurement. There are three major reasons for this state of affairs. First, an earlier (pre-exilic) metrical system was later replaced by a Babylonian sexagesimal system and later again by Greek and Roman systems of measurement (Powell 1962: *passim*). Secondly, the biblical writers of Persian and Hellenistic times frequently (but often unsuccessfully) tried to convert older measurements (of which they had no first-hand knowledge) into the systems of their own times, causing even more confusion in the process. Thirdly, these writers sometimes did not wish to convey 'information' but to *picture* an object or indicate its *value* by giving its measurements with reference to the customary *symbolic* value of certain figures (see, in this regard, Hoyrup 1993; Rochberg-Halton 1991; Parpola 1993).

Following Powell (1962) the following summary may be given of Hebrew Bible measurements and their approximate 'meaning' in terms of the metric system.

Referent	Unit and relationship	Approximate value	Notes
Distance	A day's journey	20 km	
	A bowshot	180 m	
	A *gomed*	Unknown	Only Judg. 3.16
	A pace/step	Unknown	Only 2 Sam. 6.13
Length	Finger	21 mm	Only Jer. 52.21
	Palm (4 fingers)	83 mm	
	Span (3 palms)	250 mm	
	Cubit (2 spans)	500 mm	Basic unit of length, however in relation to Solomon's temple given in Babylonian sexagesimal ratios
	Reed	Unknown	Only in Ezekiel, derived from Babylonian scientific system
Surface	Yoke	25,000 m^2	Only Isa. 5.10
	Kab	104 m^2	All areas here according to Late Babylonian system
	Seah (6 kab)	625 m^2	
	Kor (30 seah)	18,800 m^2	
Volume: dry measure	*Omer/issaron*	1–2 litres	
	Ephah (10 omer)	10–20 litres	In Kings sometimes adapted to post-exilic norms
	Homer (10 ephah)	100–200 litres	
Volume: liquids (pre-exilic)	*Log*	500 ml	
	Hin (12 log)	6 litres	
	Bath (4 hin)	24 litres	
Capacity: dry/liquid (post-exilic)	*Kab*	2 litres	Babylonian system did not distinguish dry/liquid capacities. In the Jewish system the liquid system seems to have remained the same
	Seah (6 kab)	12 litres	
	Ephah/Bath (3 seah)	36 litres	
	Kor/Homer (10 ephah)	360 litres	
Weight	Shekel	10–12 g	Basic weight unit with varying values
	Pim	9–10 g	Judaean/Asdod shekel
	Beka (half a heavier shekel)	6 g	
	Gerah	13–14 g	Sanctuary shekel
	Mina	500–600 g	Occurs only post-exilic sexagesimal systems
	Talent	30 kg	A sexagesimal structured weight measure

6. *Technology and Meaning*

Even though bartering had been the primary way for ordinary people of obtaining wanted goods, 'money' always played its part in the culture. Since, except for cosmetics and spices (Exod. 30.23), things sold were not weighed but sold by length or capacity, the real function of the shekel was to weigh metal fragments used as 'currency', for example, a shekel of copper, silver or gold (Weippert 1988: 584). Note, in connection with the sale of property, 'I signed the deed, sealed it, got witnesses, and weighed the money on scales' (Jer. 32.10). To weigh the metal a trader would hold a balance (מאזנים) with scales (פלס) in his hand and put a (stone) weight (אבן) from his weights' bag (Mic. 6.11) on one scale and the metal pieces on the other. This procedure is implied by the acusation in Amos 8.5, making the traders say:

> When will the new moon be over so that we may sell grain; and the sabbath, so that we may offer wheat for sale? We will make the ephah small and the shekel great, and practise deceit with false balances.

In other words they are selling less grain for more money. Such a trader might even have different sets of weights (אבן ואבן, Prov. 20.23) in his bag: a lighter set for shopping and a heavier set for selling. In an effort to stem this malpractice Lev. 19.36 says, 'You shall have honest balances, honest weights, an honest *ephah*, and an honest *hin*', that is, take the right amount for the correct measure of grain (*ephah*) or liquid (*hin* is *bath* in Ezek. 45.10). In a metaphorical sense heavily laden scales indicate intense suffering and anxiety (e.g. Job 6.2-3). Human beings themselves are also evaluated on the scale by adding qualities like power and justice. If human beings possess these qualities they will tip the balance in their favour. This was the well-known message Belshazzar received in the message written on the wall: מנא מנא תקל 'weighed, weighed, too light' (Dan. 5.25). Also, the justice of God may, at least by implication, be weighed on a scale. Professing his innocence (and implying that God has short-changed him), Job (31.5-8) says:

> If I have walked with falsehood, and my foot has hurried to deceit—let me be weighed in a just balance, and let God know my integrity!—If my step has turned aside from the way, and my heart has followed my eyes, and if any spot has clung to my hands; then let me sow, and another eat; and let what grows for me be rooted out.

So can any merit be measured? Discussing trustworthiness, Ps. 62.9 concludes that human beings are a mere puff of air (הבל). On the balance their deceitful nature (כזב) makes the measuring scale swing up. Isaiah 40.15 even goes further: measured against divine power and intelligence human beings in general compare to a negligible speck of dust on the balance. The frailty of human beings is again expressed in terms of length measures, for example, a human life is but 'a few handbreadths' (Ps. 39.5; Heb. v. 6).

Volume measures and prices may again indicate scarcity or abundance, a rip-off or a bargain. Consider the following comparison:

Time of siege (2 Kgs 6.25)	Price	Time of plenty (2 Kgs 7.1)	Price
Donkey's head	880 g silver	Whole horse (2 Chron. 1.17)	1,650 g silver
250 ml dove's dung	55 g silver	12 litres wheat meal/ 24 litres barley	11 g silver

Consider also Isaiah's prediction of doom by announcing a time when a farmer shall sow 100 litres of seed but only harvest 10 litres (Isa. 5.10). Or the difference between the yield of a hard day's gleaning for Ruth (10 litres) and Boaz's gift (50 litres) after the night on the threshing floor (Ruth 2.17; 3.15).

8. *The Technology of Writing*

In evaluating the cultural effect of writing and literacy, one has to distinguish between the first introduction of writing into a society and its general diffusion, which may lie centuries apart (Goody and Watt 1963: 40). Considering the Egyptian 'Satire on the Trades', according to which every artisan has a boss except for the scribe, who is the boss, one may say that, until at least the *late* eighth century BCE, when literacy became a more widespread phenomenon (at least in Judah [Weippert 1988: 579-84; Millard 1985]), the ability to write remained a powerful factor in the reinforcement of class distinctions (Goody and Watt 1963: 58-59) already brought about by the redistribution economy and symbolized by the architecture, town planning and possessions of the powerful. Among the powerful, so the Hebrew Bible says, notably counted was the scribe (cf. 2 Kgs 18.18; 19.2; 22.3; Neh. 8.1; cf. Ezek. 9.2). Literacy has a much more profound influence on culture, though, than merely distinguishing class. A few examples may illustrate this influence.

6. Technology and Meaning

As long as a culture is dependent on oral transmission it is a face-to-face culture (Goody and Watt 1963: 29) in which the authority of the transmitted information depends on the person and status of the transmitter (e.g. parent to child, priest to ordinary person [Tonkin 1995: 39]). However, when writing enters the scene messages, for example, can be sent in writing and read out on behalf of the sender. In such circumstances the authority of a message sent by an absent authority has to be proven. In ancient Israel the method of authorization was a seal impression on a piece of clay attached to the written document, as when Jezebel endorsed her letters to the nobles and elders of Naboth's city with the royal seal (1 Kgs 21.8) or when Esther's written wishes regarding the treatment of Jews in the empire were authorized with the impression of the king's seal ring (Est. 8.8). Moreover, readers may, in the absence of the author, interpret his intentions in different ways. Writing therefore often necessitates *authorized* interpreters on whose interpretation an illiterate audience has to depend, as when the Levites had to interpret and give meaning to (מפרש רשום שכל) the Law read out by Ezra (Neh. 8.8) and made the audience divorce their non-Israelite wives.

In oral communication there is, further, a direct relationship between symbol and referent, i.e. there are no archaisms or strange terms in need of a dictionary definition, since the meaning and possible connotations of a term or expression is well-known to and immediately experienced by all speakers of the language. Changes in meaning occur gradually and with the participation and knowledge of the speakers (Goody and Watt 1963: 29). Not so with a written text, which quickly becomes fossilized language, unintelligible to ordinary people, accessible only to the learned, and in need of explanation. Consider the note in 1 Sam. 9.9, 'Formerly in Israel, when a man went to inquire of God, he said, "Come, let us go to the seer"; for he who is now called a prophet was formerly called a seer.' Wherever written texts are looked upon as authoritative this characteristic of written tradition removes ordinary people from their tradition and alienates them from it.

In oral transmission memory plays a significant role. However, given the limited storage capacity of the human brain and the lack in an oral culture of a body of chronologically ordered statements to which reference could be made, the individual as well as collective memory tends to store only what is of critical importance for *present* social relations and finds it difficult to distinguish between what was and what is

(Goody and Watt 1963: 34). Each next generation mediates the cultural heritage by interpreting it in such a manner that new elements are authorized and rationalized. Two examples may illustrate the process. First, genealogies are mnemonic systems of social relations, privileges and duties (see Chapter 7 on social organization). If they are to carry out this function, they should be, and are, constantly adjusted. Logically, oral genealogies should increase in length as new generations are born. However, despite the addition of younger generations an oral genealogy tends to refer to as many people now as it did a century ago (Goody and Watt 1963: 32-33). The added depth caused by new births is compensated for by a process of genealogical shrinkage or structural amnesia in the middle of the list, leaving mostly only the first and the last three or four generations intact. Of these the first few define the group's *identity* and the last few the individual's *status* in the community. Once a genealogy is written down, the whole picture changes, of course, because new generations may then be added at will. This characteristic of a written genealogy identifies 1 Chronicles 1–10 as a *literary* genealogy.

The second example comes from the African kingdom of Dahomey. In Dahomian folklore the existing political and social institutions are attributed to a certain Wegbaja, who, very much like David in the Hebrew Bible, is said to have been recognized by the village chiefs as 'king' (cf. 2 Sam. 5.3) because of the lavishness of his gift-giving to them (cf. 1 Sam. 30.26-31) and because he established order (cf. 2 Sam. 4–10). Legitimizing not only Wegbaja's ascent but also the *present social and political order*, Dahomian folklore presents the time before Wegbaja as an era of general anarchy and lawlessness (Law 1997: 167-168), very much like the book of Judges does in respect of the pre-monarchical age in Israel. In this way the 'stylized' past is *incorporated* into the present as a legitimizing force. What ceases to be of contemporary relevance is often eliminated from tradition by the process of forgetting (Goody and Watt 1963: 30). It is this process of ignoring what is unimportant or trivial under present conditions that forms the background of the Hebrew Bible's notions of 'forgetting' or 'not remembering'. When a plaintiff says to God, 'Do not forget the oppressed' (Ps. 10.12), or 'Do not remember the sins of my youth' (Ps. 25.7) it means, 'Do not regard the oppressed as irrelevant' and, 'Regard the sins of my youth as trivial.'

However, once something has been *written* up, it cannot be elimi-

6. Technology and Meaning

nated from 'memory'. Hence the repeated divine command in the Hebrew Bible to write down important things (e.g. Exod. 17.14; Isa. 30.8; Jer. 36.2; Ezek. 24.2). A 'text' may simply serve as a memory aid (זכרון) by supplying the first few words or most salient points of what should be remembered, like the ten commandments is a summary of the law (cf. Exod. 17.14; Jer. 36.2). A text may, of course, also store what has to be exactly remembered (cf. Ezek. 43.11). To guarantee the authenticity of such a literary 'memory' (whether an instruction or a contract) documents were rolled up and sealed with an official stamp impression (e.g. Jer. 32.44; Dan. 8.26). It is with reference to this practice that Job fears a confrontation with God, who might have written down all his transgressions and stored the documents in a sealed container in his treasury (Job 14.17; cf. Deut. 32.34). Since a store room may catch fire or be flooded, some kinds of archival material, for example, ink written papyrus documents, were prone to damage. Really important documents were therefore sometimes written or engraved on a hard surface, such as a potsherd or clay or wooden tablet (לוח), although stone (לחת האבן) was the most secure way. In a metaphorical sense the human mind ('heart') is sometimes spoken of in the Hebrew Bible as a 'tablet' that may be inscribed with loyalty (Prov. 3.3) or sin (Jer. 17.1).

Assisted by the processes of selective memory and present need, stories about the past may be easily adjusted and conflicting reports harmonized as long as they are transmitted orally. But once such memories have been committed to writing succeeding generations are faced with a 'finality' that can only be adapted and harmonized with difficulty (Goody and Watt 1963: 44-45). A classical example of the problem that confronted ancient scribes in compiling the Hebrew Bible is the story in Genesis 37 of the selling of Joseph to certain merchants who happened to pass by. One tradition or text named the Ishmaelites (37.25; 38.1) and another Midianites (37.36). This problem was solved by having the Midianites selling Joseph to the Ishmaelites (37.28b) and by inserting the story of Judah and Tamar between two conflicting conclusions to the two versions (37.36; 39.1). It is in confrontation with such inconsistencies in the picture of life inherited from the past that literates become aware of the past as different from the present (Goody and Watt 1963: 56). This awareness not only leads to a more objective and critical attitude towards the past. It also forces the individual to become a palimpsest of layers of beliefs and attitudes belonging to different stages in historical time (Goody and Watt 1963: 57). Because this experience is typical of the literati of a community *only* they gradually become intellectually and spiritually alienated from the rest of the cultural group, for whom the indisputable past remains to be part of the present.

But the literati also have an advantage over the populace. While what is passed on by word of mouth automatically forms part of the indisputable cultural heritage, what is in writing is *not* part of the common culture. This circumstance makes it possible for literate people to be selective regarding the past. They may ignore, avoid or adjust the past and in that manner shape the present (Goody and Watt 1963: 60), also for the illiterate. Two examples may illustrate the procedure. It is, first, fairly clear that the story of Isaac's offering on Moriah (Gen. 22.1-19) originally had Shechem as its setting. This is indicated by (a) the reference to a *three days' journey* from Beersheba to a spot where one could see the place of offering *in the distance* (v. 4)—implying roughly 80 kilometers and a conspicious mountain, and (b) the reference to an unknown *land*, Moriah (v. 2). The first (geographical) indicator points to Shechem, and the second to a scribal alteration of ארץ חמרים (cf. Gen. 34.2) into ארץ המריה. The same probably happened in the case of Abraham's encounter with Melchizedek. He is said to have been king of Shalem (שלם), a place identified by the Amarna letters as Shechem. On the mere sound of the name, however, it was associated with Jerusalem (ירושלם). These alterations enabled the scribes to associate a powerful ancient tradition with Jerusalem and to legitimize the 'outsider' city as an obvious site for the sanctuary. If one, secondly, takes seriously the repeated references in the book of Kings to the *Annals of the Kings*, the scribes writing about this period must have been extremely selective with their sources. The picture of the kings they paint in their book are, consequently, very one-sided, as is clear from a comparison of the (successful and prominent) historical and (childish and godless) literary King Ahab. The fact that *their* selective picture has inhabited the minds of thousands of generations of readers of their book illustrates the power of writing. Moreover, whereas oral tradition survives by virtue of its ability to move along with the times, always adapting to new circumstances, the continued existence of an elite literate group of ritual specialists and bureaucrats depends on the maintenance of the *existing* social order. By registering, recording and rewriting they make permanent the present social order and ideological

6. Technology and Meaning

picture, and so become a powerfully conservative force in society (Goody and Watt 1963: 37).

While traditional transmission is mostly interested in the local past (Goody and Watt 1963: 47) and tends to *locate* stories with reference to an itinerary rather than to date, written 'histories' tend to have a broader view and to *periodize* events with reference to monarchs. In the words of Tonkin (1995: 34), 'If a geochronology "mimes" duration and time in terms of sequential movement over space, a dynastic account mimes social successivity as a sequence of rulers.' These two characteristics of a written account of the past explain much of the procedure followed in the writing of the Hebrew Bible. First, the Yehud scribes took a wider, 'all Israelite' perspective. Secondly, they ordered their material with reference to the succession of kings. It is the latter procedure that caused them serious problems of chronology, that is, of synchronizing events according to Ephraimite and Judaean succession.

Finally, quite apart from taking culture into directions it would not have taken had nobody been literate, writing has a powerful influence on a language itself and, consequently, also on literature. For example, writing challenges writers to be explicit and often leads to the construction of a 'literate' language, whose grammar and way of expression differ substantially from everyday language. Writing also enables a writer to construct complicated sentences or present detailed instructions and still be understood. Without the technique of writing many of the long-winded sentences in Deuteronomy or the instructions for the construction for the tabernacle in Exodus would have been unintelligible. For oral communication to be effective it has to rely on an audience's short-term memory. A written narrative or poem does not, however, have to cope with such restrictions. It was writing that made the composition of a poem like Psalm 119 and a narrative like Joshua–Kings possible. Moreover, a written text has an advantage over an oral text in that it can make its structures visible, as happened, for example, in the case of acrostic poems.

The technology of writing has not only deeply and profoundly influenced ancient Israelite society, it also made the production of the Hebrew Bible itself possible. That this text is of a late date is clear from the obvious way in which its authors accept that every individual of their readership can read and write:

> Hear, O *Israel*: The Lord is our God, the Lord alone... Keep these words [the book of Deuteronomy] that I am commanding you today in your

heart. Recite them...bind them [in written form] as a sign on your hand, fix them [in written form] as an emblem on your forehead, and write them on the door-posts of your house and on your gates (Deut. 6.5-9).

9. *Conclusion*

Just how deeply entrenched linguistic expression is in its cultural environment has become abundantly clear in this chapter. Without a sound knowledge of the technological environment presupposed by the text of the Hebrew Bible one will certainly not get very far in comprehending it, let alone arguing about better and worse interpretations. It also became clear once more that the implied culture should be viewed as an organism. The various technologies discussed are all deeply involved in the economic, social and political life of the characters, while the imagery drawn from this world clearly informed not only the imagery of religious language but most probably also the definition of God, who is now pictured as a farmer, then as this or that artisan, now as an invader, then as trader, to name a few occupations.

The tentative discussion of the technological world presupposed by the language of the Hebrew Bible also made it clear that the authors of the text had a fairly intimate knowledge of various techniques of specialized production, which probably identifies them as city dwellers.

Their further knowledge of the physical environment in which their upper-class characters live and act may further indicate that they might have originated from the same quarters. They were, after all, writers, and so have those been on whose texts and notes they based their story. This again has implications for the cosmological and religious dimensions of the text, because those cultural facets will most probably also have to be understood in relation to the views of upper-class city dwellers of the time.

Chapter 7

SOCIAL ORGANIZATION AND MEANING

In any society human cooperation is important. In a subsistence economy it is even more important, since in that environment everybody's survival depends of the full participation of all other members of the group. In order to ensure the cooperation of all its members a society has to organize itself. Such organization implies, among other things, the setting of clear collective goals, collectively acceptable mechanisms (customs) for achieving those goals, decisions on structures of authority (for effective decision-making) and assigning status, distributing tasks and responsibilities, etc. For what form of organization a community settles on largely depends on the physical environment the group finds itself in and the challenges it has to face.

1. *Collective Goals*

In a subsistence economy the goals of the community are very basic, like providing enough food and shelter for its members, caring for each other, especially for those who cannot fend for themselves, like children and the aged, and guaranteeing as far as possible the safety of the community. To achieve these goals it is necessary that there are enough hands to carry out the tasks crucial for the group's survival, that each member of the community may be relied upon to carry out the tasks assigned to him or her, to keep the peace among group members, to draw clear lines between 'us' and 'them' and to defend the integrity of the group.

In the following paragraphs we shall pay attention to some of the mechanisms commonly devised to achieve such goals. One example will therefore suffice here to illustrate the effects of goal settings on the value system of a community and the benefit of insight into such values for the interpretation of Hebrew Bible literature. One of the ways of ensuring survival in subsistence economies is securing enough hands to carry out the necessary tasks and, in view of a high infant mortality rate in such communities, a large enough offspring to take care of parents in their old age.

This motivates the high premium characters and narrators in the Hebrew Bible put on large families, and, logically, on fertility—especially female fertility. Psalm 128.3 says of the righteous, 'Your wife will be like a fruitful vine within your house; your children will be like olive shoots around your table,' that is, sprouting forth spontaneously, as it were (cf. Prov. 17.6). For that reason some curses in the Hebrew Bible involve posterity, for example, wishing a person no offspring at all, or their starvation. Consider, for example, 'You [Yahweh] will destroy their [the wicked's] offspring from the earth, and their children from among humankind' (Ps. 21.10; Heb. v. 11), and, 'May his [the godless's] children wander about and beg; may they be driven out of the ruins they inhabit' (Ps. 109.10). A family's childlessness is always blamed on the infertility of women in Hebrew Bible literature. A childless married woman is said to be 'barren' (עקרה) or simply called 'the barren one' (עקרת). Infertility and barrenness are not understood as a consequence of physical disorders or of intermarriage but as a wilful divine act. It is Yahweh who either closes (סגר 'locks') or opens (פתח) a woman's womb (cf. 1 Sam. 1.5; Gen. 29.31; 30.22; cf. Ps. 113.9). Quite understandably Prov. 30.16 lists her never-ending yearning alongside the earth's unquenchable 'thirst' for water and the insatiability of the domain of death. Superlative joy is, equally understandably, metaphorically expressed with, 'Sing, O barren one [עקרה] who did not bear; burst into song and shout, you who have not been in labour! For the children of the desolate woman will be more than the children of her that is married' (Isa. 54.1).

Without a sympathetic understanding of the personal and social implications of the term 'barrenness' it is easy to overlook its importance for the plot and meaning of several Hebrew Bible patriarchal and hero stories involving formerly barren women, whose joy-bringing children achieve great things (cf. Gen. 11.30; 25.21; 29.31; Judg. 13.2; 1 Sam. 2.5; Ps. 113.9; Prov. 30.16). It is this context, in which a woman's primary value lies in her ability to bear children and a maximum number of children is desirable, that practices like polygamy or concubinage are to be understood. Since the long periods women tended to suckle their children (cf. 1 Sam. 23–28) acted as a sort of birth control measure, more wives could provide more children to lend a hand on a farm-holding.

Although a redistribution economy, if superimposed on a subsistence economy, logically implies the same ends as subsistence economies, the primary goals of the redistribution system are different. In this environment such goals include ensuring the safety of the state, the contribution of community members to the central pool, the availability of the necessary infrastructure (Chapter 6), the security of the central authority, etc. What is important in the present context is that in a redistribution economy the formulation of a society's common goals is done centrally, far away from, and without the consent of, the contributors to the system. Although the needs of a state are partly determined by the needs of its population, other factors also play an important role, such as international power relations and trade, the image the powerful wish to project (cf. Jer. 22.14), the size and activities of the standing army, the number and remuneration of bureaucrats. Where contributors have no say in decisions and cannot audit state expenditure, the measures taken by the central authority to ensure the desired income may increasingly become intimidation rather than persuasion, let alone cooperation. This is the picture most of the prophetic books paint of the Israelite and Judaean states, for example Mic. 2.1-2:

> Alas for those who devise wickedness and evil deeds on their beds! When the morning dawns, they perform it, because it is in their power. They covet fields, and seize (גזלו) them; houses, and take them away; they oppress householder and house, people and their inheritance.

Or Ezek. 22.29:

> The people of the land (עם הארץ) have practised extortion (עשקו עשק) and committed robbery (גזלו גזל); they have oppressed the poor and needy, and have extorted from the alien without redress.

2. Mechanisms for Achieving Goals

Whether a strived-after goal involves securing sufficient food, supplying safe shelters, coercing members of the community to foot the state bill, obtaining the goodwill of an influential person or a god, or getting rid of a tyrant, the point where all goal-achieving mechanisms meet is custom. Custom is not 'decided' upon, though. Custom 'happens'. To achieve specific goals plans must be devised for securing the right materials, developing or obtaining appropriate skills, choosing the right time, and ensuring that the necessary organizational structures are in place. A plan that over time shows itself as the most successful in achieving a specific goal tends to become a 'recipe' for action. A problem arises, however, when recipes for the achievement of different goals clash (e.g. when they involve the same work force, tools, time, etc.) and cannot therefore be implemented concurrently. Securing the satisfaction of all needs in such circumstances necessitates the planning of activities. Tasks may, for example, be divided among different sections of the community (e.g. between men, women, children and the elderly), or assigned to different specialists (such as priests, elders, metal workers, shepherds, farm hands). Tasks may also be prioritized and scheduled. Once a satisfactory recipe for attaining a community's collective goals has been found it becomes a routine, which reduces the burden of constant or individual improvisation. Different groups (e.g. families) may, of course, develop different routines in attaining particular goals. Once a *specific* routine has, for some reason, been accepted by a whole cultural community as *the most effective* or *right* way of obtaining specific goals such a routine becomes a *custom*. A custom typically is 'our' way of achieving goals.

Such customs, referred to in the Hebrew Bible as חקות (sing. חק), משפט, or, more seldomly, דרך, pervade the economic, social, political and religious behaviour of a cultural unit and regulate behaviour and procedures in all things cultural: ploughing, sowing, harvesting, winnowing, making wine, buying and selling, constructing a building, manufacturing jewellery, writing (Franken 1965), dress and hair styles (cf. Lev. 21.5), initiation, marriage, sharing spoils of war (1 Sam. 30.17-25), systems of government (1 Sam. 8.11-17), inaugurating a king (2 Kgs 11.14), lamenting the dead (2 Chron. 35.25), supplicating a god (1 Kgs 18.28), and general religious behaviour (2 Kgs 17.8, 19, 34, 40). In a metaphorical way of speaking even God acts according to divine custom (Ps. 119.132).

The reasons for a routine becoming a custom may vary. It may simply be because it works best, or because doing something in a particular way symbolizes something of importance, as when dressing up in a particular manner or riding on a mule symbolizes status and authority. A fairly prominent reason is that a routine fits in with the values shared by the group. The value system of a culture consists of a number of goal-oriented 'rules' prescribing the rights, privileges and duties of each member of the group. A routine that fits 'the rules' will be more

7. Social Organization and Meaning   237

acceptable than one that would violate them. When the Deuteronomists, for example, accuse the Ephraimite tribes of having followed the customs of the 'nations' (חקות הגוים, 2 Kgs 17.8), the implication is that, in following their kings, the Ephraimites have rejected the (author's definition of the) *value system* of Yahwism, which, among other things, according to Deuteronomy, Ezra and Nehemiah, precludes exogamic marriage (cf. Deut. 7.3; Ezra 10.3; Neh. 13.23-28).

The same routine practised in different value frameworks may even acquire a contradictory meaning. For instance, the custom of ritual gift-giving in a reciprocal economy symbolizes a desirable value, like good neighbourliness. In a redistribution economy, however, gift-giving becomes bribery and symbolizes the undesirable value of disproportionate distribution of power.

The rules stating the rights, privileges and duties of community members (and thus evaluating custom) are not explicitly verbalized. They are rather implied in all actions sanctioned by the group. inculturation means, among other things, to get acquainted with the customs and, especially, the values of the group. Novices become inculturated by carefully observing customs being acted out, listening to proverbs, stories about the past, fables and myths, watching rituals being carried out, paying attention to what is sanctioned and what not, receiving instruction, etc. The fact that the authors of Deuteronomy prescribe *precise* recipes for various situations, and are bent upon *instruction* (cf. Deut. 4.10; 5.31; 11.19) as well as on promising *rewards* for customary and *punishment* for uncustomary behaviour (e.g. Deut. 4.25-26, 40; 27-28) may indicate the novelty of the religious system (monotheistic Yahwism) they introduce and/or the function and power of the institutions they represent. By advocating particular values, among which count as high priorities ethnic exclusivity, the brotherhood of all (uncontaminated) 'Israelites', and discrimination against non-members (Deist 1994), Deuteronomy motivates a (new?) set of recipes as customs. It is only in a community embracing these *values* that Deuteronomy's recipes for eating (Deut. 12.20-25; 14.3-21), sowing (22.9), ploughing (22.10), weaving (22.11), clothing (22.5), doing business (15.1-3; 23.19-20), marrying (7.3-4), and making war (7.1-2; 20.1-20) can be or become custom. How knowledge of such customs may inform the interpretation of the Hebrew Bible may be illustrated by examples from the customs of task distribution, scheduling, marriage and customs of address.

The stories of David's anointing as king (1 Sam. 16.1-13) and Joseph's relationship with his brothers (Gen. 37.2) presuppose the customary distribution of tasks among members of a family, according to which the younger male members of a household tend to the flocks. When, in some cases, teenage *girls* tend flocks, like the daughters of the priest of Midian (Exod. 2.16) and Rachel (Gen. 29.9), it is exceptional. In both cases the reader is confronted with a family whose 'name' is about to be extinguished because of a lack of male members. Because these girls have no brothers they are forced to act in an uncustomary manner. That families whose girls are forced to do 'men's work' are more than just frowned upon in Hebrew Bible literature is indicated by the rude treatment Jethro's daughters receive from the male shepherds of the community (cf. Exod. 2.16-19). Also, the female voice in Cant. 1.6, even though employing metaphor, implies the shamefulness for a woman of 'men's' work. 'Do not gaze at me because I am dark, because the sun has gazed on me. My mother's sons were angry with me; they made me keeper of the vineyards, but my own vineyard I have not kept.' When Moses then intervenes on behalf of the 'shamed' daughters his act characterizes him as a person with great sympathy, and therefore as suitably equipped for his future task. Moses is, after all, uniquely sympathetic on the face of the earth (Num. 12.3). The shame of being forced to infringe upon customary female–male task division is also the background of David's curse on Joab: 'May the house of Joab never be without one who has a discharge, or who is leprous, or *who holds a spindle...*' that is, a man busying himself with women's work (2 Sam. 3.29).

The customary scheduling and prioritizing of tasks forms the background of the well-known Gezer calendar (cf. Turkowski 1969: 27):

>Two months (October/November) for (olive) harvest
>Two months (December/ January) for planting (grain)
>Two months (February/ March) for late planting
>One month (April) for hoeing up of flax
>One month (May) for harvesting barley
>One month (June) for (wheat) harvest and festivity
>One month (August) for vine tending
>One month (September) for summer fruit.

The customary nature of such 'scheduled' times is indicated by the temporal settings of events in the Hebrew Bible with reference to, for example, 'the time when women go out to draw water?' (צאת לעת

7. *Social Organization and Meaning*

השאבת Gen. 24.11); 'the time of the barley harvest' (בימי קציר שערים, Ruth 1.22; 2 Sam. 21.9) and 'the time of the wheat harvest' (בימי קציר־חטים, Gen. 30.14; Exod. 34.22; Judg. 15.1; 1 Sam. 6.13; 12.17). A changed social environment is indicated by another formula of prioritized time, namely 'the time when kings go out to battle' (לעת צאת המלכים), 2 Sam. 11.1). Also, God is pictured as having set times for doing things. He has a time for inspecting human behaviour ('the time of their inspection' [עת פקדתם], Jer. 8.12; 10.15; 51.18), which may imply a 'time of trouble' (עת צרה) for humans (Judg. 10.14; Neh. 9.27; Job 38.23; Ps. 37.39; Isa. 37.39; Jer. 14.8); 'a time of vengeance' (עת נקמה, Jer. 51.6; see Job 14.13; Ps. 6.1); and 'a time of favour' (עת רצון, Ps. 69.13; Isa. 49.8). It is precisely about humans gaining insight into this divine 'schedule' that Eccl. 3.1-11 is sceptical.

Custom also regulates the formation of social units like families by, for instance, prescribing routines for sexual relations, finding a suitable partner and marriage. The choice of marriage partners depends, among other things, on whether, given the environment and economic system, intra- or inter-group relations are more important for a group's survival. If identity and cohesion are of primary importance, the endogamic patrilateral or matrilateral cousin marriage may be the best way to achieve those goals. But if economic and socio-political cooperation with neighbouring groups is more important, exogamic marriages might best serve the purpose. Consider, for example, the value of 'identity' reflected in Abraham's request to his servant:

> Put your hand under my thigh and I will make you swear by the Lord, the God of heaven and earth, that you will not get a wife for my son from the daughters of the Canaanites, among whom I live, but will go to my country and to my kindred and get a wife for my son Isaac (Gen. 24.2-4).

Or the reason Rebecca gives to Isaac for sending away Jacob:

> I am weary of my life because of the Hittite women. If Jacob marries one of the Hittite women such as these, one of the women of the land, what good will my life be to me? (Gen. 27.46).

Even though marriages concluded between 'Israelite' tribes would in reality have been of the exogamic sort, in the all-Israel perspective of the biblical narrators such marriages are endogamic. This is clear from Judg. 2 1. In this narrative 'Israel' punished one of their member tribes by vowing to refuse their daughters to Benjaminites in marriage. By this action they make it impossible for the Benjaminites to retain their identity as 'Israelites' (21.17). When the consequences of their decision dawn upon the other tribes, they bypass their solemn vow by allowing Benjaminite men to abduct 'Israelite' daughters during a festival. In this way the custom of endogamy is saved and the identity of Benjaminites as Israelites safeguarded (21.10-24). This story implies that custom takes precedence over persons and their wishes, especially of women. Although men have more freedom than women, their marriage choices are limited to kinsfolk. In Deuteronomic law, with its ideology of identity, a man is even obliged to marry the widow of a brother who dies childless, so as to prevent the widow from marrying outside the family and to ensure the continuation of the (male) name of the family (Deut. 25.5-10). There are exceptions, though: men are allowed to take as wives female prisoners of war from any group (Deut. 21.1-14). And Samson's exogamic marriage wishes, earning him a reprimand from his parents (Judg. 14.3), form part of a divine plan (14.4) and are therefore excusable. King Solomon's appetite for 'foreign' women is, however, not excused (1 Kgs 11.3-8; 2 Kgs 23.13; Neh. 13.26).

Marriage, whether endogamic or exogamic, is thus not a private amorous affair. It involves 'the transfer of rights between families, including rights to property, and right over children, as well as sexual rights' (Haviland 1996: 234). Since marrying a member of another household means that the particular household loses a labourer, that household has to be compensated for the loss, either through bride service (the groom working for some years for his father-in-law) or by means of a bride price (paid to the bride's household). Consequently, securing a marriage partner may involve protracted negotiations between families (cf. Matthews and Benjamin 1993: 14).

Not all marriages work out. To ensure stable relations (involving other households or groups) and to prevent individual improvisation, society also has to agree on acceptable rules for divorce. In subsistence societies the rules for divorce mirror the legal position of married women. Even though mothers and thrifty wives enjoy a high social standing their *legal* position is normally comparatively poor. In 'biblical Israel', for example, a husband can divorce a wife, but she has no access to the same escape from an unhappy marriage. In such a system the legal and social position of women is, for obvious reasons, one of vulnerability. In Deuteronomic law a woman receives some protection against false accusations by a husband seeking divorce, but the burden of proof remains squarely on her shoulders (Deut. 22.13-21). It is for

7. Social Organization and Meaning 241

this reason that in the metaphorical marriage of Yahweh to Israel in the book of Hosea his decision to 'divorce' his wife (Hos. 2.1) is put in a context demonstrating repeated adultery on her side and repeated efforts on his side to save the marriage (cf. Hos. 3). Yahweh's divorce from his wife is thoroughly justified.

A final example of the influence of custom may be taken from the domain of language. Communication also follows customary patterns. There are, for example, customary ways of opening, continuing and concluding a conversation, customary forms of address, of answering questions, emphasizing or highlighting parts of an utterance, of expressing kindness or rebuke, to thank a person, etc. In a closed society any newcomer is a stranger who may spell danger, like the 'Israelite' strangers spelled danger for Jericho (Josh. 2.1-3). Hebrew Bible conversations contain a variety of questions put to newcomers on a scene, aimed at ascertaining their identity, social status, affiliations, domicile, occupation, aims and intentions: 'Who are you?' (מי־אתה, 2 Sam. 1.8), 'What is your name?' (מי שמך, Judg. 13.17), 'Whose son/daughter are you?' (בן־מי אתה, 1 Sam. 17.58; בת־מי את, Gen. 24.23), 'To whom do you belong?' (למי־אתה, 1 Sam. 30.13), 'What do you do (for a living)?' (מה־מלאכתך; מה־מעשיכם, Gen. 46.33; Jon. 1.8), 'Where do you come from?' (מאין תבוא; אי מזה אתה, 1 Sam. 30.13; Judg. 19.17), 'Where are you heading?' (אנה תלך, Judg. 19.17), 'What do you want here?' (מה־לך; מה־לך פה; 1 Kgs 19.9; Judg. 1.14). The least one should do is to enquire whether a stranger's or an adversary's intentions were peaceful, for example, השלום באך ('Do you come in peace?', 1 Kgs 2.13). After such an enquiry the stranger may be greeted with 'peace be with you' (שלום לך, cf. Judg. 19.20). Known people are greeted with שלום לך, or with a mere שלום (2 Sam. 18.28), or by enquiring after his or her well-being by asking 'Is everything OK?' (השלום אתה, 2 Sam. 20.9). Greeting somebody involves speaking about well-being and peace, and in answering a peaceful greeting nobody uses a negative formulation. In order to get a truthful answer to one's enquiry about someone else's well-being one has to be much more explicit, for example, by directly asking 'Why do you have a long face?' (Gen. 40.7), 'Why do you cry?' (1 Sam. 1.8), etc. In more formal circumstances and when a social inferior meets a superior the wish of well-being may be formulated as 'May God bless you' (ברוך אתה ליהוה, 1 Sam. 15.13).

A conventional conversation may consist of elements like addressing the conversational partner, requesting him or her to pay attention, giving an indication of the main concern of the conversation, and formulating one's concern. Each of these elements requires a customary form. Addressing a person by merely using his or her name signals authority, as in addresses of God to a mortal (Gen. 21.17; 22.11; 31.11; 46.2; Exod. 3.4; 1 Sam. 3.10), a king to a subject (1 Sam. 17.55; 2 Kgs 9.22), a prophet to his assistant (2 Kgs 2.4; 5.25), or a husband to his wife (1 Sam. 1.8). Outside this social context, addressing a person by name signals impoliteness or disrespect (1 Sam. 26.14; 2 Kgs 9.23; Job 33.1, 31; 37.14). To ignore a person's name altogether is to treat him or her with utter contempt. Thus, for example, 'Put this fellow (את־זה 'this one there') in prison, and feed him on reduced rations of bread and water until I come in peace' (2 Kgs 22.27). It may therefore be telling when Elisha refers to the woman who has done him so much good and whose son he just revived as, 'that Shunammite woman' (הזאת השנמית, 2 Kgs 4.36).

In polite conversation a person is either addressed in his or her social capacity, for example, as father, mother, son, daughter, brother, sister, sir, man of God, king, or in his or her social capacity *and* name (e.g. 1 Sam. 3.16; 24.17; 26.17). Even when characters are introduced they are presented as, for example, 'Laban, son of Nahor' (Gen. 29.5), 'His daughter Rachel' (Gen. 29.6), 'Abigail, Nabal's wife' (1 Sam. 25.14). It is only when a character has already been introduced or it is expected that the reader (by now) knows his or her standing or affiliation that a mere name may be used. And even then close family members are referred to as, for example, 'My father Saul' (1 Sam. 19.2), 'Your brother Esau' (Gen. 27.6), 'Sir' (Gen. 18.12).

However, given the impoliteness of using a person's name without a title, and that inferiors have to indicate to superiors that they held themselves in the same low esteem as the superiors, inferiors may, in conversation with superiors, refer to themselves by their name. Consider, for example, 2 Sam. 24.23 in which Arauna says to David, 'All this, O king, Araunah gives to the king,' or 2 Sam. 7.20, where David says to Yahweh, 'And what more can David say to you? For you know your servant, O Lord God.' As these examples already indicate a social inferior addressing social superiors may, apart from other gestures of politeness, even change the grammatical construction of his or her address, such as by referring to the superior and (more frequently) to him- or herself in the third person. Thus, 'Do not let the king impute (אל־ישם המלך) anything to his servant (בעבדו) or to any member of my

7. *Social Organization and Meaning* 243

father's house; for your servant has known nothing of all this, much or little' (1 Sam. 22.15). Or the instruction Jacob gives his servant regarding Esau: 'Then you shall say, "They belong to your servant Jacob; they are a present sent to my lord Esau; and moreover he is behind us"' (Gen. 32.18). An inferior may, however, intersperse his or her third-person self-references with first person *grammatical* forms:

> Then David said to Achish, 'If I have found favour in your sight, let a place be given me in one of the country towns, so that I may live there; for why should your servant live in the royal city with you?' (1 Sam. 27.5).

After having exchanged the proper greetings, and having sketched the background to his or her being there, a speaker may, especially in more formal conversations, draw the conversational partner's attention to the real point of the conversation (often a request) by saying ועתה or והנה. A social inferior could, at this point, also add or use the formula 'please pay attention to me now' (שמע־נא, Jer. 37.20; cf. Gen. 23.6, 11). To indicate that new or unexpected information is about to be imparted a speaker uses והנה, for example, 'There we were, binding sheaves in the field. Suddenly (והנה) my sheaf rose and stood upright; then your sheaves gathered around it, and bowed down to my sheaf' (Gen. 37.7), or (often as part of an argument) ראה: 'See (ראה) I have handed Jericho over to you, along with its king and soldiers' (Josh. 6.2).

In formulating requests only those in socially inferior positions or persons who want to be extremely polite need to say 'please'. This is done in several different ways. One says 'On me, sir' (בי אדני), or 'If you would be so kind' (אם־נא מצאתי חן בעיניך), or one humbles oneself before the other by using a formula like 'Who am I?' (מי אנכי) or 'What is my household that...' (מי ביתי). In order to request something urgently or explicitly express a command, a speaker, usually a superior, may add a verb of movement to the imperative for example, 'Come, move on!' (לך ועבר, 2 Sam. 15.22); 'Come on, get moving!' (נהג ולך, 2 Kgs 4.24); 'Let us quickly flee' (קומו ונברחה, 2 Sam. 15.14). A military officer, however, does not use הלך or קום to add urgency to his commands, but סב, for example, 'Kill them *now*!' (סבו והמיתו, 1 Sam. 22.17), 'To me, on the double!' (סב התיצב כה, 2 Sam. 18.30); 'Fall in!' (אל־אחרי, 2 Kgs 9.18). In order to state a fact emphatically, one refers to the senses involved in the act of observation, for example, 'You personally heard (שמעתם באזניכם, Jer. 26.11), 'Look, I have first-hand knowledge of it' (הן־כל ראתה עיני שמעה אזני ותבן לה, Job 13.1). To indicate a superlative one may repeat the point of comparison, for example, 'huge' (מאד במאד, Gen. 17.20), 'pure gold' (והב זהב, 2 Kgs 25.15), 'fathomless' (עמק עמק, Eccl. 7.24), or state the same fact in the positive as well as in the negative (litotes), for example, 'From me Yahweh has kept this a complete secret' (העלים ממני ולא הגיד לי, 2 Kgs 4.27); 'They are such utter fools' (בנים סכלים המה ולא נבונים המה), Jer. 4.22). To confirm a request or statement one repeats the relevant verb or noun, for example, 'Will you go?... Yes!' (התלכי...אלך, Gen. 24.58), 'Shall I go up?... Yes!' (האעלה...עלה—2 Sam. 2.1); 'You are witnesses... Indeed!' (עדים עדים אתם..., Josh. 24.22). One may also say 'It is OK' (טוב הדבר, 1 Kgs 18.24), or simply 'OK' (טוב, 2 Sam. 3.13) or 'I agree' (יהי כדברך, Gen. 30.34).

These few examples merely scratch the surface of the vast field of sociolinguistics but illustrate the close connection between social position and language usage, polite and impolite speech, requesting and demanding, etc. and thereby of language and culture. To achieve common goals speakers and listeners have to communicate, and to do so successfully speakers and listeners should master the complicated field of customary linguistic usage. To understand the intentions of Hebrew Bible characters and writers readers should at the least be acquainted with the social meaning of linguistic expression.

3. *Organizational Units and Strategies*

In ancient Palestine (with its harsh climate and agricultural-cum-pastoral reciprocal economy) the family, whether nuclear or extended, formed the basic organizational unit. In the extended family mother's or father's parents as well as mother's and father's children (and their children) live together, even though not necessarily in the same shelter, tent or building. In cases of polygamy, for example, mothers with their children may live in separate shelters (cf. the reference to Sarah's tent in Gen. 24.67). For the orderly and effective functioning of a household, each position in the family is assigned its own status and function. It is therefore necessary clearly to distinguish different members of the household. In the Israelite household that one encounters in the narratives of the Hebrew Bible family members are distinguished as follows:

7. Social Organization and Meaning

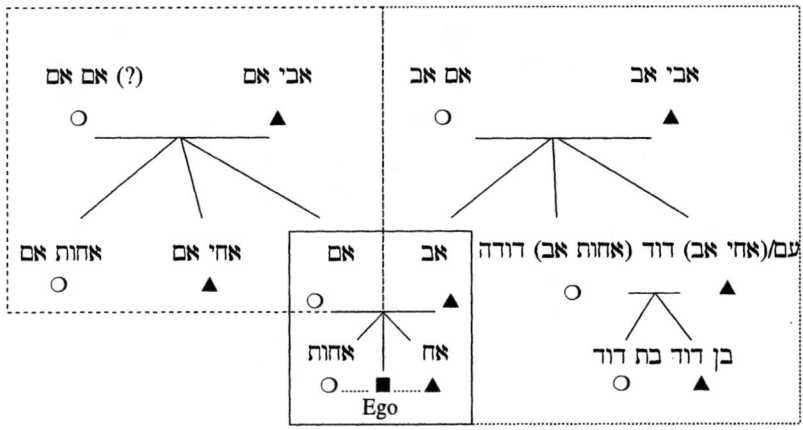

In this representation the square demarcates the immediate family and the dotted rectangles demarcate the two lineages from which Ego derives. A mere four terms allow Ego to refer to all his/her immediate family, namely 'mother', 'father', 'sister' and 'brother'. By saying 'mother's brother' or 'father's sister', 'mother's father' or 'father's father' he/she may distinguish different family members. Some of the terms are generic. For instance, although Ego may refer to his/her own brothers and sisters as אח and אחות, those terms may also be used to refer to half-brothers and half-sisters, that is, father's children with one of his other wives. אח can also be used to refer to a cousin (Gen. 13.8; 14.14, 16), a member of the same clan (Num. 16.10), or, as in Deuteronomy, to *any* fellow Israelite. אח therefore seems generically to indicate 'fellowship'. The kind of fellowship implied should be deduced from the particular speech situation. However, if a speaker wants to be specific, he/she may resort to a defining expression like בן אבי 'my father's son' (Gen. 42.32; 49.8; 1 Chron. 28.4), which may include half-brothers, or, for more preciseness, בן אמי 'the son of my mother?' (Gen. 27.29; 43.29; Deut. 13.7; Judg. 8.19; Ps. 3.20, etc.), that is, my blood brother. Even though the father of a household is the important figure as far as identity and status are concerned, a person's mother is the real distinguishing factor in a household. It is this 'branching' function of a mother in a genealogy that allowed for the metaphorical usage of 'mother' to indicate a fork in a road. Consider, '(T)he king of Babylon stands at the parting of the way (lit.: mother of the way אם הדרך), at the fork in the two roads (בראש שני הדרכים)...' (Ezek. 21.21).

The schematic representation above shows that Ego distinguishes family on the father's side terminologically from family on the mother's side. The fact that family on the father's side is referred to by a special set of terms indicates their relative importance in the *lineage* system. Although one may also refer to an uncle on the father's side as אחי אב, the term דוד is the technical term in Hebrew Bible literature. Given the relatively poor father–son relationship in extended families, the uncle on the father's side serves as a man's *confidant.* The position of the patrilineal uncle is illustrated in the case of Saul. When he returns from his search for his father's donkeys (and from Samuel) it is his *uncle* who first suspects that something significant occurred (1 Sam. 10.14-16). That דוד here refers to a Philistine governor, as has been suggested, is quite improbable, since Saul later appoints his uncle's son as head of the army (1 Sam. 14.50) to fight the Philistines. The uncle on the mother's side plays a different, perhaps more significant, role. In a patrilineal society preferring endogamy the mother's brother often is the 'supplier' of brides for his sister's sons. In endogamic societies people must marry within the family group. Since the paternal lineage defines a person's identity, marrying on the father's side is often seen as inappropriate. In this case the maternal family is the most logical 'supplier' of marriage partners, often specifically the household of the mother's brother. This explains Jacob's marriage to the daughters of his mother's brother. Moreover the amount of attention devoted to Jacob's marriage and his relation to Laban in the patriarchal narratives holds up *this* kind of marriage as the ideal solution for marriages in 'Israelite' society. The function of the matrilineal uncle is also illustrated in the story about Gideon's son Abimelech. In an effort to become king in Shechem he first secures the support of his mother's brothers and kinfolk (Judg. 9.1-6).

In the in-law relationships careful distinctions are made between the various households, because between them exist all sorts of economic and legal arrangements. Ego, if a male, calls the parents of his wife חתן ('father-in-law') and חתנה ('mother-in-law') while they speak of him as their חתן ('son-in-law'). If a female, Ego calls her husband's parents חם ('father-in-law') and חמה ('mother-in-law'), and they refer to her as כלה. The following diagram represents these relationships and the relevant terms. The patrilineal side is boxed in to indicate its priority.

7. Social Organization and Meaning 247

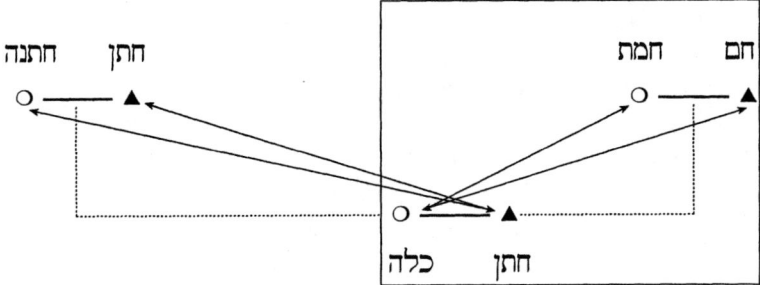

Since the different kinship terms *imply meaning derived from the social system*, they 'stand for' more than their mere translation 'equivalents'. 'In Bedouin society,' Lila Abu-Lughod (quoted by Pilch 1991: 117) says, 'one can hardly speak about 'women' in general. Every woman is a sister, daughter, wife, mother, or aunt, and it is the role and relationship that usually determines how she will be perceived and treated.' In Hebrew Bible literature, for example, 'mother', implies a series of *social duties*, such as bearing children, suckling them, preparing food, caring for and educating the young, acting as an important link in the economic system; *dependencies*, like obeying her husband, being 'divorceable' (and therefore vulnerable); and *privileges*, such as possessing dignity and influence. It is these functions and meanings that allow terms to be used in metaphorical senses. When Deborah is called 'mother in Israel' the social duties of motherhood are accentuated, because under her leadership 'the peasantry prospered in Israel, they grew fat on plunder' (Judg. 5.7). The wisdom of a mother, earning her social status, again occasions the reference to the city of Abel Bethmaacah as 'a mother in Israel' (2 Sam. 20.19; cf. v. 18).

After marriage a young couple may join either the husband's group (patrilocation) or the wife's group (matrilocation). Patrilocation normally is the rule. Where ecological factors necessitate a prominent male role in subsistence, polygamy is practised, men are the primary inheritors, warfare is prominent and men wield authority (Haviland 1996: 261). Since all these factors form part of the presupposed society of Hebrew Bible literature, patrilocation also is the norm. Where this custom is not practised abnormal circumstances are indicated, as in the cases of Moses and Jacob, who temporarily live with their fathers-in-law. Patrilocation in its turn favours patriarchy, according to which the oldest male takes the decisions for the group and has absolute authority over it.

Patrilocality and patriarchy favour patrilineal (agnatic) lines of descent, according to which a family's genealogy follows the male route from father to son to grandson, and so on. Moreover, where ecological and other factors force a social bond among various households, their interdependence and alliance may be expressed in terms of a (real or fictitious) common male genealogy. The frequency of genealogies in the Hebrew Bible and the custom of identifying a person as 'son of N', where N is male, indicate a presupposed patrilineal society. Within a male genealogy, especially when polygamy is involved, a person may be more clearly identified with reference to the relevant mother. Consider, for example, 'Jeroboam son of Nebat, an Ephraimite of Zeredah, a servant of Solomon, whose mother's name was Zeruiah, a widow, rebelled against the king' (1 Kgs 11.26; cf. 1 Kgs 14.31; 15.2; 22.42; 2 Kgs 8.26; etc.). In the case of Amasa, the situation may be different, for he is introduced as 'the son of a man named Ithra the Ishmaelite, who fathered him with Abigal (אשר־בא אל־אביגל) daughter of Nahash, sister of Zeruiah, Joab's mother' (2 Sam. 17.25). In this case Amasa's inferiority in comparison with Joab may be indicated, because his genealogy seems to identify him as an illegitimate child (בא אל nowhere means 'marry', as NRSV interprets the term here; cf. Gen. 16.4; 38.8-9; Ps. 51.2 (Heb.); 1 Chron. 7.23).

Hebrew Bible literature makes much of lineages. Just how these lineages should be interpreted is a matter of debate. Some scholars take Hebrew Bible genealogies fairly seriously as historical documents (cf. Flanagan 1981: 58-65), while others do not. Haviland (1996: 333) defines this segmentary lineage system as one 'in which a larger group is broken up into clans, which are divided into lineages'. Among the Nuer people, for example, a clan is segmented into maximal lineages, each of which is segmented into major lineages, which are segmented into minor lineages, which in turn are segmented into minimal lineages (Haviland 1996: 333). This is more or less how the Hebrew Bible pictures the social organization of 'Israel' prior to the monarchy. The twelve sons of Jacob form a segmented genealogy, while their descendants are indicated by subsegments according to lineage. As a system of *government*, and therefore as *political* system, segmentary lineage systems are rare and appear only under certain conditions, for example, when the economy is just above subsistence level and when the labour

7. Social Organization and Meaning 249

pool is just large enough to provide necessities. The system does not provide for political offices or chiefs, and constitutes a 'temporary unification of a fragmented tribal society to join in particular action' (Haviland 1996: 333). In view of the conditions for this system, as well as its temporary nature and function, it is quite unlikely that 'Israel' could have functioned as a lineage system for two hundred years. Insofar as the text pictures Israelite *political* organization in terms of segmentary lineages this picture is perhaps better interpreted in terms of meaning than of function. Law (1997: 168) observes in this regard:

> [C]laims of genealogical links between the ruling dynasties of African kingdoms are often misunderstood, if they are treated as historical statements... According to Dahomian traditions, [the two kingdoms of] Dahomey and Porto-Novo were founded by two brothers... In fact, it is clear from other evidence that Dahomey and Porto-Novo were not contemporary foundations... The traditions have been distorted for political purposes, to legitimise the authority of the kings of Dahomey.

And according to Tonkin (1995: 110) a genealogy often is a 'selective representation of demography in the light of social rules about [inheritance and] succession'. Among the Nuer, for example, institutions of authority (chiefs, jurists, priesthood) organized themselves through a genealogical grid.

> Friendship and enmity were contingent and relative states because everyone in Nuer was theoretically kin. The allies one could mobilise against an internal enemy were therefore those more closely related to oneself than to him. Socio-political identity and relative genealogical placing were aspects of each other.

That is why, in the process of transmission, genealogies are transmuted by structural amnesia (Goody and Watt 1963: 32-33). Rather than reflecting historical reality genealogies therefore often—if not mostly—are 'social' creations, shorthand demographic maps, symbolizing looser or tighter sociopolitical cohesion among groups. In view of anthropological research on the social function of genealogies, one would therefore do better to interpret encompassing Hebrew Bible genealogies as items ascribing *meaning* to social and political relations and *functionally* legitimizing privileged social positions.

There are various ways of indicating 'relatedness' through genealogies. In 'real life' a group of blood relatives or economic associates may become too large for the conditions they live in, or strife may cause a section of the larger group to break away and form a new lineage elsewhere. The resulting looser relationship may be symbolically indicated by a branching-off in the main genealogy. Consider, for example, how in the patriachal narratives of the Hebrew Bible the 'generations' of Moabites, Ammonites, Ishmaelites and Edomites 'branch' off from the 'Abrahamic' lineage, with the Israelites representing the continuation of the 'genuine' line. While a lineage genealogy may symbolize looser relations, a closer relationship may be indicated by a segmentary genealogy, that is, a genealogy according to which *all* the patriarchs of a society are pictured as stemming from one and the same arch-patriarch, as where the lineage of all twelve sons of Jacob is traced to one character. The principle is illustrated in the following genealogically constructed demographic diagram:

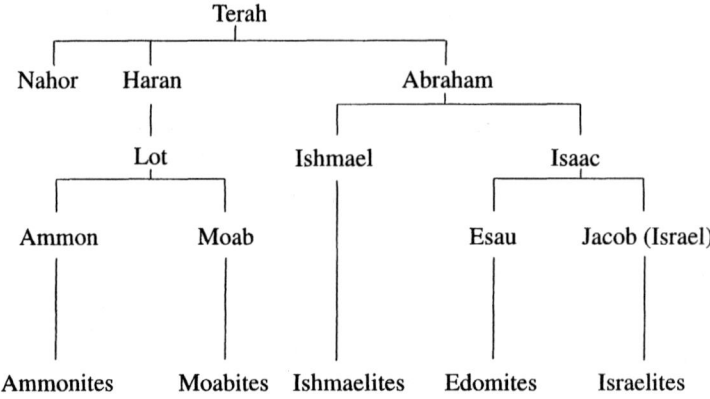

The looser (lineage) and tighter (segmentary) social relations reflected by the genealogy are explained in genealogical *narratives*. For example, the *indirectly* related Ammonites and Moabites, with whom 'Israelites' always have bad relations, stem from a relationship of incest (Gen. 19) and are therefore forbidden by custom ever to become part of 'Israel' (Deut. 23.3). The Ishmaelites, by comparison, are related through *great-grandfathers*, but their junior status is expressed as a birth from a *concubine* (Gen. 16). The Edomites and Israelites are much closer, though: their *grandfathers* were *twins* (Gen. 25.19-26). The book of Amos twice refers to this relationship as one of 'brothers' (1.9, 11). The better relations with *directly* linked lineage groups' (e.g. the Edomites and Ishmaelites) are also indicated by narratives in which representatives of the various branches pay visits to shared symbols,

7. Social Organization and Meaning 251

such as sanctuaries or graves. Consider, in this regard, the stories of Ishmael (Gen. 25.1-18) and Esau (Gen. 35.29), both representatives of branches of the main lineage, attending their fathers' funerals. The closest relationship is, however, that between 'Israelite' tribes, and is expressed with reference to a segmentary genealogy: they all have one *father*.

The symbolism may even go further. Groups mentioned as members of a segmentary genealogy do not necessarily all enjoy the same good relations. Some members may maintain better and closer relations with one another than with other (socially equal) groups. Such a closer relationship between two or more groups may be expressed in terms of a *phratry*, that is, as a lineage branch *within* a segmentary genealogy. Note in this context the relationship between Ephraim and Manasseh expressed as brothers of the same father (Joseph), who is a member of the segmentary genealogy of Jacob. This relationship is also backed up by a genealogical narrative (Gen. 41.50-52; 48.1-22), while the two groups are frequently referred to in the literature as a 'pair' (e.g. Num. 26.28; Deut. 33.17; Josh. 14.4; 16.4; Judg. 12.4).

Within any family genealogy there always are two sides, or two halves, namely on the paternal and maternal side. Differing relationships among two larger groups mentioned in the same segmentary genealogy may also be expressed with reference to such 'halves', or *moieties*. I mentioned earlier that, although in a patrilineal society identity is determined by the paternal lineage, specific individuals in an identity group may be specified by the mentioning of a mother's name. This can also be done to identify genealogical moieties. The picture that Hebrew Bible authors paint of the relationship between Israel and Judah reminds us of such 'moieties'. In Hebrew Bible literature frequent reference is made to 'the house of Joseph/Ephraim/Israel' (e.g. Josh. 17.17; 18.5; Judg. 1.22; 10.9; 2 Sam. 19.20; 1 Kgs 11.28; Amos 6.6; Hos. 5.12; 11.12) and the 'house of Judah' (Josh. 18.5; Judg. 10.9; 2 Sam. 2.4; 12.8; 1 Kgs 12.21; Jer. 3.18; 5.11). The genealogical narrative in Gen. 29.1–30.24 explains this relationship with pertinent reference to one father and two mothers:

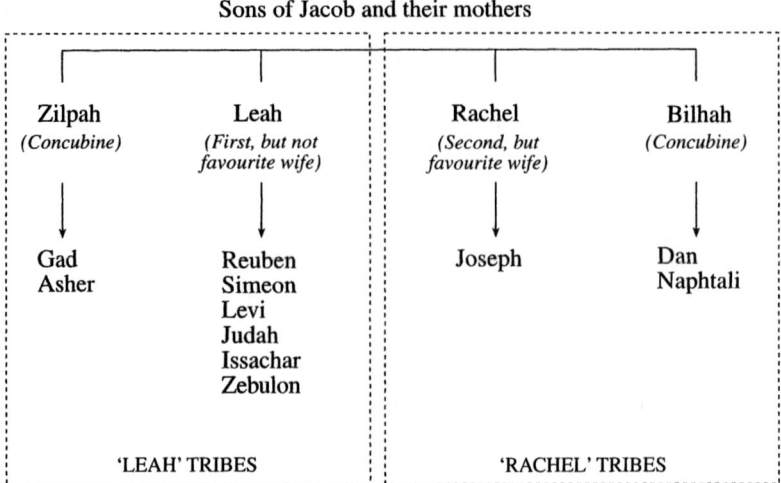
Sons of Jacob and their mothers

Even though the *historical* process of the formation of Israel and Judah most probably had been quite different, Hebrew Bible narratives (building on folkloristic convention) thus employ genealogy as a metaphor to express *social relations* among groups in the Palestinian region. To use modern, anachronistic, terms: to express looser relations they employ *lineage* as metaphor. Tighter relations are represented in terms of a *segmentary genealogy*, while relationships within the segmented genealogy are expressed in terms of *phratries* and *moieties*. The meanings of these genealogical metaphors are then mostly explicated in genealogical narratives.

The metaphor of moiety seems to have been the most powerful, since the love-hate relationship between Joseph/Israel and Judah pervades Hebrew Bible literature. Consider in this connection the perspectives from which different stories are told. Genesis 29.1–30.24, for example, pictures Joseph as (a) the first-born of (b) the beloved wife, who (c) miraculously gave birth. This narrative is clearly pro-Ephraimite and anti-Judaean (the first-born of the 'ugly duckling') in sentiment. So are the juxtaposed stories about the sexual conduct of Judah and Joseph (Gen. 38; 39), in which Joseph easily wins the contest. In comparison with Judah's disorderly household, in which custom is not even adhered to *in* the promised land, Joseph conducts himself in an exemplary fashion under trying circumstances outside the land. The Judaean perspective in Psalm 78 is completely different, though. In that perspective the Joseph group provoked Yahweh to anger with their high places and

7. Social Organization and Meaning

idols, so that he utterly rejected Israel, abandoned his dwelling at Shiloh and sent Israel in exile:

> Then the Lord awoke as from sleep, like a warrior shouting because of wine. He put...them to everlasting disgrace. He rejected the tent of Joseph, he did not choose the tribe of Ephraim; but he chose the tribe of Judah, Mount Zion, which he loves (Ps. 78.57-68).

These perspectives have, interestingly enough, not been edited out by the Yehud scribes.

The idea of Israel as a 'family' seems to have also influenced the way authors introduce characters. Although more study is needed to test the hypothesis, a cursory review of the material seems to indicate that Israelite characters are preferably introduced with reference to lineage, while non-Israelites are identified in terms of clans or regions. Consider the following examples:

Specification by lineage	*Specification by clan*
I have called by name Bezalel the son of Uri, son of Hur, of the tribe of Judah (Exod. 31.2)	Adriel the son of Barzillai the Meholathite (2 Sam. 21.8)
Achan, the son of Carmi, the son of Zabdi, the son of Zerah, of the tribe of Judah, took of the accursed thing (Josh. 7.1)	Eleazar the son of Dodo the Ahohite (2 Sam 23.19)
Othniel the son of Kenaz, the brother of Caleb (Josh. 15.17)	...but David carried it aside into the house of Obed-edom the Gittite (2 Sam 6.10)
Elophehad, the son of Hepher, the son of Gilead, the son of Machir, the son of Manasseh, had no sons (Josh. 17.3)	Abiezer of Anathoth; Mebunnai the Hushathite (2 Sam. 23.27)
After Abimelech there arose to defend Israel Tola the son of Puah, the son of Dodo, a man of Issachar (Judg. 10.1)	Then Sibbecai the Hushathite killed Saph, who was one of the descendants of the giants (2 Sam. 21.18)
There was a certain man of Ramathaimzophim of the hill country of Ephraim, whose name was Elkanah the son of Jeroham, son of Elihu, son of Tohu, son of Zuph, an Ephraimite (1 Sam. 1.1)	Over the camels was Obil the Ishmaelite. Over the donkeys was Jehdeiah the Meronothite. Over the flocks was Jaziz the Hagrite (1 Chron. 27.30)
There was a man of Benjamin whose name was Kish, the son of Abiel, son of Zeror, son of Becorath, son of Aphiah, a Benjaminite (1 Sam. 9.1)	Then David said to Ahimelech the Hittite (1 Sam. 26.6)

Returning to the social and political organization presupposed by Hebrew Bible literature, one is confronted with difficult decisions. Although it is fairly sure that grand genealogies should be interpreted as metaphorical expressions of social relations among groups, it is not so easy to decide along which lines references and allusions to social and political *customs* should be interpreted. Some of the sources on which the Hebrew Bible had been based probably originated up to three hundred years earlier than the time of their 'edition' and would have presupposed earlier social and political conditions. But these sources have been reworked by later editors living under different conditions, which might have informed their *presentation* of the earlier sources. A remark by Tonkin (1995: 105) is pertinent here:

> Nobody's ability to recall is independent of social milieu because it is through that milieu that the cognitive ability was forged. Equally, the social milieu is not independent of the cognitive operations of persons in it. Insofar as the milieu exists as practices, these practices are dialectically, structuring practices, they are active mediators of structuring representations. They may thus be conducive both to stability and to change.

The Hebrew Bible nevertheless presupposes a socio-political world, or sociopolitical worlds, of some kind. We referred earlier to the Dahomian example of presenting the era before the advent of monarchy as a time of disorderliness, and remarked that this was also the case with the Hebrew Bible's picture of pre-Davidic times. In the *literature*, therefore, we are confronted with, on the one hand, a presupposed milieu of pre-monarchical rule, and, on the other hand, a time of monarchy. It is with reference to pre-monarchical times that a cultural interpretation of the Hebrew Bible is confronted with major problems. One may fairly safely assume that the present *text* does not reflect the social system and customs of premonarchical times, since there would have been no literary records of that time and, since oral tradition always adjusts the past to the present and interprets the past for present purposes, possible oral traditions would, by the time they were committed to writing, already have distorted the original picture beyond recognition. Still, the authors were obviously aware that the pre-monarchical system differed from that of monarchical times, and made themselves a picture of that time. It is *that* picture for which a cultural interpretation of the Hebrew Bible interests itself. But precisely that picture is not clear.

The Hebrew Bible uses various undefined terms to indicate groups of

7. Social Organization and Meaning

people. The first, namely דור, may be dismissed in the context of social and political organization. This term generally refers to a 'generation' (Eccl. 1.4), that is, a collectivity of people of some sort, for example, of an era or of a particular kind, or simply to the passage of time. The kind of collectivity intended depends on the formula in which the term occurs. A group of people of a particular era may be referred to as 'that generation' (הדור ההוא, Judg. 2.10); people of a past era as the 'generation of the fathers' (דור אבות, cf. Ps. 49.19); a coming generation as 'the generation that comes after' (דור אחרון, Ps. 78.6) or 'the generation of the children' (דור בנים, Ps. 73.15). The term may also be used to indicate a group of people sharing the same attitude, whether or not they are contemporaries. There are perverse and crooked people (דור עקש ופתלתל, Deut. 32.5; cf. 32.20; Ps. 78.8; Jer. 7.29), people (דור) who curse their parents, are hypocrites, proud or unsympathetic (Prov. 30.11-14), but also upright people (דור ישרים, Ps. 112.2) living a life of devotion (Ps. 24.6). The term may also merely indicate the passage of time. While a number of generations may be stipulated to indicate a long time, for example, the tenth generation (e.g. Deut. 23.2) or a thousand generations (Deut. 7.9), a long time (past or future) may also be referred to with other formulae, for example, 'long ago' (שנות דור ודור, Deut. 32.7); or 'in times to come' (דור דורים, Ps. 72.5; דור לדור, Prov. 27.24; דור ודור, Est. 9.28; Isa. 13.20; 58.12; 60.15; 61.4; Jer. 50.39; Joel 2.2). By contrast, the terms בית אב, אלוף, משפחה, מטה and שבט seem to indicate social units. Although scholars, mostly ignoring אלף and מטה because they most frequently occur in just two texts (Gen. 36; 1 Chron. 1), have often simply equated בית אב, משפחה and שבט with the anthropological concepts of 'extended family', 'clan' and 'tribe', respectively, the referents of these terms are not at all clear. The problem is that these terms occur in varying meanings in different 'layers' of the biblical text (see Lemche 1985: 267).

A tribe Haviland (1996: 330) defines as 'a group of nominally independent [farming or herding] communities occupying a region, sharing a common language and culture, which are integrated by some unifying factor'. Unifying factors may include the need for negotiations when an increase in population density leads to quarrels over the use of resources, or an external threat to the security of the cultural group. A tribe is therefore more than a people at war, as Matthews and Benjamin (1993: 97) define the term. Although a tribe normally shares a geographical area, that territory may include non-participating groups, while participating groups may not always be able to clearly demarcate their 'territory' (Freedman 1978: 41). Tribal leaders, representing the constituting groups, come together to form a temporary and informal 'government' to take care of common challenges like the division of land, regulating the use of fountains and wells, resolving inter-group legal disputes, or putting together a joint military force.

The authority of the tribal leader rests on charismatic talents, personal bravery, generosity in redistribution, eloquence and cunning (Haviland 1996: 331; Flanagan 1981: 50). In exchange for security provided by the system, participating groups have to sacrifice some of their autonomy to the tribal authority (Haviland 1996: 330-31). The biblical picture of Israel's *twelve* tribes', rather than reflecting historical reality most probably is a later fiction. With one exception (Isa. 19.13), the term 'tribe' is exclusively used to refer to Israel as an (ideological) entity, for example, mostly שבטי ישראל, but also שבטי־יה (Ps. 122.4), שבטי נחלתך (Isa. 63.17; cf. Jer. 10.16; Ps. 74.2) and שבטי יעקב (Isa. 49.6). It may also refer to a permanent constituent of 'Israel', such as 'the tribe of Levi' or 'the tribe of Benjamin' (sometimes also מטה), or to indicate the territory occupied by such a unit (Deut. 12.5; Lemche 1985: 282). The tribes are said to be governed by elders and leaders (cf. ראשי המטות, Num. 30.2; ראשי שבטים, Deut. 1.15; זקני ישראל, 1 Kgs 8.1; זקני שבטים, Deut. 31.28). However fictitious (or symbolic!) the twelve-tribe system might be, the stories about these tribes reflect something of how a tribal system works. On the one hand, the 'Israelites' (usually one tribe at a time) are threatened by hit-and-run nomad squads or neighbouring peoples and the people belonging to the tribes are thereby forced to stand together to weather their difficulties (cf. Judg. 3.12-29; 4.1-24; 6.2–7.25; 11.4-33; etc.). On the other hand, the so-called 'judges' (see Lemche 1985) are not elected but present themselves through personal qualities. Ehud made himself a name as an elite 'left-handed' fighter (Judg. 3.15), Deborah was renowned for her wisdom (Judg. 4.4-5), Gideon was the son of a priest and knew how to thwart the Midianite invaders (Judg. 6.11); Jephthah distinguished himself as a military leader and cunning bargainer (Judg. 11.3-6, 12-27; 12.2-3), and Samson was famous for his enormous strength. Apart from the abortive effort by Abimelech (Judg. 9) to establish permanent leadership tribal leadership is temporary.

Lemche (1985: 260-72) is correct in saying that, apart from in genealogies, משפחה (sometimes referred to as אלף or אלוף) is not often

7. Social Organization and Meaning

referred to in the Hebrew Bible. Yet there are indications that this term refers to a fairly basic cultural group, looked after by the ראשי אלף (Num. 1.16). Its anthropological equivalent is, however, not clear. Genesis 10.32 suggests that a nation or larger social unit consists of משפחות. This also seems to be implied by other texts. Consider, for example, 'All the ends of the earth shall remember and turn to the LORD; and all the משפחות גוים shall worship before him (Ps. 22.27; Heb. v. 28; cf. משפחות עמים, Ps. 96.7). In like manner the 'people' (עם; בית יעקב) of Israel is said to consist of משפחות (Jer. 2.4; 31.1). In some texts the reference to a 'nation' is dropped and a larger group merely indicated by its constituent members, for example, משפחת האדמה (Gen. 12.3; Amos 3.2). That a משפחה may branch off in smaller units is indicated by the expression עקר משפחת גר 'a branch of a foreigner's משפחה' (Lev. 25.47) and may be implied in some other cases (Gen. 24.38; Num. 3.20). In some instances, however, the referent of משפחה comes very close to that of בית־אב (cf. Exod. 6.14; Judg. 9.1; Ps. 107.41), and in other cases to that of גוי or even דור (e.g. Jer. 10.25). If we are right that משפחה is to be viewed as the basic *social* unit, it might explain why the term may also be used to indicate either larger or smaller groups.

That the term בית־אב indicates a nuclear or extended family (and their property) is clear from many passages (e.g. Gen. 7.1; 24.23, 38, 40; 31.14, 37; 38.11; 46.31; Exod. 12.3; Lev. 33.13; Num. 30.3; Deut. 15.16; 22.21; Judg. 9.5; 11.2; 14.19; 19.2; 1 Sam. 1.21; 18.2; 22.1, 15, 21; 27.3; 2 Sam. 14.9; 24.17; 1 Kgs 2.31). It would seem that this unit, with a senior male person at its head (Gen. 7.1; 24.38, 40; 38.11; 46.31; Lev. 22.13; Num. 30.3; Deut. 15.16; Judg. 9.5; 14.19; 1 Sam. 1.21; 18.2; 22.1; 27.3; cf. ראשי בית־אבות, Exod. 6.14; נשיאי האבות, 1 Kgs 8.1), determines property rights (Gen. 31.14, 37; Judg. 11.2) and is responsible for the maintenance of order in the community (Deut. 22.21; 1 Sam. 24.21; 2 Sam. 3.29; 14.9; 24.17; 1 Kgs 2.31). There are, however, instances in which בית־אב means as much as 'lineage' (cf. Gen. 18.19), or in which its referent approaches that of משפחה (Exod. 1.1; Gen. 24.7; 2 Sam. 3.29; Ps. 45.10, Heb. v. 11).

In view of the foregoing discussion one may perhaps say that the בית־אב is basically a unit of *social and economic responsibility*, for example, for bringing children into the world (thereby functioning as a unit in the minimal lineage system), educating them, marrying them off, producing food, keeping order and arranging inheritance. The משפחה would then basically be unit of *relationship* (maximal lineage [cf.

Lemche 1985: 264]) and *status*. In that capacity the משפחה has to protect the 'name' of its members, for example, by resolving disputes between households, avenging the murder of a member (Num. 35), ensuring offspring for a male member who dies childless (Deut. 25.5-10), standing in for a family suffering economic difficulties (Lev. 25.35-55), or protecting households against enemies. The tribe functions as a unit *identifying* a person as belonging to Israel and as a *safety net* ensuring a broad affiliation to the larger group.

Just how these terms are to be interpreted with reference to political and anthropological categories is difficult to say. In his studies on the evolution of the state, Service (1962) distinguishes four stages, namely the formation of bands, tribes, chiefdoms and, finally, the archaic state. Haviland (1996: 327-38) classifies the first two as uncentralized and the latter two as centralized political organizations. A band, usually only found among food foragers, is a fairly loose system functioning on the basis of consensus decisions and trust. A clan also consists of a fairly loosely organized group of families who believe themselves to share a common ancestry (Haviland 1996: 332-33). Leadership in this kind of organization is temporary, informal and normally rests on men respected for their 'age, integrity, and wisdom' (Haviland 1996: 331). Although we must not underestimate the difficulties involved in dating biblical texts and the problematic relationship between text and reality, we might suggest that, at least in the biblical texts in which they are frequently mentioned, the definition and role of elders alter as the monarchical system of government unfolds in the narrative. In many texts the elders function very much as in a clan system, while in other texts they are no longer representatives of clans but rather wealthy property owners and merchants with very limited powers (variously referred to as זקני העיר, זקני ישראל or זקני בית [המלך]). The status and function of elders can thus be represented as follows:

7. Social Organization and Meaning

	Earlier monarchy	Later monarchy
Composition	1. The body of heads of households and clans	1. The well-to-do and important citizens of a town or city 2. Landowners
Function	1. Represent the male assembly of the people 2. Elect a leader 3. Constitute a decision-making body/part of the royal council 4. Military, economic, religious, judicial, and executive powers	1. Judicial powers of a limited nature. 2. Report back to 'the people'
Relationship with other officers	Mentioned with the heads of households (נסיאים) and officials (שטרים)	Mentioned with the royal officials, especially the שׂרים

In view of the differences between the two 'types' of elders, the mere mentioning of them in the Hebrew Bible does not suggest clan or tribal organization. Whether an author mentioning elders wished to suggest to his readers a clan or tribal background depends on the *function* of elders in the story. The qualities Hebrew Bible texts like to associate with elders are respect of the community, wise advice in difficult matters, and the administration of justice. This is shown, negatively, in the implied social shaming of God's judgment upon the house of Eli in 1 Sam. 2.31, 'Behold, the days are coming, when I will cut off your strength and the strength of your father's house, so that *there will not be an old man in your house*... There shall *not be an old man in your house for ever*.' Trusted and respected as they are, the authority of tribal elders and leaders is neither absolute nor permanent. Their authority rests on the respect people have for them. 'Grey hair is a crown of glory,' says Prov. 16.31. Bemoaning the collapse of the social order, Lam. 5.12 observes that 'no respect is shown to the elders'. Misbehaviour on their side causes people to gossip about them and so to undermine their authority. Consider, for example, the shaming effect of the Ephraimite gossip about the conduct of the Judaean patriarch in Genesis 38. Respectable elders ensure safety, stability and justice in a community. This is, however, not the picture of elders throughout the Hebrew Bible. Once they are coopted in the monarchical political order, they become part of an oppressive system. In Isaiah and Jeremiah one finds them on the side of the corrupt, wealthy officialdom, as in Isa. 3.14-15:

> The Lord enters into judgment with the *elders* and princes of his people: 'It is you who have *devoured* the vineyard, the spoil of the poor is in *your* houses. What do you mean by *crushing my people*, by grinding the face of *the poor*?'

In Deuteronomy the elders merely have some kind of judicial function (Deut. 21.2, 19; 22.15-18; 25.7-9). Except for the book of Joel, the so-called Minor Prophets ignore the elders completely.

4. *Status Groups, Social Roles and Symbols*

'Status', Pilch (1991: 119) says, 'refers to a *position* in a social system which is evaluated in terms of what others perceive that position to be. Essentially, status defines *who* a person is: man, woman, farmer, shepherd, artisan, carpenter, etc.' A role he defines as 'what a person is expected *to do* socially on the basis of status' (Pilch 1991: 119). Often the role a person plays in society already symbolizes his or her status. But certain statuses in society are marked by specific symbols, for example, dress, living quarters, forms of address. In biblical literature one may distinguish various statuses ranked according to age, gender, marriage status, position in a family, economic or political position, occupation and purity.

Although old age is not always praised, it is nevertheless valued. There are various remarks about the problems of ageing, such as losing eyesight (Gen. 27.1; 48.10; 1 Sam. 3.2; 1 Kgs 14.4), getting deaf and the failure of taste (2 Sam. 19.35 [Heb. v. 36]), difficulty in walking (1 Sam. 4.18), a drop in body temperature or in activity (1 Kgs 1.1) and a deterioration of the mental faculties (2 Sam. 19.36). But these symptoms indicate real old age, and one could be reckoned among the 'aged' long before they set in, because the mean life expectancy at birth was in the vicinity of 30 years. In biblical literature women are reckoned as 'old' as soon as menopause sets in, while male characters retire at the age of 50, and the age of 60 is looked upon as really old. The short life expectancy certainly contributed to the high value attached to old age, which often forms part of a divine reward for good

7. Social Organization and Meaning 261

conduct (cf. Gen. 15.15; Deut. 5.33; 11.9) or a wish, for example, 'May you see your children's children' (Ps. 128.6). The same experience contributed to the conception that a person who did manage to live long was 'satisfied' (שׂבע; שׂבע ימים, cf. Gen. 25.8; 1 Chron. 23.1; Job 42.17). Just how much old age was appreciated is indicated by the fact that ideal ages were calculated by means of magical numbers, for example, 110 ($5^2 + 6^2 + 7^2$) or 120 ($2 \times 3 \times 4 \times 5$) and ascribed to very special people, like Joseph (110, Gen. 50.26), Moses (120, Deut. 34.7; cf. Gen. 6.3) and Joshua (110, Josh. 24.29). The age of hyper-old people, like the mythical generations before the flood, might, as Labuschagne suggests, perhaps also have been calculated on the basis of the ideal age of 120. If 840 (120×7) is subtracted from the phenomenal ages one reaches in many of these cases a 'normal' old age, for example, Adam (90), Seth (72), Enosh (65), Kenan (70), *et al*. After all, 'The days of our life are seventy years, or perhaps eighty, if we are strong' (Ps. 90.10). Given the short life expectancy it is understandable that an old person would be valued more than a young person, since everybody could be young but few grew old. Moreover, a person who has lived twice the time most people do must have had the opportunity to collect more wisdom in the art of living than most people are able to. In fact, according to the Papyrus Insinger (Instruction P) the art of living only takes effect after the age of 40. In spite of Job's and Elihu's scepticism (Job 12.12; 32.9) wisdom is, irrespective of gender, generally seen as the outstanding characteristic of old age (cf. Ezek. 7.26). For all the reasons advanced, it is only natural that old people formed a status group in society. Their role in biblical literature is that of recounting the past, giving advice and administering justice, and their symbol is grey hair. It is from among their numbers that the 'elders' of the Hebrew Bible come (see Matthews and Benjamin 1993: 121-24).

The second age group is that of the adults, that is, the generation in charge of life and on whose shoulders rests the continuation of culture. They beget children, educate them (see Pilch 1991: 71-94), are economically active, pay taxes and build cities, and are to be respected for that. Children have to obey them: 'The eye that mocks a father and scorns to obey a mother will be pecked out by the ravens of the valley and eaten by the vultures' (Prov. 30.17). Their status symbols are, for male members, owning property (אישׁ חיל) and wearing a beard (זקן), and for female members a large, obedient and well-behaved family living in a well-run household (אשׁת חיל). The third age group is constituted by the unmarried teenagers (בחורים; בתולות) respected for their vitality and physical abilities: 'The glory of youths [בחורים] is their strength [כחם], but the beauty of the aged is their grey hair' (Prov. 20.29). They form part of the workforce and from their male ranks the soldiers (בחורים) are recruited, while specific household tasks, such as fetching water and firewood, grinding meal, spinning and weaving accrue to the female members of the group (בתולות). Their distinguishing symbols are thrift (חרוצים; opposite עצל), bravery (אמיץ לב, גבורה, for the male members) or virginity (בתולים, for the female members). The duties of the females of this group are indicated in the metaphor for an upside-down world: 'Young men [בחורים] are compelled to grind, and boys [נערים] stagger under loads of wood' (Lam. 5.13).

The fourth age group are the children (בנים; בנות) and consists of all children before puberty, including babies [(תעלולים; עוללים; ינקים)]. The really young are sometimes grouped together as עולל ויונק (cf. Ps. 8.3; Lam. 2.11; Joel 2.6) and were characterized by their dependence and vulnerability (cf. Isa. 65.20; Lam. 4.4). That a newborn child first had to be adopted by his or her father or else was considered stillborn, as Matthews and Benjamin (1993: 10) contend, is neither likely in a subsistence economy in which children are important as status symbol (Ps. 128.3) and as a source of labour, nor is it attested anywhere in Hebrew Bible literature. The metaphor of the foundling in Ezek. 16.3-5, to which they refer, also does not imply such a *custom*. On the contrary, the relationship between society and newborns is depicted quite differently. Children are depicted as a divine gift (cf. Ps. 37.26; 13.9; 115.14; 128.3) for whom a father has compassion (רחם, Ps. 103.13) and whom a mother will never 'forget' (Isa. 49.15). Consider also the compassion reflected in the following poetic line 'My eyes are spent with weeping; my stomach churns; my bile is poured out on the ground because of the destruction of my people, because infants and babes [עולל ויונק] faint in the streets of the city' (Lam. 2.11). Depending on their age, children's role is to assist the household in its tasks, for example, young boys may herd sheep, while girls may assist their older sisters in their tasks. Children's status symbol is belonging to an honourable, disciplined and well-run household. Each of these age grades constitutes a social group, and the passage from one group to another is marked by rites of passage: for males, circumcision, marriage, and perhaps some puberty rite later in Judaism redefined by the status of bar-mitzvah; for females menstruation, then marriage, and at many steps a legal transfer from the property or care of one man to that of another (father, husband, then perhaps son or brother?).

The superior status of males as a social group is undisputed in Hebrew Bible literature. Given the patriarchal society, with its customs of patrilocality and patrilineality, dictated by the physical surroundings (requiring 'man-power') and hostile environment, it could hardly have been otherwise. Men therefore do not have to acquire status. They own it and may only lose it temporarily through uncustomary conduct. Yet some men have more status than others. A higher status may be obtained by acquiring more property (e.g. flocks, herds, donkeys), having larger households (e.g. more than one wife, many children), being a valiant warrior or behaving wisely (and earning a place among the 'elders'). While the status of men is quite clear, that of women is complicated and often misunderstood. A 'biblical' woman has very little, if any, legal rights. It is perhaps already symbolic of women's rights that Lady Ashera's name, which may simply mean 'wife', probably derives from 'she who follows' (Margalit 1990: 269, 273). In the household she is dominated by the status of her husband, whom she would have called 'sir' (בעלי, Hos. 2.16), *if* she would address him personally, which never happens in Hebrew Bible literature. Her husband has a right to divorce, but not she. Even inheriting her father's property in the absence of a male heir creates a major incident (Num. 26.33; 27.1-11).

Yet women's legal position, which, like labour pains, is pictured as a curse (Gen. 3.16; cf. 2.24) should not be confused with their *status*. In biblical literature women enjoy a high social status. 'He who finds a wife finds a good thing, and obtains favour from the Lord' (Prov. 18.22). 'House and wealth are inherited from parents, but a prudent wife is from the Lord' (Prov. 19.14). 'A capable wife who can find? She is far more precious than jewels' (Prov. 31.10). This status endowed her with an awful lot of power. Her conduct can make or break her husband: 'A good wife is the crown of her husband, but she who brings shame is like rottenness in his bones' (Prov. 12.4). Even though the Hebrew Bible contains no example of a wife addressing her husband, it is clear that she, in her status as wife and mother, could make life difficult for him at home. Otherwise the following proverbs would not have existed: 'It is better to live in a desert land than with a contentious and fretful wife' (Prov. 21.19); 'It is better to live in a corner of the housetop than in a house shared with a contentious wife'

(Prov. 25.24). More seriously, children should equally honour their father and mother (Exod. 20.12; Prov. 10.26; 20.20; 23.22; 23.25; 28.24) and equal punishment is meted out by society for serious violations of customary behaviour towards any parent (Deut. 21.18-19). Consider, in this context, Ps. 35.14: 'As though I grieved for a friend or a brother; I went about as one who laments for a mother, bowed down and in mourning,' from which the special position of the mother figure is well illustrated. Women's wisdom and courage are often acknowledged and praised (cf. Judg. 4.4-5, 21; 5.24-31; 9.52-54; 2 Sam. 14.2; 20.16, 22). As in the Gilgamesh epic, the story of the liberation from Egypt hinges on the juxtaposition of male murders jeopardizing and female wisdom saving the situation (cf. Exod. 1.15-22; 2.1-10, 16-22; 4.24-26; cf. 1 Sam. 19.12). And, as I shall argue below, queen mothers play a major role in Judaean politics.

Moreover, women constitute the deposit of honour of the household and of the cultural group. When Dinah is raped by Shechem her brothers fiercely revenged that act (Gen. 34). And if a conqueror wants publicly and decisively to humiliate a *group*, it treats its *women* badly (cf. Isa. 13.16; 47.2; Ezek. 16.37; 23.10). Much of this high esteem for women may be, and probably is, informed by their ability to bear children and administer a household, and is therefore based on their contribution rather than on their person (see, however, Matthews and Benjamin 1993: 22-31). This is, of course, not a 'condonation' (from a present-day perspective) of the position of 'biblical' women, but merely to draw a clear distinction between their *legal* position and social *status*, which are often confused in discussions of 'biblical' women.

A mother, then, enjoys little legal but a high social status. It is this status, and the legal position of her children, that may be interfered with in a polygynous environment and that may therefore lead to strife in the household. It is often assumed that, because of the costs involved, polygyny had not been the rule in ancient Israel. This might be true. In the Hebrew Bible, however, the practice is often referred to or presupposed. Consider the number of Hebrew Bible narratives with a polygynic household as setting, that Deuteronomy regulates inheritance in cases of polygyny and that אהובה 'the preferred' and שנואה 'the non-preferred' seem to have been technical terms for 'first' and 'second' wife, respectively, while the relation between two wives of the same husband seemed to have been technically referred to as צרה ('competitor', 1 Sam. 1.6; Sir. 37.11). It is precisely in an effort to avoid strife between wives that subsistence societies often, like in the case of Leah and Rachel, prefer sororal polygyny, that is, a man taking his wife's sister(s) as a second (or further) wife. But not even that always helped. Note the conversation between Leah and Rachel, of whom Rachel was favoured above the first wife:

> Then Rachel said to Leah, 'Please give me some of your son's mandrakes.' But she said to her, 'Is it a small matter that you have taken away my husband? Would you take away my son's mandrakes also?' Rachel said, 'Then he may lie with you tonight for your son's mandrakes.' When Jacob came from the field in the evening, Leah went out to meet him, and said, 'You must come in to me; for I have hired you with my son's mandrakes.' So he lay with her that night (Gen. 30.14-16).

Apart from the problem of hierarchy created by polygyny there is also the problem of inheritance. In ancient Near Eastern subsistence agricultural economies the eldest son (first-born) usually got twice the share of each of his brothers. First-born was, however, not necessarily a chronological position, but a status conferred on any son of the father's choice. This is also the case in Hebrew Bible literature (cf. Gen. 48.13-20, 22; 49.3-4; 1 Chron. 5.1-2). Even though the most logical thing to do would perhaps have been to let the eldest son be the 'first-born', a mother could never be sure which son would receive that status—even less so in cases of polygyny. Consider, in this regard, Sarah's remark with reference to Ishmael, 'Cast out this slave woman with her son; for the son of this slave woman shall not be heir with my son Isaac' (Gen. 21.10). The practice of choosing the son of the favoured wife must have been so common that the Deuteronomic legislator found it necessary to stipulate in 21.15-17:

> If a man has two wives, one of them loved and the other disliked, and if both the loved and the disliked have borne him sons, the firstborn being the son of the one who is disliked, then on the day when he wills his possessions to his sons, he is not permitted to treat the son of the loved as the firstborn in preference to the son of the disliked, who is the firstborn. He must acknowledge as firstborn the son of the one who is disliked, giving him a double portion of all that he has; since he is the first issue of his virility, the right of the firstborn is his.

The first-born is the one who carries the 'name' of the family forward and, in the case of extended families, wields authority over the family after the father's death. This status, however, falls away when the economic system changes, as in larger cities.

Apart from age and sex, economic and legal position may also define social status. Status groups that are based on a legal definition include the widow (אלמנה), the orphan (יתום), the slave (עבד) and the foreigner (גר). Widows and orphans are frequently mentioned together in the Hebrew Bible (cf. Job 22.9; 24.3; Ps. 68.5; Isa. 1.17, 23; 9.17; 10.2; Jer. 49.11; Lam. 5.3), while some texts, quite often Deuteronomic in origin, mention together the widow, the orphan, slave and foreigner (cf. Deut. 10.18; 14.29; 16.14; 24.17, 19-21; 27.19; 26.11, 13; Ps. 94.6; 146.9; Jer. 7.6; 22.3; Ezek. 22.7; Zech. 7.10; Mal. 3.5). Given the legal status of women in 'biblical' society, the death of a husband leaves his wife defenceless: she does not have the rights of property or inheritance, nor any means of sustaining herself. Even if her parents would still be alive, she could hardly return to them, as Tamar does (Gen. 38.11), for her husband's household would have paid a bride-price for her. She is practically in the hands of the inheritor of her husband's property, who is not necessarily her own son. If she also has children to support, her position is worse, but if she has none, her position, especially in her old age, is critical (cf. 2 Sam. 14.6-7; 1 Kgs 17.17-19; 2 Kgs 4.18-37). It is this hopeless position that is employed as a metaphor in the prophecy against Babel: 'both these things shall come upon you in a moment, in one day: the loss of children and widowhood' (Isa. 47.9). The fact that legal texts and wisdom literature so often remind people to look after widows and orphans is an indication that they were often forgotten by society and left to fend for themselves and to live by their wits. However, to call widowhood a 'social institution' standing between the exploiter and the exploited, as Matthews and Benjamin (1993: 133) do, seems far-fetched. Rather than a 'social institution' widowhood means to be vulnerable, exploitable, insecure (cf. 1 Kgs 17.10-12; Job 24.3, 21; Ps. 94.6; Isa. 1.23), sometimes even disgraced (cf. Isa. 54.4). A child of a widow who has 'made it' in life is therefore specifically called 'a widow's child' (e.g. 1 Kgs 7.14; 11.26), and to wish someone really bad luck one wishes his wife to become a widow (Ps. 109.9).

Slavery in the ancient Near East is a problematic issue, because, as in the Hebrew Bible, anybody who served in some or other capacity was called a 'slave' of the employer. 'Slave' is, for that reason, not a suitable translation of עבד, which often has rather to be rendered by 'servant'. Moreover, the term 'slave' should not be understood in terms of Greek and Roman custom or, worse still, in terms of the nineteenth-century European and American slave trade. In that sense the ancient

7. Social Organization and Meaning

Near East did not know slavery (Gelb 1973: 96). A wealthy household might have had a slave in service. Such a person would, however, not work in the fields but would, like Joseph in the house of Potiphar, instead be employed as a domestic servant. A more common form of slavery was debt slavery. While household slaves would generally have been foreigners, debt slaves would have been from among the circle of the creditor's acquaintance, 'To guarantee loans for a stranger (זר) brings trouble, but there is safety in refusing to do so' (Prov. 11.15). A debtor who could not supply security for or repay his debts sometimes had to supply the creditor with a servant for a period of time to 'work off' the debt. Once the debt has been paid in this manner the servant would again be 'set free' (cf. 2 Kgs 4.1; Exod. 21.2-11; Deut. 15.12-18; Lemche 1985). Not all of these servants would be full-time 'slaves'. Some would work for a creditor on certain days of the week or when labour was needed, for example, during harvest time. Part-time debt slaves had to hand their upper cloak to the creditor as pledge. Referring to this practice Deut. 24.12-13 rules: 'If the person is poor, you shall not sleep in the garment [rather: "you should not keep his garment overnight" (לא תשכב בעבטו)] given you as the pledge. You shall give the pledge back by sunset, so that your neighbour may sleep in the cloak and bless you...' (see Matthews and Benjamin 1993: 203).

That this ruling does not reflect custom is clear from the accusation against the powerful in Amos 2.8: 'They lay themselves down beside every altar on garments taken in pledge...', Eliphaz's remark to Job, 'You have exacted pledges from your family for no reason, and stripped the naked of their clothing' (Job 22.6), and the early sixth-century BCE Meṣad Hashavyahu ostracon on which a worker complains to the 'governor' of the settlement about his pledged garment that has not been returned to him in exchange for work done. The practice of claiming a debtor's garment is also presupposed by Prov. 20.16. According to this text ('Take the garment of one who has given surety for a stranger [זר]; seize the pledge given as surety for foreigners [נכרים])' granting loans to unknown people or guaranteeing loans for foreigners in most cases leads to the creditor having to seize the debtor's garment. To reward the creditor for his stupidity in having granted the loan in the first place, one should rather confiscate his garment instead. As a debt slave a person would count among the עניים whom we shall discuss below, and therefore among those with a very low social status. If such a person would succeed in rehabilitating his household, its status would, or course, change for the better. It is precisely because it would have been terribly difficult to elevate oneself from this position to a higher social status that Deuteronomy urges creditors to assist debt slaves who have repaid their debts through service to get on their feet again (Deut. 15.13-15).

Slavery was also practised on a broader scale by the state. On the one hand, there was the practice of 'forced labour', that is, as part of their annual tax citizens had to render service to the crown. The state could, however, also employ prisoners of war as slaves. But neither were these people 'slaves' in the meaning of the English term. In subsistence economies, which could not feed extra mouths, war captives were simply killed (Gelb 1973: 73-74). At the most women and (perhaps) children would be taken prisoner and distributed among the households of military officers and state officials as concubines and household slaves (cf. Deut. 21.10-14). It is only in cases where the state had enough central supplies to feed prisoners of war that men were not killed off and became state property. Viewed in this light 2 Samuel 8 suggests that David's 'kingdom' was halfway to a real state that could deal with male prisoners of war: 'He also defeated the Moabites and, making them lie down on the ground, measured them off with a cord; he measured two lengths of cord for those who were to be put to death, and one length for those who were to be spared' (2 Sam. 8.2).

But even these captives were not 'slaves' after the Greek and Roman fashion or in the common meaning of the term (Gelb 1973: 94-96). After a period of humiliating captivity surviving male prisoners of war would be semi-freed and deployed in various capacities. Some would be utilized as a labour force on state farms or in building projects, others as soldiers. Some would be redistributed to temples, some as servants to individual households of, for example, generals and nobles. Since chiefs and kings always had to be on their guard against usurpers, they often employed foreigners, also prisoners of war, as part of the king's bodyguard (cf. 1 Sam. 28.2) or, like Joseph in Egypt and Ebedmelech in Jerusalem (Jer. 38.7), in posts of confidence (Gelb 1973: 81, 92-94). Some were even deployed as part of an elite troop for rapid military action (cf. David's Cherethites and Pelethites [2 Sam. 8.18]). Such slaves, even though they remained state property and would be known as 'released slaves' (חפשי), could, depending on the tasks entrusted to them, climb up the social ladder. Of course, very few

7. *Social Organization and Meaning* 269

would succeed in doing so and would have remained in the 'released slave' category.

Another group whose 'identity' is of a legal nature is the 'stranger'. The Hebrew Bible distinguishes between two kinds of strangers, namely the 'sojourners' or 'strangers' (גרים) and the 'foreigners' (נכרים; נכריות, cf. Judg. 19.11; 1 Kgs 11.1), that is, a citizen of a foreign country. A foreigner, unless identified as belonging to a royal court, like the queen of Sheba (1 Kgs 10.1), can hardly be spoken of in terms of social status. Apart from the fact that such a person would be eyed and treated with suspicion, they would not in any way fit into the existing social structure, and in any case nobody would know in what social bracket such unknown people belong. Laban's daughters feel themselves treated as such statusless 'foreigners' by their father and are therefore eager to leave his household (Gen. 31.15), while Ruth is surprised at the treatment she receives from Boaz, even though she/he is a foreigner (Ruth 2.10).

The situation with the stranger is quite different, though. A stranger is not of foreign nationality. Anybody who does not belong to 'us' and 'our community' is a stranger. A person travelling through a village or who resettles in a new village or district is, for example, treated as a stranger. Should a person be but a passer-by or a temporary visitor, custom prescribes that he or she should, like Abraham and Lot do (Gen. 18.1-5; 19.1-3), be treated with hospitality and offered shelter. To illustrate the chaotic conditions in Israel in premonarchical times, Judges 19 tells a story whose plot hinges on 'strangers'. A Levite originally from the territory of Benjamin resettles in the hills of Ephraim and after some time pays his father-in-law in Benjamin a visit. On his journey back he first thinks of turning into Jebus for the night, but then decides not to, because Jebus is a foreign city (עיר נכרי). He then turns into Gibeah of Benjamin, where he now has the status of a 'stranger'. Yet nobody offers him shelter (Judg. 19.11-15). Finally, an old man who originally lived in the hills of Ephraim (where the Levite 'stranger' now lives as stranger) but now resides as a stranger in Gibeah (הוא־גר בגבעה) offers him shelter. So one stranger (the old man) offers his hospitality to another stranger (the Levite) who lives as a stranger in the old man's district of origin. During the night, though, the men of Gibeah command the old man to hand the stranger over to them so that they can sodomize him (Judg. 19.22; cf. Gen. 19.5). After some time of negotiation the Levite's concubine is handed over to the men, who then rape her to death (Judg. 19.25-27). This story illustrates the vulnerability of a stranger as well as the rationale of the custom of hospitality to strangers. It also illustrates, though, that a person (like the old man) who resettles in a new district is always seen as a 'stranger' and that a stranger does not enjoy civil rights. That is why the men of Sodom and the men of Gibeah can demand that Lot and the old man hand over their guests, which they could not have demanded from one of their own group.

It is, however, not only individuals who may become 'sojourners'. After the assassination of Abner the troops in the service of Saul's son flee from Beeroth to Gittaim where they 'have been living as strangers to this day' (2 Sam. 4.3). Because such people are not part of the social structure of the group among whom they live, they do not fit in anywhere and can consequently not rely on the 'security net' of the social system. They are therefore vulnerable and exploitable as the story in Judges 19 illustrates. The Hebrew Bible consequently ranks 'strangers' with the vulnerable, like orphans and widows, and repeatedly reminds its readers to show kindness to this group. Hence, 'When you reap your harvest in your field and forget a sheaf in the field, you shall not go back to get it; it shall be left for the alien [i.e. 'stranger'], the orphan, and the widow' (Deut. 24.19).

Status groups that are based on economic distinctions presuppose a redistribution economy, which applies in 'biblical' Israel to the time of the monarchy. At the top of the economic status scale stand the well-to-do, that is, the freeman (עשיר), big man (איש חיל, Lev. 19.15) or officials (שרים, Job 34.19). This class is its own boss, owns property and/or many possessions and other people look up to them with respect and awe. When God promises Solomon both riches (גם־עשר) and honour (גם־כבוד), and Lady Wisdom the same to her followers (Prov. 3.16; cf. 8.18; 11.16; 22.4; Eccl. 6.2), these are promises with an implication of high social standing. People of this social standing probably are also not on the king's conscription list. For when David enquires about the reward for killing Goliath, he is informed, 'The king will greatly enrich [יעשרנו עשר גדול] the man who kills him, and will give him his daughter and make his family free (ואת בית אביו יעשה חפשי) in Israel' (1 Sam. 17.25). At the other end of the scale stand the 'poor' (רש or דל). These are often mentioned together: 'The rich [עשיר] and the poor [רש] have this in common: the Lord is the maker of them all' (2 Sam. 12.1; Prov. 22.2; cf. Prov. 13.8; 18.23; 22.7); 'The rich [עשיר] shall not give more, example, said to give his vassals the 'breath of life', and the *Israel Stela* says that, at the sight of Merneptah, 'breath enters our nostrils'. Against this backdrop some statements in Ecclesiastes, whose narrator is himself a king (Eccl. 1.1), seem to refer to the king and the circle in the royal court closest to him as the circle of 'the living'. To begin with, 'For what advantage have the wise [חכם 'the educated'], over fools (הכסיל 'the uneducated')?: How do the poor (עני, who are generally thought of by the educated to be a little stupid) know how to conduct themselves before "the living" (החיים, i.e. court personnel and king, Eccl. 6.8)?' Again, in Eccl. 4.13-16 the argument is that a wise poor youngster is better off than an old, foolish king who does not take advice. For the prudent youngster works his way from the rags of prison to the riches of the court and takes the king's place (by assassinating him?). And suddenly all the living (כל־החיים, i.e. those who served the old, foolish king), join the youngster: the king is dead, long live the king! Also, with the court as background, Ecclesiastes 9 argues that rich and poor, wise and foolish, pure and impure all die in the same manner. Death is not only inevitable, it is also the great equalizer. Then follows an interesting remark: 'But whoever is elected (יבחר) to be among the living (or: 'is joined' [יחבר; LXX: κοινωνεῖ] with all the living) has hope, for a living dog is better than a dead lion' (9.4). 'The living' here clearly refers to all people. In view of death as the great equalizer even a 'living *dog*' is better off than a 'dead *lion*'. This remark seems to be a pun. Addressing the king (the lion) ordinary people refer to themselves as 'dead dogs'. But when 'the lion' dies, he is nothing. Then the 'living dog' is better off than the 'dead lion'. Like ethical qualities (righteousness–wickedness; goodness–evil) and religious qualities (clean–unclean; to sacrifice–not to sacrifice) also status (dead dog–living lion) does not survive death. All human 'classifications' of people are vanity.

Another person with a high social standing in the court is the queen mother (גבירה) frequently referred to in Judaean literature (1 Kgs 14.21; 15.2, 13; 22.42; 2 Kgs 8.26; 10.13; 11.1; 12.1; 14.2; 15.2, 33; 18.2; 21.1, 19; 22.1; 23.31, 36; 24.8, 18). She holds a position independently of the king and, retaining it after his death, she may mediate between political factions in the nation and even act as regent (cf. 2 Kgs 11.1-3). Even though the king has the authority to remove her from office (1 Kgs 15.13), she plays an important role in the cult, participates in political, military and economic affairs of the court and is sufficiently powerful even to oppose the king on issues of state. The fact that the literature never uses the title for an Israelite queen may be the result of the scribes' down-playing of Israel as a 'kingdom', because it seems as if Jezebel assumes the queen mother's regent role at the death of her son when she heard of the assassination of the king 'she painted her eyes, and adorned her head, and looked out of the window' and challenged Jehu when he reached the palace: 'Is it peace, Zimri, murderer of your master?' (2 Kgs 9.30-31).

In the royal court serve various officials, for example, royal advisers, the king's 'friend', the chief priest, the diviners, the messenger/scribe, the interpreter, the chief of military staff, the chief of forced labour, councillors, etc. The social status of belonging to the court is dictated by loyalty rather than by competence. To lose the king's trust is like a death sentence. 'A king's anger,' says Prov. 19.12, 'is like the growling of a lion, but his favour is like dew on the grass.' That is why Ahitophel, even though an extremely competent adviser, when he realizes that the self-appointed King Absalom prefers the advice of Hushai to his, goes home and commits suicide (2 Sam. 17.23). Other officials are too late. When Solomon comes to power, he swiftly acts against those whom his father advised him not to trust, among whom count the chief priest and the chief of military staff (1 Kgs 2.26-34). He has them killed and in their place he appoints new individuals (2.35).

In the court is also 'the king's friend' (רעה המלך, Gen. 26.26; 2 Sam. 3.8; 16.16; cf. 15.34; 16.19; 1 Kgs 4.5; 16.11; cf. 2 Sam. 13.3), a Hebrew term for which the translation 'friend' is in fact misleading. This officer, who is regarded as part of the royal family and is often also chosen from among the collaterals of the royal house, serves as a close *confidant* and political adviser to the king. It is this officer whom David sends back to Jerusalem after Absolom's coup not only to keep him informed about developments in the court but also to counter the able advice of another royal adviser (cf. 1 Sam. 16.23), who has switched allegiances (2 Sam. 15.31-37).

Already, the few remarks above on the implications of 'living together' and 'getting organized' show that the implied meaning of biblical terms, customs, actions and consequently texts relating the actions of characters are embedded in the social organization of ancient Israel, not to speak of similes and metaphors drawn from the sphere of social organization. Also, that knowledge of the social organization of ancient Israel is intimately involved with other cultural domains. The *environ-*

ment plays a role in determining the kind of organization necessary to survive in a region; distinguishing age and status groups may involve *religious* ritual (rites of passage); marrying a person has *economic* consequences; while the rules of conduct imply measures of *social control*.

Chapter 8

POLITICAL ORGANIZATION AND MEANING

The purpose of organizing a community is, among other things, to exercise some form of control over individual members in order to ensure the proper functioning of society. Since ancient Israel had over time developed from a clan society into a state, it experienced different forms of political organization, a fact which has to be taken into account when interpreting Hebrew Bible stories.

Anthropologists distinguish four basic political systems, namely bands, tribes, chiefdoms and states (Haviland 1996: 328). It would seem that, apart from bands (normally only occurring among hunters and gatherers), the three other systems had all functioned at different stages in the history of ancient Israel. In Haviland's definition a tribal system normally occurs in herding and farming economies and is one in which a number of villages, sharing a common language and culture, are integrated by such factors as clans, associations that cross-cut kinship, or territorial boundaries, and in which a degree of household autonomy is sacrificed to the tribal authority in exchange for security (Haviland 1996: 330-31). Although groups under tribal authority share a geographical area, they need not be the only inhabitants of that area or be able to demarcate their 'territory' (Freedman 1978: 41).

Whether the biblical picture of Israel's 'twelve tribes' should be viewed as historically accurate or as a later fiction is debatable. The fact, however, that many Hebrew Bible narratives and some of its poems represent Israel as in terms of a tribal system seems to suggest that this kind of political organization had been in place at some stage, and that knowledge of the workings of a tribal political system is essential for the interpretation of such narratives and poems.

8. *Political Organization and Meaning*

1. *Tribal Authorities*

Tribal authorities come into being where population density increases and with it quarrels, adultery, theft and other forms of anti-social behaviour that threaten the social fabric of society (Haviland 1996: 330), and/or when an external threat of some sort forces autonomous social entities to seek closer cooperation with each other. In spite of the formation of a larger (tribal) system the seat of political authority normally remains the clan, which is represented on the tribal level. The clan leadership, and therefore also the tribal leadership, may be age-graded, typically consisting of old men of the various clans, while the tribal leader normally is a person respected for his age and wisdom.

The narratives of the Hebrew Bible frequently mention clan and tribal elders in various functions, such as representing the people at certain occasions (e.g. Exod. 3.16-18; 12.21; Judg. 8.16; 1 Kgs 8.1), mediating or giving decisions in cases of family and other community issues and administering justice (e.g. Deut. 21.2, 19; 22.15-18; 25.7-9; Jer. 26.17); giving advice (Ezek. 7.26); appointing a military leader (Judg. 11.5); mourning the dead (Josh. 7.6; Lam. 2.10); negotiating with outsiders (2 Sam. 3.17-18), etc. That an elder had been a trusted person of honour is clear from texts like Job 12.20, Lam. 4.16; 5.12,14; and Prov. 20.29. Job, in speaking of God's power to turn the human order upside down, says that he 'deprives of speech *those who are trusted* (נאמנים) and takes away the discernment ('advice') *of the elders* (זקנים)', which reflects the normal position held by elders. Lamentations 4.16 bemoans the fact that God showed 'no honour to the priests, no favour to the elders'; and 5.12 that 'princes are hung up by their hands' and 'no respect is shown to the elders'. These texts see the sociopolitical order turned upside down, thereby implying what had, even up to the fall of Jerusalem, been the position of elders in the community.

The authority that rests in tribal elders and leaders is, however, not absolute and permanent, but rests on the respect people have for them. Misbehaviour on their side may cause people to start gossiping about them and may in the end cost them their position. One does not need a great deal of imagination to picture the faces of the 'Josephite' narrator and his audience when he related to them Genesis 38's story of the leader of the Judah group, and what effect that story must have had on their view of Judah as a clan or tribe.

Against the background of the sociopolitical position and function of elders a pronouncement like Isa. 3.14-15 pictures a society in which the total *social order* has collapsed:

> The Lord enters into judgment with the elders and princes of his people: 'It is you who have *devoured* the vineyard, the spoil of the poor is in *your* houses. What do you mean by *crushing my people*, by grinding the face of *the poor*?'

Consider also the implied shaming social effect of God's judgment upon the house of Eli in 1 Sam. 2.31:

> Behold, the days are coming, when I will cut off your strength and the strength of your father's house, so that *there will not be an old man in your house*. Then in distress you will look with envious eye on all the prosperity which shall be bestowed upon Israel; and *there shall not be an old man in your house for ever*.

And the implications of the imagery in Lam. 5.14: 'The old men have quit the *city gate*' (where they used to attend to all sorts of community problems and represented their households or clans).

2. Chiefdoms

Another kind of political organization is that of a *chiefdom*. In the biblical text Saul, David and Solomon are all called 'kings', thereby suggesting that a kingdom was suddenly substituted for 'Israel's' tribal political organization, which, of course, is a literary *representation* of social reality as the *authors* conceived of it. However, as Flanagan (1981) has convincingly argued, the political situation presupposed by the Saul and David narratives seems to suit better the anthropological category of 'chiefdom'. A chiefdom is a first move towards *centralized* government. The need for a centralized government normally arises under two conditions, namely environmental and social circumscription (Carneiro 1970: 734-38). Environmental circumscription occurs when increased production, necessitated by, for example, population growth or tributes extracted from the region, is inhibited by scarce natural resources. Social circumscription occurs when a single indigenous, foreign group succeeds in securing the use of natural resources for itself, thereby denying other groups access to these resources. In such circumstances the groups living in a region may go under, migrate or unite. Both these conditions are met in the Saul, David (and Solomon) narratives. Already, in Josh. 17.14, the Joseph people complain about too little space for too many people: 'Why have you [Joshua] given me

8. Political Organization and Meaning

[Joseph] but one lot and one portion as an inheritance, since we are a numerous people...?' And according to 1 Kgs 4.20 'Judah and Israel were as numerous as the sand by the sea'. This is environmental circumscription. According to the book of Judges, various neighbouring groups, and according to Judges 13–16 and 1 Samuel 4–8 especially the Philistines, caused social circumscription. It is under these circumstances that Saul becomes 'king', or, rather, 'chief'.

A chiefdom is characterized by a number of features distinguishing it, on the one hand, from tribal rule, and on the other hand, from royal rule (Flanagan 1981: 50-55). First, like tribal leaders, chiefs are normally leaders of a localized descent or territorial group and often achieve the status of leader by being wealthy, generous, successful, admirable, eloquent, physically brave and sometimes also skilled in dealing with the supernatural (Haviland 1996: 331). Likewise, Saul is said to have been a tall man of a well-known family and brave at war (1 Sam. 9.1; 1 Sam. 11), while David, according to tradition, distinguished himself as a military hero (1 Sam. 17; 23; 27), cunning negotiator, able musician (1 Sam. 16.16; 2 Sam. 1; 22), and a generous redistributor of the spoils of war among the leaders of the southern clans (1 Sam. 30.26-31 [Flanagan 1981: 57]). But, unlike tribal leadership and like a monarch, the chiefdom is a permanent institution around which political power is centralized. However, even where the custom of father–son succession, typical of monarchical systems, apply in chiefdoms (Haviland 1996: 334) the system is unstable and haunted by power struggles kindled by aspiring high-ranking officials or even family members (see Haviland 1996: 335). This explains Saul's paranoid (?) fear and hence persecution of the military star David (1 Sam. 18–31). Rebuking Jonathan's naive friendship with David, Saul says, 'You son of a perverse, rebellious woman! Do I not know that you have chosen the son of Jesse *to your own shame*, and to the shame of your mother's nakedness?' (1 Sam. 20.30). Consider also the strife preceding David's succession to Saul (1 Sam. 2.12–3.1) and the protracted power struggle among David's children for his 'throne' (2 Sam. 15–1 Kgs 1).

Secondly, unlike a tribal society but very much like a kingdom, a chiefdom has a social ranking system consisting of major and minor authorities linking leaders on every level to form a chain of command. Describing an African chief, Haviland (1996: 335) notes:

> In keeping with his exalted station in life, a paramount chief has at his disposal uniformed messenger, a literate clerk, and the symbols of

wealth: many wives, embroidered gowns, and freedom of manual labour... [B]eneath each paramount chief are several lesser chiefs; one for each district within the chiefdom, one for each town within a district In this status chain the people closest to the chief, usually his family or war heroes, occupy a higher rank than people further away from him (Haviland 1996: 334).

Note, for example, Saul appointing his uncle (1 Sam. 14.50) and David and Absalom their cousins (2 Sam. 8.16; 17.25) as chiefs of the army. Consider also the term שׁליש (officer), used to indicate the officials in David's 'administration' (2 Sam. 23.8) and which probably means 'of the third rank', that is, after the chief and his chief of staff (Na'aman 1995: 71). Yet unlike a kingdom, a chiefdom does not have a specialized bureaucracy or the machinery to physically coerce subjects into contributing towards the central pool of the redistribution economy. Although David is said to have had quite a few officials (שׁלישׁים, 2 Sam. 23.8-39; cf. Na'aman 1995), these officials are mere former war heroes rewarded for their services and *not professional administrators* geared to extracting taxes, as, for example, Solomon's administrative personnel. Fourthly, unlike a tribal leader but like a king, the more conspicuous the dichotomy between the chief's centre and the dependent settlements develop, the more the chief is portrayed as divinely elected and appointed (Flanagan 1981: 51). Of both Saul and David it is said that they built themselves palaces (cf. Gibeah of Saul, 1 Sam. 11.4; 15.34; 2 Sam. 6.9; 7.2) and are said to have been divinely appointed (1 Sam. 9; 16.1-13).

Typical of most African chiefdoms is the official praise singer, whose job it is to publicly sing the praises of the chief and declare his divine status. Certain so-called 'royal psalms' strongly resemble these praise songs. In Psalm 2 (cf. also Ps. 45.2-7; Ps. 110), for example, the assembled petty chiefs (or subject kings?) are ridiculed for even considering rebellion against the Big Man, for the Big Man reigns by divine fiat. God himself calls him his 'son' and takes care of rebels. Therefore (Ps. 2.12, although admittedly a very difficult verse to translate), 'kiss his feet, lest he be angry, and you perish in the way; for his wrath is quickly kindled. Blessed are all who take refuge in him.' Moreover, unlike a temporary tribal leader but like a king, a chief may accumulate status symbols and a great deal of wealth that may then be passed on to his heirs. Saul as well as David are said to have worn a crown (נזר, 2 Sam. 1.10; עטרת, 12.30), while David accumulated wealth and wives in Jerusalem. 2 Samuel 5.10-13 says:

8. *Political Organization and Meaning* 281

And David became greater and greater... King Hiram of Tyre sent messengers to David, along with cedar trees, and carpenters and masons who built David a house... In Jerusalem, after he came from Hebron, David took more concubines and wives; and more sons and daughters were born to David.

3. *States*

Not all chiefdoms develop into states but some do. State formation may be primary (i.e. a spontaneous development), or secondary (i.e. resulting because of outside pressures); pristine (i.e. self-made) or modelled (i.e. constructed along the lines of existing examples) Cohen and Service 1978: 154-55). In the case of primary state formation, the process is normally driven by the inner logic of chiefdoms, that is, a chiefdom's hierarchical social and economic structuring of society becomes a 'centripetal' force favouring 'its own strengthening and perpetuation' (Cohen and Service 1978: 8). More often, though, the emergence of states is caused by external factors. Carneiro (1970: 738), for example, views the emergence of a state as 'a predictable response to certain specific cultural, demographic and ecological conditions'. As in the case of chiefdoms, these conditions are continued and perhaps intensified environmental, and especially social circumscription. For a state to function properly there is another set of prerequisites, such as a surplus production of food, which in turn rests upon substantial improvements in agricultural technology (e.g. the building of terraces), the managing of rotation cycles, clearly demarcated territory, and a rural population large enough to support market systems and a specialized urban sector. Once these conditions are met, 'corporate groups that stress exclusive membership proliferate, ethnic differentiation and ethnocentrism become more pronounced, and the potential for social conflict increases dramatically' (Haviland 1996: 336).

Reading Hebrew Bible narratives in the theoretical context of state formation an interesting picture emerges. With the Philistine threat, which caused the tribal system to become a chiefdom, removed (2 Sam. 5.17-25; 8.1) and all other potential enemies subdued (2 Sam. 8.2-15), the chiefdom of Jerusalem spontaneously develops into a kingdom modelled on the examples of Canaanite city states and of neighbouring states like Syria and Egypt. According to Hebrew Bible narratives the principle of dynastic succession immediately becomes institutionalized. With the single exception of the rule of Queen Athaliah (2 Kgs 11) the reigning king's son is installed in his place, and even in cases where the king is assassinated his son is installed in his place (2 Kgs 12.20-21; 14.1; 14.19-21). However, even though the narrator can state that 'during Solomon's lifetime Judah and Israel lived in safety, from Dan even to Beer-sheba, all of them under their vines and fig trees' (1 Kgs 4.25), the inevitable problems of becoming a state are present between the lines of the story. Haviland (1996: 336), as we have seen, refers to the potential for social conflict increasing when, with the advance of a state, corporate groups, stressing exclusive membership, proliferate and ethnic differentiation and ethnocentrism become more pronounced. Note, in this context, the conspicuous absence of Judah among Solomon's tax districts (1 Kgs 4.7-19), the priority of Judah in the phrase 'Judah and Israel' (1 Kgs 4.20, 25), and the remark: 'King Solomon conscripted forced labour out of all Israel; the levy numbered thirty thousand men' (1 Kgs 5.13; cf. the apologetic correction in 9.20-22). It is this differentiation that finally leads the Israelites to say, 'What share do we have in David? We have no inheritance in the son of Jesse. To your tents, O Israel! Look now to your own house, O David' (1 Kgs 12.16, and note the mentioning of David's name without title, which we have already identified as a customary way of insulting a person).

Israel, so the text seems to suggest, would not accept the custom of hereditary succession and remained an unstable chiefdom with its crises of succession (1 Kgs 15.27-28; 16.9-10) until the advance of the Aramaean and Assyrian military might forced it in the time of Omri (1 Kgs 16.16-23) and Ahab also to become a kingdom. This kingdom, then, is a secondary state modelled after the example of the Judaean and perhaps other states. But the formation of the state in both Israel and Judah seems to have induced a sharp distinction between 'national' ideologies, such as the creation of supposed ethnic groups of 'Canaanites' and 'Israelites'. Some of the harsh ethnocentric sentiments reflected in a book like Deuteronomy echo these developments. Reading the stories of Elijah and Elisha as a literary representation of an involved cultural conflict in times of political change (from a chiefdom to statehood) may enhance a reader's depth of perspective and prevent her from viewing the plot of the narrative in terms of a purely religious, or still worse, 'theological', conflict.

No ancient Near Eastern state was conceivable without a very close relationship between king and temple, as is also illustrated by the huge amount of narrating time (*Erzählzeit*) devoted to Solomon's construc-

8. *Political Organization and Meaning* 283

tion of the temple and palace complex (1 Kgs 5–8) compared to the time devoted to his administrative and economic undertakings (1 Kgs 4.1-19; 9.10-19, 24-28). There are good reasons for this emphasis on the central sanctuary. One is that the temple has a specific function in a redistribution economy; another has to do with the role of religion in the legitimization of the institution of kingship. Even though his study was conducted in a different culture, Heitzman's investigation into the function of the temple in the 'ritual polity' of mediaeval South India (Heitzman 1991) concurs on so many points with investigations into the function in the state economy of ancient Near Eastern and Greek temples (cf. Blenkinsopp 1991; Hoglund 1991; Carter 1994) that the model may be used to explain the function of the temple in the political and economic set-up of an ancient Near Eastern state and to interpret the function of the central sanctuary in Hebrew Bible literature.

In this model the early state was not so much about administration and control over territory as about the king as universal overlord linking together constellations of small political and economic units (Heitzman 1991: 23). The king and his capital were at the centre of the universe, from where he directed divine (cosmic) righteousness to the material world. The belief that the central temple of the state stood on the 'centre of the earth' was widespread in the ancient Near East and may also be implied by the reference to the 'centre of the earth' (טבור הארץ) in Ezek. 38.12. The link between the temple and justice is also attested by the documents from the Uruk temple, where temple officials dealt with a wide range of matters, such as marriage and property and the hearing of petitions and grievances (Blenkinsopp 1991: 32). The connection between king and justice is also well attested. Proverbs 20.8 says, 'A king who sits on the throne of judgement winnows all evil with his eyes.' Note also, 'So David reigned over all Israel; and David administered justice and equity to all his people' (2 Sam. 8.15); 'All Israel heard of the judgment that the king had rendered; and they stood in awe of the king, because they perceived that the wisdom of God was in him, to execute justice' (1 Kgs 3.28; cf. Ps. 72.1-2; 89.14 [Heb. v. 15]). The prerequisite for the survival of the state, says Amos, is the administration of justice: 'Hate evil and love good, and establish justice in the gate; it may be that the Lord, the God of hosts, will be gracious to the remnant of Joseph' (Amos 5.15). But justice implies more than a courtroom. The equitable distribution of goods is, after all, the rationale behind the link among the central shrine, taxes, the erection of storehouses and the appointment of administrative staff. It is in this context that the chief or king is often referred to as the 'shepherd' of the people. Consider the elders' speech when they ask David to become king: 'In times past, when Saul was king over us, it was you that led out and brought in Israel; and the Lord said to you, "You shall be shepherd of my people Israel, and you shall be prince over Israel" ' (2 Sam. 5.2). Psalm 78.71 looks back on this event by comparing David's two statuses as 'shepherd', 'from tending the ewes that had young he [Yahweh] brought him [David] to be the shepherd of Jacob his people, of Israel his inheritance'. But it is exactly the accusation of the prophets that the kings and their officials have not lived up to that standard. Consider, for example, 'Therefore thus says the Lord, the God of Israel, concerning the shepherds who shepherd my people: "It is you who have scattered my flock, and have driven them away, and you have not attended to them" ' (Jer. 23.2). Or 'So they (Israel) were scattered, because there was no shepherd; and scattered, they became food for all the wild animals' (Ezek. 34.5).

To display his support of the religious institutions and his power to suppress chaos, and to be continually legitimized, the king had to perform regular rites (e.g. taking part in daily sacrifices, religious festivities and processions, and annual military campaigns). With the temple at the centre, the kingdom spreads with an ever weakening royal presence to a periphery (in the ancient Near East, to vassal states) that was only nominally tied to the king and that therefore had to be ritually reintegrated on a regular basis by military campaigns. Anthropologists describe this kind of administrative system in terms of the so-called 'central place' theory, according to which the 'relationships between and among sites may be represented by a series of hexagons, with influence from large, central sites radiating outward, incorporating intermediate and smaller-sized sites' (Carter 1994: 116). Applying this theory to the distribution of, and relationships among, ancient Near Eastern administrative centres, it was found that, owing to geological and environmental factors, a hexagonal rather than a rhomboidal pattern was followed in Mesopotamia and an elliptical pattern in Achaemenid Palestine (Carter 1994: 116). Whatever pattern might have been followed, each such zone of influence had an area of political centralization (administrative centre) to which donors from dominant social groups could bring their gifts 'in the manner of the king' (cf. 1 Kgs 5.5-6, 11-18) in order legitimately to share in the political power and to

8. Political Organization and Meaning 285

remain integrated into the total organizational system. Consider, in this regard, the value of the gifts the leaders (הנשאים) donate for the construction of the wilderness sanctuary compared to those of the ordinary people (Exod. 35.27-28). To enable them to make their donations and so to demonstrate their personal devotion and protection of justice, notables in outlying areas erected smaller sanctuaries, thereby creating their own spheres of influence and coming to dominate local production systems (Heitzman 1991: 25-26). This was, according to the archaeological finds, also the case in ancient Israel and Judah, where administrative complexes often contained small sanctuaries (cf. Weippert 1988: 620-31) and officials dominated the production processes. In terms of the Persian empire the Second Temple in Jerusalem would have been a similar 'local' sanctuary with its own area of influence (cf. Blenkinsopp 1991: 37-40). Throughout the Persian empire foundries had, for example, been constructed at local sanctuaries, also in Jerusalem, for melting and casting metal donations into forms convenient for transportation to the central royal treasury (Schaper 1995: 531).

In Southern India Rajaraja I, from an originally minor dynasty, suddenly shot to prominence in the tenth century CE. Celebrating his triumph, he constructed a huge temple in his capital city and created an elaborate infrastructure for the support of the temple rituals (Heitzman 1991: 27). For the building project the king and high officials made spectacular donations from his private wealth and from booty amassed in wars (Heitzman 1991: 29; cf. 1 Kgs 5.5-18). Careful arrangements were made for, and records kept of, the funding and staffing of the temple. Much earlier, the temple records of Uruk reveal the remarkable variety of professions required to operate the temple system, for example, musicians, exorcists, porters, scribes, bakers and carpenters (Blenkinsopp 1991: 31). The staff of the Indian temple, for example, priests, dancers, artisans, service workers, watchmen and administrators, were recruited from local sanctuaries and outlying villages (Heitzman 1991: 32). Consider the elaborate description the Chronicler gives of the personnel of the Solomonic temple (1 Chron. 23–26). In India the supplies for the temple services and its personnel were secured in several ways. Animals were donated to villages in the central area of the kingdom and the villages then made responsible for supplying oil manufactured from milk. Courtiers, military personnel and representatives of the temple treasury further arranged for an annual income by regularly collecting from the villages the prescribed donations according to standardized measures. Consider, in this context, the collection of donations for the tabernacle (Exod. 35.1-29), the expression 'according to the shekel of the sanctuary' (בשקל הקדש, Exod. 30.13, 24; 38.24, 25, etc.) indicating a sanctuary standard, the personal levies ordinary Israelites are commanded to pay to the sanctuary (Exod. 30.11-16) and the right of priests to consume most of the sacrificial animals (Lev. 6.16-18, 26; 7.6, 15-16, 31-38, etc.).

Furthermore, in the case of Rajaraja's temple, land taxes ensured the temple of an income: agricultural villages had to pay in kind and merchant villages in gold (Heitzman 1991: 32), very much as the Hebrew Bible prescribes tithing as a sanctuary tax (e.g. Num. 18.21, 26; Deut. 12.17; 2 Chron. 31.5; Neh. 10.38) and as the taxes due to the Persian empire had to be paid in kind and in metal (Schaper 1995). The system of ensuring income for the temple in Southern India created a transactional network throughout the kingdom. Primary transactions consisted of outgoing messages identifying the creator and primary donors of the temple (the king and nobility) as the leading citizens of the kingdom (Heitzman 1991: 33). Their donations ensured them their positions and the well-being of the whole kingdom, including every one of its subjects. On an administrative level the transactions consisted of produce and people coming from all over the kingdom to the centre and money and production material (e.g. animals) going from the centre to the kingdom. Heitzman presents the integrating function of the Indian system with the following diagram:

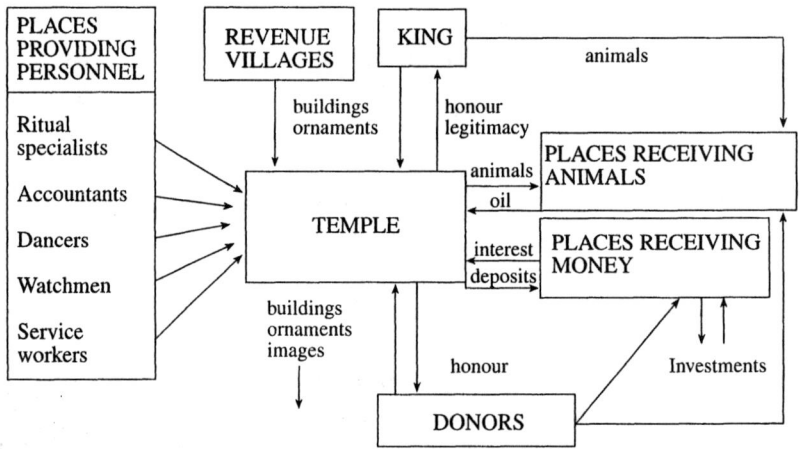

The Indian system had several functions, which may also be asserted in the case of ancient Near Eastern temples. First, through the transactional network the temple integrated the whole economic, social, political and religious life in the kingdom and tied together the local leaders into a single administrative system headed by the king. In his investigation Blenkinsopp (1991: 26) finds that temples of the Achaemenid period also 'served as catalysts of economic exchange and promoters of social cohesion'. Secondly, the architecture of the temple, the recruitment of personnel from older sacred sites, the engraving of donations, and even the preambles of the inscriptions show the king as the focus of the kingdom's devotion to its god and the protection of *dharma* (righteousness).

Blenkinsopp (1991: 26) sees the Achaemenid temple as also being the 'point of convergence for the symbolic structures of the region, an emblem of collective identity'. Thirdly, the temple was in the end not a mere 'ideological' institution legitimizing royalty and nobility but—as a redistribution economy is supposed to function—encouraged investment and agricultural development in backlying areas (Heitzman 1991: 45, 50-51), very much like the Achaemenid policies of ruralization enhanced the resettlement of earlier abandoned rural areas (Hoglund 1991: 57-60).

The relationship between king and priest, palace and temple, runs like a golden thread through the narrative of the Judaean kingdom. In the light of the foregoing discussion this comes as no surprise. In the ancient Near Eastern state the temple was the central point not only of cosmology and religion, but also of status, economy, and politics. This explains why the temple plays such an important role in the psalms, which are not mere 'liturgical' or 'theological' literature, but 'literature of complete existence'. Hence, 'Because of your temple at Jerusalem kings bear gifts to you' (Ps. 68.29; Heb. v. 30), or

> As we have heard, so have we seen in the city of the Lord of hosts, in the city of our God, which God establishes forever. We ponder your steadfast love, O God, in the midst of your temple. Your name, O God, like your praise, reaches to the ends of the earth. Your right hand is filled with victory (Ps. 48.8-10; Heb. vv. 9-11).

As long as the temple exists, society exists. Note the reassurance Jeremiah's opponents get from the magic formula 'The temple of the Lord, the temple of the Lord, the temple of the Lord!' (Jer. 7.4). But if the temple is removed, society collapses. Consider the shocking nature of the announcement, 'I will do to the house that is called by my name, in which you trust, and to the place that I gave to you and to your ancestors, just what I did to Shiloh [whose temple is no more]' (Jer. 7.14).

In view of the importance of a central temple for a state, the picture Hebrew Bible literature paints of the kingdom of Israel is quite peculiar in that, unless the sanctuary at Bethel is supposed to have served that purpose, there is no talk of a central shrine. The temple at Bethel is once called 'a royal sanctuary' (מקדש־מלך, Amos 7.13) and a priest there says to the king, 'Amos has conspired against you *in the very center* [בקרב] of the house of Israel; the land is not able to bear all his words' (Amos 7.10), thereby perhaps suggesting that Bethel is the centre of the kingdom. This might also be indicated by the fact that Jehu's 'cleansing programme' involves Jezreel, but not Bethel. But there is a much clearer indication in Judg. 9.37 of the historical site of Shechem as the northern 'navel of the earth' (טבור הארץ). Moreover, quite different from the situation in Jerusalem, the Bethel priesthood is never said to have been involved in the intricacies of succession, and there are no clear indications of the economic and political functions of temple at Bethel (or any other northern temple for that matter). This paucity of information on a central shrine in Israel has two consequences for the interpretation of stories about that kingdom. First, it suggests that, in the eyes of the narrators, even though they call the northern leaders 'king', the Israelites never really succeeded in founding a *kingdom* (and there therefore remained for them a kind of chiefdom). Secondly, it identifies the 'northern kingdom' as illegitimate compared to the 'southern kingdom', where *Yahweh* lived together with his 'son' (Ps. 2.7), whom he protected through his priests for four hundred years. It is this perspective that informs a formulation like 'since the day that Ephraim departed (סור, 'turned away, degenerated') from Judah' (Isa. 7.17). This perspective also explains some of the narrated wars between Judah and Israel (cf. 1 Kgs 12.21; 14.30; 15.7, 16) as efforts to incorporate Israel into the Judaean system, and the repeated (idealized?) efforts of southern kings to involve Israelites in Judaean 'religious' programmes (2 Kgs 23.15-23; 2 Chron. 30.5-6). The essential importance of the combination of palace and temple for the 'survival' of the kingdom also renders Ezekiel's vision of the new temple complex a devastating blow to monarchists:

8. Political Organization and Meaning

> Mortal, this is the place of my throne and the place for the soles of my feet, where I will reside among the people of Israel forever. The house of Israel shall no more defile my holy name, neither they nor their kings, by their whoring, and by the corpses of their kings at their death. *When they placed their threshold by my threshold and their doorposts beside my doorposts, with only a wall between me and them*, they were defiling my holy name by their abominations that they committed; therefore I have consumed them in my anger (Ezek. 43.7-8).

While Zechariah still expects the restoration of king and priest as a team (Zech. 6.12), in Ezekiel's vision the 'plans' of the architectural palace-temple unit symbolizing the state is torn up and the state cancelled.

In spite of the temple symbolizing perfect harmony and justice, and therefore the continued existence of the state, kings still had to make plans to ensure the safety of the state. Apart from the erection of city walls and strongholds and sustaining a well-equipped army, they also took other measures. For example, to ensure stable internal and external political relations both chiefs and kings used 'marriage' as an instrument. For the sake of stability in the court a new chief or king often incorporated the wives and concubines of his predecessor into his harem. This action symbolized the transfer of power and rights to him. Thus, just as Saul feared (1 Sam. 20.30), David takes Ahinoam, Saul's wife, into his harem (1 Sam. 14.50; 25.43; cf. 2 Sam. 12.8). She bears Amnon (2 Sam. 3.2), who would have been a strong contender to succeed David, but is killed by Absalom in the succession race. To demonstrate the transfer of all the royal rights to him, Absalom publicly takes David's concubines (2 Sam. 16.21-22; cf. 3.6-10; 1 Kgs 2.13-25). To ensure internal stability, the chief or king would marry into the most important clans of the region, as David is said to have married Abigail, the wife of a Calebite chieftain (1 Sam. 25.2-42]). International relations are also stabilzed by interstate marriages. Observe Solomon marrying an Egyptian (1 Kgs 3.1), Ahab a Phoenician (1 Kgs 16.31) and Jehoram of Judah an Israelite princess (1 Kgs 8.18).

Apart from the fact that insight into Israelite and Judaean political organization could be of assistance in assessing the culturally inscribed *meaning* of the literary representations of Israelite history, it is also of importance to note that the political systems in Israel served as the 'breeding ground' for various religious metaphors, whose meanings are partly constituted by (presupposed knowledge of) a *particular* political system. In the religious language of the Hebrew Bible Yahweh is, for instance, pictured as a powerful but benevolent and just chief (e.g. Deut. 10.17-18), a king of a vast kingdom (Ps. 22.28; 103.9; 145.11-13), a victoriously returning warrior king (e.g. Ps. 24.7). Yahweh also 'sits enthroned forever, he has established his throne for judgement. He judges the world with righteousness; he judges the peoples with equity' (Ps. 9.7-8). As king 'winnows all evil with his eyes' (Prov. 20.8), Yahweh's 'eyelids test the children of men' from his holy palace (Ps. 11.4). Moreover, God (or rather El) is pictured as the chairperson of a divine assembly (Ps. 82.1) and his 'household' as a council (Ps 89.7; Jer. 23.18; cf. 2 Kgs 9.5; 25.1).

Chapter 9

SOCIAL CONTROL AND MEANING

Every society must ensure that its members behave in such a way that the fabric holding it together is, in spite of individual's goals and characters, not endangered. Therefore, every society has some form of social control. Depending on the kind of community (e.g. household, clan, tribe, chiefdom, state) social control may be internalized or externalized, informal or formal, positive or negative. Where there is no central political authority, the mechanism to enforce a particular kind of behaviour is normally lacking. In such societies the control is more internalized than externalized, rather informal than formal. Centralized authority normally has to resort to coercion. Therefore the social control in this kind of society is predominantly externalized and formal.

One is, however, not working here with airtight compartments of social control. In ancient Israel, for example, households and clans and their forms of social control coexisted with centralized state authority and its mechanisms of social control. The *extent of authority* exercised by the heads of households and clans had, of course, been diminished after the introduction of centralized authority, but the *mechanisms* of internal and informal social control remained in place in these smaller units. Moreover, centralized authority may also succeed in internalizing social control through various means, such as religion.

'Internalized social control' means that members of a society are educated to take personal responsibility for their own conduct and to expect some form of punishment should they transgress against what they know is right. Certain actions are, for example, looked upon by everybody in disgust. For Egyptians, so the narrator tells us, it was disgusting to eat with Hebrews or to be shepherds (Gen. 43.22; 46.34). Also, in Israel certain things were 'simply not done' (cf. 2 Sam. 13.12). It would, for example, be disgusting for a dealer to have false scales or weights (Prov. 11.1; 20.10, 23), for a chief, king or officer to act unjustly (Prov. 16.12, 15), to tell lies (Prov. 12.22), be arrogant (Prov. 16.5) or to scoff (Prov. 24.9). In the same manner certain sexual acts were looked upon as disgusting (Lev. 18). Thus conduct in every sphere of culture (e.g. economy, social and political life) was controlled through the internalization of certain rules of 'do' and 'do not', and watching over people's adherence to such rules was God. For that reason most of the acts of 'abomination' were described as 'abominations to Yahweh'. Consider, for example, Prov. 16.5: 'Every one who is arrogant is an abomination to the Lord; be assured, he will not go unpunished.' Or Prov. 6.16-19:

> There are six things that the Lord hates, seven that are an abomination to him: haughty eyes, a lying tongue, and hands that shed innocent blood, a heart that devises wicked plans, feet that hurry to run to evil, a lying witness who testifies falsely, and one who sows discord in a family.

In this way fear of (external) supernatural revenge ideally prevented a breach of the social code. But not only that: through divine intervention an abominable act committed in private would somehow be made public. A typical case in point would be Achan, who secretly secured for himself a few pieces from the spoil during the fall of Jericho. When the whole community suffered defeat after that act, they knew that *someone* must have acted against the code. So they used divination to get at the transgressor and punished him (Josh. 7). Stories relating things that are 'not done in Israel' would function as additional motivation to act according to the 'ways of Israel' (cf. Gen. 34.7; 2 Sam. 13.12; Judg. 20.6, 10; etc.).

External control over the behaviour of individuals was achieved through two means, namely negative and positive sanction. Negative sanction consists of disapproving public reaction against a transgressor of the social code. Such a negative reaction could be expressed in words, by simple gestures or, where the necessary authority was in existence, through public punishment. Consider, for example, Eli's admonition of his two sons (1 Sam. 2.22-25) and Tamar's plea to Absalom (2 Sam. 13.12-13). A person acting against the code also became the topic of village gossip, and in that manner brought shame on him- or herself as well as on his or her household, that had obviously failed to instil in such a person a sense of responsibility. In this manner people's criticism of the conduct of Hophni and Phinehas finally reached the ears of their father (1 Sam. 2.22). Gestures of negative sanction included whispering (Ps. 41.7), pushing out the lip (Ps. 22.8),

9. Social Control and Meaning

shaking the head (Ps. 64.8; 109.25), wagging or clapping the hands (Lam. 2.15; Zeph. 2.15), whistling (1 Kgs 9.8; Jer. 19.8; Lam. 2.16) and saying 'Ha! Ha!' (Ps. 40.6; 70.4). Negative public censure took the form of public humiliation, such as cutting off a man's beard (2 Sam. 10.4-5), flogging (Deut. 25.3), maiming (Deut. 25.12; Judg. 1.6-7; 2 Sam. 4.12), execution (Exod. 30.33; 31.14) or banning.

The categories of 'honour' and 'shame' also belong to the mechanisms of social control. Guilt and shame are, however, as Keesing (1966: 305) already warned, 'modal tendencies of great generality, and both may be operative in different zones of conduct within the same society'. Shame and guilt are *universal* social control mechanisms and should not, for example, be used to distinguish Mediterranean 'shame' cultures from industrialized Western 'guilt' cultures, as sometimes happens. As will be argued below, shaming is a negative and honouring a positive mechanism used in all non-legal and informal systems of social control.

Biblical Hebrew has quite a number of words and expressions for 'shame' or 'shaming' as well as for 'honour' and 'honouring'. An interesting example occurs in Ps. 69.19 (Heb. v. 20): 'You know my reproach (חרפתי), my shame (בשתי), and my dishonour (וכלמתי).' Other terms include קלון (cf. Ps. 83.16), באש and חפר (see Prov. 13.5: 'a wicked man causes disgust (יבאיש) and shame (יחפיר)'. Interestingly enough, these terms frequently occur in causative form, that is, 'X shames Y'. And supplicants often beg God not to let them be *shamed*. Shame, like honour, is something the community does or gives to people who deserve such treatment, and does not refer to a mere 'red face'. To be 'shamed' is to be 'ostracized', gossiped about and jeered at. In this respect there is sometimes some misunderstanding about shame and guilt, as if a *feeling* of shame (i.e. to be ashamed) substitutes in some cultures for a *feeling* of guilt, and as if a feeling of shame only arises when and if one is 'caught out'. But shame is not a *feeling*. It is a social status, as 'guilt' is a legal status. That is why one can only be shamed *after* one has been 'caught out'. When Jer. 2.26 says, 'As a thief is shamed when caught, so the house of Israel shall be shamed: they, their kings, their princes, their priests, and their prophets...' it does not mean that the kings, princes, priests and prophets will, when caught out some day, feel ashamed of themselves, but that these officials will be dealt with as a thief is dealt with when caught.

Consider also the following proverbs: 'A son who gathers in summer is prudent, but a son who sleeps in harvest brings shame' (Prov. 10.5); 'A good wife is the crown of her husband, but she who brings shame is like rottenness in his bones' (12.4); and: 'He who does violence to his father and chases away his mother is a son who causes shame and brings reproach' (19.26). Since the conduct of the son or wife indicates that the father of the household has been unable to control his household, people censure that father by 'talking' about him and avoiding him. A remark by Haviland (1996: 345) is to the point here, when he says that 'figures of authority are vulnerable to their dependants because their positions rests on the respect these people are willing to give them'. When the conduct of a father's son or wife shows that they do not respect him, he loses face in the community. The community may then sanction him, negatively gossiping, labelling him as a fool, avoiding him, etc. A final example: When an Israelite supplicant begged God not to let him be shamed, it was a prayer for remaining *integrated* in community life as an honoured (i.e. acceptable and accepted) person. Since a person is honoured as long as he or she complies with what is expected of a person in that position, supplicants often insist on their innocence: they did not *deserve* to be shamed, and yet people shake their heads, clap or wave their hands, or whistle when they pass by the supplicant's house, *as if* he or she deserved avoidance or scorning.

Cultures thus differ from each other not by virtue of any 'inherent' or 'essential' characteristic like 'shame' or 'guilt', but in the way they deal with transgressors against social norms and settle disputes. One of the mechanisms of social control operative in non-legal or non-centralized political environments is 'shaming', a mechanism that has disappeared from the *public* face of Western societies, where legal coercion is the norm, but is alive and well in smaller and closer communities, or wherever group gossip can flourish, or certain ways of 'looking' at people, avoidance, etc.

In dealing with disputes, non-legal systems tend to resort to negotiation and mediation, while legal systems tend to make use of adjudication. For instance, in the dispute between David and Absalom Joab obtained the services of a wise woman from Tekoa to negotiate a truce between father and son. The role of a mediator is directly referred to in some biblical texts. In admonishing his sons, Eli says, 'If a man sins against a man, God will mediate for him (פללו) but if a man sins against the Lord, who can intercede for him?' (1 Sam. 2.25). This is also Job's problem with God. While Elihu is certain that, under certain circumstances, there is a mediator (or interpreter מליץ) for a sufferer, Job's experience is otherwise: 'There is no umpire [מוכיח; LXX μεσίτης] between us, who might lay his hand upon us both' (Job 9.33). The story about the appointment of 'able men...who fear God,...are trustworthy and who hate a bribe' (Exod. 18.21) to assist Moses in his task of settling disputes probably also has 'mediators' in mind.

An adjudicator's task is different, though. As an authorized third party this person hears evidence and gives a binding decision, as happens in courts of law. Since Israelite culture did not know police investigations of crime, the adjudicator had to rely on the witnesses brought before him. Since there was hardly any possibility of appeal to a higher court, and since the judgment had to be carried out immediately after it had been passed, it was absolutely essential that the adjudicator was incorruptible and that witnesses spoke the truth. While there seemingly was little other than custom to ensure upright adjudicators, certain measures were in place to ensure the relative trustworthiness of witnesses. Two or three concurring witnesses were necessary before a sentence could be passed (Deut. 17.6; 19.15), while false witnesses had to reckon with the rule 'then you shall do to him as he had meant to do to his brother; so you shall purge the evil from the midst of you' (Deut. 19.19).

While the main aim of non-legal social control is the *reintegration* of offenders into society, legal social control metes out punishment to create fear and coerce people into cooperation. Consider, for instance, the motivation for the *quid pro quo* rule for false witnessing referred to above:

> And the rest shall hear, and fear, and shall never again commit any such evil among you. Your eye shall not pity; it shall be life for life, eye for eye, tooth for tooth, hand for hand, foot for foot.

Social control is, however, also exercised positively. If shaming is a negative form of control, honouring a person is its positive opposite. If a person behaves wisely, that is, according to the norms and customs of society, members of that society hold that person in high esteem and express their appreciation by accepting his or her authority, following his or her advice, etc. The ideal man in Israelite culture was, for example, a wealthy person who owned property, controlled his household, was kind and generous towards the poor and vulnerable, made a positive contribution at the city gate, where the elders gathered to discuss matters of common concern, was a brave soldier and well-represented his household in religious matters. Such a cultural all-rounder was a גבור חיל (cf. Judg. 11.1; Ruth 2.1; 1 Kgs 11.2; 2 Kgs 5.1). The ideal woman was one who could give birth to children (especially male children), obeyed her husband, looked well after the needs of the household, instilled in her children the customs of the group, etc. Such a woman was an אשת חיל (Ruth 3.1; Prov. 12.4; 31.10).

There are quite a few indications in the Hebrew Bible of the ideal conduct of an 'upright' person. Job, for example, uses examples of his social conduct to convince his friends that he did not deserve the public shaming Yahweh had brought on him. Consider, for example, Job 29.12-20:

> Because I delivered the poor who cried, and the fatherless who had none to help him. The blessing of him who was about to perish came upon me, and I caused the widow's heart to sing for joy. I put on righteousness, and it clothed me; my justice was like a robe and a turban. I was eyes to the blind, and feet to the lame. I was a father to the poor, and I searched out the cause of him whom I did not know. I broke the fangs of the unrighteous, and made him drop his prey from his teeth. Then I thought, 'I shall die in my nest, and I shall multiply my days as the sand, my roots spread out to the waters, with the dew all night on my branches, my glory fresh with me, and my bow ever new in my hand.'

Or Ps. 37.18-40, here schematically represented:

The Righteous		*The Unrighteous*	
18-19:	their heritage will abide for ever; they are not put to shame in evil times, in the days of famine they have abundance	20:	the wicked perish; the enemies of the Lord are like the glory of the pastures, they vanish—like smoke they vanish away
21b:	is generous and gives	21a:	borrows, and cannot pay back
22a:	shall possess the land	22b:	shall be cut off
25:	not seen forsaken or his children begging bread.		
26:	ever giving liberally and lending, and his children become a blessing.		
30:	utters wisdom and speaks justice		
31:	the law of his God is in his heart	32:	watches the righteous, and seeks to slay him
33:	not condemned when he is brought to trial		

9. Social Control and Meaning

Consistently acting according to the rules accumulated one's honour. Prov. 22.4 and 27.18 say, 'The reward for humility and fear of the Lord is riches and honour and life'; 13.18: 'Poverty and shame *will come* to him who neglects discipline, but he who regards reproof will be honoured'; 20.3: 'It is an honour for a man to keep aloof from strife; but every fool will be quarrelling,' while the supplicant in Ps. 71.21 asserts of Yahweh, 'Thou wilt increase my honour, and comfort me again.' Similarly, after the birth of her sixth son Leah said, 'Now my husband will honour me' (Gen. 30.20). Like shaming honouring was an act of the community, so that honour, even though it could be shared by members of an honoured household (Prov. 17.6; 20.7) was not something that 'belonged' to a position of authority, but a reward for good conduct. Once the community withdrew their respect, honour made way for shame.

In the biblical text a variety of references to social control mechanisms are used as metaphors for the way Yahweh deals with his people. Consider, for example, the threat in Hos. 9.11: 'Ephraim's glory shall fly away like a bird—no birth, no pregnancy, no conception!' In a society in which the number of children, especially sons, was considered as part of a family's honour (cf. Ps. 128.3-6), the threat of making the whole group infertile meant threatening it with public shaming. To express acceptance of guilt in a situation, Jer. 3.25 (cf. 3.22-25) says, 'Let us lie down in our shame, and let our dishonour cover us; for we have sinned against the Lord our God.'

In other texts individuals complain about undeserved negative sanctioning, for example, Ps. 69.8-12:

> I have become a stranger to my brethren, an alien to my mother's sons...
> When I humbled my soul with fasting, it became my reproach. When I made sackcloth my clothing, I became a byword to them. I am the talk of those who sit in the gate, and the drunkards make songs about me.

Some psalms describe the psychological effects sanctioning has on the individual, for instance, Ps. 22.14-17:

> I am poured out like water, and all my bones are out of joint; my heart is like wax, it is melted within my breast; my strength is dried up like a potsherd, and my tongue cleaves to my jaws; thou dost lay me in the dust of death. Yea, dogs are round about me; a company of evildoers encircle me; they have pierced my hands and feet—I can count all my bones—they stare and gloat over me.

This kind of description is sometimes taken by scholars to depict physical illness. But the bodily references rather seem to be 'externalized' descriptions of psychological processes. In this case, for example, the supplicant says '*I am* poured out [נשפכתי] like water', while expressions like 'my skeleton' (עצמותי), 'my heart/chest' (לבי), 'my bowels' (מעי), 'my strength' (כחי), 'my tongue' (לשוני), 'my hands' (ידי) and 'my feet' (רגלי) often serve to refer to functions of the self, psyche or mind. Also, the metaphor of being surrounded by wild dogs in hyena-like fashion (סבבוני כלבים) seems to confirm psychological distress rather than physical illness. The extent and severity of the negative feelings and thoughts is, so it would seem, expressed by 'a company of evildoers' (עדת מרעים).[1]

In some instances, as in Ps. 69.5-6, a supplicant pleads with God to prevent his stupid actions from bringing disgrace over his household or group, 'O God, thou knowest my folly; the wrongs I have done are not hidden from thee. Let not those who hope in thee be put to shame through me, O Lord God of hosts; let not those who seek thee be brought to dishonour through me, O God of Israel.'

It is clear that insight into the workings of social control mechanisms of ancient Israelite culture can considerably enhance the interpretation of texts in which there are allusions to such mechanisms, as well as the interpretation of metaphors reckoning with the reader's acquaintance with the world of social control.

---

1. For the reaction of 'my bones' as a description of psychological reaction to stressful situations, compare Job 4.14; Ps. 35.10; Isa. 38.13; Jer. 20.9; 23.9). For 'my heart' as 'I', compare Judg. 5.9; 1 Sam. 2.1; Job 23.16, etc.; for 'my bowels' and 'my strength' as 'my psyche/vitality', consider Job 30.27; Ps. 40.9; Jer. 4.19; Lam. 1.20 and Gen. 31.6; Job 6.11–12; Ps. 31.10; Lam. 1.14, respectively; and for 'my hands' and 'my feet' as 'my actions' and 'my inclination', see Job 21.2; 31.25; Ps. 18.21, 25; 89.21, and Job 23.11; 31.5, 7; Ps. 56.14; 119.59.

CONCLUDING EDITORIAL REMARKS

In what would have appeared as Chapter 10 'World View and Meaning' Ferdinand Deist's manuscript contained only one page plus a further sentence on another page. It was therefore impossible for me to extend such a brief beginning into a further 50–80 pages of closely argued analysis in order to guess what Ferdinand would have wanted to say by way of a grand finale to his work. While it would be easy enough to extrapolate from his many comprehensive analyses of the material culture of the world constructed by the ancient biblical writers, such an extrapolation would have been mine and not his. I have no wish to transform (or to transmogrify) Deist on the material culture of the Bible into Carroll on the material culture of the Bible. Other opportunities may present themselves in the future for such a production, but in this book I would like to preserve and protect Ferdinand Deist's own work—as best I can. Readers of this book may if they wish extrapolate from what Deist has written to what he might have written, but I shall leave that task for them to perform for themselves. Death ought to count for something in this world, so I shall allow Deist's death to have the last word by robbing all of us of what we might have learned had he lived to complete and to revise this work as a totality on the cultural materialism of the Bible. As Qoheleth has stated the case: 'This is an evil in all that is done under the sun, that one fate comes to all...' A man of such sterling qualities as Ferdinand Deist was would undoubtedly have appreciated having some of the words of Qoheleth applied to his own end and there I shall leave the matter.

RPC

BIBLIOGRAPHY

Aharoni M.
    1996   'An Iron Age Cylinder Seal', *IEJ* 46: 53-54.

Ahlström, G.W.
    1991   'The Role of Archaeological and Literary Remains in Reconstructing Israel's history?', in D.V. Edelman (ed.), *The Fabric of History* (JSOTSup, 27; Sheffield: JSOT Press): 116-41.
    1996   *The History of Ancient Palestine from the Palaeolithic Period to Alexander's Conquest* (JSOTSup, 146; Sheffield: Sheffield Academic Press, 1993).

Albertz, Rainer
    1994   *History of Israelite Religion in the Old Testament Period.* I. *From the Beginnings to the End of Exile*; II. *From the Exile to the Maccabees* (London: SCM Press).

Alonso-Schökel, L.
    1971   *Das Alte Testament als literarisches Kunstwerk* (Cologne: Bachem).

Alter, R.
    1990   'The Art of Biblical Poetry' (Edinburgh: T. & T. Clark).

Amiran R.
    1976   'The Lion Statue and the Libanon Tray from Tell Beit Mirsim', *BASOR* 222: 29-40.

Amitai, J. (ed.)
    1985   *Biblical Archaeology Today: Proceedings of the International Congress of Biblical Archaeology, Jerusalem, April 1984* (Jerusalem: Israel Exploration Society).

Anderson, W.T.
    1996   Four Different Ways to be Absolutely Right', in Anderson (ed.) 1996: 106-12.

Anderson, W.T. (ed.)
    1996   *The Fontana Postmodernism Reader* (London: Fontana).

Ayer, A.J.
    1974   *Language, Truth and Logic* (London: Penguin).

Banks, M.
    1996   *Ethnicity: Anthropological Constructions* (London: Routledge).

Barbour, I.G.
    1974   *Myths, Models and Paradigms: The Nature of Scientific and Religious Language* (London: SCM Press).

Bar-Efrat, S.

Bibliography

Barstad, H.M.
    1989   *Narrative Art in the Bible* (Sheffield: Almond).

    1996   *The Myth of the Empty Land: A Study in the History and Archaeology of Judah During the 'Exilic' Period* (Symbolae Osloenses Fasc. Suppl., 28; Oslo: Scandinavian University Press).

Barton, John (ed.)
    1998   *The Cambridge Companion to Biblical Interpretation* (Cambridge: Cambridge University Press).

Bauman, Zygmunt
    1978   *Hermeneutics and Social Science: Approaches to Understanding* (London: Hutchinson).

Bedford, P.R.
    1991   'On Models and Texts: A Response to Blenkinsopp and Petersen', in Davies 1991: 154-62.

Bellinger, L.
    1962   'Cloth', *IDB*, I: 650-55.

Ben-Barak, Z.
    1981   'Meribaal and the System of Land Grants in Ancient Israel', *Biblica* 62: 73-91.

Ben-Tor, A.
    1997   'The Yigael Yadin Memorial Excavations at Hazor, 1990–1993: Aims and Preliminary Results', in Silberman and Small 1997: 107-27.

Berg, W.,
    1988   'Israels Land, der Garten Gottes. Der Garten als Bild des Heiles in Alten Testament', *BZ* 32: 35-51.

Bernstein, R.J.
    1983   *Beyond Objectivism and Relativism: Science, Hermeneutics, and Praxis* (Oxford: Basil Blackwell).

Bhabha, Homi K.
    1994   'The Location of Culture' (London: Routledge).

Biran, A., and J. Naveh.
    1993   'An Aramaic Stele Fragment from Tel Dan', *IEJ* 43: 81-93.

Blenkinsopp, Joseph
    1995   *Sage, Priest, Prophet: Religious and Intellectual Leadership in Ancient Israel* (Library of Ancient Israel; Louisville, KY: Westminster/John Knox Press, 1995).

Blenkinsopp, J.
    1991   'Temple and Society in Achaemenid Judah', in Davies 1991: 22-53.

Bogdal, K.-M. (ed.)
    1990   *Neue Literaturtheorien: Eine Einführung* (Opladen: Westdeutscher Verlag).

Bohanan, Paul
    1995   *How Culture Works* (New York: Free Press).

Borowski, D.
    1979   'Agriculture in Iron Age Israel' (PhD dissertation, University of Michigan).

Botterweck, G.J., and H. Ringgren (eds.)
    1982   *Theologisches Wörterbuch zum Alten Testament* (Stuttgart: W. Kohlhammer) ET, *Theological Dictionary of the Old Testament* (Grand Rapids: Eerdmans, 1974).

Bourdieu, Pierre
    1993   *The Field of Cultural Production: Essays on Art and Literature* (ed. Randal Johnson; Oxford: Polity Press).

Brett, Mark G. (ed.)
    1996   *Ethnicity and the Bible* (Biblical Interpretation, 19; Leiden: E.J. Brill).

Brettler, M.
    1989   'Ideology, History and Theology in 2 Kings xvii 7-23', *VT* 39: 268-82.

Buksinski, T.
    1985   'Die Begründung des historischen Wissens', *Zeitschrift für allgemeine Wissenschaftstheorie* 16: 1-18.

Bultmann, C.
    1992   *Der Fremde im antiken Judäa* (FRLANT, 153; Göttingen: Vandenhoeck & Ruprecht).

Button, G. (ed.)
    1991   *Ethnomethodology and the Human Sciences* (Cambridge: Cambridge University Press).

Cahill, J.M.
    1995   'Rosette Stamp Seal Impressions from Ancient Judah', *IEJ* 45: 23-52.

Caird, G.B.
    1980   'The Language and Imagery of the Bible' (Philadelphia: Westminster Press).

Callaway, J.A.
    1985   'Response to Mazar', in Amitai 1985: 72-78.

Cancik-Kirschbaum, E.
    1995   'Konzeption und Legitimation von Herrschaft in nachassyrischer Zeit. Mythos und Ritual in VS 24, 92', *Die Welt des Orient* 26: 5-20.

Carasik, M.
    1994   'Who Were the "Men of Hezekiah" (Proverbs xxv)?', *VT* 44: 289-300.
    1995   'Ruth 2,7: Why the Overseer was Embarrassed', *ZAW* 107: 493-94.

Carneiro, R.L.
    1970   'A Theory of the Origin of the State', *Science* 169: 733-38.

Carroll, M.D. *et al.* (eds.)
    1995   *The Bible in Human Society: Essays in Honour of John Rogerson* (JSOTSup, 200; Sheffield: Sheffield Academic Press, 1995).

Carroll, R.P.
    1991   *Wolf in the Sheepfold: The Bible as a Problem for Christianity* (London: SPCK).
    1992   The Myth of the Empty Land', *Semeia*: 79-93.
    1993   'The Hebrew Bible as literature—a misprision?', *Studia Theologica* 47: 77-90.
    1996   'He-Bibles and She-Bibles: Reflections on the Violence done to Texts by Productions of English Translations of the Bible', *BibInt* 4: 257-69.
    1997   *Wolf in the Sheepfold: The Bible as Problematic for Theology* (London: SCM Press).

1998	'Biblical Ideolatry: Ideologiekritik, Biblical Studies and the Problematics of Ideology', in Cook, Kruger and Cornelius 1998: 101-14.

Carter, Charles E.
1994	*The Province of Yehud in the Post-Exilic Period: Soundings in Site Distribution and Demography*, in Eskenazi and Richards 1994: 106-45.
1999	*The Emergence of Yehud in the Persian Period: A Social and Demographic Study* (JSOTSup, 294; Sheffield: Sheffield Academic Press).

Casson, R.W.
1983	'Schemata in Cognitive Anthropology', *Annual Review of Anthropology* 12: 429-62.

Castelli, E. *et al.* (eds.)
1995	*The Postmodern Bible* (New Haven: Yale University Press).

Caws, P.
1994	'Identity: Cultural, Transcultural, and Multicultural', in Goldberg (ed.) 1994: 371-87.

Childs, B.S.
1972–73	'Psalm Titles and Midrashic Exegesis', *Journal of Semitic Studies* 16: 137-50.
1979	*Introduction to the Old Testament as Scripture* (London: SCM Press; Louisville: Westminster Press).

Clark, W.M.
1968	'The Animal Series in the Primeval History', *VT* 18: 433-49.

Clements, R.E.
1989	'Israel in its Historical and Cultural Setting', in Clements (ed.) 1989: 3-16.
1995	'Wisdom, Virtue and the Human Condition', in M.D. Carroll 1995: 139-57.

Clements, R.E. (ed.)
1989	*The World of Ancient Israel: Sociological, Anthropological and Political Perspectives* (Cambridge: Cambridge University Press).

Clifford, J.
1986	'Introduction: Partial Truths', in J. Clifford and G.E. Marcus (eds.), *Writing Culture: The Poetics and Politics of Ethnography* (Berkeley: University of California Press).

Cogan, M.
1995	'A Lamashtu Plaque from the Judean Shephelah', *IEJ* 45: 155-61.

Cohen, R.
1985	'Response to Mazar', in Amitai 1985: 78-80.

Cohen, R., and E.R. Service (eds.)
1978	*The Origins of the State* (Philadelphia: Institute for the Study of Human Issues).

Collini, S.
1994	'Escape from DWEMsville. Is Culture too Important to be Left to Cultural Studies?', *Times Literary Supplement*, 27 May: 3-4.

Cook, J., P.A. Kruger and I.A. Cornelius (eds.)
1998	*Journal of Northwest Semitic Languages* 24.1 (Deist Memorial Volume).

Cooper, J.S.
1993 'Sumerian and Aryan. Racial Theory, Academic Politics and Parisian Assyriology', *Revue de l'Histoire des Religions* 210: 169-205.

Coote, R.B., and K.W. Whitelam
1987 *The Emergence of Early Israel in Historical Perspective* (Sheffield: Almond Press).

Coulter, J.
1991 'Cognition: Cognition in an Ethnomethodological Mode', in G. Button, *Ethnomethodology and the Human Sciences* (Cambridge: Cambridge University Press): 176-95.

Cross, F.M.
1962 'Epigraphic Notes on Hebrew Documents of the Eighth–Sixth Centuries BC: II. The Murabba'at Papyrus and the Letter Found near Yabneh-Yam, *BASOR* 165: 44-46.

Crüseman, F.
1992 *Die Tora: Theologie und Sozialgeschichte des alttestamentlichen Gesetzes* (Munich: Chr. Kaiser Verlag).

Cryer, F.H.
1994 'On the Recently Discovered "House of David" Inscription', *SJOT* 8.2: 3-19.

Currid, J.D.
1984 'The Deforestation of the Foothills of Palestine', *PEQ* 116: 1-11.

Dalley, S.
1990 'Yahweh in Hamath in the 8th Century BC: Cuneiform Material and Historical Deductions', *VT* 40: 21-32.

Dalman, G.
1937 *Arbeit und Sitte in Palästina.* V. *Webstoff, Spinnen, Weben, Kleidung* (Repr.: Hildesheim: Georg Olms).

D'Andrade, R.
1995 *The Development of Cognitive Anthropology* (Cambridge: Cambridge University Press).

Dar, S.
1986 *Landscape and Pattern: An Archaeological Survey of Samaria, 800 BCE– 636 CE with a Historical Commentary by Shimon Applebaum, Part 1–2* (*BARev* International Series, 308: Oxford: British Archaeological Reports).

Davies, M.
1995 'On Prostitution', in M.D. Carroll *et al.* 1995: 225-48.

Davies, Philip R.
1992 *In Search of 'Ancient Israel'* (JSOTSup, 148; Sheffield: Sheffield Academic Press).
1994 'The Society of Biblical Israel', in Eskenazi and Richards 1994: 22-33.
1998 *Scribes and Schools: The Canonization of the Hebrew Scriptures* (Library of Ancient Israel; Louisville, KY: Westminster/John Knox Press).

Davies, Philip R. (ed.)
1991 *Second Temple Studies 1: Persian Period* (JSOTSup, 117; Sheffield: Sheffield Academic Press).

Day, P.L.
  1992 'Anat: Ugarit's "mystress of animals" ', *JNES* 51: 181-90.
Deist F.E.
  1986 'Who Is to Blame: The Pharaoh, Yahweh or Circumstance? On Human Responsibility and Divine Ordinance in Exodus 1-14', *Ou Testameniese Werkgesmeenskap van Suid-Afrika* 29: 91-112.
  1988 'Parallels and Reinterpretation in the Book of Joel: A Theology of the Yom Yahweh?', in W. Claassen (ed.), *Text and Content: Old Testament and Semitic Studies for F.C. Fensham, 1988* (JSOTSup, 48; Sheffield: JSOT Press).
  1989 'Heads I Win, Tails you Lose: Yahweb and the Editor of the Exodus Story. An Historico-Aesthetic Interpretation of Exodus 1-12', *OTE* 2: 36-52.
  1993a 'On Presuppositions and Bible Translation', *JNSL* 19: 13-23.
  1993b 'The Nature of Historical Understanding', *OTE* 6: 384-98.
  1993c 'Coincidence as a Motif of Divine Intervention in 1 Samuel 9', *OTE* 6: 7-18.
  1994 'The Dangers of Deuteronomy. A Page from the Reception History of the Book', in F. García Martínez *et al.* (eds.), *Studies in Deuteronomy in Honour of C.J. Labuschagne on the Occasion of his 65th Birthday* (Leiden: E.J. Brill): 13-29.
  1995 *Ervaring, rede en metode in Skriftuileg: 'n Wetenskapshistoriese ondersoek na Skrifuitleg in die Ned. Geref. Kerk 1840–1990* (RGN-Studies in Metodologie; Pretoria: RGN).
  1996a 'Prophetic Discourse: Dialogue, Disaster, or Opportunity?', *Scriptura* 57: 179-92.
  1996b ' "Murder in the Toilet" (Judges 3: 12-30): Translation and Transformation', *Scriptura* 58.3: 263-72.
Dennett, D.C.
  1995 *Darwin's Dangerous Idea: Evolution and the Meanings of Life* (London: Penguin).
Dennis, P.A., and W. Aycock (eds.)
  1989 *Literature and Anthropology* (Fort Worth: Texas Christian University Press).
Derrida, J.
  1996 'The Play of Substitution', in Anderson (ed.) 1996: 82-87.
De Saussure, F.
  1983 *Course in General Linguistics* (trans. and annotated by Roy Harris; London: Duckworth).
Dever, W.G.
  1991a 'Archaeology, Material Culture and the Early Monarchal Period in Israel', in Edelman (ed.) 1991: 103-15.
  1991b 'Archaeological Data on the Israelite Settlement: A Review of Two Recent Works', *BASOR* 284: 77-90.
  1997 'Philology, Theology and Archaeology: What Kind of History Do We Want, and What Is Possible?', in Silberman and Small 1997: 290-310.

Diebner, B.J.
    1992–93   'The "Old Testament"—Anti-Hellenistic Literature?', *Dielheimer Blätter* 28: 10-40.

Diebner. B.J., and H. Schult
    1975   'Thesen zu nachexilischen Entwürfen der frühen Geschichte Israels im Alten Testament', *Dielheimer Blättner* 10: 41-47.

Dörner, A., and L. Vogt
    1990   'Kultursoziologie (Bordieu—Mentalitätsgeschichte—Zivilisationstheories)', in Bogdal 1990: 131-53.

Dothan, T.
    1997   'Tel Miqne-Ekron: An Iron Age I Philistine Settlement in Canaan', in Silberman and Small 1997: 96-106.

Doughtery, J.W.D. (ed.)
    1985   *Directions in Cognitive Anthropology* (Urbana: University of Illinois Press).

Duke, R.K.
    1990   *The Persuasive Appeal of the Chronicler: A Rhetorical Analysis* (Sheffield: Almond Press).

Duranti, A.
    1993   'Truth and Intentionality: An Ethnographic Critique', *Cultural Anthropology* 8.2: 214-45.

Dyson, M.E.
    1994   'Essentialism and the Complexities of Racial Identity', in Goldberg (ed.) 1994: 218-29.

Edelman, D.V.
    1991   'Doing History in Biblical Studies', in Edelman (ed.) 1991: 13-25.

Edelman, D.V. (ed.)
    1991   *The Fabric of History: Text, Artefact and Israel's Past* (JSOTSup, 127; Sheffield: JSOT Press).

Eph'al, I., and J. Naveh
    1989   'Hazael's Booty Inscriptions', *IEJ* 39: 192-200.

Elon, A.
    1997   'Politics and Archaeology', in Silberman and Small 1997: 34-46.

Eskenazi, T.C., and K.H. Richards (eds.)
    1994   *Second Temple Studies 2: Temple Community in the Persian Period* (JSOTSup, 175; Sheffield: Sheffield Academic Press).

Exum, J. Cheryl, and Stephen D. Moore (eds.)
    1998   *Biblical Studies/Cultural Studies: The Third Sheffield Colloquium* (JSOTSup, 266; GCT, 7; Sheffield: Sheffield Academic Press, 1998).

Exum, J. Cheryl, and D.J.A. Clines
    1993   *The New Literary Criticism and the Hebrew Bible* (Sheffield: Sheffield Academic Press).

Fabian, J.
    1991   'Dilemmas of Critical Anthropology', in Nencel and Pels 1991: 180-202.

Feyerabend, P.
    1996   'Anything Goes', in Anderson (ed.) 1996: 195-99.

Finkelstein, I.
    1985   'Reponse to Mazar', in Amitai 1985: 80-83.

1990	'A Few Notes on Demographic Data from Recent Generations and Ethnoarchaeology', *PEQ* 130: 47-52.
1997	'Pots and People Revisited: Ethnic Boundaries in the Iron Age I', in Silberman and Small 1997: 216-37.

Finkelstein, I., and Y. Zilberman
1995	'Site Planning and Subsistence Economy. Negev Settlements as a Case Study', in Holloway and Handy 1995: 213-26.

Finnegan, R.
1970	*Oral Literature in Africa* (Nairobi: Oxford University Press, 1970).

Flanagan, J.W.
1981	'Chiefs in Israel', *JSOT* 20: 47-73.

Fleischman, J.
1992	'The Age of Legal Maturity in Biblical Law', *JANES* 21: 35-48.

Fokkelman, J.P.
1975	*Narrative Art in Genesis* (Assen: Van Gorcum).

Foley, B.
1990	'Marxism in the Poststructuralist Moment: Some Notes on the Problem of Revising Marx', *Cultural Critique* 15: 5-37.

Foster, B.R.
1995	'Humor and Wit in the Ancient Near East', in J.M. Sasson (ed.), *Civilizations of the Ancient Near East*, IV (New York: Charles Scribner's Sons): 2459-69.

Franken, H.J.
1965	'A Note on How the Deir 'Alla Tablets Were Written', *VT* 15: 150-52.

Freedman, M.
1978	*Main Trends in Social and Cultural Anthropology* (New York: Holmes & Meier).

Fretz, M.J.
1982	'Weapons and Implements of War', in Botterweck and Ringren 1982: 893-95.

Frick, F.S.
1991	'Sociological Criticism and its Relation to Political and Social Hermeneutics. With a Special Look at Biblical Hermeneutics in South African Liberation Theology', in D. Jobing, P. Day and G.T. Sheppard, *The Bible and the Politics of Exegesis: Essays in Honor of Norman K. Gottwald on his Sixty-Fifth Birthday* (Cleveland: Pilgrim Press): 225-349.

Friis, H.
1968	*Die Bedingungen für Errichtung des Davidischen Reichs in Israel und seiner Umwelt* (trans. B.J. Diebner; Dielheimer Blätter zum Alten Testament Beihefte, 6; Heidelberg: Dielheimer Blätter).

Gabel, J.B., and C.B. Wheeler
1986	*The Bible as Literature: An Introduction* (Oxford: Oxford University Press).

Geertz, C.
1973	*The Interpretation of Cultures: Selected Essays* (New York: Basic Books).
1983	*Local Knowledge: Further Essays in Interpretive Anthropology* (New York: Basic Books).

Gelb, I.J.
    1973   'Prisoners of War in Early Mesopotamia', *JNES* 32: 70-98.

Gelinas, M.W.
    1995   'United Monarchy—Divided Monarchy: Fact or Fiction?', in Holloway and Handy 1995: 227-37.

Ginev, D., and A. Polikrov
    1988   'The Scientification of Methodology of Science', *Zeitschrift für allgemeine Wissenschaftstheories* 19: 18-27.

Glock, A.E.
    1985   'Tradition and Change in Two Archaeologies', *American Antiquity* 50.2: 464-77.

Goldberg, T.G.
    1994   'Introduction: Multicultural Conditions', in Goldberg (ed.) 1994: 1-41.

Goldberg, T.G. (ed.)
    1994   *Multiculturalism: A Critical Reader* (Oxford: Basil Blackwell, 1994).

Goodenough, W.H.
    1981   *Culture, Language and Society* (Menlo Park: Benjamin/Cummings, 2nd edn).

Goody, J., and I. Watt
    1963   'The Consequences of Literacy', *Comparative Studies in Society and History* 5: 304-45.

Gordis, R. *The Word and the Book: Studies in Biblical Language and Literature* (New York: Ktav, 1976).

Gorelick, L., and A.J. Gwinnet
    1990   'The Ancient Near Eastern Cylinder Seal as Social Emblem and Status Symbol', *JNES* 49.1: 45-56.

Gottwald, Norman K.
    1979   *The Tribes of Yahweh: A Sociology of the Religion of Liberated Israel, 1250–1050 BCE* (Maryknoll, NY: Orbis Books; London: SCM Press).
    1985   *The Hebrew Bible. A Socio-Literacy Introduction* (Philadelphia: Fortress Press).
    1993   *The Hebrew Bible in its Social World and in Ours* (SBL, Semeia Studies; Atlanta: Scholars Press).

Gottwald, Norman K., and Richard A. Horsley (eds.)
    1993   *The Bible and Liberation: Political and Social Hermeneutics* (Maryknoll, NY: Orbis Books; London: SPCK, rev. edn).

Gould, S.J.
    1989   *Wonderful Life: The Burgess Shale and the Nature of History* (New York: Norton).

Grabbe, Lester L.
    1995   *Priests, Prophets, Prophets, Diviners: A Socio-Historical Study of Religious Specialists in Ancient Israel* (Valley Forge, PA: Trinity Press International).

Grabbe, Lester L. (ed.)
    1997   *Can a 'History of Israel' Be Written?* (European Seminar in Historical Methodology, 1; JSOTSup, 245; Sheffield: Sheffield Academic Press).

1998	*Leading Captivity Captive: 'The Exile' as History and Ideology* (European Seminar in Historical Methodology, 2; JSOTSup, 278; Sheffield: Sheffield Academic Press).

Grimshaw, A., and K. Hart
1996   *Anthropology and the Crisis of Intellectuals* (Cambridge: Prickly Pear Press).

Gruber, M.I.
1987   'Hebrew *da ʾbân nepes* "dryness of throat": From Symptom to Literary Convention', *VT* 37: 365-67.

Gudeman, S., and M. Penn
1982   'Models, Meaning and Reflexivity', in Parkin 1982: 89-106.

Hadley, J.M.
1987   'The Khirbet et-Qom Inscription', *VT* 37: 50-62.

Hall, S.
1993   'Culture, Community, Nation', *Cultural Studies* 7.3: 349-73.

Halpern, B.
1997   'Text and Artifact: Two Monologues?', in Silberman and Small 1997: 311-41.

Hamp, V.
1982   'חָרַשׁ haraš I', in Botterweck and Ringgren 1982: 234-37, 777-87.

Handy, L.K.
1995   'Historical Probability and the Narrative of Josiah's Reform in 2 Kings', in Holloway and Handy 1995: 252-75.

Harding, S.
1994   'Is Science Multicultural? Challenges, Resources, Opportunities, Uncertainties', in Goldberg (ed.) 1994: 344-70.

Harris, Marvin
1979   *Cultural Materialism: The Struggle for a Science of Culture* (New York: Vintage Books)

Harris, O.
1991   'Time and Difference in Anthropological Writing', in Nencel and Pels 1991: 145-61.

Harris, R.
1991   'Inanna-Ishtar as Paradox and Coincidence of Opposites', *HR* 30.3: 261-78.

Haviland, W.A.
1996   *Cultural Anthropology* (Fort Worth: Harcourt Brace College, 8th edn).

Heitzman, J.
1991   'Ritual Polity and Economy: The Transactional Network of an Imperial Temple in Medieval South India', *Journal of the Economic and Social History of the Orient* 34: 23-54.

Herzog, Z.
1992a   'Administrative Structure in the Iron Age', in Kempinski and Reich 1992: 223-30.
1992b   'Settlement and Fortification Planning in the Iron Age', in Kempinski and Reich 1992: 231-74.

Hesse, B., and P. Wapnish
    1997   'Can Pig Remains Be Used for Ethnic Diagnosis in the Ancient Near East?', in Silberman and Small 1997: 238-70.

Hestrin, R.
    1987   'The Lachish Ewer and the "Asherah" ', *IEJ* 37: 212-23.

Hill, J.H.
    1998   'Language, Culture, and Worldview', in F.J. Newmeyer (ed.), *The Cambridge Survey*. IV. *Language: The Socio-Cultural Context* (Cambridge: Cambridge University Press): 14-36.

Hoglund, Kenneth
    1991   The Achaemenid Context', in Davies 1991: 54-72.
    1992   *Achaemenid Imperial Administration in Syria-Palestine and the Missions of Ezra and Nehemiah* (Atlanta, GA: Scholars Press)

Hole, F.A.
    1995   'Assessing the Past through Anthropological Archaeology', in Sasson 1995: 2715-27.

Holland, D., and N. Quinne
    1987   *Cultural Models in Language and Thought* (Cambridge: Cambridge University Press).

Holloway, S.W., and L.K. Handy
    1995   *The Pitcher Is Broken. Memorial Assays for Gösta W. Ahlström* (JSOTSup, 190; Sheffield: Sheffield Academic Press, 1995).

Horsley, R.A.
    1991   'Empire, Temple and Community—But Not Bourgeoisie. A Response to Blenkinsopp and Petersen', in Davies 1991: 163-74.

Hosfeld, F.-H., and E. Zenger
    1996   'Neue und alte der Psalmenexegese. Antworten auf die Fragen von M. Millard und R. Rendtorff', *BibInt* 4: 332-43.

Hough, G.
    1969   *Style and Stylistics* (London: Routledge & Kegan Paul).

House, P.R. (ed.)
    1992   *Beyond Form Criticism: Essays in Old Testament Literary Criticism* (Winona Lake, IN: Eisenbrauns).

Hoyrup, J.
    1993   ' "Remarkable Numbers" in Old Babylonian Mathematical Texts: A Note on the Psychology of Numbers', *JNES* 52.4: 281-86.

Isserlin, B.S.J.
    1984   'Israelite Architectural Planning and the Question of the Level of Secular Learning in Ancient Israel', *VT* 34: 169-78.

Ivic, M.
    1965   *Trends in Linguistics* (trans. M. Heppell; The Hague: Mouton).

Jakobson, R.
    1960   'Linguistics and Poetics', in T.A. Seboek (ed.), *Style in Language* (Cambridge, MA: Harvard University Press): 350-77.

Jamieson-Drake, D.W.
    1991   *Scribes and Schools in Monarchic Judah* (JSOTSup, 109; Sheffield: Sheffield Academic Press).

Janowski, B., U. Neumann-Gorsolke and U. Glessmer
  1993 *Gefährten und Feinde des Menschen: Das in Tier in der Lebenswelt des Alten Israels* (Neukirchen–Vluyn: Neukirchener Verlag).
Jobling, D.
  1991 'Text and the World—An Unbridgeable Gap? A Response to Carroll, Hoglund and Smith', in Davies 1991: 174-82.
Jencks, C.
  1996 'What Is Post-Modernism?', in Anderson (ed.) 1996: 26-30.
Johnson, T., C. Dandeker and C. Ashworth
  1984 *Structure of Social Theory: Dilemmas and Strategies* (London: Macmillan).
Joubert, D.
  1992 *Reflections on Social Values* (Pretoria: HSRC).
Jung, W.
  1990 'Neuere Hermeneutikkonzepte: Methodische Verfahren oder geniale Anschauung?', in Bogdal 1990: 154-75.
Kallai, Z.
  1993 'The King of Israel and the House of David', *IEJ* 43: 248.
Kaminsky, J.S.
  1995 'Joshua 7: A Reassessment of Israelite Conceptions of Corporate Punishment', in Holloway and Handy 1995: 315-46.
Keel, O.
  1997 'Leben aus dem Wort Gottes? Vom Anspruch und vom Umgang mit den Schiften des Alten und Neuen Testaments', in A. Schifferle (ed.), *Pfarrerei in der Postmoderne? Gemeindebildung in nachchristlicher Zeit. Für Leo Karrer* (Freiburg: Herder): 95-109.
Keesing, F.M.
  1966 *Cultural Anthropology: The Science of Custom* (New York. Holt, Rinehart & Winston).
Kempinski, A.
  1966 'Two Recent Books on the Archaeology of Early Palestine', *IEJ* 45: 55-64.
Kempinski, A., and R. Reich
  1992 'The Iron Age: Introduction', in Kempinski and Reich 1992: 191-92.
Kempinski, A., and R. Reich (eds.)
  1992 *The Architecture of Ancient Israel: From the Prehistoric to the Persian Periods* (Jerusalem: Israel Exploration Society).
Kent, S., and H. Vierich
  1987 'The Myth of Ecological Determinism—Anticipated Mobility and Site Spatial Organisation', in S. Kent (ed.), *Farmer and Hunters: The Implications of Sedentation* (Cambridge: Cambridge University Press): 96-103.
Kessler, M. (ed.)
  1994 *Voices from Amsterdam: A Modern Tradition of Reading Biblical Narrative* (Atlanta: Scholars Press).
Kezich, G.
  1996 'The Phenomenology of Improvisation: Ethics and Aesthetics. The Case of the *"Ottava Rima"* ', *Journal of Mediterranean Studies* 6.1: 15-27.

Knauf, E.A.
    1991   'From History to Interpretation', in Edelman (ed.) 1991: 26-64.

Knierim, R.
    1985   'Criticism of Literary Features, Form, Tradition and Redaction', in D.A. Knight and G.M. Tucker (eds.), *The Hebrew Bible and its Modern Interpreters* (Philadephia: Fortress Press): 123-65.

Koenen, K.
    1994   ' "...denn wie der Mensch jedes Tier nennet, so soll es heissen" (Gen 2, 19). Zur Bezeichnung von Rindern im Alten Testament', *Biblica* 75: 539-46.

Kuhrt, A.
    1983   'The Cyrus Cylinder and the Achaeminid Imperial Policy', *JSOT* 25: 83-97.

Laato, A.
    1995   'Assyrian Propaganda and the Falsification of History in the Royal Inscriptions of Senacherib', *VT* 45: 198-226.

Labuschagne, C.J.
    1982   'The Pattern of Divine Speech Formulas in the Pentateuch. The Key to its Literary Structure', *VT* 32: 86-96.
    1984   'Additional Remarks on the Pattern of Divine Speech Formulas in the Pentateuch', *VT* 34: 91-95.

Lakoff, G., and M. Johnson
    1985   *Metaphors We Live By* (Chicago: University of Chicago Press).

Lang, B.
    1985   'The Social Organisation of Peasant Poverty in Biblical Israel', in Lang (ed.) 1985: 83-99.

Lang, B. (ed.)
    1985   *Anthropological Approaches to the Old Testament* (Philadelphia: Fortress Press).

Law, R.
    1997   'Oral Tradition as History', in Msiska 1997: 159-73.

Lee, A.
    1990   'Genesis I and the Plagues Tradition in Psalm cv', *VT* 40: 257-63.

Lee, J.
    1991   'Language and Culture: The Linguistic Analysis of Culture', in Nencels and Pels 1991: 192-226.

Lelyveld, A.J.
    1984   *The Unity of Contraries: Paradox as a Characteristic of Normative Jewish Thought* (Syracuse: Syracuse University Press).

Lemche, N.P.
    1985   *Early Israel* (VTSup, 37; Leiden: E.J. Brill).
    1991   *The Canaanites and their Land* (Sheffield: JSOT Press).
    1993   'The Old Testament—A Hellenistic Book?', *SJOT* 7: 163-93.

Lemche, Niels Peter
    1998   *The Israelites in History and Tradition* (Library of Ancient Israel; London: SPCK; Louisville, KY: Westminster/John Knox Press).

Levin, C.
    1993   *Der Jahwist* (FRLANT, 157; Göttingen: Vandenhoeck & Ruprecht).

Levinson, B.
1991 'The Right Chorale: From the Poetics to the Hermeneutics of the Hebrew Bible', in J.P. Rosenblatt and J.C. Sitterman Jr (eds.), ' *"Not in Heaven": Coherence and Complexity in Biblical Narrative* (Bloomington: Indiana University Press, 1991): 129-53, 241-47.

Levinson, B.M.
1994 'The Case of Revision and Interpolation within the Biblical Legal Corpora', in B.M. Levinson (ed.), *Theory and Method in Biblical and Cuneiform Law. Revision, Interpolation and Development* (Sheffield: Sheffield Academic Press): 37-59.

Lewis, T.J.
1991 'The Ancestral Estate (nah^{a}lat 'elohîm) in 2 Samuel 14:16', *JBL* 110: 597-612.

Liid, D.C.
1992 'Gate of the Guard', in *ABD* II: 908.

Long, B.O.
1997 'Historical Imaginings, Ideological Gestures: W.F. Albright and the "Reasoning Faculties of Man" ', in Silberman and Small 1997: 82-94.

Lutz, C.
1985 'Ethnopsychology Compared to What? Explaining Behavior and Consciousness Among the Ifaluk', in White and Kirkpatrick 1985: 35-79.

Marais, J.
1998 *Representation in Old Testament Narrative Texts* (Biblical Interpretation Series, 36; Leiden: E.J. Brill).

Maren-Grisebach, M.
1970 *Methoden der Literaturwissenschaft* (Munich: Francke Verlag).

Margalit, B.
1989 'Some Observations on the Inscription and Drawing from Khirbet el-Qôm', *VT* 39: 371-75.
1990 'The Meaning and Significance of Asherah', *VT* 4: 264-97.

Margulies, H.
1974 'Das Rätsel der Biene im Alten Testament', *VT* 24: 56-76.

Matthews, V.H.E., and D.C. Benjamin
1993 *Social World of Ancient Israel 1250–587 B.C.E.* (Peabody, MA: Hendrickson Publishers).

Mayes, A.D.H.
1989 'Sociology and the Old Testament', in Clements (ed.) 1989: 39-63.

Mazar, A.
1985 'The Israelite Settlement in Canaan in the Light of Archaeological Excavations, in Amitai 1985: 61-71.
1990 *Archaeology of the Land of the Bible, 10,000–586 BCE* (Garden City, NY: Doubleday, 1990).
1996 The Excavations at Tel Beth Shean during the years 1989–1994', in Silberman and Small 1996: 144-64.

McClaren, P.
1994 'White Terror and Oppositional Agency: Towards a Critical Multiculturalism', in Goldberg (ed.) 1994: 45-74.

Meadow, R.H.
1983 'The Study of Faunal Remains from Archaeological Sites', *BA* 46: 49-52.
Meek, T.J.
1951 'Archaeology and a Point in Hebrew Syntax', *BASOR* 154: 31-33.
Meja, V.
1975 'The Sociology of Knowledge and the Critique of Ideology', *Cultural Hermeneutics* 3: 57-68.
Meshel, Z.
1992 'The Architecture of the Israelite Fortresses in the Negev', in Kempinski and Reich 1992: 294-301.
Meyers, C.
1995 'An Ethnoarchaeological Analysis of Hannah's Sacrifice', in D.P. Wright, D.N. Freedman and A. Hurvitz (eds.), *Pomegranates and Golden Bells: Studes in Biblical, Jewish and Near Eastern Ritual, Law, and Literature in Honor of Jacob Milgrom* (Winona Lake, IN: Eisenbrauns): 77-91.
Millard, A.R.
1985 'Assessment of the Evidence for Writing in Israel', in Amitai 1985: 301-12.
Millard, M.
1996 Von der Psalmenexegese zur Psalterexegese. Anmerkungen zum Neuansatz von Frank-Lothar Hossfeld und Erich Zenger', *BibInt* 4: 311-28.
Miller, J.M.
1986 'The Israelite Occupation of Canaan', in J.M. Miller and J.H. Hayes, *A History of Ancient Israel and Judah* (Philadelphia: Westminster Press): 213-45.
1991 'Is it Possible to Write a History of Israel without Relying on the Hebrew Bible?', in Edelman (ed.) 1991: 93-102.
Mittmann, S.
1976 'Amos 3, 12-15 und das Bett der Samarier', *ZDPV* 92: 149-67.
Moore Stephen D. (ed.)
1997 'The Bible and New Historicism', *BibInt* 5.4: 289-481.
Moser, P.K.
1986 'On Justification by Consensus', *ZAW* 17: 154-61.
Msiska, M.-H., and P. Hylands (eds.)
1997 *Writing and Africa* (London: Longman).
Mulder, M.J.
1982 'יַעַר ja 'ar', in Botterweck and Ringgren 1982: 778-87.
Mullen, E. Theodore Jr
1993 *Narrative History and Ethnic Boundaries: The Deuteronomistic Historian and the Creation of Israelite National Identity* (SBL, Semeia Studies; Atlanta: Scholars Press).
Müller, H.
1990 'Systemtheories und Literaturwissenschaft', in Bogdal 1990: 201-207.
Müller, J.E.
1990 'Literaturwissenschaftliche Rezeptions- und Handlungstheorien', in Bogdal 1990: 176-200.

Na'aman, N.
1995 'The Debated Historicity of Hezekiah's Reform in the Light of Historical and Archaeological Research', *ZAW* 107: 179-95.

Nencel, L., and P. Pels
1991 *Constructing Knowledge: Authority and Critique in Social Science* (London: Sage).

Netzer, E.
1992 'Domestic Architecture in the Iron Age', in Kempinski and Reich 1992: 193-201.

Neu, R.
1990 '*Patrilokalität und Patrilinearität in Israel*', *BZ* 34: 222-33.

Niditch, S.
1993 *Folklore and the Hebrew Bible* (Philadelphia: Fortress Press).

Nielsen, K.
1989 'עץ 'es', in Botterweck and Ringgren 1989: 283-98.

Niemann, H.H.
1993 'Heerschaft, Königtum und Staat: Skizzen zur soziokulturellen Entwicklung im monarchischen Israel (Forschungen am Alten Testament, 6; Tübingen: J.C.B. Mohr).

O'Connor, M.
1987 'The Poetic Inscription from Khirbet el-Qôm', *VT* 37: 224-30.

Orr, H.A.
1996 'Dennett's Dangerous Idea', *Evolution* 50.1: 467-72.

Otto, E.
1993 'Town and Rural Countryside in Israelite Law: Reception and Redaction in Cuneiform and Israelite Law', *JSOT* 57: 3-22.

Panopoulos, P.
1996 'Revitalising the Past, Contextualising the Present: Cultural Responses to the Tradition of Improvised Singing in Aegean Greece', *Journal of Mediterranean Studies* 6.1: 56-69.

Parkin, D.
1982 *Semantic Anthropology* (London: Academic Press).

Parpola, S.
1993 'The Assyrian Tree of Life: Tracing the Origins of Jewish Monotheism and Greek Philosophy', *JNES* 52.3: 161-208.

Perdue, Leo G., J. Blenkinsopp, J.J. Collins, and C. Meyers
1997 *Families in Ancient Israel* (The Family, Religion, and Culture; Louisville, KY: Westminster John Knox Press).

Peters, F.E.
1983 'Hellenism and the Near East', *The Biblical Archaeologist* 46: 33-39.

Pilch, J.
1991 *Introducing the Cultural Context of the Old Testament* (New York: Paulist Press).

Pilch, J.J., and B. Malina
1993 *Biblical Social Values and their Meaning: A Handbook* (Peabody, MA: Hendrickson).

Pohlmann, L.
1971   *Literaturwissenschaft und Methode.* I. *Theoretischer Teil und methodegeschichtlicher Überblick* (Frankfurt-am-Main: Athenäum).

Posner, R.
1971   'Strukturalismus in der Gedichtinterpretation. Textdeskription und Rezeptionsanalyse am Beispiel von Baudelaires "Les Chats" ', in J. Ihwe, *Literaturwissenschaft und Linguistik*, II.1 (Frankfurt-am-Main: Athenäum, 1971): 224-66.

Postgate, J.N.
1971   'Land Tenure in the Middle Assyrian Period: A Reconstruction', *BSOAS* 34: 508-12.

Powell, M.A.
1962   'Weights and Measures', in *IDB*, IV: 829-39.

Rainey, A.F.
1982   'Wine from the Royal Vineyards', *BASOR* 245: 57-62.
1983   The Biblical Shephelah of Judah', *BASOR* 251: 1-22.

Ramírez, G.
1996   'The Social Location of the Prophet Amos in the Light of the Group/Grid Cultural Anthropological Model', in S.B. Reid (ed.), *Prophets and Paradigms: Essays in Honour of Gene M. Tucker* (JSOTSup, 229; Sheffield: Sheffield Academic Press): 112-24.

Rand, H.
1991–92   'Numerological Structure in Biblical Literature', *The Jewish Bible Quarterly* 20: 50-56.

Reeves, J.C.
1992   'The Feast of the First Fruits of Wine and the Ancient Canaanite Calendar', *VT* 42: 350-61.

Reich, R.
1992   'Palaces and Residences in the Iron Age', in Kempinski and Reich 1992: 202-22.

Rendsburg, G.
1995   'On the Writing of ביתדוד in the Aramaic Inscription from Tel Dan', *IEJ* 45: 22-25.

Rendtorff, R.
1988   *Das Alte Testament: Eine Einführung* (Neukirchen–Vluyn: Neukirchener Verlag) ET, *The Old Testament. An Introduction* (London: SCM Press, 1985)..
1996   'Anfragen an Frank-Lothar Hosfeld und Erich Zenger aufgrund der Lektüre des Beitrags von Matthias Millard', *BibInt* 4: 329-31.

Renfrew, C., and E.B.W. Zubrow
1994   *The Ancient Mind: Elements of Cognitive Anthropological* (Cambridge: Cambridge University Press).

Richardson, M.
1989   'Point of View in Anthropological Discourse', in Dennis and Aycock 1989: 31-39.

Rochberg-Halton, F.
1991   'Between Observation and Theory in Babylonian Astronomical Texts', *JNES* 50.2: 107-20.

Rogerson, J.W.
1970 'The Hebrew Conception of Corporate Personality. A Re-examination', *JTS* 21: 1-16.
1978 *Anthropology and the Old Testament* (Oxford: Basil Blackwell).
1989 'Anthropology and the Old Testament', in Clements 1989: 17-37.

Rogerson, J.W., and P.R. Davies
1989 *The Old Testament World* (Cambridge: Cambridge University Press; Englewood Cliffs, NJ: Prentice Hall).

Rorty, R.
1996 'Ironists and Metaphysics', in Anderson (ed.) 1996: 96-102.

Rosen B., and I. Finkelstein
1992 'Subsistence Patterns, Carrying Capacities and the Settlement Oscillations in the Negev Highlands', *PEQ* 124: 42-58.

Rosman, A., and P.G. Rubel
1992 *The Tapestry of Culture: An Introduction to Cultural Anthropology* (New York: McGraw–Hill, 4th edn).

Routledge, B.
1995 ' "For the Sake of Argument": Reflections on the Structure of Argumentation in Syro-Palestinian Archaeology', *PEQ* 127: 41-49.

Roux, Jurie le
1992 'Once Again, Methods: A Taste of Deistian Hermeneutics', in Wessels and Scheffler 1992: 3-19.

Salmond, A.
1982 'Theoretical Landscapes: On a Cross-Cultural Conception of Knowledge', in Parkin 1982: 65-88.

Sass, H.-M. 'The Quest for Humanism in a Scientific Society', *Zeitschrift für allgemeine Wissenschaftstheorien* 11 1980: 45-53.

Sasson, J.M. (ed.)
1995 *Civilizations of the Ancient Near East*, IV (New York: Simon & Schuster).

Schaper, J.
1995 'The Jerusalem Temple as an Instrument of the Achaemenid Fiscal Administration', *VT* 45: 528-39.

Schenker, A.
1990 'Zeuge, Bürge, Garant des Rechts. Die drei Funktionen des "Zeugen" im Alten Testament', *BZ* 34: 87-90.

Schopman, J.
1986 'Negative Cross-Fertilization', *Zeitschrift für allgemeine Wissenschaftstheorien* 17: 59-67.

Scott, J.
1990 *Dominance and the Arts of Resistance: The Hidden Transcript* (Newhaven: Yale University Press).

Service, E.R.
1962 *Primitive Social Organization: An Evolutionary Perspective* (New York: Random House).

Seybold, K.
1982 'חָשַׁב hašab', in Botterweck and Ringgren 1982: 243-62.

Shavit, Y.
    1997   'Archaeology, Political Culture, and Culture in Israel', in Silberman and Small 1997: 48-61.

Shea, W.H.
    1985   'Israelite Chronology and the Samaria Ostraca', *ZDPV* 101: 9-20.
    1990   'The Khirbet el-Qom Tomb Inscription Again', *VT* 40: 110-16.

Shiloh, Y.
    1983   'Jerusalem, City of David', *IEJ* 33: 129-31.
    1992   'Underground Water Systems in the Land of Israel in the Iron Age', in Kempinski and Reich 1992: 275-93.

Shmueli, E.
    1970   'How is Objectivity in the Social Sciences Possible? A Re-evaluation of Karl Mannheim's Concept of "Relationism" ', *Zeitschrift für allgemeine Wissenschaftstheorien* 10: 107-18.

Shore, C.
    1995   'Anthropology, Literature and the Problem of Mediterranean Identity', *Journal of Mediterranean Studies* 5.1: 1-13.

Silberman, N.A.
    1997   'Structuring in the Past: Israelis, Palestinians, and the Symbolic Authority of Archaeological Monuments', in Silberman and Small 1997: 62-81.

Silberman, N.A., and D. Small (eds.)
    1997   *The Archaeology of Israel: Constructing the Past, Interpreting the Present* (JSOTSup, 237; Sheffield: Sheffield Academic Press).

Simkins, R.A.
    1994   *Creator and Creation* (Peabody, MA: Hendrickson).

Simonds, A.P.
    1975   'Mannheim's Sociology of Knowledge as a Hermeneutic Method', *Cultural Hermeneutics* 3: 81-104.

Slomovic, E.
    1979   'Toward an Understanding of the Formation of Historical Titles in the Book of Psalms', *ZAW* 91 (1979): 350-80.

Small, D.B.
    1997   'Group Identification and Ethnicity in the Construction of the Early Stage of Israel: From the Outside Looking In', in Silberman and Small 1997: 271-88.

Smelik, K.A.D.
    1992   *Converting the Past: Studies in Ancient Israelite and Moabite Historiography* (OTS, 28; Leiden: E.J. Brill).

Sollors, W.
    1996   'The Idea of Ethnicity', in Anderson (ed.) 1996: 54-61.

Sowayan, S.A.
    1996   'The Bedouin Oral Historical Narrative as a Literary Product and Historical Source', *Journal of Mediterranean Studies* 6.1: 45-55.

Stam, R., and E. Shohat
    1994   'Contested Histories: Eurocentrism, Multiculturalism, and the Media', in Goldberg (ed.) 1994: 296-324.

Stager, L.E.
    1985   'Response to Mazar', in Amitai 1985: 83-87.

Stegler, Shweder and Herdt (eds.)
  1990   *Cultural Psychology: Essays on Comparative Human Development* (Cambridge: Cambridge University Press).
Stern, E.
  1992   'The Phoenician Architectural Elements in Palestine During the Late Iron Age and the Persian Period', in Kempinski and Reich 1992: 302-309.
  1997   'Discoveries at Tel Dor', in Silberman and Small 1997: 128-43.
Stern, P.
  1995   'The "Blind Servant" Imagery of Deutero-Isaiah and its Implications', *Biblica* 75: 225-32.
Sternberg, M.
  1985   *The Poetics of Biblical Narrative: Ideological Literature and the Drama of Reading* (Bloomington: Indiana University Press).
  1992   'Biblical Poetics and Sexual Politics: From Reading to Counterreading', *JBL* 111.3: 463-88.
Stetkevytch, J.
  1989   'Arabic Hermeneutical Terminology: Paradox and the Production of Meaning', *JNES* 48.2: 81-96.
Stewart, J.
  1989   'The Literary Document as Cultural Document: A Caribbean Case', in Dennis and Aycock 1989: 97-112.
Talmon, S.
  1958   'Divergencies in Calender-reckoning in Ephraim and Judah', *VT* 8: 48-74.
Thomas, D.W.
  1960   'KELEBH "dog": Its Origin and Some Usages of It in the Old Testament', *VT* 10: 410-27.
Thompson, T.L.
  1991   'Text, Context and Reference in Israelite Historiography', in Edelman (ed.) 1991: 65-102.
  1994   *Early History of the Israelite People: From the Written and Archaeological Sources* (Studies in the History of the Ancient Near East; Leiden: E.J. Brill).
  1999   *The Bible in History: How Writers Create a Past*, (London: Jonathan Cape, 1999).
Tonkin, E.
  1982   'Language Versus the World: Notes on Meaning for Anthropologists', in Parkin 1982: 107-22.
  1995   *Narrating our Past: The Social Construction of Oral History* (Cambridge: Cambridge University Press, 2nd edn, 1995).
Toorn, K., van der
  1996   'Ancestors and Anthroponyms: Kinship Terms as Theophoric Elements in Hebrew Names', *ZAW* 108: 1-11.
Tsevat, M.
  1981   'Response to Mazar', in Amitai 1981: 87-89.
Turkowski, L.
  1969   'Peasant Agriculture in the Judaean Hills', *PEQ* 101: 21-33, 101-12.

Turner, T.
1994 'Anthropology and Multiculturalism: What Is Anthropology that Multiculturalists Should Be Mindful of It?', in Goldberg (ed.) 1994: 406-25.

Vansina, J.
1985 *Oral Tradition as History* (Madison: University of Wisconsin Press).

Verloren van Themaat, W.A.
1989 'Universal or Culture-Bound Science? *Zeitschrift für allgemeine Wissenschaftstheories* 20: 116-23.

Wagner, R.
1996 'The Idea of Culture', in Anderson (ed.) 1996: 49-53.

Walls, N.H.
1992 *The Goddess Anat in Ugaritic Myth* (SBL dissertation, 135; Atlanta: Scholars Press).

Walton, J.H.
1989 *Ancient Israelite Literature in its Cultural Context: A Survey of Parallels between Biblical and Ancient Near Eastern Texts* (Grand Rapids: Zondervan).

Waterman, J.T.
1970 *Perspectives in Linguistics* (Chicago: University of Chicago Press, 2nd edn, 1970).

Weinberg, Joel
1992 *The Citizen-Temple Community* (JSOTSup, 151; Sheffield: JSOT Press, 1992).

Weinfeld, Moshe
1972 *Deuteronomy and the Deuteronomic School* (Oxford: Clarendon Press).

Weippert, H.
1985a 'Amos, seine Bilder und ihr Milieu', in Weippert 1985b: 1-29.
1985b *Beiträge zur prophetischen Bildsprache in Israel und Assyrien* (OBO, 64; Freiburg: Universitätsverlag).
1985c 'Die Bildsprache der neuassyrischen Prophetie', in Weippert 1985b: 55-93.
1988 *Palästina in vorhellenistischer Zeit* (Munich: Beck).

Weiss, M.
1961 'Wegen der neuen Dichtungswissenschaften und ihre Anwendung auf den Psalmenexegese', *Biblica* 42: 255-302.

Wellhausen, J.
1905 *Prolegomena zur Geschichte Israels* (Berlin: W. de Gruyter).

Wells, R.S.
1966 'De Saussure's System of Linguistics', in M. Joos (ed.), *Readings in Linguistics. I. Development of Descriptive Linguistics, 1925–1956* (Chicago: University of Chicago Press, 4th edn): 1-18.

Wessels, Willie, and Eben Scheffler (eds.)
1992 *Old Testament Science and Reality: A Mosaic for Deist* (Pretoria: Verba Vitae).

White, G., and J. Kirkpatrick
1985 'Exploring Ethnopsychologies', in White and Kirkpatrick 1985: 3-32.

White, G., and J. Kirkpatrick (eds.)
    1985   *Person, Self and Experience: Exploring Pacific Ethnopsychologies* (Berkeley: University of California Press).

Whitelam, Keith W.
    1996   *The Invention of Ancient Israel: The Silencing of Palestinian History* (London: Routledge, 1996).
    1995   'Sociology or History: Towards a (Human) History of Ancient Palestine?', in J. Davies, G. Harvey and W.G.E. Watson (eds.), *Words Remembered, Texts Renewed: Essays in Honour of John F.A. Sawyer* (JSOTSup, 195; Sheffield: Sheffield Academic Press): 149-63.

Whitley, C.F.
    1969   *The Genius of Ancient Israel: The Distinctive Nature of the Basic Concepts of Israel Studied against the Cultures of the Ancient Near East* (Amsterdam: Philo Press).

Wimsatt, W.K.
    1968   'Genesis: a Fallacy Revisited', in P. Demetz (ed.), *The Disciplines of Criticism: Essays in Literacy Theory. Interpretation, and History* (New Haven and London: Yale University Press): 193-225.

Wiseman, D.J.
    1992   'Medicine in the Old Testament World', in B. Palmer (ed.), *Medicine and the Bible* (Carlisle: Paternoster, 2nd edn, 1992).

Wolff, H.W.
    1973   *Anthropologie des Alten Testaments* (Munich: Chr. Kaiser Verlag, 1973).

Yardeni, A.
    1991   'Remarks on the Priestly Blessing on two Ancient Amulets from Jerusalem', *VT* 41: 176-85.

Yeivin, S.
    1969   'Weights and Measures of Varying Standards in the Bible', *PEQ* 101: 63-68.

Young, I.
    1992   'The Style of the Gezer Calendar and Some "Archaic Biblical Hebrew" Passages', *VT* 42: 362-75.

Zertal, A.
    1995   'Three Iron Age Fortresses in the Jordan Valley and the Origin of the Ammonite Circular Towers', *IEJ* 45: 253-73.

INDEXES

INDEX OF REFERENCES

OLD TESTAMENT

Genesis		17.20	244	24.38	257
1	48, 52, 106, 107	18.1-5	269	24.40	257
		18.6	186	24.58	244
1.2	48	18.8	182	24.67	244
1.28	107	18.12	242	25.1-18	251
1.36	52	18.19	257	25.6	167
2	156, 157	18.23-33	168	25.8	261
2.24	263	19	250	25.19-26	250
3.11-12	209	19.1-3	269	25.21	234
3.15-19	157	19.5	269	26.1-15	125
3.16	263	21.10	265	26.14	119
4.7	112	21.14-21	127	26.19-32	127
6–9	76	21.14	184	26.19-22	127
6.3	261	21.15-16	127	26.26	274
7.1	257	21.17	242	26.33	75
7.4	125	21.30	127	27.1	260
9.20-25	196	21.33	141	27.6	242
10.32	257	22.1-19	230	27.9	184
11.3	206	22.2	230	27.29	245
11.30	234	22.3	159	27.37	167
12.3	257	22.4	230	27.46	239
12.6	140	22.11	242	29.1–30.24	251, 252
12.10-20	125	22.14	75	29.2-10	127
12.16	158, 159	22.17	202	29.2	143
13.8	245	23	168	29.5	242
13.10	124, 156	23.6	243	29.6	242
14.10	166	23.11	243	29.7	111
14.14	245	23.17-18	203	29.9	238
14.16	245	24	158	29.31	234
14.23	217	24.2-4	239	30.14	239
15.1-4	168	24.7	257	30.20	297
15.9	159	24.11-18	127	30.22	234
15.15	261	24.11	239	30.32	162
16	250	24.23	241, 257	30.34	244
16.4	248	24.35	119, 159	30.37-43	168

Index of References

30.37	140	43.11	133	17.12	120
30.43	158, 159	43.22	291	17.14	229
31.6	298	43.29	245	18.21	180, 295
31.11	242	46.2	242	20.12	264
31.14	257	46.6	123	21.2-11	267
31.15	269	46.31	257	21.2	179, 272
31.17	158	46.33	241	21.32	184
31.37	257	46.34	291	22.7-8	196
31.40	123	47.26	75	22.9-12	163
32.5	119, 159	48.1-22	251	22.9	158
32.7	158	48.10	260	22.15	271
32.14-15	166	48.13-20	265	22.25	179
32.18	243	48.15	163	23.3	271
32.31	120	48.22	265	23.4	158, 160
32.32	75	49.3-4	265	23.8	180
33.11	167	49.8	245	23.11	271
34	264	49.12	183	25.5	184
34.2	230	49.24	164	25.33	140
34.5	143	50.26	261	26–28	218
34.7	292			26.1	220
35.4	140, 214	*Exodus*		26.36	219
35.8	140	1.1	257	27.17	220
35.20	75	1.11	204	27.20	193
35.29	251	1.15-22	264	28.9	213
36	255	2.1-10	264	28.11	213
37	229	2.15-20	127	28.36	213
37.2	238	2.16-22	264	29.2	186
37.7	143, 243	2.16-19	238	30.11-16	286
37.24-28	127	2.16	238	30.13	286
37.25	158, 176, 229	3.4	242	30.15	271
		3.8	133	30.23	225
37.28	229	3.16-18	277	30.24	286
37.36	167, 229	4.20	159	30.33	293
38	252, 259, 277	4.24-26	264	31.2	253
		6.14	257	31.14	293
38.1	229	8.15	110	32.2-4	214
38.8-9	248	9.3	143, 158	33.4	214
38.11	257, 266	9.12	110	34.7	112
39	252	9.33	125	34.22	239
39.1	229	10.13	123	35.1-29	286
40.7	241	10.15	218	35.22	214
41–45	125	11.5	194	35.27-28	285
41.50-52	251	11.15	193	35.30-35	212
41.53-57	174	12.3	257	37.20	140
42.9	173	12.5	162	38.24	286
42.26	159	12.21	277	38.25	286
42.32	245	15.17	156	39.3	220
43.11-26	167	16.21	120	39.6	213

Leviticus		17.23	140	11.10	124
2.11	133	18.20	145	11.14	125
2.30-32	182	18.21	286	11.17	125
6.16-18	286	18.26	286	11.19	237
6.26	286	19.6	140	11.30	140
7.6	286	21.17-18	126	12.1-19	146
7.14	166	22.21	159	12.5	256
7.15-16	286	24.5-7	156	12.17	286
7.31-38	286	26.6	139	12.20-25	237
11	132, 134	26.28	251	12.29	181
11.13-19	142	26.33	263	13.7	245
11.32	184	27.1-11	263	14	132
14.4	140	27.17	163	14.3-21	237
18	292	30.2	256	14.4	162
18.25	119	30.3	257	14.22-29	146
18.28	119	31.28	256	14.27	145
19.9-10	145	31.50	213, 214	14.28-29	182
19.10	271	33.55	147	14.29	266
19.15	270, 271	35	258	15.1-3	237
19.22	271	36.3	144	15.4	145
19.23	149			15.12-18	267
19.35-36	169	Deuteronomy		15.12	179
19.36	225	1.44	133	15.13-15	268
20.18	127	2.7	110	15.16	257
20.22	119	2.22	75	15.18	179
21.5	236	3.14	75	16.11-14	146
22.13	257	4.10	237	16.14	266
23.13	185	4.16-18	107	16.19	180
25.3	150	4.19	120	17.5	203
25.21	167	4.21	145	17.6	295
25.34	144	4.25-26	237	19.10	145
25.35-55	258	4.40	237	19.14	144
25.36-37	179	5.31	237	19.15	295
25.47	257	5.33	261	19.19	295
26.5	187	6.5-9	232	20.1-20	237
26.6	163	7.1-2	237	21.1-14	240
33.13	257	7.1	181	21.2	260, 277
		7.3-4	237	21.10-14	268
Numbers		7.3	237	21.15-17	265
1.16	257	7.9	255	21.18-19	264
3.20	257	8.7-9	124, 156	21.19	260, 277
5.2	272	8.8	133, 185	22.5	237
7.3	159	8.9	209	22.6-7	134
11.8	193	9.5	181	22.9	237
12.3	238	10.17-18	290	22.10	160, 237
13.23	156	10.17	182	22.11	237
13.32	124	10.18	266	22.13-21	240
16.10	245	11.9	261	22.15-18	260, 277

Index of References

22.21	257	33.13-14	156	*Judges*	
23.2	255	33.16	156	1.6-7	111, 293
23.3	250	33.17	161, 251	1.14	241
23.9	131	33.19	217	1.21	75
23.19-20	179, 237	33.28	185	1.22	251
23.24-25	145	33.29	222	1.26	75
23.25	192	34.7	261	1.27	200
24.6	193			2.1	239
24.10-13	179	*Joshua*		2.10	255
24.12-13	267	2.1-3	241	3.12-29	256
24.12	271	2.15	217	3.13	200
24.14-15	271	4.9	75	3.15	256
24.17	179, 266	5.9	75	3.16	224
24.19-21	145, 266	6.2	243	3.17	167
24.19	270	6.24	210	3.19-22	168
24.20	152	6.25	75	4.1-24	256
25.3	293	7	292	4.4-5	256, 264
25.4	151	7.1	253	4.19	184
25.5-10	240, 258	7.6	277	4.21	264
25.7-9	260, 277	7.25-26	148	5.7	247
25.11	111	7.26	75	5.9	298
25.12	293	8.28	75	5.24-31	264
26.11-12	146	8.29	75	6.1-5	200
26.11	266	9.27	75	6.2–7.25	256
26.12-15	182	10.12	121	6.2	200
26.13	266	13–22	145	6.5	132, 158
27–28	237	13.13	75	6.6	186
27.17	144	14.4	251	6.11	140, 151, 256
27.19	266	14.14	75		
28.12	121, 125, 166, 181	15.17	253	6.18	167
		15.18	159	6.19	141, 186
28.24	125	15.19	167	6.24	75
28.30	149	15.36	75	7.12	158
28.40	155	16.4	251	7.13	186
28.49	135	16.10	75	8.16	277
28.51	185	17.3	253	8.19	245
29.23	124	17.14	278	8.23	182
32.2	125	17.17	251	9	256
32.5	255	18.5	251	9.1-6	246
32.7	255	19.33	140	9.1	257
32.8-9	76	21.12	143	9.4	272
32.9	145	23.13	147	9.5	257
32.13-14	183	24	121	9.6	140
32.14	161	24.13	149	9.8-15	141
32.20	255	24.22	244	9.15	123
32.34	229	24.26	141	9.33	120
32.42	130	24.29	261	9.37	288
33.13-16	166			9.52-54	264

Judges (cont.)		Ruth		10.27	167
9.53	193	1.22	186, 239	11	279
10.1	253	2.1	296	11.2	111
10.4	159	2.2	146	11.4	280
10.9	200, 251	2.3	143, 157	11.9	120
10.12	200	2.7	146	12.3	180
10.14	75, 239	2.10	269	12.17	186, 239
11.1	296	2.17	151, 226	13.1-2	200
11.2	257	2.23	186	13.6	200
11.3-6	256	3.1	296	13.19-21	209
11.3	272	3.10	271	13.19-20	191
11.4-33	256	3.15	186, 226	13.21	192
11.5-11	168	4.1-12	203	13.22	222
11.5	277			14.50	246, 280,
11.12-27	256	1 Samuel			289
11.30-32	168	1.1	253	15.3	158
12.2-3	256	1.5	234	15.13	241
12.4	251	1.6	264	15.27	167
12.6	184	1.8	241, 242	15.34	280
12.14	159	1.21	257	16.1-13	238, 280
13–16	279	1.34	184	16.16	279
13.2	234	2.1	298	16.20	159, 184
13.17	241	2.5	234	16.23	274
14.3	240	2.7	271	17	279
14.4	240	2.12-31	279	17.7	219
14.19	257	2.22-25	292	17.23	159
15.1	186, 239	2.22	292	17.25	270
15.19	75	2.25	294	17.34-36	129
16.7-9	217	2.31	259, 278	17.40	125
16.9	217	3.2	260	17.45	222
16.13-14	219	3.10	242	17.47	222
18.12	75	3.16	242	17.55	242
19	269, 270	4–8	279	17.58	241
19.2	257	4.18	260	18–31	279
19.11-15	269	5.5	75	18.2	257
19.11	269	6.13	186, 239	18.8	137
19.16	143	6.18	75	18.22-27	177
19.17	241	8.3	180	19.2	242
19.20	241	8.11-17	170, 236	19.12	264
19.22	269	9	280	19.22	126
19.25-27	270	9.1	253, 279	20.1	144
20.6	292	9.5-10	110	20.25	202
20.10	292	9.7	166, 167	20.30	279, 289
20.18	121	9.9	227	22.1	257
21.10-24	240	9.10-13	127	22.5	137
21.17	240	9.14-15	110	22.6	141
		10.3	140	22.7-8	173
		10.14-16	246	22.15	243, 257

Index of References

22.17	243	3.2	289	13.27 LXX	178
22.19	158	3.6-10	289	13.29	159
22.21	257	3.8	131, 274	14.2	264
23–28	234	3.13	244	14.6-7	266
23	279	3.17-18	277	14.9	257
24.14	131	3.26	126	14.26	172
24.17	242	3.29	216, 238,	15–1 Kgs 1	279
24.21	257		257	15.14	243
25.2-42	289	4–10	228	15.22	243
25.3-21	167	4.2	272	15.31-37	274
25.7	158	4.3	75, 270	15.34	274
25.11	184	4.12	293	16.1-4	174
25.14	242	5.2	284	16.6	148
25.15-16	167	5.3	228	16.16	274
25.16	200	5.10-13	280	16.19	274
25.20	159	5.17-25	281	16.21-22	289
25.42	159	6.8	75	17.10	130
25.43	289	6.9	280	17.18	196
26.6	253	6.10	253	17.23	159, 274
26.13	168	6.13	224	17.25	248, 280
26.14	242	6.19	184	17.28	185
26.17	242	6.67	109	17.29	182
27	279	7.2	139, 280	18.8-9	141
27.1-6	177	7.7	164	18.9	159
27.3	257	7.20	242	18.17	148
27.5	243	8	268	18.18	75
27.9	158	8.1	281	18.28	241
28.2	268	8.2-15	281	18.30	243
28.22-25	184	8.2	167, 268	19.20	251
28.24	186, 196	8.15	283	19.25-31	174
30.10	126	8.16-18	171	19.26	159
30.13	241	8.16	280	19.35	260
30.17-25	236	8.18	268	19.36	260
30.17	158	9.7	174	20.6	200
30.23-31	167	9.8	131, 272	20.9	241
30.25	75	9.11	173	20.16	264
30.26-31	228, 279	10.4-5	293	20.18	247
31.13	141	11.1	239	20.19	247
		11.8	168	20.22	264
2 Samuel		12.1	120, 270	20.23-26	171
1	279	12.2	119	20.24	206
1.8	241	12.8	251, 289	21.1	125
1.10	280	12.11-12	120	21.2	219
1.24	210	12.30	210, 280	21.8	253
2.1	244	12.31	176	21.9	239
2.4	251	13.3	274	21.18	253
2.18	132	13.12-13	292	22	279
2.24	132	13.12	291, 292	22.2	271

2 Samuel (cont.)		5.15	206	11.28	206, 251
22.6	217	6.4	206	12.4	191
22.51	208	6.7	206	12.16	144, 282
23.6-7	147	6.29	205	12.18	206
23.6	138	6.32	205	12.19	75
23.8-39	280	6.35	205	12.21	251, 288
23.8	280	7.1-14	205	13.7	167
23.19	253	7.3	206	13.13	159
23.20	129	7.5	205	13.27	159
23.27	253	7.7	205	13.29	159
24	175	7.8	205	14.4	260
24.9	222	7.10	206	14.11	131
24.17	257	7.11	206	14.21	273
24.23	242	7.12	206	14.25-26	180
		7.14	213, 266	14.26	176
1 Kings		8.1	256, 257, 277	14.30	288
1.1	260			14.31	248
1.19	184	8.2	125	15.2	248, 273
2.7	173	8.8	75	15.4	219
2.13-25	289	8.18	289	15.7	288
2.13	241	8.37	132	15.13	273
2.26-34	274	9.8	293	15.16	288
2.28-35	173	9.10-19	283	15.18	176
2.31	257	9.11	177	15.19	167, 168
2.40	159	9.13	75	15.27-29	174
3.1	289	9.15-19	175	15.27-28	282
3.28	283	9.15	206	16.4	131
4.1-19	171, 283	9.19	172	16.9-11	174
4.5	274	9.20-22	175, 282	16.9-10	282
4.6	206	9.20-21	206	16.11	274
4.7-19	282	9.24-28	283	16.16-23	282
4.20-25	170	9.26	177	16.17-23	174
4.20	279, 282	10.1	269	16.31	289
4.22-23	175	10.2	158	17	123, 125
4.24-25	175	10.5-6	174	17.6	184
4.25	282	10.5	173	17.7	125
4.26-28	175	10.11	210	17.10-12	266
4.33	107, 137	10.12	141	17.12	186
4.38	125	10.14	177	17.17-19	266
5–8	283	10.19-20	129, 205	18.5	126, 127
5.5-18	285	10.21-22	177	18.24	244
5.5-6	284	10.27	139	18.25-29	109
5.8-10	142	10.28-29	177	18.28	236
5.11-18	284	11.1	269	19.9	241
5.11	176, 185	11.2	296	19.11-12	122
5.13-16	175	11.3-8	240	19.19	158
5.13	175, 206, 273, 282	11.24	272	20.14	121
		11.26	248, 266	20.30	201

Index of References

21	131	10.14	184	21.19	273
21.3	144	10.27	75	22.1	273
21.4	144	11	281	22.3	226
21.8	227	11.1-3	273	22.27	242
22.6	121	11.1	273	23.5	120
22.11	161	11.13-16	174	23.7	218
22.15	121	11.14	236	23.8	202
22.17	163	12.1	273	23.11	120
22.19-23	109	12.12	206	23.13	240
22.39	206	12.18	210	23.15-23	288
22.42	248, 273	12.20-21	282	23.31	273
		13.7	154	23.36	273
2 Kings		13.21	272	24.8	273
1.8	184	14.1	282	24.14	213
2.4	242	14.2	273	24.16	213
2.22	75	14.7	75	24.18	273
3.4	176	14.19-21	282	25.1	290
3.19	142, 148	15.2	273	25.3	125
4.1	267	15.33	273	25.7	111
4.9-10	195	16.6-8	180	25.15	244
4.18-37	266	16.6	75		
4.24	159, 243	16.8	167, 168,	*1 Chronicles*	
4.27	244		176	1–10	228
4.36	242	17.3-4	180	1	255
4.38-44	186	17.8	236, 237	4.23	215
4.38-41	109	17.9	208	5.1-2	265
5.1	296	17.16	120	5.18	222
5.15	167	17.19	236	7.23	248
5.25	242	17.34	75, 236	8.8	206
6.24-32	125	17.40	236	10.12	140
6.25	184, 226	17.41	75	11.23	219
6.26-27	174	18–19	53	12.8	222
7.1	185, 226	18.2	273	12.24	222
8.8	167	18.8	208	12.34	222
8.9	167	18.13	209	12.40	158
8.22	75	18.14-16	180	16.29	167
8.26	248, 273	18.15	176	19.7	182
9–10	174	18.16	210	20.5	219
9.5	290	18.18	226	21.5	222
9.17	208	18.32	185	21.20	186
9.18	243	19.2	226	22.3-4	201
9.22	242	19.23	142	23–26	285
9.23	242	19.28	190	23.1	261
9.30-31	274	20.12-18	173	26.27	176
9.30	218	20.12	167	27.25	208
9.37	182	20.13	172	27.30	158, 253
10.7	184	21.1	273	28.4	245
10.13	273	21.3	120		

Reference	Page	Reference	Page	Reference	Page
2 Chronicles		8.1	226	14.17	229
1.15	139	8.8	227	15.32	111
1.17	226	9.27	239	16.15	161
2.7	212	10.34-39	181	19.17	197
2.10	185	10.38	286	19.20	222
2.15	185	10.39	181, 185	19.24	213
8.4-6	175	12.25	172	20.17	182
9.27	139	12.39	203	20.29	144
14.13	176	13.5	185	21.2	298
14.15	158	13.12	185	21.10	161
16.4	172, 204	13.23-28	237	21.18	154
17.12	172, 204	13.26	240	21.22-26	183
17.17	222			22.6	267
19.5	199	*Esther*		22.9	266
20.25	176	1.7	177	22.16	111
21.3	167, 209	2.18	167, 168	23.10	212
24.6	168	8.8	227	23.11	298
24.12	213	8.15	218	23.16	298
25.5	222	9.22	271	24.3	178, 266
26.6-10	176	9.28	255	24.4	271
26.10	157, 208			24.9	271
27.5	185	*Job*		24.21	266
28.8	176	1.3	158, 159	24.24	271
30.5-6	288	3.3-10	120	28.1-19	209
31.5	286	4.2	151	28.15-17	210
32.6	202	4.14	298	28.19	210
32.27	205	4.18-19	204	28.21	134
32.28	172, 185, 204	5.5	152	29.6	183, 184
		5.26	153	29.7-8	203
33.14	136	6.2-3	225	29.12-20	296
35.25	75, 236	6.4	222	29.45	183
		6.5	161	30.11	191
Ezra		6.11-12	298	30.14	200
2.67	158	6.12	210	30.25	271
4.6-1	71	6.14	112	30.27	298
4.13	180	7.6	219	30.29	131
4.20	177, 180	8.17	148	30.30	197, 218
7.24	173, 180, 181	9.33	295	31.5-8	225
		10.8-12	183	31.5	298
10.3	237	10.9	215	31.7	298
		10.16	130	31.21-22	203
Nehemiah		11.10	219	31.24	210
5.1-5	181	11.19	163	31.25	298
5.3	125, 143, 179	12.12	261	31.26-27	121
		12.20	277	32.9	261
5.5	179	13.1	243	33.1	242
5.11	185	14.7-10	140	33.31	242
6.5-7	71	14.13	239	34.19	270

Index of References

34.28	271	18.25	298	37.31	296
36.8	217	18.28	120	37.32	296
36.29	122	18.35	223	37.33	296
37.1-5	122	19.10	210	37.35-36	139
37.14	242	20.5	209	37.39	239
38.14	215	20.8	290	38.2	222
38.22-23	121	21.10	194, 234	38.3	112
38.22	181	22.2-22	168	38.4	190
38.23	239	22.8	292	39.1	151
39.23	222	22.13	161	39.5	226
40.17	139	22.14-17	297	40.6	293
41.1	136	22.16	131	40.9	298
41.7	136	22.26	271	40.17	271
41.24	193, 194	22.27	257	41.7	292
41.30	193	22.28	290	44.11	163
42.12	119	23.1	164	44.13	145
42.17	261	23.2	163	45.2-7	280
		24.6	255	45.9	210
Psalms		24.7	290	45.10	257
1.3	126	25.7	228	46.9	223
2	280	26.5	156	46.10	222
2.7	288	26.10	180	48.1-7	51
2.9	216	28.9	164	48.8-10	287
2.12	280	29	76	48.8	123
3	52	29.3-10	123	49.15	163
3.3	223	29.4	190	49.19	255
3.20	245	29.6	160	50.3	122
5.12	223	31.10	298	51.2	248
6.1	239	31.16	111	52.8	156
7.12-13	222	31.21	222	56.14	298
8	239	32.6	111	58	148
8.3	262	32.9	190	58.9	148
9.7-8	290	32.10	112	59.6	131
10.2	271	33.5	112	60.3	187
10.5	111	35.2	222, 223	60.4	209
10.9	271	35.3	222	61.3	208
10.12	228	35.10	298	62.9	225
11.2	222	35.14	264	64.8	293
11.4	290	37.14	222	65.9-13	127
12.5	271	37.18-40	296	65.12	163
12.6	212	37.18-19	296	66.10	212
13.9	262	37.20	163, 196, 296	68.5	266
14.6	271			68.23	131
15.5	180	37.21	296	68.29	287
16.6	144, 145	37.22	296	69.5-6	298
18.2	223	37.25	296	69.8-12	297
18.10	123	37.26	262, 296	69.12	203
18.21	298	37.30	296	69.13	239

Psalms (cont.)		102.14	111	128.6	261		
69.19	293	103.4	112	129.3	149, 157		
70.4	293	103.5	135	129.4	217		
71.9	111	103.9	290	129.6	153		
71.21	297	103.13	262	133.1	196		
72.1-2	283	103.16	123	135.7	121, 181		
72.4	271	104	76, 127	137	68		
72.5	120, 255	104.3	123	139.11-12	120		
72.12	271	104.14-15	156	139.13	219		
72.21	271	104.26-29	136	140.12	271		
73.15	255	105	52	141.2	168		
74.2	256	105.28	52	142.6	145		
74.13-14	136	105.29	52	145.11-13	290		
74.19	135, 271	105.30-31	52	146.9	266		
75.8	187	105.31	132	147.10	202		
76.3	222	105.32-35	52	147.13-19	202		
76.12	166	106.3	111	147.13	201, 202		
77.17	122	106.23	201	147.16-18	121		
78	252	107.37	156	148.10	107		
78.6	255	107.41	257				
78.8	255	109.9	266	*Proverbs*			
78.20	184	109.10	234	1.17	134		
78.45	132	109.14	112	1.21	203		
78.52	163	109.25	293	2.24	206		
78.57-68	253	110	280	3.3	112, 229		
78.71	164, 284	112.2	255	3.10	187		
80.1	163, 164	112.9	271	3.14	210		
80.2-8	168	113.3	120	3.16	270		
80.14	156	113.9	234	4.18	120		
81.17	186	115.14	262	5.15-20	127		
82	76	118.12	133, 148	5.22	112		
82.1	290	119	231	6	133		
83.12	182	119.57	145	6.5	132, 134		
83.16	293	119.59	298	6.12-13	168		
84.11	120	119.72	210	6.16-19	292		
89.3	112	119.82-83	197	6.18	110		
89.7	290	119.110	132	7.11	110		
89.14	283	119.119	212	7.16	218		
89.15	112	119.132	236	7.22	132		
89.21	298	119.176	163	7.23	134		
90.10	261	122.4	256	8.18	270		
91.4	222	124.7	134	9.2	187		
91.13	129	126.5	151, 155, 157	9.5	187		
92.2	139			10.5	185, 294		
92.10	161	127.5	203, 223	10.10	110, 168		
92.12	156	128.3-6	297	10.15	271		
94.6	266	128.3	156, 234, 262	10.16	112		
96.7	257			10.26	197, 264		

11.1	291	20.16	267	28.1	130
11.15	267	20.17	152	28.3	125, 271
11.16	270	20.20	264	28.7	110
11.18	151	20.23	169, 225, 291	28.11	271
11.22	210, 214			28.15	130, 131
11.25	167	20.28	112	28.24	264
12.4	263, 294, 296	20.29	262, 277	29.4	272
		20.26	154	29.7	271
12.22	292	21.1	126	29.14	271, 272
13.5	293	21.4	219	30.11-14	255
13.8	270	21.13	271	30.16	234
13.18	297	21.14	168	30.17	110, 261
13.23	271	21.17	187	30.19	135
14.4	160	21.19	263	30.20	183
14.20	271	21.23	110, 196	30.25	185
15.1	196	22.2	270	30.29-31	272
15.17	174, 184	22.4	270, 297	30.30	129, 130
15.19	138	22.5	138	30.32	110
15.27	180	22.7	270, 271	31	218
16.5	292	22.16	271	31.10	263, 296
16.12	292	22.17–24.33	76	31.19	216
16.15	292	22.22	203, 271	31.20	271
16.30	168	23.5	135	31.22	218
16.31	259	23.22	264	31.23	203
17.3	211	23.25	264	31.31	203
17.5	271	23.29-31	186		
17.6	297	24.7	203	*Ecclesiastes*	
17.8	180	24.9	292	1.1	273
17.9	234	24.30-31	150	1.4	255
17.23	168, 180	25	52, 53	3.1-11	239
18.10	208	25.4	211	3.5	148
18.11	200	25.11	210	4.12	216
18.15	167	25.12	210	4.13-16	273
18.16	166	25.13	111	4.14	271
18.21	110	25.14	125, 166, 167	5.1-2	110
18.22	263			6.2	270
18.23	270, 271	25.18	222	6.8	271, 273
19.4	271	25.24	264	7.6	148
19.6	167	25.26	128	7.24	244
19.7	271	26.1	125	9	273
19.12	274	26.2	134	9.2	132
19.14	144, 263	26.3	161, 190	9.4	273
19.26	294	26.11	131	10.20	134
20.2	272	26.20	194	11.4	150
20.3	297	26.28	110	12.4	194
20.7	297	27.18	297	12.11	192
20.8	154, 283	27.24	255		
20.10	291	27.25-27	182		

Song of Songs		5.10	224, 226	19.9	220		
1.2	188	5.11	71	19.10	219		
1.6	238	5.12	178	19.13	256		
1.11	210	5.17	162, 163	21.5	222		
1.15	135	5.18	112, 217	21.7	158		
2.9	132	5.20	120	21.15	222		
2.14	135	5.23	180	22	201		
2.17	132	7.4	127	22.4	201		
3.10	210	7.15	183	22.6	222		
4.1-6	135	7.17	288	22.10-11	201		
4.1	135	7.18	133	22.13	184		
4.10	188	7.22	183	22.17-18	218		
4.11	182	7.23-24	138	23.18	182		
4.15	132	7.23	151	24.2	119		
5.1	187, 188	7.25	149, 150, 163	24.4	119, 149		
5.2	135			24.7	187		
5.12	183, 184	9.4	192	24.13	155		
5.21	135	9.10	140, 204, 206	25.4-5	123		
6.9	135			26.9	216		
7.2	188	9.17	266	27.1	136		
7.3	132	10.1-19	147	27.10	163		
7.7-8	156	10.2	266	27.12	154		
8.2	187, 188	10.13	160	28.7	187		
		10.16	148	28.8 RSV	71		
Isaiah		10.17-18	148	28.10 RSV	71		
1.3	161	11.1-10	272	28.23-25	149		
1.17	266	11.6-8	129	28.25	185		
1.18	218	11.6-7	163	28.26-28	154		
1.22	187	13.10	120	28.27	151		
1.23	180, 266	13.12	210	28.28	159		
1.25	211, 212	13.14	163	29.5	154		
2.4	191, 223	13.16	264	29.6	122		
2.12-13	139	13.17	210	30.1	112		
2.15	200, 208	13.19	124	30.8	229		
2.22	272	13.20	163, 255	30.13	201, 222		
3.14-15	260, 271, 278	13.21	135	30.14	127, 215, 216		
		13.22	111				
3.15	194	14.8	142	30.16	120		
3.16	217	14.30	163	30.23-26	165		
3.18-23	178	14.31	202	30.24	152, 160, 193		
3.19-22	213, 214	16.2	134				
3.24	178, 197	16.3	123	31.4	129, 130		
3.26	202	16.8	148	32.2	123		
4.6	123	16.10	155	33.9	119		
4.7	213	17.2	163	33.12	147		
5	150	17.6	155	34.11	135		
5.2	151	18.3	208	34.13-14	131		
5.6	138, 150	18.5	150	34.13	138		

35.6	132	60.15	255	7.18	120, 193
35.9	129	60.16	183	7.29	255
36.16	127	60.17	211	8.2	120, 182
36.17	185	61.4	255	8.7	134
37.39	239	63.1	217	8.12	239
38.8	120	63.17	256	8.20	187
38.12	220	64.8	215	9.1	131
38.13	298	65.10	163	9.7	211
38.14	135	65.20	262	9.10	163
39.2	186	65.25	129	9.22	153, 182
40.11	163, 164			10.3-16	214
40.15	226	*Jeremiah*		10.9	210, 218
40.20	212	1.10	156	10.13	121
40.31	135	1.11	140	10.15	239
41.6-7	214	2.2	112	10.16	145, 256
41.7	213	2.4	257	10.20	217
41.15	193	2.21	156	10.22	131
41.16	123, 154	2.23	161	10.25	257
41.17	271	2.26	293	11.16	156
41.18	128	2.32	214	12.2	156
41.19	140	3.18	251	12.3	163
41.25	215	3.22-25	297	12.4	119
44.12-20	214	3.24	271	12.11	119
44.12	211	3.25	297	12.12	150
44.14	140	4.3	147, 149	12.13	151
44.28	164	4.5	199	12.14	145
45.7	114	4.6	208	14.8	239
45.9	216	4.11	123	15.18	128
47.2	194, 264	4.19	298	16.16	136
47.9	266	4.20	218	17.1	229
48.10	212	4.22	244	17.11	213
49.2	222	4.28	119	17.12	203
49.6	256	4.29	222	18.1-6	216
49.15	262	4.30	210, 214, 218	18.6	216
51.1	183, 207			18.9	156
51.9-10	52	5.4	271	18.11	216
51.9	136	5.5	192	19.1-2	216
54.1	234	5.11	251	19.8	293
54.2	217	5.16	222	19.10-13	216
54.4	266	6.23	222	20.9	298
55.1	183	6.27	211	22.3	266
56.3	140	6.28	210	22.7	142
58.6	192	6.29-30	212	22.13-14	206
58.7	271	6.29	211	22.13	206
58.12	201, 255	7.2	203	22.14	217, 235
59.11	135	7.4	287	22.15	139
60.6	158	7.6	266	23.2-4	164
60.9	210, 211	7.14	288	23.2	284

Jeremiah (cont.)		49.16	135	3.16	152
23.9	298	49.18	124	3.48	126
23.10	119, 149, 163	49.19	130	4.1-2	210
		49.22	135	4.2	215
23.18	290	49.27	222	4.4	262
23.29	207	49.29	158	4.7	183
24.1	213	49.31	202	4.16	277
24.6	156	50.2	209	4.20	272
25.10	194	50.16	192	5.3	266
25.30	155	50.39	255	5.10	195, 197
26.10	203, 205	50.42	222	5.12	259, 277
26.11	243	51.2	154	5.13	262
26.12	205	51.3	222	5.14	277, 278
26.17	277	51.6	239		
26.18	149	51.14	132	*Ezekiel*	
27.2	191	51.18	239	2.6	138
29.2	213	51.21	158	4.2	222
29.5	156	51.27	132	4.9	185
31.1	257	51.33	153	6.13	140
31.5	156, 157	51.58	200	7.19	210
31.8	160	52.10	184	7.26	261, 277
31.10	164	52.21	224	8.16	120
31.12	185	52.33	173	9.2	226
31.28	156			11.3	185
32.10	225	*Lamentations*		13.4	131
32.41	156	1	112	13.19	186
32.44	144, 229	1.1	112	16	214
36.2	229	1.2	112	16.3-5	262
36.10	203	1.3	112	16.10	184
37.14-21	203	1.6	112	16.13	186, 210
37.20	243	1.8	112	16.21	184
38.6	217	1.9	112	16.37	264
38.7	268	1.10	112	17.24	140
39.3	202	1.11	112	19.1-9	130
39.10	271	1.13	112	21.21-22	109
40.5	167	1.14	112, 298	21.21	121, 245
41.7	184	1.15	112, 155, 193	21.22	222
41.8	185			22.7	266
41.9	126	1.17	112	22.12	180
42.10	156	1.19	112	22.18	210, 211
44.17-25	120	1.20	112, 298	22.20	211
46.3	222	1.22	112	22.29	235
46.9	222	2.10	277	22.30	201
46.23	132	2.11	262	23.6	185
48.11	187	2.15	293	23.9-12	185
48.26	71	2.16	293	23.10	264
48.40	135	2.18	201	23.14	217
49.11	266	3.13	222		

Index of References

23.20	122, 161, 183	8.26	229	2.6	262
				2.13-14	167
23.24	222	*Hosea*		2.19	185
23.25-26	218	1.7	222	2.21	149
23.40	214	2.1	241	2.24	187
24.2	229	2.5	122	3.10	191
24.3-5	185	2.16	263	3.13	153, 155, 192
26.8	222	2.18	163		
27	177	2.23	150, 156	3.18	183
27.5-7	139	2.25	156		
27.12	210	3	241	*Amos*	
27.17	186	3.2	186	1.2	119, 163
28.6	156	4.3	119	1.3	153, 193
28.13	209	4.13	124, 140	1.7	203
28.24	147	5.12	251	1.9	250
29.3	136	6.5	207	1.10	203
30.12	145	6.6	112	1.11	250
32.2	136	7.4-7	195	2.7	271
33.21	209	7.8	195	2.8	179, 267
34	164	7.11	134	2.9	139
34.2-6	164	7.12	134	2.13	153, 192
34.5	284	7.14	185	2.15	222
34.10	164	8.7	151	3.2	257
34.11-16	164	9.11	297	3.12	129, 163
34.17-24	164	9.13	156	4.1	161
36.35	157	10.1	156	4.3	222
38.4	222	10.4	150	4.9	132
38.11	202	10.11	149	5.10	203
38.12	283	10.12	149, 151	5.11	167, 178, 204
38.20	107	11.4	217		
40.3	217	11.10	129	5.12	180, 203
43.7-8	289	11.12	251	5.15	203, 283
43.8	206	12.7	112, 169	5.18	120
43.11	229	13.3	154, 197	5.19	196
44.30	167	13.7	130	5.24	126, 179
45.10	225	13.12	112	6.1-6	178
46.5	167	13.15	127	6.4	184
46.11	167	14.6	156	6.6	187, 251
46.16-17	167	14.8	141	6.12	161
46.16	167			7.7	201
46.17	167	*Joel*		7.10-17	169
47.1-12	128	1–2	133	7.10	288
47.7-12	157	1.4	132	7.13	288
47.10	136	1.10	149, 185, 187	7.14	158
				8.5	169, 225
Daniel		1.12	119	8.8	119
5.7	218	1.19-20	165	8.9	120
5.25	225	2.2	255	9.9	155

Amos (cont.)		1.13	192	2.5	200, 201
9.13	158, 187	2.5	222	3.9	213
9.14-15	156	2.7	135	3.10	157
		2.9	210	6.12	289
Obadiah		2.11	130	7.10	266
1.4	135	3	132	9.10	222
		3.3	222	9.17	185
Jonah		3.8	200	10.2	163
1.8	241	3.14	200	11	181
		3.15-17	132	11.4	164
Micah				11.13	181
1.8	131, 135	*Habakkuk*		13.9	212
2.1-2	53, 178,	1.8	135	14.8	128
	235	2.6	179	14.10	176
2.4	145	2.9-11	207	14.15	158
2.12	163	3.17	148, 165		
3.3	184			*Malachi*	
3.6	218	*Zephaniah*		1.11	120
3.11	180	1.10	136	3.3	212
4.4	157	1.18	210	3.5	266
4.12	153	2.6	163	3.10	121, 167,
4.13	210	2.7	163		182
5.8	163	2.14	139	4.2	160
6.8	112	2.15	293		
6.11	225	3.3	131	*Ecclesiasticus*	
6.15	155, 193	3.4	272	15	213
7.3	180	3.13	163	15.6	215
7.4	138			27.3	155
7.14	163	*Haggai*		37.11	264
7.20	112	1.11	187		
				1 Maccabees	
Nahum		*Zechariah*		8.2	210
1.10	138	2.4	201		

INDEX OF SUBJECTS

Afrikaans 74
Afrikaner 74
Afrikaner identity 73
Ammonites 176, 250
Anat 114
Anglo-Boer War 72, 73
animals 107, 128, 136, 137, 158
Aramaeans 158
Ashera 114, 141
Assyria 65, 76, 147, 202, 207, 209

Ba'al 76, 114, 122, 123, 141
Babylon 63, 65, 68, 70-72, 109, 130, 186, 194, 200, 202
Barley Letter 69
Beth Shean 69
birds 134, 135
bit hilani 205
Book of Jashar 121
bureaucrats 170

cattle 159, 160, 182
chiefdoms 276, 279-82
cities 197-200
city gate 202, 203
civic-temple-community 66, 67
cognitive anthropology 91
concubinage 234
configurationalist approaches 84, 90
custom 116, 235, 236, 239, 241
Cyrus cylinder 65

diachrony/diachronic 35-37
divorce 240
dyeing 217

Edomites 250
Egypt 52, 67, 70, 71, 130, 136, 177, 194

El 114, 290
emic 83, 84
empiricism 95
ethnicity 99
ethnohistorical approaches 84, 92
ethnolinguistics 91
etic 83, 84
evolutionary theories 86
evolutionist approaches 84, 85

family 244, 245
fish 136
functionalist approaches 84, 88, 99

genealogy 228, 248-51
Gezer calendar 116, 238
Gibeon 121
Gilgamesh 175, 264
goats 162, 164, 182
gold 210-13
Gomorrah 156
guilt 293, 294, 297

harvesting 151-53, 155, 162
Hazor 205
Hirbet Shehadah 190
Hymn to the Sun 75

idealism 95
intentionality 101
ironist 47
Ishmaelites 158, 250
Israel Stela 273

Jerusalem 51, 67, 70, 77, 109, 119, 147, 177, 180, 203, 219, 230, 268, 288
Ketef Hinnom 69
Khirbet el-Qôm 69

Kuntillet 'Ajrud 69, 77

language 241
langue 35, 36, 38, 87
Leviathan 136, 194
lmlk jar handles 69

marriage 239, 240, 246, 247
Marx 98
Massoretes 36
materialism 95
meat 184, 185
Megiddo 205
Memes 85
Mesad Hashavyahu 267
Midianites 158
milk 183
Moabite Stela 69
Moabites 250
Mot 114
Mount Zion 51
Murabba'at 69

oil 186, 193
oral communication 227, 231
oral tradition 230, 254

paradigm 26, 27
parole 35, 36, 38, 87
patrilocation 247, 248
pesher 76
Philistines 113, 133, 176
plants 106, 137, 138
ploughing 148, 149
polygamy 234, 244
polygyny 264, 265
postmoderism 24, 39
pottery 214-16

qualitative probabalism 45, 61
queen mother 273
Qumran 76

Rahab 52, 136
rain 106, 125, 126
rationalism 95, 96
realism 54, 55
relevance theory 28, 31, 32
rivers 125, 126

Samaria 69, 77, 131, 144, 147, 161, 174, 180, 190, 194, 205
Samaria ostraca 175
Samaritans 67, 146
Satan 115
shame 238, 293, 294, 297
sheep 162, 164, 182
siege 221
Siloam inscriptions 69
silver 210, 212, 213
slavery 266-68
society of knowledge 33
Sodom 156
sowing 150, 151
speech 244
spinning 216
states 276, 281, 282
strangers 267, 269, 270
structuralist approaches 84, 87, 90
subjectivism 95, 96
substantialism 95, 100
Sumeria 71, 175
synchrony/synchronic 35-39, 57, 58
syntagm 26, 27

Tel Dan 69
Tel Dan Stele 76
temple 283-89
threshing 153, 154
towns 197, 198
trees 137, 139-42
tribal elders 277
tribes 276
tribute 167

Ugaritic 113, 114

value studies 92

weaving 218-20
wine 186-88, 193
Wisdom of Amenemope 76
writing 229-31

Yavne Yam 69

Zaphon 51
Zion 68, 208
Zoroastrian 76

INDEX OF HEBREW TERMS

אב 119, 245, 246
אביון 271
אביר 159, 160
אבן 225, 229
אגם 126
אדמה 119, 165
אהובה 264
אולם־הכס 205
און 168
אוצר 181, 182, 205
אור 108
אח 245, 246
אחון 159
אחות 245
אחזה 144
איתן 126
אי 128
איל 129, 162
איש־חיל 261, 270
אכר 157
אלון/אלה 137, 141
אלמנה 266
אלוף/אלף 159, 160, 165, 255, 256
אם 245
אמיץ 262
אניה/אני 108
אספי־השערים 172
אפעה 129
אפיק 125
אצבע 108
ארבה 132
ארג 212, 219, 220
ארגות 218
ארגמן 217
ארז 137
ארי/אריה 129
ארמנה 203

ארץ 108, 119
אשל 137
אשפה 221
אשת־חיל 262, 296
אש 108
את 191

באר 108, 126, 127
באש 293
בד 108
בוקר 158
בורה 262
בור 126, 127
בחור 262
בחון/בחן 211, 221
ביר 126
בירניות 207
בית־אבות/בית־אב 80, 255, 257
בית־האוצר 172
בית־האספים 172
בית־הכלי 172
בית־נכאת 172
בלו 180
בליעל 168
בעל 263
בן 245
בן־קשת 221
בצורה 197
בצר 208
בקר 158, 159, 160
ברוש 137
ברזל 193, 209, 213
בריח 202
ברכה 167
בשת 293
בתולים/בתולה 214, 262

גאון 137
גבור־חיל 296
גבירה 273
גבר 108
גדודים 272
גדי 162
גדר 199, 206, 213
גוים/גוי 106, 237
גורל 144
גזית 206
גזל 235
גזם 132
גזר 280
גל 192
גלגל 221
גמל 158
גר 266, 269
גרון 221
גשם 106, 124
גת 193

דב 129
דבק 213, 221
דבש 182
דגן 185
דוד 245, 246
דום 121
דור 218, 255
דחן 151
די 162
דל 270, 271
דלה 218
דרבן 192
דרך 236
דרך־ענבים 157

הבל 225
הד 137
הלך 180
הנה 243
הר 108
הרוץ 192

זאב 128
זהב 218
זונה 131
זכרון 229
זית 137, 151

זקן 256, 258, 261, 277
זר 157, 267
זרם 106, 124
זרע 157

חבל 144, 217
חבר 107
חברת 107
חוט 216
חולם־פעם 213
חומה 199, 200, 201, 203
חזיר 158
חטאת/חטאה 112
חטים 185, 239
חטין 151
חיק 221
חכם 273
חלב 182, 184
חלון 205, 206
חלק 144
חם 246, 247
חמאה 182
חמה 246
חמר 158, 159, 204
חמת 247
חנית 221
חסיל 132
חפר 293
חפשי 268, 270
חץ 221
חצב 206, 213
חצי 221
חצן 221
חצר 200
חק 236, 237
חרוץ 193, 262
חרב 108, 130, 141, 221
חרט 211
חרפה 293
חרש 212
חרש 137, 157, 191, 213
חשב 212, 220
חתן 246, 247
חתנה 246, 247

טבור 283, 288
טל 106, 124, 125
טלה 162

Index of Hebrew Terms

יד 108, 121, 299
יהודית/יחודי 107
יוצר 181
יורה 106, 124
ילק 132
ינק 262
יער 137, 182
יצהר 185
יקב 193
ירח 121
יתד 221
יתום 266
יתרים 217

כבש 162
כדור 218
כהן 171
כובע 221
כור 211
כח 299
כחם 262
כידון 221
כלב 131, 299
כלה 246, 247
כלמה 293
כמן 151
כסיל 273
כסמים 151
כפיר/כפר 129, 197
כר 221
כשב 162
כשבה 182
כתף 108

לב 110, 299
לביא 129
לבנה 137
לבנים 206
לוז 137
לוח/לח 137, 229
לויתן 136
לולם 205
לשון 299

מאזנים 225
מבוע 126
מגדל 199, 207
מגל 192

מגן 221
מגרש 143
מרה 180
מוכיח 295
מוסרות 191
מזכיר 171, 172
מזרה 193
מחליק-פטיש 213
מחנים 197
מחרשה 191
מטה 151, 191. 92, 255
מטר 106, 124, 125
מים 126, 128
מיתרים 217
מכרה 221
מלאכת 241
מליץ 295
מלקוש 106, 124
מנדה 180
מנחה 167, 168
מסגר 213
מסכנות 172, 204
מסכת 219
מסמר 213
מסע 221
מעוז-ראש 221
מעים 299
מעין 126, 127
מעלות 205
מפח 211
מפיץ 221
מפץ 221
מצור 221
מצחה 221
מצרף 211
מקבות 213
מקדש 288
מקור 126, 127
מקל-יד 221
מרכבה/מרכב 221
משאת 167, 168
משכב 219
משפחה 80, 255, 256, 257, 258
משפט 236
מתג 190
מתנה/מתן 166, 167
מתת 167

ענבים 151	נאמנים 277
עני 267, 271, 273	נהר 108, 125, 126
ענילים 214	נזז 157
עץ 137	נזם 214
עצל 262	נחל 125, 126
עצם 299	נחלה 143, 144
עקרה 234	נחש/נחשת 129, 136, 200, 209
ערי־המסכנות 172	נטע 157
עש 235	ניר 219
עשיר 270	נכר 267, 269
עתור 162	נמר 129
	נעל 108
פול 151	נער 262
פוך 218	נצב 171, 172, 173
פחז 272	נקד 158
פחם 211, 213	נשאים 259
פטיש 207, 213	נשיא 257, 285
פי 121, 130	נשק 220
פיפיות 193	
פישור 216	סב 243
פלג 125	סבך 137
פלח־רכב 193	סגים 211
פלס 225	סגר 221
פלך 216	סגריר 106, 124
פעם 213	סוס 158, 221
פר 159, 160	סחרה־שלם 221
פרי 141	סכה 219
פרד 158	סללה 221
פרה 159	סריון 221
פרזות 201	
פרשים 221	עבד 108, 266
פשתים/פשתה 151, 220	עבים 137
פתיל 217	עבריה/עברי 107
פתן 129	עגלה/עגל 159, 160, 184, 221
	עדי 214
צאן 162, 164	עדשים 151
צב 171	עוללים 262
צבי 129	עז 162, 182
צהר 193	עטין 183
צלצל 221	עטרת 214, 280
צנה 221	עיר 108, 165, 197, 208
צנפה 218	עכשוב 129
צפעני 129	על 191, 192
צפצפה 137	עליה 205
צרה 264	עם־הארץ 235
צרף 211, 213	עמוד 205
צוף 182	עמיד 214
	עמרים 146

Index of Hebrew Terms

קבול 221
קובע 221
קון 221
קיר 199
קלון 293
קלע 221
קמח 185
קצח 151
קציר 239
קצר 157
קרדום/קרדם 191, 221
קריה 197
קשת 221

ראם 159
ראש 256
רביבים 106, 124, 125
רביד 214
רגל 299
רהל 162
רוח 48, 108
רחים 193, 194
רחת 193
רכוב/רכב 194, 221
רמו 137
רמח 221
רסן 190
רקם 219, 212
רקם־ארג 216
רש 270, 271
רשע 108
רתם 137

שדד 149
שדה 143, 182
שה 162
שנואה 264
שער/שעיר 108, 125, 151, 162
שרד 220
שרים 259, 270
שריקות 220
שרף 129

שאול 108

שבט 80, 151, 191, 192, 221, 255, 256
שבלים 146
שבר 185
שדמות 148
שור 159, 160, 161
שחד 167, 168
שטה 137
שטרים 259
שטם 221
שיר, שירה 108
שכם 191, 192
שלום 241
שלח 220
שליש 280
שמן 137
שמש 108, 120, 121
שנים 217, 218
שפיפן 129
שערה/שער 185, 199, 202, 239
שקל 286
שקמה 137
שקמים בולס 158
שריה 221
שריון 221
שתי 219
שתת 219

תאנה 137
תאשור 137
תדהר 137
תולע 217, 218
תותח 221
תירוש 185
תיש 162
תכלת 217
תלי 221
תמר 137
תן 128
תנור 194, 195
תנין 136
תעלולים 262
תרומה 181
תרזה 137
תשורה 167

INDEX OF AUTHORS

Abu-Lughod, A. 247
Adams, R. 79
Albertz, R. 59
Albright, W.F. 59, 62
Alter, R. 57
Amiran, R. 129
Ayer, A.J. 27

Bal, M. 113
Banks, M. 80-82, 99, 100
Barrois, A.G. 96
Barstad, H.M. 70
Bauman, Z. 12
Bedford, P.R. 66
Bellinger, L. 217, 220
Ben-Tor, A. 69
Benjamin, D.C. 147, 163, 164, 240, 255, 261, 264, 266, 267
Benzinger, I. 96
Berg, W. 156
Bernstein, R.J. 44
Bertholet, A. 96
Biran, A. 69
Blenkinsopp, J. 66, 283, 285, 287
Brown, H. 43
Buksinski, T. 45, 61

Carasik, M. 52
Carneiro, R.L. 278, 281
Carroll, R.P. 10, 16, 50, 57, 59, 70, 299
Carter, C.E. 56, 65-67, 71, 72, 283, 284
Childs, B.S. 52, 57
Clark, W.M. 107
Cohen, R. 281
Collini, S. 81
Cross, F.M. 69
Cryer, F.H. 69

Currid, J.D. 119

Dalman, G. 216-20
Dar, S. 56, 143, 144, 146, 148, 176, 189, 190, 195
Davies, M. 50, 51, 53
Davies, P.R. 12, 50, 57, 61-67, 70-72, 74, 75, 115
Deist, F.E. 9-13, 15, 16, 34, 59, 64, 71, 110, 133, 205, 299
Delitzsch, F. 96
Dennett, D.C. 85
Derrida, J. 24, 41
Dever, W.G. 50, 58
Diebner, B.J. 57, 58, 63, 64
Douglas, M. 84
Duranti, A. 78, 101

Eph'al, I. 76
Evans-Pritchard, E.E. 84
Exum, J.C. 57, 113

Feyerbend, P. 39, 41, 49, 50
Finkelstein, I. 118
Finnegan, R. 68
Flanagan, J.W. 248, 256, 279, 280
Foster, B.R. 71, 72, 175
Franken, H.J. 236
Frazer, J.G. 93
Freedman, M. 25, 68, 93, 256, 276
Fretz, M.J. 220, 221
Freud, S. 34
Friis, H. 57

Gelb, I.J. 176, 267, 268
Gelinas, M.W. 67
Glock, A.E. 46

Index of Authors

Goldberg, T.G. 81
Goodenough, W.H. 83, 84, 108, 110
Goody, J. 63, 68, 226-31, 249
Gottwald, N.K. 57, 58, 97
Gould, S.J. 78
Grabbe, L.L. 12
Grimshaw, A. 56, 60, 80, 90
Gudeman, S. 83

Halpern, B. 54, 63
Harding, S. 44
Harris, M. 84
Harris, R. 114
Hart, K. 56, 60, 80, 90
Haviland, W.A. 75, 78, 82, 143, 165, 177, 240, 247-49, 255, 256, 258, 276, 277, 279-82, 294
Heitzman, J. 66, 283, 285-87
Herzog, Z. 195, 197-200, 202-205, 221
Hesse, B. 63, 158
Hoglund, K. 65, 71, 283, 287
Horsley, R.A. 65, 66
Hough, G. 34, 38
Hoyrup, J. 223

Isserlin, B.S.J. 69, 204

Jakobson, R. 26, 27
Jamieson-Drake, D.W. 69, 70
Jobling, D. 66
Johnson, M. 111, 112
Johnson, T. 95
Joubert, D. 92

Kallai, Z. 63
Kant, I. 42
Keel, O. 59
Keesing, F.M. 293
Keil, C.F. 96
Kempinski, A. 56, 195
Kent, S. 118
Kessler, M. 59
Knierim, R. 58
Koenen, K. 159
Kuhn, T. 43, 58, 80
Kuhrt, A. 65

Laato, A. 53, 54, 76

Labuschagne, C.J. 36
Lakoff, G. 111, 112
Law, R. 68, 228, 249
Lee, A. 52
Lelyveld, A.J. 114
Lemche, N.P. 57, 62, 67, 80, 255, 256, 258, 267, 272
Lévi-Strauss, C. 87
Levin, C. 57
Levinson, B.M. 35
Liid, D.C. 203
Long, B.O. 46, 50, 59, 62

Marais, J. 113
Maren-Grisebach, M. 34
Margalit, B. 77, 263
Margulies, H. 63, 133
Marx, K. 98
Matthews, V.H.E. 147, 163, 164, 240, 255, 261, 264, 266, 267
Mayes, A.D.H. 80
Mazar, A. 69
Meek, T.J 130
Meshel, Z. 204, 208
Millard, A.R. 69, 226
Mittmann, S. 129
Moser, P. 43-45
Mulder, M.J. 137

Na'aman, N. 280
Naveh, J. 69, 76
Netzer, E. 195, 196, 204
Nielsen, K. 140
Niezsche, F. 34
Nötscher, F. 96

Otto, E. 76

Parpola, S. 223
Paul, H. 35
Pederson, J. 96
Penn, M. 83
Pilch, J. 247, 260, 261
Pohlman, L. 34
Posner, R. 26
Postgate, J.N. 173
Powell, M.A. 223

Rainey, A.F. 69, 176
Rand, H. 36
Reeves, J.C. 77
Reich, R. 195, 204-207
Rendtorff, R. 57
Richter, W. 39
Rochberg-Halton, F. 223
Rogerson, J.W. 79
Rorty, R. 44, 47
Routledge, B. 24, 45, 46
Roux, J. le 10, 62, 64

Sapir, E. 91, 97
Sass, H.-M. 44
Saussure, F. de 34-38, 87
Schaper, J. 66, 180, 181, 285, 286
Scheffler, E. 10
Schopman, J. 97
Schult, H. 58
Scott, J. 98
Service, E.R. 258, 281
Seybold, K. 223
Shavit, Y. 59
Shea, W.H. 175
Shiloh, Y. 69, 199
Shmueli, E. 43
Silberman, N.A. 59
Simonds, A.P. 33
Slomovic, E. 52
Small, D.B. 65, 72, 75
Smelik, K.A.D. 54, 63
Spitzer, L. 34
Stern, E. 205, 206
Sternberg, M. 57, 117
Stetkevytch, J. 114

Steward, J. 86

Talmon, S. 76
Themaat, W.V. van 43
Thomas, D.W. 105, 131, 133
Thompson, T.L. 67, 69
Tonkin, E. 68, 227, 231, 249, 254
Toulmin, S. 43
Turkowski, L. 148-52, 158, 165, 185, 189-93, 238
Turner, T. 81

Vansina, J. 68
Vaux, R. de 96

Vierich, H. 118
Wagner, R. 49, 50, 100
Wapnish, P. 63, 158
Watt, I. 63, 68, 226-31, 249
Weinberg, J. 12, 69
Weinfeld, M. 76
Weippert, H. 57, 65, 66, 71, 118-20, 130, 143, 152, 153, 161, 163, 172, 176, 184-86, 195, 196, 199, 204, 206, 208, 213, 215, 225, 226, 285
Wellhausen, J. 67
Wells, R.S. 36
Wessels, W. 10
White, L. 85
Whitelam, K.W. 67
Whorf, B.L. 91, 97
Wimsatt, W.K. 24, 31

Yardeni, A. 69
Yeivin, S. 172

THE BIBLICAL SEMINAR

1. John W. Rogerson, *Anthropology and the Old Testament*
2. Athalya Brenner, *The Israelite Woman: Social Role and Literary Type in Biblical Narrative*
3. J.H. Eaton, *Kingship and the Psalms*
4. Mark Kiley, *Colossians as Psuedepigraphy*
5. Niels Peter Lemche, *Ancient Israel: A New History of Israelite Society*
6. J. Høgenhaven, *Problems and Prospects of Old Testament Theology*
7. Benedikt Otzen, *Judaism in Antiquity: Political Developments and Religious Currents from Alexamder to Hadrian*
8. Bruce D. Chilton, *God in Strength: Jesus' Announcement of the Kingdom*
9. Albrecht Alt, *Essays on Old Testament History and Religion*
10. Jack M. Sasson, *Ruth: A New Translation with a Philological Commentary and a Formalist-Folklorist Interpretation (Second Edition)*
11. Douglas A. Knight (ed.), *Tradition and Theology in the Old Testament*
12. J.P. Fokkelman, *Narrative Art in Genesis: Specimens of Stylistic and Structural Analysis (Second Edition)*
13. Elizabeth Struthers Malbon, *Narrative Space and Mythic Meaning in Mark*
14. S. Mowinckel, *The Psalms in Israel's Worship*
16. Dean W. Chapman, *The Orphan Gospel: Mark's Perspective on Jesus*
17. Larry J. Kreitzer, *The New Testament in Fiction and Film: On Reversing the Hermeneutical Flow*
18. Daniel C. Fredericks, *Coping with Transience: Ecclesiastes on Brevity in Life*
19. W.D. Davies, *Invitation to the New Testament: A Guide to its Main Witnesses*
20. Terence Collins, *The Mantle of Elijah: The Redation Criticism of the Prophetical Books*
22. Cecil Hargreaves, *A Translator's Freedom: Modern English Bibles and their Language*
23. Karel van der Toorn, *From Her Cradle to Her Grave: The Role of Religion in the Life of the Israelite and the Babylonian Woman*
24. Larry J. Kreitzer, *The Old Testament in Fiction and Film: On Reversing the Hermeneutical Flow*
25. W.D. Davies, *The Gospel and the Land: Early Christianity and Jewish Territorial Doctrine*
26. Michael Prior, CM, *Jesus the Liberator: Nazareth Liberation Theology (Luke 4.16-30)*
27. Neil Elliott, *Liberating Paul: The Justice of God and the Politics of the Apostle*
28. Jane Schaberg, *The Illegitimacy of Jesus: A Feminist Theological Interpretation of the Infancy Narratives*
29. Volkmar Fritz, *The City in Ancient Israel*

30 Frank Moore Cross, Jr, *The Ancient Library of Qumran (Third Edition)*
31 Craig A. Evans and Stanley E. Porter (eds.), *The Synoptic Gospels: A Sheffield Reader*
32 Stanley E. Porter and Craig A. Evans (eds.), *The Johannine Writings: A Sheffield Reader*
33 Craig A. Evans and Stanley E. Porter (eds.), *The Historical Jesus: A Sheffield Reader*
34 Stanley E. Porter and Craig A. Evans (eds.), *The Pauline Writings: A Sheffield Reader*
35 Daniel Smith-Christopher (ed.), *Text and Experience: Towards a Cultural Exegesis of the Bible*
36 James H. Charlesworth (ed.), *Qumran Questions*
37 Andrew Parker, *Painfully Clear: The Parables of Jesus*
38 Stephen H. Smith, *A Lion With Wings: A Narrative-Critical Approach to Mark's Gospel*
39 John W. Rogerson (ed.), *The Pentateuch: A Sheffield Reader*
40 J. Cheryl Exum (ed.), *The Historical Books: A Sheffield Reader*
41 David J.A. Clines (ed.), *The Poetical Books: A Sheffield Reader*
42 Philip R. Davies (ed.), *The Prophets: A Sheffield Reader*
43 Craig A. Evans and Stanley E. Porter (eds.), *New Testament Backgrounds: A Sheffield Reader*
44 Stanley E. Porter and Craig A. Evans (eds.), *New Testament Text and Language: A Sheffield Reader*
45 Stanley E. Porter and Craig A. Evans (eds.), *New Testament Interpretation and Methods: A Sheffield Reader*
46 Michel Desjardins, *Peace, Violence and the New Testament*
47 David J. Chalcraft (ed.), *Social-Scientific Old Testament Criticism: A Sheffield Reader*
48 Michael Prior, CM, *The Bible and Colonialism: A Moral Critique*
49 Alexander Rofé, *Introduction to the Prophetic Literature*
50 Kirsten Nielsen, *Satan—The Prodigal Son? A Family Problem in the Bible*
51 David J.A. Clines, *The Bible and the Modern World*
52 Robert Goldenberg, *The Nations that Know Thee Not: Ancient Jewish Attitudes towards Other Religions*
53 N. Wyatt, *Religious Texts from Ugarit: The Words of Ilimilku and his Colleagues*
54 Luis Alonso Schökel, *A Manual of Hermeneutics*
55 Detlev Dortmeyer, *The New Testament among the Writings of Antiquity*
57 Louis Stulman, *Order amid Chaos: Jeremiah as Symbolic Tapestry*
58 Alexander Rofé, *Introduction to the Composition of the Pentateuch*
59 James W. Watts, *Reading Law: The Rhetorical Shaping of the Pentateuch*
60 Yairah Amit, *History and Ideology: Introduction to Historiography in the Hebrew Bible*
61 Larry J. Kreitzer, *Pauline Images in Fiction and Film: On Reversing the Hermeneutical Flow*

62 Sandra Hack Polaski, *Paul and the Discourse of Power*
64 R.S. Sugirtharajah, *Asian Biblical Hermeneutics and Postcolonialism: Contesting the Interpretations*
65 Harold C. Washington, Susan Lochrie Graham and Pamela Thimmes (eds.), *Escaping Eden: New Feminist Perspectives on the Bible*
66 Norman K. Gottwald, *The Tribes of Yahweh*
67 Alec Gilmore, *A Dictionary of the English Bible and its Origins*
69 Allan Millard, *Reading and Writing in the Time of Jesus*
70 Ferdinand E. Deist, *The Material Culture of the Bible: An Introduction* (edited with a preface by Robert P. Carroll)
71 Tod Linafelt (ed.), *Strange Fire: Reading the Bible after the Holocaust*